Sexuality, Society, and Feminism

Sexuality, Society, and Feminism

Edited by

Cheryl Brown Travis and
Jacquelyn W. White

American Psychological Association
Washington, DC

Published by
American Psychological Association
750 First Street, NE
Washington, DC 20002

Copies may be ordered from
APA Order Department
P.O. Box 92984
Washington, DC 20090-2984

In the U.K., Europe, Africa, and the Middle East, copies may be ordered from
American Psychological Association
3 Henrietta Street
Covent Garden, London
WC2E 8LU England

Typeset in Goudy by EPS Group Inc., Easton, MD

Printer: Automated Graphic Systems, White Plains, MD
Jacket Designer: Minker Design, Bethesda, MD
Technical/Production Editor: Eleanor Inskip

Library of Congress Cataloging-in-Publication Data
Travis, Cheryl Brown, 1944–
Sexuality, society, and feminism / Cheryl B. Travis, Jacquelyn W. White.
  p. cm.—(Psychology of women; 4)
 Includes bibliographical references and index.
 ISBN 1-55798-617-7 (hbk.)
 1. Sex. 2. Sexual ethics. 3. Sex (Psychology)
4. Feminism. I. White, Jacquelyn W. II. Title. III. Series: Psychology of women
book series; v. 4.
HQ21.T67 1999
306.7—dc21

               99-44905
               CIP

British Library Cataloguing-in-Publication Data
A CIP record is available from the British Library.

Printed in the United States of America
First Edition

CONTENTS

CONTRIBUTORS

Kristin M. Bardari, Private Practice, Pawleys Island, South Carolina

Vanessa M. Bing, Women's Center, Borough of Manhattan Community College, City University of New York

Barrie Bondurant, Psychology Department, Lyon College, Batesville, Arkansas

Laura S. Brown, Private Practice, Seattle, Washington

Mary Crawford, Psychology Department, University of Connecticut, Storrs

John DeLamater, Sociology Department, University of Wisconsin, Madison

Patria L. N. Donat, Division of Education & Human Sciences, Mississippi University for Women, Columbus

Janet Shibley Hyde, Psychology Department, University of Wisconsin, Madison

Arnold S. Kahn, Psychology Department, James Madison University, Harrisonburg, Virginia

Myra Christen Kawaguchi, The Guidance Center, Murfreesboro, Tennessee

Suzanne B. Kurth, Sociology Department, University of Tennessee, Knoxville

Virginia Andreoli Mathie, Psychology Department, James Madison University, Harrisonburg, Virginia

Kayce L. Meginnis, Psychology Department, University of Tennessee, Knoxville

Danny S. Moore, Psychology Department, St. Leo's College, St. Leo, Florida

Patricia J. Morokoff, Psychology Department, University of Rhode Island, Kingston

Mary Beth Oliver, Department of Communication Studies, Penn State, University Park

Pamela Trotman Reid, Institute for Research on Women and Gender, University of Michigan, Ann Arbor

Sharon S. Rostosky, Counseling Department, University of Kentucky, Lexington

Bethany B. Spiller, Psychology Service, Veterans Administration Medical Center, Memphis, Tennessee

Leonore Tiefer, Private Practice, New York City

Cheryl Brown Travis, Psychology Department, University of Tennessee, Knoxville

Deborah P. Welsh, Psychology Department, University of Tennessee, Knoxville

Jacquelyn W. White, Psychology Department, University of North Carolina, Greensboro

Sexuality, Society, and Feminism

INTRODUCTION

Issues relating to sexuality are constantly in the headlines, are the topic of heated controversies, and are the focus of national policy decisions. A perusal of almost any forum of our society underscores the highly volatile nature of these issues. Recent jury verdicts have awarded millions for a woman sexually harassed by a law firm. A Supreme Court decision on a case originating in Nashville, TN, held that plaintiffs did not have to demonstrate psychological harm in order to prove sexual harassment. Researchers have found their study protocols debated on the floor of Congress. The former Speaker of the House, in an oblique allusion to the menstrual cycle, stated that women could not serve in combat trenches. And even the former Surgeon General of the United States, Jocelyn Elders, was removed from her position following her endorsement of the idea of including information about masturbation in sex education. Beyond these examples, we find that the meaning and experience of sexuality is changing for individuals. For example, a new survey found that approximately 37% of teen females have first intercourse primarily because of peer pressure rather than out of affection for their partners. Furthermore, there are differences of opinion regarding what behaviors are included in having sex. Clearly, cultural notions of what constitutes sexuality and the elements deemed acceptable affect not only individuals, but also aspects of larger social agendas.

Women's sexuality is a topic of increasing importance for several reasons. First, psychology as a science has only recently begun to include women as primary participants, rather than as comparisons to a male standard. For this reason, research on women's sexuality is in need of a careful reflection with regard to epistemology, life course development, and the social order. Second, political economics and social changes in society have affected women's lives tremendously. It is important to determine the extent to which these forces have affected women's personal development and interpersonal experiences, especially with respect to sexuality.

The intent of this volume on sexuality, society, and feminism is not to provide advice about how to have more and better sex, but rather to transform our understanding of sexuality: how it is negotiated, developed, and evoked; and what it means in a contemporary social framework. The role of society in women's sexuality has been to suppress and deny, and, more important to set the framework and rules by which sexuality is negotiated and thus has determined the forms of sexuality that are possible. For example, Sue Wilkinson and Celia Kitzinger (1993) have suggested that a hidden assumption of heterosexuality frames all relationships. Further, the assumption is not only that the framework is heterosexual but that it is between women and masculine men, thus implicitly reproducing issues of dominance and subordination.

For this volume, we have followed a number of guidelines similar to those outlined by Judith Worell and Claire Etaugh (1994) as key components in transforming knowledge, including

1. challenging traditional knowledge;
2. focusing on the experience of women's lives;
3. acknowledging power as a basis for social arrangements;
4. recognizing gender as having multiple conceptions that are socially constructed;
5. attending to language and creating a public awareness of hidden phenomena; and
6. promoting social activism.

We take a pluralistic position with respect to methodology. We do not look for the uniquely best form of feminist methodology. We suggest that it is better to ask whether or how epistemology operates in the service of feminism. We assume that language is particularly important in the process of conceptualizing sexuality and that examination of language can highlight contradictions that reveal hidden meanings and assumptions.

Our general approach to sexuality follows the idea others have applied to gender (Crawford, 1995; Crawford & Unger, 1995; West & Zimmerman, 1977). Specifically, sexuality is a meaning system that organizes interactions and governs access to power and resources. Sexuality is not so much an attribute of persons, but rather exists in transactions between people. We further agree with Mary Jacobus and her colleagues, E. F. Keller and

S. Shuttleworth (1990), that the arena of the body (masculine or feminine) is often a battlefield where a variety of struggles, not all having to do with gender or sexuality, are played out and that the body reflects the matrices of power at all levels.

It is the purpose of this volume to contribute to contemporary feminism by extending the discourse of constructionist accounts in psychology. In a sense, this entire volume is a way of going forward to new understanding of sexuality. We adopt the view that sexuality is actively constructed and emergent within contexts. In other words, sexuality is repeatedly negotiated and redefined; sexuality changes developmentally over the life span (explored in section II); it has various meanings and manifestations (as exemplified in section III); and it can be used in a larger sense to reinforce violence against women (see section IV). We also believe that new constructions of sexuality have the potential to transform the way women themselves think, feel, and behave.

SECTION I: EPISTEMOLOGY

Chapters in this section focus on aspects of epistemology, especially chapter 1, and other chapters review evolutionary and biological approaches to sex and gender, meta-analytic approaches to human sex differences in sexuality, and feminist considerations of sexology and the medicalization of sexuality. In chapter 2, Danny Moore and Cheryl Travis point out that even when standard criteria of logical positivism are applied, much of the gender-focused work in neuroanatomy and sociobiology is deeply flawed in both logic and methodology. The fact that gender-biased facts remain a favorite topic of science journals and popular media reveals the social and political nature of these constructions. In chapter 3, Janet Hyde and Mary Beth Oliver review a number of other theoretical models of gender including the perspectives of the neoanalytic theorist Nancy Chodorow, social learning theory, social role theory and script theory, and feminist theory. Hyde and Oliver then apply empiricist methods of meta-analysis to gender differences in sexuality as a way of clarifying their extent and relative size. A major conclusion of this review is that sociobiological models of gender are driving the research agenda and that feminist researchers must consider how to recapture it. In chapter 4, Leonore Tiefer points out that the contemporary public tends to rely on sex experts who are assumed to be professional and neutral with regard to sexual values. Thus, in some ways the experts create frameworks of meaning and reality for the public. In contrast, she proposes that it is naive to believe that sex experts have no particular ax to grind and instead illustrates how theory and research formulations actively promote particular constructions of sexuality. This sexological model is not simply a "mirror held up to nature" but rather promotes a distinct perspective that privileges biological factors while making universal claims.

SECTION II: LIFE COURSE DEVELOPMENT

One strategy for escaping the pervasive focus on gender difference is to formulate questions and models that address the development of sexual phenomena over the life course of girls and women. In chapter 5, the authors summarize the literature on the developing sexuality of adolescent girls, observing that virtually all of the research and federal funding for research on adolescent girls focuses on how to contain, delay, or otherwise deny identity development that includes sexuality. The authors suggest that this negation may be a factor contributing to teen pregnancy and sexually transmitted disease. In chapter 6, the authors explore the diverse ways in which meaning can emerge by looking at ethnocultural variation, in particular mother–daughter relationships. This is an especially complex relationship because mothers themselves are not free agents of gender or sexuality and therefore may reproduce for their daughters some aspect of the oppression already imposed on the mothers. In chapter 7, Hyde and DeLamater address a hidden aspect of women's sexuality associated with pregnancy. It is ironic that many women experience a blossoming of sexuality during pregnancy and early motherhood, yet the pregnant woman's public cultural role is treated as asexual. Finally, in chapter 8, Rostosky and Travis take up the issues of sexuality, aging and medical models of menopause, concluding that illness models of menopause and aging effectively label women as the "other," as weak, and inferior. Views of older women as wise agents who are entitled to voice their knowledge are offered as alternatives.

SECTION III: MEANING AND FUNCTION

The third section of this volume builds on the perspective that sexuality is socially constructed and that meanings are negotiated and renegotiated. Sexuality is elicited, expressed, maintained, or suppressed by virtue of societal context. Furthermore, the meaning and function of sexuality vary according to this context. In chapter 9, Crawford explores the ways in which humor operates as a political and social mechanism to construct these meanings, and in chapter 10, Travis, Meginnis, and Bardari examine the body as an arena where a variety of social struggles are played out. The authors argue that if women do not have control of their bodies, they cannot own their sexuality, or have an unfettered identity. In chapter 11, Laura Brown reviews the conflicting and conflicted ways in which society constructs lesbians as simultaneously dangerous and powerful as well as impotent. She illustrates how what is shameful, what is acceptable, and how one represents one's own sexuality all are derived from the general social discourse. Goals of and barriers to a sexual assertiveness in women are then discussed by Patricia Morokoff in chapter 12. Morokoff points out that cultural definitions of sexuality that foil assertiveness among women have broad-ranging implications for women's roles in society, their health, and their satisfaction in relationships.

SECTION IV: SEXUALITY AND THE SOCIAL ORDER

The consequences for women of current constructions of sexuality are not matters of benign variations in satisfaction or convenience. There is a dark side that operates to exclude and marginalize women by virtue of demeaning harassment and implicit as well as explicit threats to physical safety. In chapter 13, Kurth, Spiller, and Travis explore the power of prevailing sexual scripts to bypass consent and to divert power away from women. The authors argue that the meaning and significance of harassment has to do primarily with power, but that this power dynamic is frequently disguised from both parties. It is disguised from women to the extent that men control the meaning of social discourse, and it may be disguised from men in a motivated way because it allows men to engage in behavior that would otherwise be labeled as reprehensible. Issues of consent are explored in more detail in chapter 14 in the growing incidence of acquaintance rape. Donat and White argue that social and legal definitions of rape, constructed from a male perspective, deny women a voice in labeling and explaining rape. Finally, in chapter 15, Kahn and Mathie take up the seeming anomaly of the unacknowledged rape victim. Nonconsensual intercourse is a widespread phenomenon and may not rely so much on threat or force as the strategy whereby men simply ignore their victims and "just do it." The authors review data that indicate that date and acquaintance rape are widespread and that the victims do not consciously acknowledge a high percentage of these incidents. Failure among the women themselves to recognize and label such events as violations, despite the fact that they meet legal definitions of rape, has myriad consequences, not the least of which is that the assailant is likely to engage in additional sexual assaults on other women. These issues of physical safety and sexual consent hold vast significance for the well-being of women. If women are going to speak and act with authority, they must be psychologically and emotionally free to do so. Availing themselves of the right to be knowers and doers should not require them to risk physical and emotional violence.

There is a woeful lack of dialogue or scholarship on the social context of sexuality. Absent, but badly needed, is a drawing back to look at sexuality in social context as it is evidenced for both the individual and society. There is a pressing need for scholars to be actively involved in the formulation of conceptual models, the development of appropriate methods of inquiry, and the bringing forth of knowledge in this area. In this book we will frame the direction of scholarly efforts to develop a knowledge base relevant to science, educational practice, and public policy issues. A major benefit will be to focus the attention of researchers and scholars and to provide them with a platform from which to pursue their programs of related research. The volume has the potential to influence practice in a variety of ways, because it will educate clinicians about some of the primary issues women face about their sexuality.

The volume will contribute to the development of an integrated body of scholarly research and will provide an arena for the discussion and sharing of newly emerging approaches that offer better understanding of gender, sexuality, and culture. Taking stock of what we know (and don't know) on these topics can be enriched by integrating findings from other disciplines.

The volume will serve primarily as a reference for scholars, academics, and practitioners in the field of psychology at the advanced undergraduate, graduate, and postgraduate levels, and also will be relevant to audiences in the field of women's studies and sociology. As in other feminist works, this volume is geared toward creating change. Thus, it is hoped that those who read it will be inspired to pursue change in research endeavors, professional applications, and political arenas.

REFERENCES

Crawford, M. (1995). *Talking difference: On gender & language.* Newbury Park, CA: Sage.

Crawford, M., & Unger, R. (1995). *Women and gender: A feminist psychology.* New York: McGraw-Hill.

Jacobus, M., Keller, E. F., & Shuttleworth, S. (1990). *Body–politics: Women and the discourses of science.* New York: Routledge.

West, C., & Zimmerman, D. (1977). Women's place in everyday talk: Reflections on parent-child interaction. *Social Problems, 24,* 521–529.

Wilkinson, S., & Kitzinger, C. (Eds.). (1993). *Heterosexuality: A feminism and psychological reader.* Newbury Park, CA: Sage.

Worell, J., & Etaugh, C. (1994). Transforming theory and research with women. *Psychology of Women Quarterly, 18,* 443–450.

I

EPISTEMOLOGY, THEORY, AND METHODS

1

SOCIAL CONSTRUCTIONS OF SEXUALITY: UNPACKING HIDDEN MEANINGS

JACQUELYN W. WHITE, BARRIE BONDURANT, AND
CHERYL BROWN TRAVIS

Sexuality is an ambiguous term. It can refer to a variety of phenomena, including sexual identity, sexual preference, and sexual behavior. Depending on one's theoretical perspective, sexuality may be defined in physiological, intrapersonal, or interpersonal terms. Following from these perspectives there are questions regarding what constitutes sexuality. Is sexuality to be defined by physiological reactions in certain body parts, but not others? When does one experience sexuality? Is it lodged in one's sense of identity as a woman or man? Or must it be defined by the sex of one's intimate partner? And what does it mean to be intimate with another? These questions have been addressed within frameworks derived from conventional wisdom and traditional science. However, increasingly there is a dissatisfaction with modern scientific traditions. There is a desire for theories, methods, and results that encompass an array of phenomena, including, for example, patterns of relating, language, consciousness, intentionality, and meaning. From feminist perspectives, there is a desire to develop a science for, as well as about, women. We propose that sexuality is interactive and contextual; as such, it requires a social account. It is this social, emergent, and dynamic quality of sexuality that is the focus of this volume.

Approaching sexuality from a social and political context as well as from a personal context leads to a criticism of traditional science and conventional wisdom. These criticisms, when applied to the study of sexuality, reveal numerous ways that the traditional study of sexuality has supported and reproduced gender inequalities in society. Deconstructing sexuality within a social framework enables alternative conceptions of sexuality that may promote equality and provide an understanding of the limits of both traditional and modernist epistemologies.

In the first part of this chapter we review problems associated with modernism and present a summary of social constructionism. We then discuss feminism and social constructionism, as well as modernist and constructionist approaches to sexuality. We conclude with a summary of how social constructionist approaches to sexuality can transform knowledge.

PROBLEMS OF MODERNISM

Approaches to knowledge have varied over the centuries, with reliance on combinations of superstition, animism, religion, or meditation, and, more recently, rationality, logic, and empiricism. Each approach is characterized by certain kinds of procedures, rules of inference, and values regarding what constitutes the most compelling source of information or data. In some cultures, for example, altered states of consciousness are thought to be the process by which the most valuable knowledge is revealed to an individual. Revelations usually occur during periods of isolation and involve a disciplined passivity by the recipient of knowledge. Approaches to knowledge, otherwise known as epistemology, have embedded within them elements of the host culture, including values, expectations, and politics. Thus, the kinds of questions that are asked, the kinds of information sought, and the subsequent interpretation and use of knowledge all are shaped and colored by the social and political context. Because of this confounding of culture, values, and politics, it is more accurate to say that knowledge is created, received, or constructed rather than discovered.

Modernism has been the prevailing epistemology of the 20th century. The signature belief of modernism is that objective reality can be discovered, given the right tools. Related features of modernism include the search for universal, unchanging laws that govern events, laws that can be used to reliably predict and eventually control events. This approach has worked with moderate success in the natural and physical sciences, although even here there is considerably more variability than is commonly appreciated. Early efforts at self-reflection on this modern scientific tradition suggested that scientific progress is linear (i.e., logical) within, but not between, paradigms (Kuhn, 1970). However, even within a paradigm, "pure science" is much messier and more nonlinear than claimed by modernist science (Latour & Woolgar, 1979).

In an effort to reach success and cultural stature similar to the physical sciences, the social sciences have adopted modernist approaches. Virtually all American psychologists have been trained in traditional modernist perspectives, such as logical positivism. There is, however, a growing unease with modernist assumptions about the nature of science. There is a growing, postmodern challenge arguing that reality is not objective, static, or separate from the observer.

Mary Gergen (1988) and Janis Bohan (1990a, 1990b) have articulated many of the basic problems of modernist approaches to knowledge:

1. Facts are not independent of theory or method.
2. The scientist and the subject of study are not independent.
3. Value-free, neutral science does not exist.
4. Knowledge cannot be understood separate from the context in which it is embedded.
5. Knowledge or truth cannot be gained through disengaged observation.
6. Traditional modern science limits the vision and usefulness of psychology.

A full examination of the critiques of modernism is beyond the scope of this chapter. Thus, to provide a basic foundation for understanding the social constructionist approach to sexuality, we will briefly discuss just two critiques: the independence of scientist and participant, with the assumption of the value-free nature of science, and context-free knowledge.

Although objectivity is the cornerstone of the modern scientific tradition, postmodernism suggests that objective understanding of the world is impossible because each individual must view the world from a particular vantage point. The methods of science do not protect scientists from their own subjectivity or bias. Since the researcher must choose the topic of study, methodology to use, and the interpretation of results, there are many opportunities for subjectivity to enter objective research. The researcher and the researched cannot be separated in scientific inquiry (Wallston & Grady, 1985). This lack of objectivity can be seen in numerous scientific endeavors. Researcher bias and social consensus are major, although often unrecognized, influences on science. Modernistic approaches tend to disguise the value-laden underpinnings of hypotheses, methods, and interpretations. This results in a blurring of that which is descriptive and that which is prescriptive (Bohan, 1990b). Thus, it is really more appropriate to view knowledge as socially constructed rather than discovered.

Furthermore, a focus on the atomistic, derived from models in the natural and physical sciences, and the search for unchanging facts have encouraged psychologists to strip behavior of its context. All too often, larger social and political frameworks are ignored. For modernism, context is a source of confound and error. For example, Lederman and Teresi (1993) state that "nature hides the simplicity in a thicket of complicating circumstances, and the experiment's job is to prune away these complications" (p. 71). They conclude that famous scientists of history were successful because they could "strip complications away from simplicity." However, modernism doesn't work particularly well for many areas of psychology, precisely because the social context of behavior is key to understanding thoughts, feelings, and behavior.

Social constructionism argues that not only knowledge but reality itself is created in an interactive process. Constructionism recognizes knowledge as embedded in social context and that language reflects that embeddedness. Constructionism sees human thoughts, feelings, language, and behavior as the result of interchanges with the external world, a world that is social and political. Because knowledge is socially constructed, only views of reality on which the most powerful agree are accorded the status of truth. Other constructions are marginalized or denied. The emphasis on process allows the influence of power relations in the construction of knowledge to become visible. Indeed, examining the nature of power is part of social constructionism.

Social constructionism encourages the examination of researcher subjectivity, the underlying social processes, and power relations that determine which truths will be accepted by the dominant (more powerful) group. Stephanie Riger (1992) points out that "the fact that Helen Thompson Woolley's data about women's intellectual competence have had to be repeatedly rediscovered (reinvented) demonstrates that power, not truth, determines which version of reality will prevail" (p. 736). In a similar vein, Celia Kitzinger (1990) argues that the acceptance or rejection of scientific evidence depends not on the quality of the experimental design and data collection techniques, but on whether the results serve a useful ideological and political function. She suggests that deconstructing the role of ideology and politics in the scientific method is a more fruitful avenue for feminists than reliance on the scientific method to refute oppressive theories.

Social constructionism additionally argues that there is no separation between subjectivity and objectivity and that the dichotomy between the person and the situation is false. The person is intimately and intricately bound within social, cultural, and historical forces and cannot be understood fully without consideration of these social forces. The analysis of variance techniques that separately examine person, situation, and their interaction are seen as inappropriate because of the assumption of the statistical independence of person and situation.

Social constructionism highlights the role of language in the creation of meaning. Traditional language and usual categories are derived from the experiences of the dominant group. Deconstruction is a tool used by social constructionists to analyze texts (Derrida, 1976; Foucault, 1979, 1982). Deconstruction examines text for contradictions between rhetoric and logic, as well as what is left out or silenced, that which is not said. Derrida (1976) asserts that knowledge is constructed out of differences, between what a text means to say and what it is construed to mean. When a text is searched for omissions and contradictions, the hidden assumptions and meanings become clearer. The expectations and judgments of others are reflected in language and constitute part of the context (Unger, 1988). Thus it is helpful to clarify and publicly identify the group or entity implicitly represented as the voice of authority within a text. One can then make apparent the implicit assumptions and hidden voice of authority (Brown, 1997): Deconstruction challenges us to ask: "Supposed" by whom? "Different" in what ways? "Opposite" to what? "Truth" according to whose authority?

This approach can be applied instructively to many essentialist statements about gender. For example, in his popular press book about Venutian women and Martian men, John Gray (1992) states that "without the awareness that we are supposed to be different, men and women are at odds with each other. We usually become angry or frustrated with the opposite sex because we have forgotten this important truth." (p. 10).

SOCIAL CONSTRUCTIONISM AND FEMINISM

There are numerous links between social constructionism and feminism. Feminists have recognized that traditional, modernist approaches to science have rendered women invisible in significant ways. This invisibility of women in science has discouraged women from being knowers (i.e., scientists in search of knowledge), restricting them to being objects of knowledge (Henwood & Pidgeon, 1995). "The feminine body functions as the imaginary site where meaning (or life) is generated; yet, in this scheme, women can never be meaning makers in their own right" (Jacobus, Keller, & Shuttleworth, 1990, p. 7). Feminists have responded to these epistemological concerns in three fundamentally different ways: feminist empiricism, standpoint epistemology, and feminist postmodernism (Harding, 1986; Riger, 1992). Each is described below. A major distinction between each rests on the primary research methods advocated. However, all argue that knowledge generated by traditional modernist methods is seriously flawed, operates to disadvantage women, and reproduces basic inequalities. These problems are elucidated in the area of sexuality in later chapters.

Feminist empiricists endorse using the scientific method toward the feminist goal of achieving greater equality for women. They contend that androcentric biases can be eliminated in traditional scientific methods. Feminist empiricism advocates for nonsexist research as a starting point, while recognizing that all science is value laden (McHugh, Koeske, & Frieze, 1986). In addition, this approach suggests that the research endeavor should include an examination of one's own subjectivity or biases. Feminist empiricists argue that despite postmodern critiques, quantitative data serve useful functions in knowledge construction (Unger, 1995; Weisstein, 1993). Experimental methods are powerful tools that should be used. Science has the potential to address feminist as well as patriarchal concerns (Unger, 1995; Weisstein, 1993). Rhoda Unger (1995) argues that feminist empiricism is necessary for social change within psychology and society at large. She argues for researchers to transcend the empiricist feminist dilemma of how to be a social constructionist and still use data. Feminists must be comfortable with contradictions between theory and social activism. These contradictions should not stop us from using a tool that is valued and respected by our society. The feminist empiricism called for by Unger is one informed by social constructionism, is reflexive and skeptical, but dares to have values and fight for a social agenda. Chapter 2 in this volume on biological models and the meta-analysis of gender differences in sexuality presented in chapter 3 reflect feminist empiricist approaches.

In contrast, *feminist standpoint epistemologies* argue that all research reflects the researcher's perspective. Therefore, oppressed people have the potential to better see their own and their oppressors' position than do other groups of people (Nielsen, 1990). Minorities who live in both their own culture as well as in the larger White community are sometimes said to be bilingual or to possess a double consciousness. It is this ability to understand two cultures or to be the outsider within that offers unique insights for science (Collins, 1986). Standpoint theorists argue that researchers and participants from oppressed groups offer a valuable perspective, and in this volume both chapter 6, which focuses on ethnocultural experience, and chapter 11, which focuses on heterosexism, reflect elements of cultural standpoint feminism. It is now accepted that ethnic cultural diversity is a fundamental component of any feminist approach (Landrine, 1995). Standpoint theorists rely extensively on interviews, narratives, or other methods that allow people to describe their experiences and points of view (Riger, 1992). Inherent in feminist standpoint theories is a belief in objective reality (Nielsen, 1990). Some people are more oppressed than others. Some people through their oppressed position can see the true state of affairs more clearly than others. Thus, standpoint theory differs from social constructionism by asserting that there is an objective reality. It relies primarily on atheoretical subjective experience as the basis of knowledge.

Feminist postmodernism, in contrast to feminist empiricism and standpoint epistemology, allows for the heterogeneity of voices, multiple perspectives, and multiple methods. Postmodern feminists question the nature of reality and objectivity in research. They argue that attention to power relations and the political implications of research are essential (Riger, 1992). Thus, postmodernist feminist analyses tend to be distinguished by attention to the personal, social, and political context (see chapter 9, this volume, on humor and chapter 10, this volume, on body politics). Some researchers suggest using traditional methodologies while recognizing that the results will be just one of many competing truths (Gergen, 1985). These researchers have used traditional Q-sort methodologies (Kitzinger, 1987), story completion tasks (Kitzinger, 1995), and surveys (Unger, Draper, & Pendergrass, 1986), as well as discourse analysis (Crawford, 1995; Gavey, 1989; Potter & Wetherell, 1987), interviews, and emancipatory research (Lather, 1986). In short, how methods are used, not the type of method, guides classification of research. Indeed, empirical methods are forms of discourse. Social constructionist practices can include any type of method, as long as one does not claim to have discovered a singular truth.

Language and the power of language have been aspects of the sociopolitical context that have received considerable attention by postmodern feminists. Traditional language and usual categories are derived from the experience of the dominant group and therefore simply are not adequate to bring forward women's experience. Linguistic arrangements also reflect social architecture. Language and convention limit what can be said and how it can be said. Postmodern feminists recognize that modern science reflects a worldview based on dualities, such as rational–irrational, logical–intuitive, objective–subjective, public–private. Susan Heckwood (1990) has argued that these dualities are really variations of one underlying duality: masculinity–femininity, the first side being associated with men, the second with women. She suggests that this formulation privileges men over women. She concludes that the denigration of women is integral to the entire system of modern science. Language thus often marks that which is out of place, as indicated by woman doctor or female executive (Unger, 1988). Language also can function to keep certain things hidden. For example, linguistic reference to sexual harassment did not come into regular use until approximately 1982, although the behavior certainly flourished prior to that time (see chapter 13, this volume). Mary Crawford illustrates these points with respect to humor and sexuality in chapter 9. In chapter 11, Laura Brown discusses language as a mechanism of constructing the social and points out that one hidden assumption in traditional theory is the assumption of heterosexuality.

Along with focusing on language, postmodern feminists have used deconstruction as a way to illuminate androcentric biases. For example, a deconstruction of the use of terms for sexual dysfunction in men and women, *impotence* and *frigidity*, respectively, reveals that both terms are from a man's perspective. The legal definition of consent in rape trials typically also comes from a man's perspective, as discussed by Patricia Donat and Jacquelyn White in chapter 14, this volume.

Not surprisingly, each of these feminist epistemologies has been subject to criticism by the others. For example, feminist standpoint views argue that women's subjective experiences cannot be understood in the context of laboratory studies and numbers. Conversely, standpoint epistemology has been criticized for its atheoretical approach: "Some (all?) narratives (yes, even women's) are so saturated with denial, gaps, and invisible privilege, that their stories dare not stand alone without benefit of theory" (Fine & Bertram, 1995, p. 464).

Although each of the feminist approaches has limitations, each approach has contributed to scholarship and activism. Feminist postmodernism is clearly aligned with social constructionism and offers new perspectives on sexuality. In the next segment of this chapter we review how traditional science historically functioned as a tool to construct sexuality. This is followed by a brief presentation of several examples that challenge traditional views. As a means of reconciling these examples, we show how social constructionism can be used to deconstruct the traditional view of sexuality and offer alternative constructions. We conclude with recommendations for feminists who want to use social constructionism to transform knowledge and promote social change to enhance the lives of women.

THE SCIENTIFIC METHOD: A TRADITIONAL TOOL TO CONSTRUCT SEXUALITY

In earlier periods of human history the social and political organization of sexuality was accomplished largely by religion. However, there has been a gradual shifting of this function to secular realms and the information age of facts. This movement of sexuality from the realm of the religious to the secular was accomplished largely by making sexuality something that is scientific and medical. Mary Boyle (1994) outlines four major themes characteristic of 20th-century literature on sexuality:

1. Sexuality is associated closely with gender relations.
2. Sexuality can be understood through science.
3. Sexuality is an energy system.
4. Sexuality is a property of individuality.

Implicit in this body of literature are messages that men are naturally dominant and women are naturally submissive. It additionally implies that achieving femininity lies in surrendering the body (and the self) to men; that women are a sexual problem and need men to teach them mature sexual responsiveness. Finally, it conveys the message that women who reject these roles will be psychologically flawed (Boyle, 1994). Just as 20th-century literature has reinforced gender relations, it has also reflected a growing trust in science and medicine.

During the 20th century, initial scholarly interest in sexual life developed from a medical perspective. Although seen as objective and scientific, the medical perspective on sexuality perpetuates political and social ideology. The earliest medical concerns with sexuality dealt with pathology and treatment. Early advocates of a more encompassing approach, such as Hirschfeld (Hirschfeld & Lombardi-Nash, 1991) who in 1910 advocated for the decriminalization of homosexuality, were not popular with their contemporaries. They were seen as confusing science and propaganda (Haeberle, 1981; see also chapter 4, this volume). The tools of science, as they were then understood (i.e., anatomy, physiology, biology), were used to avoid (or in some cases disguise) social and political issues.

Nevertheless, social and political issues did underlie developments then just as they underlie developments now. Jacobus et al. found that "scientific formulations of sexual differences shift in accordance with changes in the economic organization of society—but also . . . in response to technological developments" (Jacobus et al., 1990, p. 5). "Despite shifting technological, economic, and political forces, however, there has been an historical persistence of certain aspects of gender ideology that have been subtly retained, revived, or recast in different eras" (Jacobus et al., 1990, p. 6). It appears that prevailing social and political forces denied acknowledgment of certain aspects of human sexual behavior that research had suggested (i.e., multiple orgasms in women and homosexual experiences among men). Early efforts to stop more psychosocial approaches to sexuality were largely successful. This persistent gender ideology helped naturalize scientific constructions of sexuality.

Leonore Tiefer (1988) evaluated both the impetus and the consequences of efforts to keep sex research apolitical. She noted that "sex research has developed a profoundly neutral, studiously apolitical, and what I would term ultra scientific stance" (p. 20). An essentially biological account of sexual behavior resulted: "Sexuality has been constructed as the sort of thing both animals and people have and do: behavior, orgasm, hormones, brain-behavior relationships" (p. 22). "In the process, what has been ignored are the historical, cultural, and interpersonal dimensions of sexuality. Human sexuality is construed as a universal, inherent, biologically driven essence expressed in numerous direct and indirect ways" (p. 21).

This approach views sex as a biological process, rooted in anatomical differences and in the reproductive cycle. Different proportions of male and female hormones entering the brain exert masculinizing and feminizing influences on the personality and behavior of the developing child. This developmental pattern is seen as part of the natural scheme of evolution. Sex differences present at birth are cited as supporting evidence. This perspective acknowledges that humans are flexible enough to manifest differences in gender roles, but "the evidence presented . . . indicates that the learning of a gender role is a culturally fostered ontogenetic phenomenon of development superimposed on a prenatally determined pattern and mechanism of sexual behavior" (Diamond, 1965, p. 166). The argument continues that hormonal processes are set in motion by genetic determinations. These processes not only influence the development of internal sex organs and external genitalia, but also enter the brain and alter its anatomic structure and, eventually, cognitive function. Thus, certain masculine and feminine characteristics, as well as sexual orientation, are congruent with each other and natural in origin. From this perspective sexuality is assumed to be a biological given that shapes sexual desires, including choice of love objects.

Sexuality also began to be conceptualized as an expression of pleasure and of individual identity in the late 19th and early 20th centuries. The emphasis in traditional, context-free science on the biological determination of sexuality fit in nicely with the growing rhetoric on the naturalness of sexual pleasure. As pleasure was accepted as a natural part of human behavior, it became an important marker of individual identity. Any deviation from perceived normalcy was seen as an indication of a character flaw. This individualistic view of the self, especially in psychological research, led to an emphasis on the individual to the exclusion of the social and cultural context (Henriques, Holloway, Urwin, Venn, & Walkerdine, 1984; Kitzinger, 1988). Individualization decontextualizes and depoliticizes sexuality, lends support to the dominant group, and obscures power dynamics and their consequences.

From this perspective, constructing sexuality as a central aspect of a person serves to control that person's behavior. Even the current reconstructions of lesbianism from a pathological disorder to a life-style choice is suggested to be another expression of an individualist bias that serves to decontextualize an inherently political activity (Kitzinger, 1987). Research and therapy focusing on the lesbian's self and identity emphasize individual sources of distress and individual avenues for change while minimizing institutional, social, and cultural sources of oppression and the need for social change. This individualistic bias serves as a method of social control for lesbians just as the pathological model did in the past (Kitzinger, 1987). Scientific debates on homosexuality have revolved around methodological issues instead of discussing the social and political function of beliefs about homosexuality (Kitzinger, 1990). These discussions reinforce science as the norm, ignore the "invalidity of positivist-empiricism" and fail to "create practical alternatives which will offer real opportunities for radical social and political change" (Kitzinger, 1990, p. 75).

The idea that the self is realized most fully in terms of individualism free of context and the idea that sexuality is a central component of selfhood lead to a conclusion that sexuality is similarly individualistic and independent of context. The individualistic conception of the self also figures in the psychological assumption that sexual intercourse is healthy and should be engaged in by normal individuals. The prevailing logic is that the self is primarily an individualistic phenomenon; sexuality is a core characteristic of the self; therefore, sexuality is an individualistic phenomenon. It follows that sexual intercourse is healthy and should be engaged in by normal individuals and likewise that heterosexuality is natural. A primary assumption of this perspective is the naturalness of heterosexuality. Within this perspective, homosexuality is problematized because it departs from the natural course of development. The press for a sexuality located within a decontextualized individual is very strong, although the everyday language regarding sex consistently implies (at minimum) a relational context. For example, the man with a bad back says he will have to forgo sex for a time; the divorced man says he urgently needs sex. What is meant in each case is intercourse with a partner.

This individualistic perspective not only defines, but restricts, what is viewed as acceptable sexual behavior. Furthermore, male behavior is taken as the norm and female behavior is understood in comparison, usually with the conclusion that women are deficient in some way. Such a perspective also argues for inevitable differences in male and female sexuality. This "anatomy is destiny" perspective relies on studies of animals across the phylogenetic scale, human infant sex differences, anthropological studies in search of universal sex differences, and studies of hormone-behavior relationships.

A number of other implicit assumptions about sexuality that derive from a modern scientific approach can be seen in the work of some of the most well-known sex researchers. For example, Alfred Kinsey's (Kinsey, Pomeroy, & Martin, 1948) work is clearly based on the idea that sex consists chiefly of those behavioral acts associated with intercourse (Miller & Fowlkes, 1980). Other behaviors are not real sex. Masters and Johnson refined this same implicit and unacknowledged assumption by admitting to their initial studies only those participants who regularly had orgasm during coitus (Masters & Johnson, 1966). That is, orgasm is natural or real sex—studying anything else would not be studying sex. Although these studies assumed a cloak of objectivity and empiricism, the most androcentric bias can be found in the imbuing of will and intentionality to genital body parts (Boyle, 1994). For example, Masters and Johnson (1966) described the female physiological response of vasocongestion as an "invitation to mount" (1966, p. 69) and stated that a full erection of a penis is the physiological evidence of a psychological "demand" for intromission (Masters & Johnson, 1970, p. 195).

CHALLENGES TO BIOLOGICAL CONSTRUCTIONS
OF SEXUALITY

There are, however, challenges to this mechanistic, biological view of sex. Alternative perspectives described below suggest that the postnatal environment makes a huge contribution to one's gender identity and subsequent sexuality. The focus is on the social context of behavior and suggests that women and men are essentially alike, except in basic reproductive functions (menstruation, impregnation, ejaculation, lactation, etc.). Socialization accounts for all other differences. This point of view examines sexuality in terms of power differentials, and how hierarchical social arrangements between women and men define sexual behavior.

Margaret Mead's (1961) work challenged traditional scientific constructions by arguing that cultural arrangements were powerful enough to alter sexual preferences across different life stages. Studies of congenital hermaphrodites with similar degrees of hermaphrodism who were assigned different sexes are used to support the claim of the importance of environmental over genetic and hormonal influences (Money, 1970). Money and Ehrhardt (1972), for example, in discussing a genetic male hermaphrodite reared as a girl, concluded that the eroticization of gender developed independently of biological influences. In its extreme form, this perspective assumes that all aspects of sexuality are imposed on individuals, suggesting that if socialization practices were different, sexual arrangements could look very different from what is considered normal in Western culture. As another example, Adrienne Rich (1980) problematizes heterosexuality by proposing that heterosexuality is not due to nature but due to social arrangements in which heterosexuality is compulsory, demanded by men in a male-dominated, autocratic system.

Leonore Tiefer (1995) has argued compellingly that sex is not a natural act; rather, it is socially constructed and repeatedly negotiated. Tiefer's assertion challenges the traditional biological approach to understanding human sexuality and is supported by a number of phenomena. In some cases, these phenomena offer evidence directly contradictory to natural biological models of sexuality derived from traditional science approaches; in other cases the model of a homogeneous natural sexuality is shown to be inadequate for dealing with applied problems. The socially negotiated nature of sexuality is illustrated in the following five examples that were chosen to highlight cross-cultural issues, transgenderism within gender differences, historical concerns, class and ethnic diversity, and sexually transmitted diseases.

Cross-Cultural Differences

Numerous studies have documented different cultural patterns of erotic development and sexual orientation, challenging the notion of sexuality as a universal biological given. The work of Herdt (1984) is particularly illustrative. He identified 53 distinct societies in the Pacific and New Guinea that have "age structured homosexual practice." In a longitudinal study of the Sambia of Highlands Papua, New Guinea, Herdt (1991) described an elaborate pattern of sexual identity development, marked by what Westerners would see as a dramatic discontinuity. Same-sex erotic contact between 7-year-old boys and adolescent unmarried youths is encouraged, in the belief that the male body cannot spontaneously produce sperm. "Insemination functions like an externally introduced androgen to secure maleness maturation" (Herdt, 1991, p. 7). Youths are forbidden to engage in male-female interactions or contacts until their late teens when arranged marriages occur. Married men are permitted homosexual activities until their wives give birth, after which all homosexual activity is forbidden. Herdt (1991) points out that the Sambia pattern (followed by 95% of the men studied) provides an alternative to the Western cultural construction of sexual orientation, its locus, and the meaning of sexual preference. It is worth noting that the Sambians have no categories for homosexual or heterosexual. Herdt concludes, "The Sambia pattern of coercive and obligatory homosexual activity is simply a more extreme form of the many social influences that regulate sexuality across all societies, ours included, perhaps, especially ours, with our strong ideas of individualism, romantic love, and 'the right to orgasm'" (p. 9).

Within Gender Differences: Transgenderism

One need not look to the sexual practices of other cultures to find sexual practices that deviate from what the traditional perspective defines as normal. Transgenderists provide a particularly good example. *Transgender* is a term used to describe individuals who challenge the categories of sex and gender in a variety of ways. Transgenderists are men who present social identities as women and include transsexuals, transvestites, cross-dressing male prostitutes, drag queens, and female impersonators. Inquiries into these men's motives, investment in their gender role, their audiences, and frequency of behavior provide dramatic challenges to traditional assumptions regarding the natural cooccurrence of biological sex, gender identity, and behavioral expressions of sexuality (Gagne & Tewksbury, 1996; Tewksbury & Gagne, 1994).

The study of these persons reveals the possibilities for the independence of one's biological sex, gender identity, and socially presented gender. For example, evidence suggests that many male cross-dressers are heterosexual (Hirschfeld & Lombardi-Nash, 1991; Peo, 1988), although much of this behavior occurs in private because of the social stigmatization men accrue when publicly adopting "feminine" behaviors. Furthermore, researchers also suggest that contrary to the stereotypes, cross-dressing is not necessarily erotically motivated (Bullough & Bullough, 1993). Marjorie Garber's (1992) analyses show how cross-dressing has existed within a heterosexual population for centuries, and has influenced culture in a number of significant ways, in the arts in particular. Cross-dressing also may permit men to engage in behaviors that the "masculine" otherwise prohibits, such as more open emotional displays, elaborate use of clothing and jewelry, and engaging in domestic activities. Unfortunately, the price they pay, relative to the dominant culture's values, is that observers hold their sexuality suspect, and assume they are gay. Although transgenderists demonstrate the distinctions among biological sex, gender, and sexuality, a common cultural response is to fuse these together and label any deviation from the socially prescribed norm as homosexual.

Historical Changes in Lesbian and Gay Identities

Changes across time in the way people think about homosexuality also challenge the traditional notion of a universal, unchanging sexuality. Until the late 19th century, passionate romantic friendships between women were seen as a normal and a healthy part of a middle-class woman's life (Jeffreys, 1985 as cited in Kitzinger, 1994). On the rare occasion when sex between women was discussed it was regarded as a preparation for marriage (Cook, 1979, as cited in Kitzinger, 1994).

A greatly revised view of sexual activities between women emerged at approximately the same time as the first wave of feminism in the early 20th century. Passionate relationships between women became identified with sexuality and seen as a fundamental aspect of the individual that indicated pathology (Kitzinger, 1994). Thus, concepts of sexuality are connected to social and political changes and facilitate maintenance of the status quo. Similarly, outspoken feminist activists of today are often stigmatized as lesbians. This is ironic, because one would think that the women and men who embrace traditional gender-related values would vehemently deny that their sexual intimacies have any political overtones whatsoever, yet they readily discern the potential subversive political subtexts in the intimate sexualities of women who oppose traditional gender arrangements. This leads to the questions: If resistance is political, what is acquiescence? If political resistance is linked (according to traditional logic) to intimate sexuality, how can it be that the embodiment of traditional sexuality within a mainstream culture is devoid of political causality?

A similar pathologizing of gay male relationships began in the late 19th century (D'Emilio & Freedman, 1988). By the end of the 19th century, homosexual behavior among men was seen "not as a discrete, punishable offense, but as a description of the person, encompassing emotions, dress, mannerisms, behavior, and even physical traits" (D'Emilio & Freedman, 1988, p. 226). As homosexual behavior began to be seen as a pathological behavior that defined the person, physicians began to hypothesize about the etiology of homosexuality. Initially, researchers suggested that homosexuality was an acquired type of insanity or a degenerative disease, but it was later reconceptualized as congenital in the writings of Havelock Ellis (1898–1928). Subsequently, the influence of Freud shifted the construction of homosexuality back to the belief in an acquired etiology. Thus, both lesbian and gay male identities have been constructed or reconceptualized as homosexual activity that is a central defining characteristic of a person.

Within Group Differences: Class and Ethnicity

Within group sexual differences present another challenge to the traditional biological perspective. Feminist wisdom has begun to benefit from the recognition that knowledge is pluralistic and that women do not constitute a homogeneous class. Expectations, resources, and the experience of oppression can and do vary depending on age, culture, class, ethnicity, physical ability, and sexual preference. Attention to diversity throughout feminist scholarship has been promoted by feminists (Landrine, 1995; Reid & Kelly, 1994; Pamela Reid offers a variety of new viewpoints with respect to ethnicity, social class, and sexuality in chapter 6, this volume). Some of the possible complexities are highlighted by findings that although African American women may hold more permissive attitudes about sexual behavior than their Anglo counterparts, they may be less likely to engage in sexual intercourse, especially middle-class African American women (Robinson, Ruch-Ross, & Watkins-Ferrell, 1993). Understanding something of these subtleties can lead to a model of sexuality that is more likely to include distinctions between permissive attitudes and promiscuous behavior. Failure to take these variations into account can result in inadequate translations for interventions. The notes of Michele Fine (1989) on the interaction of social class and ethnicity on women's reactions to public systems designed to help rape victims is a clear example of just how critical it is to include diversity.

Issues surrounding class and ethnicity are expressed in a variety of ways in traditional models of sexuality. The sexual discourse was a way to distinguish classes and justify racial privilege. European settlers in North America defined Native Americans as sexual savages. European Americans described African Americans as possessing an animal sexuality, and the 19th-century European American middle class defined working-class men and women as promiscuous and morally depraved. In each case, the definition of sexuality justified the superiority of the middle class and facilitated oppressive public policies toward Native Americans, African Americans, and working-class people. The changing sexual discourse that moved the focus from reproduction to pleasure also reinforced hierarchies between classes (D'Emilio & Freedman, 1988).

Sexually Transmitted Diseases

Just as class and ethnic concerns are related to the discourse on sexuality, they also affect the definition and treatment of social problems. Looking at culture, class, ethnicity, and variations in sexualities is important in developing models of sexuality that have practical applicability. Ignoring within group differences has seriously undermined efforts to prevent HIV infection among women (Amaro, 1995). Whereas most men contract HIV from homosexual activity, most women contract HIV from drug use or heterosexual contact. Not only do women contract HIV through the use of infected needles, but women who use drugs are more likely to engage in high risk sexual behaviors. Furthermore, prevention programs often do not consider the role of gender and assume that the use of condoms, the decision when and if to have sexual contact, and the meaning of sexual activities are the same for men and women. Whereas a man decides to wear or not wear a condom, a woman decides whether to ask a man to wear a condom and whether to refuse sex if he does not. Theoretical models and prevention programs also disregard the fact that women do not always have a choice about sexual activity and that women grow up in a society that encourages them to be passive sexual partners in relationships where they have less power than their partner. Hortensia Amaro (1995) encourages researchers to integrate into theoretical models of HIV risk behavior women's social status, the importance of relationships to women, the role of male partners and the male gender role, and women's fear of and experiences with abuse.

ALTERNATIVE CONSTRUCTIONS OF SEXUALITY

Social constructionism offers theorists a way to get beyond simplistic debates. If we recognize that humans are biological beings born into a social world, biological and social factors cannot be considered in separation. The question becomes how do social and political environments interact with the biologically developing organism to socially construct a woman or man with given attitudes and behavior. The focus is not on the causal role of biological phenomena, but rather on their socially constructed meanings. Behaviors that result in reproduction have no psychological or social meaning without a context to name and shape them for individuals.

Social constructionism suggests examining the social processes involved in generating concepts such as the self, gender, and sexuality. This approach requires questioning taken-for-granted notions, searching for how we come to establish knowledge, and determining what proof structures are used to validate knowledge. Within this perspective sexuality is constructed through the interplay of social, cognitive, and biological factors. Sexuality becomes a process negotiated in social interactions, as revealed in the two following deconstructions.

Deconstruction of Freud on Incest

One of the earliest modern discourses on women's sexuality can be found in Freud's writings. In his early years, he encountered many patients beleaguered by physical disorders for which there was no apparent cause. Using free association, he found dramatic evidence of widespread incest in middle-class European society. However, he later declared (some argue in response to massive criticism from his colleagues) that in fact these women's reports were fantasies rooted in intense sexual desire for their fathers, not recollections of genuine repressed experiences. He described this in the classic case of Dora. Critics of Freud suggest that his original acknowledgment of incest can be supported by large numbers of documented cases of child rape in France and Britain at the time of Freud's writings (Sulloway, 1979). "When we look at Freud's classic case of Dora (Freud, 1905/1963) from a deconstructive perspective, we can see it as a therapist's attempt to adjust the meaning a client attaches to her experience to match the prevailing meanings of the patriarchal society in which she lives ... we might surmise that the cultural belief in the primacy of men's sexual needs prevented Freud from seeing Dora's revulsion as genuine" (Hare-Mustin & Marecek, 1988, p. 461). In a different approach to understanding Freud's diagnosis of Dora, Slipp (1995) used psychoanalytic concepts and logic to examine Freud's own gender identity. He suggests that Freud's gender theories were strongly influenced by his mother's emotional abandonment of him. By deconstructing Freud's writings on incest, his entire theory of the psychosexual stages of development can be seen in new ways that were shaped by possible interactions between Freud's personal psychological make-up, social pressures, and cultural beliefs.

Deconstruction of Childhood Sexuality

Just as deconstructing Freud's views on incest provides opportunities for new interpretations of sexuality, so does Kenneth Plummer's (1991) deconstruction of current conceptualizations of childhood sexuality. Plummer presents a model that explores how a biological potential becomes scripted as the child develops a sense of self. Plummer recognized that sexuality has a physiological and behavioral base, but "nothing automatically translates itself for the child into sexual meaning" (p. 237). He cites as an example the physiological change called orgasm. The meaning of that experience would be quite different for a 5-month-old baby, a 5-year-old child, a 15-year-old adolescent, and a 50-year-old adult. He proposes that sexuality is scripted in childhood by caretakers, peers, the media, and the child's own earlier acquired meanings. He then identifies four common themes in contemporary Western culture's sexual scripts for children: the scripting of absences (i.e., much is left unsaid); values (mainly negative, especially guilt); secrecy (i.e., not a matter of public discussion); and the social uses of sexuality (i.e., to challenge authority, to control others, as play, or an expression of anger). He concludes that "the issue of whether the child *is* sexual or not need not be of concern. What matters is how the child interprets sexuality" (1991, p. 240). His deconstruction of childhood sexuality, as does the deconstruction of Freud's theories, suggests that sexuality is a process developed through interactions.

GOING FORWARD

We argue that to accept research findings as situated or contextual and as open to alternative interpretation and revision marks a psychology that is contextually aware. A focus on context removes some of the dangers of research that fosters individual blame for social problems. We additionally argue that deconstructions of sexuality do not have to be value free; the acceptance of multiple perspectives does not free researchers from making value decisions (Bohan, 1993). Rather, as researchers, it is important to be aware of and state our values and how they may influence us. In the case of Dora, a woman's claim of incest and the response of her family is not to be reduced to the individual pathology of the woman, but examined from multiple perspectives.

Methodologically, incorporating social constructionism into psychology would necessitate stating the values and goals of the research process at the outset for others to examine. The researcher would be obligated to take a critical stance toward the research, evaluating how assumptions and values may influence the research at every stage. The use of the scientific method can be most objective, ironically, when "the subjectivity of the researcher and the researched is recognized and incorporated into research activity and consequent theorizing" (Prince & Hartnett, 1993, p. 222). Acknowledgment of the social, historical, and cultural context also would be required. Research findings can be compared to make generalizations, but care is required not to overgeneralize, or universalize, results. All work would be subject to a critical assessment based on the historical, cultural, and social factors that influenced the research. In short, social constructionism could lead to a more self-critical, reflexive psychology.

Social constructionists hold that all science is political because it is subjective and privileges some ideas, hypotheses, and methods of analysis over others. The feminist researcher, informed by social constructionism, can go beyond recognizing that science is politics to analyze the social forces operating and then make changes in these power relations (Morawski, 1988). Both postmodern feminism and postmodernism in general assert that traditional knowledge and the ways of acquiring it are fundamentally flawed and should be replaced. From this perspective, the modernist assumption that knowledge is grounded in absolute truth having a universal, pan-historical, and constant nature waiting for discovery is simply wrong. Postmodern feminism argues that dismantling the rhetoric of traditional theory and method will produce a public illumination of the social and political values that drive the research. By focusing on the many ways that sexuality is socially constructed, an awareness of alternate realities and methods of construction becomes possible. Illuminating multiple perspectives while considering social, cultural, and historical contexts will transform knowledge.

REFERENCES

Amaro, H. (1995). Love, sex, and power: Considering women's realities in HIV prevention. *American Psychologist, 50,* 437–447.

Bohan, J. A. (1990a). Social constructionism and contextual history: An expanded approach to the history of psychology. *Teaching Psychology, 17,* 82–89.

Bohan, J. A. (1990b). Contextual history: A framework for re-placing women in the history of psychology. *Psychology of Women Quarterly, 14,* 213–227.

Bohan, J. S. (1993). Regarding gender: Essentialism, constructionism, and feminist psychology. *Psychology of Women Quarterly, 17,* 5–21.

Boyle, M. (1994). Gender, science, and sexual dysfunction. In T. R. Sarbin & J. I. Kitsuse (Eds.), *Constructing the social* (pp. 101–118). Thousand Oaks, CA: Sage.

Brown, L. (1997, August). And we're all from Bajor: Giving away feminist psychology: To whom and how. Div. 35 presidential address presented at the annual meeting of the American Psychological Association, Chicago, IL.

Bullough, V., & Bullough, B. (1993). *Cross-dressing, sex and gender.* Philadelphia: University of Pennsylvania Press.

Collins, P. H. (1986). Learning from the outsider within: The sociological significance of black feminist thought. *Social Problems, 33,* 514–532.

Crawford, M. (1995). *Talking difference: On gender and language.* Thousand Oaks, CA: Sage.

D'Emilio, J., & Freedman, E. (1988). *Intimate matters: A history of sexuality in America.* New York: Harper & Row.

Derrida, J. (1976). *Of grammatology.* Baltimore, MD: Johns Hopkins University Press.

Diamond, M. (1965). A critical evaluation of the ontogeny of human sexual behavior. *Quarterly Review of Biology, 40,* 147–175.

Ellis, H. (1898–1928). *Studies in the psychology of sex* (Vols. 1–7). Philadelphia: F. Davis. (Revised edition in 4 vols., 1936. New York: Random House)

Fine, M. (1989). Coping with rape: Critical perspectives on consciousness. In R. Unger (Ed.), *Representations: Social constructions of gender* (pp. 186–200). Amityville, NY: Baywood Publishing.

Fine, M., & Bertram, C. (1995). Feminist futures: A retrospective. *Feminism and Psychology, 5,* 460–467.

Foucault, M. (1979). *Discipline and punish: The birth of the prison,* translated by Alan Sheridan. New York: Vintage Books.

Foucault, M. (1982). The subject and power. Afterward to H. Dreyfus and P. Rabinow, *Michel Foucault: Beyond Structuralism and Hermeneutics.* Hassocks, Sussex: Harvester Press.

Freud, S. (1905/1963). *Dora: An analysis of a case of hysteria.* New York: Collier Books. (Original work published 1905)

Gagne, P., & Tewksbury, R. (1996). No "Man's" Land: Transgenderism and the stigma of the feminine man. In V. Demos & M. T. Segal (Eds.), *Advances in gender research* (Vol. 1, pp. 115–155). Greenwich, CT: JAI Press.

Garber, M. (1992). *Vested interests: Cross-dressing and cultural anxiety.* New York: Harper Perennial.

Gavey, N. (1989). Feminist poststructuralism and discourse analysis: Contributions to a feminist psychology. *Psychology of Women Quarterly, 13,* 459–476.

Gergen, K. J. (1985). The social constructionist movement in modern psychology. *American Psychologist, 40,* 266–275.

Gergen, M. M. (1988). Toward a feminist metatheory and methodology in the social sciences. In M. Gergen (Ed.), *Feminist thought and the structure of knowledge.* New York: New York University Press.

Gray, J. (1992). *Men are from Mars, women are from Venus.* New York: Harper Collins.

Haeberle, E. J. (1981). Swastika, pink triangle and yellow star—The destruction of sexology and the persecution of homosexuals in Nazi Germany. *Journal of Sex Research, 17,* 270–287.

Harding, S. (1986). *The science question in feminism.* Ithaca, NY: Cornell University Press.

Hare-Mustin, R. T., & Marecek, J. (1988). The meaning of difference: Gender, theory, postmodernism and psychology. *American Psychologist, 43,* 455–464.

Heckwood, S. J. (1990). *Gender and knowledge: Elements of a postmodern feminism.* Cambridge, England: Polity Press.

Henwood, K., & Pidgeon, N. (1995). Remaking the link: Qualitative research and feminist standpoint theory. *Feminism and Psychology, 5,* 7–30.

Herdt, G. H. (Ed.). (1984). *Ritualized homosexuality in Melanesia.* Berkeley & Los Angeles: University of California Press.

Herdt, G. (1991). Commentary on status of sex research: Cross-cultural implications of sexual development. *Journal of Psychology and Human Sexuality, 4,* 5–12.

Henriques, J., Holloway, W., Urwin, C., Venn, C., & Walkerdine, V. (1984). *Changing the subject: Psychology, social regulation, and subjectivity.* London: Methuen.

Hirschfeld, M., & Lombardi-Nash, M. A. (Trans.). (1991). *Transvestites: The erotic drive to cross dress.* Buffalo, NY: Prometheus Books.

Jacobus, M., Keller, E. F., & Shuttleworth, S. (1990). *Body/Politics: Women and the discourse of science.* New York: Routledge.

Kinsey, A. C., Pomeroy, W. B., & Martin, C. E. (1948). *Sexual behavior in the human male.* Philadelphia: Saunders.

Kitzinger, C. (1987). *The social constructionism of lesbianism.* London: Sage.

Kitzinger, C. (1988). Individualism and the feminist challenge. *Contemporary Social Psychology, 13,* 38–46.

Kitzinger, C. (1990). The rhetoric of pseudo science. In I. Parker & J. Shotter (Eds.), *Deconstructing social psychology* (pp. 61–75). New York: Routledge.

Kitzinger, C. (1994). Problematizing pleasure: Radical feminist deconstructions of sexuality and power. In H. L. Radtke & H. J. Stam (Eds.), *Power/Gender: Social relations in theory and practice* (pp. 194–209). London: Sage.

Kitzinger, C. (1995). Engendering infidelity: Essentialist and social constructionist readings of a story completion task. *Feminism and Psychology, 5,* 345–372.

Kuhn, T. S. (1970). *The structure of scientific revolutions.* Chicago: University of Chicago Press.

Landrine, H. (Ed.). (1995). *Bringing diversity to feminist psychology: Research, theory, and practice.* Washington, DC: American Psychological Association.

Lather, P. (1986). Research as praxis. *Harvard Educational Review, 56,* 257–277.

Latour, B., & Woolgar, S. (1979). *Laboratory life: The social construction of scientific facts.* Beverly Hills, CA: Sage.

Lederman, L., & Teresi, D. (1993). *The god particle: If the universe is the answer, what is the question.* New York: Houghton Mifflin.

Masters, W. H., & Johnson, V. E. (1966). *Human sexual response.* Boston: Little Brown.

Masters, W. H., & Johnson, V. E. (1970). *Human sexual inadequacy.* London: J. & A. Church.

McHugh, M. C., Koeske, R. D., & Frieze, I. H. (1986). Issues to consider in conducting nonsexist psychological research. *American Psychologist, 41,* 879–890.

Mead, M. (1961). Cultural determinants of sexual behavior. In *Sex and internal secretions* (pp. 1433–1479). Baltimore, MD: Williams and Wilkins.

Miller, P. Y., & Fowlkes, M. R. (1980). Social and behavioral construction of female sexuality. *Signs, 5,* 783–800.

Money, J. (1970). Sexual dimorphism and homosexual gender identity. *Psychological Bulletin, 74*, 425–440.

Money, J., & Ehrhardt, A. A. (1972). *Man and woman, boy and girl: Differentiation and dimorphism of gender identity from conception to maturity*. Baltimore, MD: John Hopkins University Press.

Morawski, J. G. (1988). Impasse and feminist thought? In M. M. Gergen (Ed.), *Feminist thought and the structure of knowledge* (pp. 182–194). New York: New York University Press.

Nielsen, J. M. (1990). Introduction. In J. M. Nielsen (Ed.), *Feminist research methods: Exemplary readings in the social sciences* (pp. 1–37). Boulder, CO: Westview.

Peo, R. (1988). Transvestism. *Journal of Social Work and Human Sexuality, 7*, 57–75.

Plummer, K. (1991). Understanding childhood sexualities. In T. Sanfort (Ed.), *Male intergenerational intimacy* (pp. 231–249). New York: Haworth Press.

Potter, J., & Wetherell, M. (1987). *Discourse and social psychology: Beyond attitudes and behaviour*. London: Sage.

Prince, J., & Hartnett, O. (1993). From 'Psychology constructs the female' to 'females construct psychology'. *Feminism and Psychology, 3*, 219–224.

Reid, P. T., & Kelly, E. (1994). Research on women of color. *Psychology of Women Quarterly, 18*, 477–486.

Rich, A. (1980). *On lies, secrets, and silence: Selected prose*. New York: Norton.

Riger, S. (1992). Epistemological debates, feminist voices. *American Psychologist, 47*, 730–740.

Robinson, W. L., Ruch-Ross, H. S., & Watkins-Ferrell, P. (1993). Risk behavior in adolescence: Prediction and prevention. *School Psychology Quarterly, 8*, 241–245.

Slipp, S. (1995). *The Freudian mystique*. New York: New York University Press.

Sulloway, F. J. (1979). *Freud, biologist of the mind: Beyond the psychoanalytic legend*. Cambridge, MA: Harvard University Press.

Tewksbury, R., & Gagne, P. (1994). Transgenderists: Products of non-normative intersections of sex, gender, and sexuality. *Journal of Men's Studies, 5*, 105–129.

Tiefer, L. (1988). A feminist perspective on sexology and sexuality. In M. M. Gergen (Ed.), *Feminist thought and the structure of knowledge* (pp. 16–26). New York: New York University Press.

Tiefer, L. (1995). *Sex is not a natural act and other essays*. Boulder, CO: Westview Press.

Unger, R. (1988). Psychological, feminist, and personal epistemology: Transcending contradiction. In Mary Gergen (Ed.), *Feminist thought and the structure of knowledge* (pp. 125–141). New York: New York University Press.

Unger, R. K. (1995, March). *How I looked at the psychology of women literature and what I didn't find there*. Invited address for the meeting of the Association for Women in Psychology, Indianapolis, IN.

Unger, R. K., Draper, R. D., & Pendergrass, M. L. (1986). Personal epistemology and personal experience. *Journal of Social Issues, 42*, 67–79.

Wallston, B. S., & Grady, K. (1985). Integrating the feminist critique and the crisis in social psychology: Another look at research methods. In V. E. O'Leary, R. K. J. Unger, & B. S. Wallston (Eds.), *Women, gender, and social psychology* (pp. 7–35). Hillsdale, NJ: Lawrence Erlbaum.

Weisstein, N. (1993). Power, resistance and science: A call for a revitalized psychology. *Feminism and Psychology, 3*, 239–245.

2

BIOLOGICAL MODELS AND SEXUAL POLITICS

DANNY S. MOORE AND CHERYL BROWN TRAVIS

Distortions of sexuality couched in the language of neuroanatomy, hormones, and sociobiology seem to be reinvented every few years, despite numerous scholarly efforts to expose the conceptual bias, methodological limitations, and practical inadequacies of these models. From what should be thorough discrediting and debunking, they rise like a phoenix. In this chapter we focus on the technical limits of biological models that become apparent when strict scientific criteria for methods, data, and analysis are applied. However, before exploring these flaws, it is helpful to give some thought as to why these biological frameworks retain such appeal.

Apparently these models persist in part because they offer a framework for understanding and managing sexuality that has the appearance of being especially scientific. Biological models are judged, by Western sensibilities, to be inherently more scientific (i.e., precise, objective, and factual) than models that deal with large-scale variables. Importantly, the science of biological models is perceived to be demonstrably accurate and in some fundamental sense true. Hence, any science that relies on biological precepts is also apolitical. We argue here that biologically based science has the nice quality of disguising politics. In fact, it is the disguise of political agendas, the camouflage of differential power, and the general denial of the effects of these that is a recurrent theme in the social construction of sexuality and gender.

The appearance of science has been used to add credence to a number of expectations about sexuality and gender roles. Cast in the language of biological science, "bio-proof" has been offered for what are believed to be immutable differences between men and women. The use of biological models commonly is believed to make psychology more scientific. Thus, in order to be able to make scientific pronouncements about sex, psychology should study sex as one would study the "science" of any other phenomena. Psychology, therefore, has contributed to the viewing of sexuality and gender roles as categorically distinct and biologically determined.

In a dedication to their book that says as much about the future as the past, Hubbard, Henifin, and Fried (1979) allude to the costs of such a biologically driven model: "To the many women, past and present, who have constricted their aspirations to fit within what they were told were the limitations of their biology" (p. v). Since the constrictions of our roles have the potential to affect men and women alike, we also would add a concern for the men who have aspired in directions that their officially sanctioned biology proscribed, compelled to exclude the nurturance of those closest to them.

It is our task within the discipline to recognize the beliefs of convenience and popular myth. We contend that these myths derive from political agendas that are camouflaged as natural science. In this chapter we dismantle the misapplication biological models on which sexist expectations of gender and sexuality are based and give particular attention to the areas of neuroanatomy, hormones, and sociobiology. We challenge the belief in a naturally nurturant, dependency driven, sexually coy female, biologically unsuited for competitiveness, and dispel the notions of the naturally ardent, sexually driven, promiscuous male, biologically equipped for intense competition and success.

NEUROANATOMY: A CASE STUDY IN "SCIENCE" AND MEDIA

The connection of brain size, neuroanatomy, and physiology to personal style, intellect, behavior, and complex features of sexuality has been popularly viewed as a well-established fact. In this section we challenge the process by which some findings are given superordinate attention beyond scientific basis, and by which these are indirectly supported by virtue of frequent repetition. We have taken research reported by Simon LeVay (1991) as a case in point. In addition to noting a number of serious flaws in the study itself, we examine the context provided for the article both prior to its publication and within the issue of *Science* in which it appeared.

Notably it was the subsequent replay and repetition of the study that accorded the study significance beyond its technical merit. The mechanisms of social construction are revealed by the way in which the article was paired with other animal studies designed within a biological framework. The process of social construction is also revealed by later hype associated with the study. We suggest that the excessive attention accorded a limited study of questionable merit was due to the fact that it allowed writers to publish their own cherished beliefs as if these beliefs were scientifically based.

LeVay, 1991

LeVay's (1991) study was roughly 2 1/2 published pages, and appeared in the back of the issue with other technical reports. In it, he reported findings from analyses of four separate interstitial nuclei of the anterior hypothalamus (INAH), thought to be associated with sexual behavior. A total of 41 tissue samples were taken from the hypothalamic area of the brain and included samples from 19 homosexual men who had died of AIDS, 6 presumed heterosexual men who died of AIDS, 10 presumed heterosexual men who had died from causes other than AIDS, and 6 presumed heterosexual women. The number of cells in each nuclei, and the area contained within the nuclei (spatial dispersal of cells) were measured. For three of the nuclei (INAH-1, INAH-2, and INAH-4), no differences were found on any measure for any group. For one nuclei (INAH-3), there was no difference in the number of cells, but there was a slight shift in the measurement for total area or volume, measured as the spatial dispersal of cells. The scores (in cubic millimeters) for presumed heterosexual men ranged from .02 to .21, with an average of .12, whereas those of homosexual men with AIDS ranged from .005 to .19, with an average of .051. The scores for the 6 women ranged from .02 to .16, with an average of .056. There was virtually complete overlap in the two distributions, with some heterosexual men having scores lower than the lowest scores among homosexual men. Had LeVay chosen to base his analysis on the actual number of cells rather than on how they were distributed in space, he would have reported no differences between the two groups. Despite numerous uncertainties about the validity of the data, in regard to staining techniques or the appropriateness of the measurement (spatial dispersal of cells as opposed to number of cells), the study was widely viewed as providing a neurological basis for homosexuality.

Certainly a study design using so few participants in any one condition would warrant skepticism. In any case, it is entirely possible that the ravages of a disease such as AIDS and the related regimens of medications could have caused the changes in the nuclei. With only six heterosexual men having died from the disease, valid comparisons would be almost impossible within the AIDS group. Most important, the heterosexual group serving as control, including the sample of six women, was actually of undetermined sexual orientation. There is no way to know if the control sample constituted an exclusively heterosexual group. Also, it is known that testosterone levels are affected by AIDS, and thus it is possible that the hormone levels resulting from the disease caused the questionably measured differences (Byne, 1994). As of yet, the results of LeVay's study have not been subject to replication.

The details of laboratory research often are lost or supplanted by cultural myth (Latour & Woolgar, 1979), and they were clearly lost in this case. Even though scientists such as LeVay often provide disclaimers in their work, these disclaimers, almost without exception, are not emphasized adequately or are completely ignored in the popular media: a media seemingly preoccupied with establishing biological origins for sexual preference. In the case of LeVay, limitations concerning the design of the study were buried by the sensationalism of the popular press. The publication context of the original LeVay article established a prolog that would decrease criticism and increase the likelihood of acceptance. A chronology of media coverage additionally illustrates the amount of energy invested in the popular image of a deterministic, biological model for sexuality.

The Prolog

The original outlet for LeVay's study, *Science*, holds a premier reputation, but it clearly emphasizes the natural, life, and physical sciences with less emphasis on the social and behavioral sciences. The journal was no stranger to the debate concerning a biological basis for sex differences in the human brain. *Science* previously had published at least four similarly flawed studies (Cherfas, 1991; de Lacoste-Utamsing & Holloway, 1982; Gladue, Green, & Hellman, 1984; Swaab & Fliers, 1985) in which purported dimorphic male and female brain structures had been found in humans, all suggesting a link between the differences in structure and differences in male and female behavior. One (Cherfas, 1991) went so far as to specifically link these differences to sexual orientation. All contained one or more problems in method, analysis, or interpretation: small sample size (de Lacoste-Utamsing & Holloway, 1982); over-generalization from men to women (Gladue et al., 1984); over-generalization from animals to humans (Cherfas, 1991; Swaab & Fliers, 1985).

Strong editorial support for biological models of human sexuality also was demonstrated, by the inclusion of other major review articles related to the neurological basis for sexuality, in the same issue that contained LeVay's report. These lengthy articles, featured in the early pages of the issue, focused on laboratory animal research having the appearance of more rigor, and by association, conveyed a sense of rigor about LeVay's work that did not exist. If LeVay's actual article was not explicit in suggesting that he had found a cause for homosexuality, the lead article of the issue promoted that conclusion (Barinaga, 1991). This featured color reproductions of the photos presented in his report, and a color photograph of LeVay, the "Brain Man" himself (p. 956). Two other articles, one regarding the "Brain as Sexual Organ" (Gibbons, 1991), and one describing the neurobiological evidence for a narrowing of the gender gap (Holden, 1991a), were conjoined with the Barinaga article. In the same issue Holden (1991b) also offered a short briefing on the progress of brain scanning and mapping, illustrating the expertise of contemporary science in dealing with the once impenetrable brain (p. 964). Whether intentional or not, that issue of *Science* had the effect of allowing the sensationalizing of the study while preserving the scientific tone of the actual article which was placed among the more technical reports.

The Hype

On August 31, the day following the publication of LeVay (1991), *Science News* scooped the other large popular periodicals and reported: "A comparison of 41 autopsied brains has revealed a distinct difference between homosexual and heterosexual men in the brain region that controls sexual behavior" (Ezzell, 1991, p. 134). Even though the article went on to include the makeup of the participant pool, and also included LeVay's own caution about making assumptions regarding the origins of the difference, the opening sentence quoted above easily upstaged LeVay's suggestion for caution.

The high profile accorded to LeVay's work continued into September 1991, with at least five articles appearing in major magazines. On September 4, *The Chronicle of Higher Education* published a short piece (Wheeler, 1991) that would prove to be one of the rare objections to the study, as voiced by Anne Fausto-Sterling (1985), but the popular press ignored the objections. On September 5, John Maddox published an article in *Nature*, in which he suggested that although inconclusive LeVay's results needed to be taken seriously.

On September 9, *Newsweek*, *Time*, and *U.S. News and World Report* all ran articles on LeVay's findings. *Newsweek* posed the question: "What Causes People to Be Homosexual?" and implied an answer to the question with, "A study pinpoints a difference in the brain" (Begley & Gelman, 1991, p. 52). *Time* ran an article (Gorman, 1991) with a photo depicting two presumably gay men in a happy embrace. The photograph was accompanied by bold text, with the suggestion that a structural difference had been found in the brains of homosexual and heterosexual men. *U.S. News and World Report* in a short article (Crabb, 1991) ran the photographs comparing slices of brain tissue but failed to offer any explanation of the complexity involved in interpreting the photos, only noting that the slices came from the hypothalamus, and that the hypothalamus "controls sexual behavior" (p. 58).

Later, in January of 1992, *Discover* reprinted the above-mentioned photographs (Grady, 1992), and *Time* referred to LeVay's study in a cover story that discussed the biological basis for men and women being fundamentally different (Gorman, 1992). In February of 1992 the cover of *Newsweek* bore a sensational, larger-than-life photo of a newborn, and a headline "Is This Child Gay?" The article was anchored by references to the LeVay study, with repeated citations of his findings, and frequent comments on LeVay's own homosexuality. Throughout 1992, LeVay's work received further media attention in *Newsweek* (Gelman & Foote, 1992), *Science* (Marshall, 1992), and *New Statesman and Society* (Kohn, 1992). The following year, LeVay's (1993) new book was reviewed in *Science*, with further reference to the original study (Livingston, 1993). In 1994, *Discover* ran an extensive five-page account of LeVay's rise to fame, his research, and the aftermath of his notoriety (Nimmons, 1994). All this coverage is in contrast to the 2 1/2 pages allocated to the original article.

The power of the media in this example is astounding, considering that LeVay acknowledged the problems with his sample in the original study. He would later (LeVay, 1993) seem to further de-emphasize the results of his 1991 study in terms of cause and effect, albeit far after the fact, and long after the flurry of, in his words, "media attention and public interest" (p. xiii). "Time and again I have been described as someone who 'proved that homosexuality is genetic' or some such thing. I did not. My observations were made only on adults who had been sexually active for a considerable period of time. It is not possible, purely on the basis of my observations, to say whether the structural differences were present at birth and later influenced the men to become gay or straight, or whether they arose in adult life, perhaps as a result of the men's sexual behavior" (p. 122). However, LeVay did not dispute the inference of a biological basis for sexual orientation. His views are all too apparent elsewhere in the same volume, when he suggested that "gay men simply don't have the brain cells to be attracted to women" (p. 121).

A subsequent publication has further bolstered the popular appeal of LeVay's 1991 findings and maintained interest in the topic. In the May 1994 issue of *Scientific American*, LeVay and Hamer (1994) entered into what was billed as a debate about homosexuality with William Byne (1994). LeVay and Hamer recounted LeVay's original study, and cited the addition of one more specimen (this included tissue reported to have been retrieved from a gay man who had died of non-AIDS related causes). The same results were reported for this additional case, and it was offered as support for the original assumption, that AIDS pathology was not responsible for observed differences. In tandem with Hamer's research on the heritability of homosexuality, the article purported to offer "Evidence for a Biological Influence in Male Homosexuality" (p. 44).

Seeming to fall victim to the repetition of his own work, LeVay became more emphatic in his statements. He surmised that the difference in hypothalamic structure between gay and straight men, as compared with the difference between men and women overall, "suggests a difference related to male sexual orientation about as great as that related to sex" (p. 46). Byne (1994) argued that genetic studies such as Hamer's have serious limitations, that there are some important flaws in sexuality research in general, and that LeVay's study was an example of those flaws. He also noted that genetic studies are inherently confounded with nature and nurture effects; that is, it is impossible to interpret the genetic family tree without considering the soil in which it was grown.

Although many of the articles that appeared in the popular media noted the limitations and the methodological problems of LeVay's study, the popular formats gave the study credence. Such pervasive media attention to questionable findings does little for the public understanding of sexuality, and overemphasizes biologically based conclusions.

HORMONES AND BEHAVIOR

It would appear that popular culture wishes to attribute much of sexual behavior in humans to biology. These simplified views rely on a picture of human sexuality that allows for little variation, and concomitantly little variation in sexual and related gender relationships. These deterministic views of sexuality are often supported by reliance on a highly selective set of examples from animal models, and are elaborated by biased interpretations of findings in human research. Arguments are made to seem scientific by the introduction of details about biological mechanisms, especially the endocrine system and its hormones.

In this section we review some of the assumptions implicit in popularized views about a natural sexuality and its biological basis, and present evidence that discredits them. This evidence is organized according to two principal points: (a) There is a wide range of variation in animal bonding, mating, fertilization, and gestation that contradicts the direct-drive model linking hormones and behavior, and (b) there often is bidirectional influence between behavior and hormones including environmental factors, such as the social and cultural context of behavior and biology. The following discussion highlights variation across a range of species and is designed to provide a framework for rebutting a cavalier reliance on scientific explanations for sexuality.

Range of Variation Across Species

The popularized view is that hormones create and regulate an invariant sequence of biological reproduction characterized by the production of sperm and ova, followed by heterosexual mating behavior of two distinct sexes, followed by genetic cross fertilization, gestation or incubation. In fact, there are numerous exceptions to even the most fundamental assumptions about the basics of biological reproduction.

Reproduction does not require courtship or mating (physical joining), and for that matter, does not necessarily involve an exchange of the genetic material that is definitive of sexual reproduction. There are many species that thrive and function quite well by reproducing in an asexual format, that is, parthenogenesis. For example, in some hermaphroditic species such as earthworms and sea bass, individuals are both male and female, and simultaneously produce both egg and sperm (Crews, 1992). Other hermaphrodites, including many tropical reef fish, produce gametes in sequence, and are actually male and female individuals at respective times. Hermaphroditic species can be first male then female later in life (protandrous), and others, as in many varieties of the teleost fishes, are protogynous, being first female and subsequently male (Demski, 1987). Still other species are parthenogenic reproducers that do not rely on the genetic combination of sperm and ova, and all individuals in the species are female. For example, the Amazon Molly, a popular aquarium fish, engages in mating behavior with males from similar species who actually deposit sperm, but there is no genetic contribution of DNA from the donor males. Although the mere presence of sperm may be necessary for the development of the eggs, it is the social behavior associated with mating rituals that stimulates the reproductive biological cycle. Still other parthenogenic species, such as whiptail lizards, require no sperm at all (Crews, 1992).

Direction of Influence: Environmental and Social Factors

It is also a popular assumption that only hormones influence sexual behavior, when in reality research has revealed that often the environment, both physical and social, affects the secretion and production of hormones. Often, only an environmental cue is necessary to initiate behavior that leads to nesting and reproduction in some species of birds. The zebra finch of Australia, for example, occupies one of the harshest habitats on earth, with droughts lasting as long as three years. Both female and male zebra finches are in a state of reproductive readiness during these arid months, with developed ova and sperm, and begin mating within 10 minutes of the long awaited rain. The finch then proceeds to nest building and egg laying within a week (Arnold, 1975).

There is strong evidence to suggest that environmental factors affect hormonal levels in animals. External environmental factors can produce changes in hormonal levels and reproductive rhythms. Auditory stimuli provide one such example. When laboratory rats were exposed to one minute intervals of bell ringing every 10 minutes around the clock (Zondek & Tamari, 1967), the effect was associated with increased production of germ cells in both males and females, increased organ weight for uterus and ovaries, and prolonged estrous. It has also been established that for ferrets light has some similar effects (Donovan, 1967). The social environment also can have profound effects on reproduction in laboratory animals. For example, male rats housed in isolated individual cages exhibited lower levels of plasma testosterone than those housed in groups (Dessi-Fulgheri, Lupo di Prisco, & Verdarelli, 1976). The mere lack of exposure of male to female rats has resulted in impaired testicular function compared with socially active rats (Jean-Faucher, Berger, De Turkheim, Veyssiere, & Jean, 1978). Overcrowding can have an effect on animal reproduction as well, resulting in lower ovulation rates among free-ranging rabbits (Lloyd, 1967). Such synchrony of biology and environment clearly has survival value, but in these cases it is the environment that is the controlling factor.

In non-human primates, a rise in social status precipitates a rise in plasma testosterone levels, as in the rhesus monkey (Mazur, 1976; Rose, Bernstein, & Gordon, 1975). A similar phenomenon has been observed in humans. A study of male tennis players linked mood, changes in social status, and subsequent changes in hormone levels (Mazur & Lamb, 1980). The change in testosterone levels from pretest to posttest was examined in relation to their having been victorious, or having lost (presumably affecting mood). In decisive tennis matches, winners showed significantly more increase in testosterone than did losers. No difference was found in players who simply were designated as winners of a lottery style contest with identical rewards. The results imply that the fluctuations in testosterone were tied to some effort on the part of the victors, but more important to our discussion, the results also suggest two other important processes. First, simply having won a contest may increase testosterone. Elevated levels of testosterone do not necessarily increase performance, but perhaps it is performance that increases (or decreases) testosterone. Second, it is possible that increased levels of plasma testosterone may not put men "in the mood," and perhaps being in the mood elevates testosterone. Clearly the direction of influence is arguable, and the simplistic notion that our hormones elicit natural behavior (including promiscuity in males for example) is misguided. This is especially important considering the vast opportunities for change in social status, and as well as mood changes, in the daily life of our culture. It also clearly suggests that cultural determinants play a vital role in our behavior whether it be competitive or sexual.

The human body is indeed a sophisticated system. Minor hormonal influences can affect the sexual phenotype greatly, but the environment, especially with regard to the gender role in which one is immersed, can have a perhaps greater impact than simple biology. That is, the social definitions and expectations of others can elicit behavior and personal styles that are generally consistent with those expectations, even when chromosomal makeup is at variance with the imposed social definitions. In one case, a genetic female with male external genitalia, internally possessing a uterus, fallopian tubes, and partially developed ovaries, was raised as a boy (Money, Hampson, & Hampson, 1955). The young man eventually had operations to remove the internal female reproductive organs, but the memorable aspect of this example is the determination with which as a young adult he would pursue his established gender role. At the time of his first contact with the authors he had met and fallen in love with the young girl who would one day be his wife, and was determined to be married to her despite facing repeated operations to correct his underdeveloped penis, along with the maintenance of male hormone therapy. Even though this young man sometimes experienced concern over his apparent differences throughout his childhood (as when he began to develop breasts), and was aware of the removal of female structures, his male role was well established. When he was at college, a homosexual advance by another young man, made him, by his own report, nauseated. He had always known that he wanted to be married someday; he later married a young woman and they conceived children by artificial insemination.

SOCIOBIOLOGY

In this section we briefly review examples of a bias in favor of biological explanations and identify key sociobiology terms and their applications in "pop sociobiology," as well as in more respectable formulations. In the following examples some flaws and contradictions are pointed out, while general flaws in sociobiology also are offered, and alternative analyses are explored.

Basic Definitions

The general principles of natural selection are not inherently sexist and simply stated propose that individuals vary; some variations are more favorable than others; some of this variation is heritable; differential reproductive success may occur; and differing gene frequencies may result. Sociobiology is the study of social behavior as determined by biology, and is essentially based on elements of evolutionary theory emphasizing natural selection as a mechanism by which evolution can occur (Dunbar, 1982; Simpson, 1972). However, sociobiology as applied to humans (Lumsden & Wilson, 1981; Wilson, 1975) is seriously flawed. The concepts of sexual selection and parental investment which have grown out of theories of natural selection, now encompassed by the larger rubric of sociobiology, have been particularly subject to sexist constructions, and have been accorded a certain degree of legitimacy by virtue of frequent repetition, even prior to the advent of sociobiology.

Sexual selection refers to selective pressure on particular traits through conspecifics rather than other environmental factors. The cornerstone of sexual selection is competition (occurring most frequently among males) for access to mating partners (females). The mechanism of sexual selection is thought to account for spectacular physical ornamentation and exotic courtship behavior exhibited by males. Parental investment is a concept closely related to sexual selection regarding the "behavior of a parent toward its offspring that increases the chances of that offspring's reproductive success at the cost of the parent's investment in other offspring" (Barash, 1982, p. 393). Trivers' paper outlining the parental investment concept (1972) has become an institution in itself, and still emanates through the natural and life sciences literature, being cited as often as 100 times per year. Trivers used Bateman's (1948) work with *Drosophila*, conjoined with the theory of sexual selection, in his contention that males and females differ significantly in the likelihood of reaching their maximum breeding potential.

The gist of parental investment theory is that males and females incur different initial biological costs and opportunity costs in the conception and incubation of offspring. It is argued that males benefit by mating with as many females as possible, whereas females benefit most by taking special care in choosing a mate that can provide protection, if not direct support, for the rearing of offspring. Males have the potential for a high breeding rate by courting, mating, and then leaving one female for another, whereas (mammalian) females, once pregnant, have committed their biological resources and any other breeding opportunities. The bottom line, according to parental investment theory, is that optimal mating strategies are not equivalent for females and males. Naturally, if one sex (female) is seen as contributing more to reproduction, then that sex also can be seen as having more to lose. Presumably, this would foster cautious mating behavior on the part of females and impulsive sexual behavior on the part of males. In the following sections we address the misapplication of these ideas and their general flaws.

Misapplications of Sociobiology

A group of writers has been very successful in popularizing sociobiological concepts, and therefore promoting myths regarding human sexual behavior. Fox (1972) argued that the evolution of increased brain size in humans was linked to the ability of the son to control his sexual approaches to his father's females. The evolution of the female neocortex was accorded to the serendipitous passing along of male intellectual prowess. This serves the interests of those who would view male superiority as justification for dominance in almost any cultural configuration, whether it be economic, political, or sexual.

Desmond Morris (1967), in his book *The Naked Ape*, proposed that man's (sic) hunting past necessitated male group bonding and the eventual development of the male-female pair-bond in service of male-male cooperation. That is, males would not bond in a cooperative hunting unit unless the more powerful males were willing to assure junior, or less powerful, members of a female mate. The necessary male-female bond in turn developed into the intense emotional bond that we have come to know as love. Morris proposed that humans evolved in stages, from fruit-picking primates to hunting carnivore primates, and he believed that the desire for sex was situationally controlled in the small, close-knit, communal, tree-dwelling primates. With the evolution toward hunting, the absence of many of the males and the roaming of the male hunters became a factor. Social and cultural rules had to develop to maintain a pair-bond, which is presumed to have been necessary for survival of the fledgling species. The pair-bond also implies the strength of the sexual urge, as well as a necessary control of both sexes, and a particular benefit to marauding men in the control of the women.

> To start with, he owes all his basic sexual qualities to his fruit-picking, forest-ape ancestors. These characteristics were then drastically modified to fit in with his open-country, hunting way of life. . . . The first of these changes, from a sexual fruit-picker to a sexual hunter, was achieved over a comparatively long period of time and with reasonable success. The second change [adapting to a culturally determined social structure] has been less successful. It has happened too quickly and has been forced to depend on intelligence and the application of learned restraint rather than on biological modifications based on natural selection. It could be said that the advance of civilization has not so much molded modern sexual behavior, as that sexual behavior has molded the shape of civilization. (Morris, 1967, p. 24)

Sociobiological concepts have been misapplied not only in the realm of the theoretical evolution of humans, but also in more observable aspects of human society (Barash, 1982; Buss, 1989; Dawkins, 1976). Complex human interactions, such as bride price, differential age of marriage, sexual double standards for behavior, and extramarital sexual activity are seen as being explained by sexual selection and parental investment (Buss, 1989; Daly & Wilson, 1978; Rushton & Bogaert, 1987; Wilson, 1978). Scholarly literature, and popular literature as well, has described marriage and kinship systems as primarily a contract among men regarding the rules of exchange of women (Daly & Wilson, 1978).

One of the cardinal human rules in the exchange of women, a taboo against rape, was likely established by men to protect their investments. However, selective biological examples lend credence to rape as a naturally occurring phenomenon. For example, Barash (1982) observed that in mallard ducks, a paired female may be raped by unattached males, usually provoking another copulation by her mate, with the second copulation serving to decrease the likelihood that the mated male will invest in another male's offspring. On the basis of this example, it may be inferred that humans rape as a reproductive strategy to increase the chances of passing on their genes, or that spousal rape is a naturally occurring strategy as well. The danger of such misguided assumptions is that they serve to explain rape in humans as a biological problem, a problem to be punished but still expected in certain unavoidable numbers of occurrences, rather than a social problem with the possibility of social remediation.

Finally, in a recent rendition of sexual selection theory and human marriage systems offered by Buss (1989), similarities in reported attitudes (not observed behavior) across 37 samples were taken as support for an evolutionary basis for human mate preferences, especially with respect to earning capacity and physical attractiveness. In 36 out of 37 samples, women were reported to value the financial prospects of potential mates to a significantly greater degree than men. One exception, that of the country of Spain, was not explained. In 92% of the samples women expressed a high value for industriousness, but in three sample cultures, Colombia, Spain, and Zulu, women showed the opposite effect. All samples reportedly showed a male preference for attractiveness. Economics, industriousness, and especially attractiveness all are culturally defined, yet the differences were seen as support for the "evolution-based hypothesis" (p. 12).

General Flaws of Sociobiology

A number of scholars well versed in biology and evolutionary theory have critiqued sociobiology (Gould, 1976; Gould & Lewontin, 1979; Kitcher, 1987; Lewontin, 1979; Travis & Yeager, 1991). In brief, they argue that the major flaws of a simplistic sociobiology include (a) errors in description, such as arbitrary clustering of disparate elements of behavior into common categories; (b) the concept of progressive optimization which suggests that everything observed is adaptive; (c) reconstructing versions of prehistoric arrangements that are unknowable; and (d) reasoning by tautology and the argumentative technique which suggests that if a causal connection is plausible then it must hold true.

The misapplication of sociobiology involves taking the description of the individual and the unique and making leaps of interpretation and application to the general and the universal. This most often takes the form of what has been called pop sociobiology, a form that detracts from the serious interpretation of the subdiscipline (Kitcher, 1987). Kitcher argues that it is obviously more difficult to defend a generalized application of theory than it is to support singular examples or the behavior of individual species, and criticizes those who have popularized simplistic explanations. Kitcher further argues that it is impossible to separate the possibility of cultural transmission from biological determinants, and therefore it is unlikely that any one evolutionary theory can explain the behavior of all humans.

Pop sociobiologists believe that fundamentals of human nature can be discovered, that they can be shown to be universal, that if universality can be established it must be adaptive, and that anything universal must be inherited (Hubbard, 1990). As applied to human culture, this view supports the notion of promiscuous behavior in men as being adaptive, when in reality there is no evidence that promiscuous men have more offspring than men who invest heavily in the nurturing of their children.

Even before sociobiological concepts were formalized into a new discipline they were apparent in standard psychological research and theory. For example, Kinsey, Pomeroy, Martin, and Gebhard (1953) commented in their volume, *Sexual Behavior in the Human Female*, on the apparent "naturalness" of extramarital affairs among men, but not women. (Presumably the women with whom these men have affairs are excluded from the psychological analysis that makes illicit sex abhorrent to women.) They commented that "it may be a fact that the males' extra activities do not do so much damage to a marriage, or the wives may be more tolerant of their husbands' extramarital relations, or the wives may not comprehend the extent to which the male activities are actually affecting the stability of their marriages. Contrawise, like the true mammal that he is, the male shows himself more disturbed and jealous and more ready to take drastic action if he discovers that his wife is having extramarital relations" (p. 436). They implied that men and women are more accepting of male permissiveness, and that perhaps women do not have the mental capacity to comprehend the true nature of the situation. Obviously Kinsey and his cohorts were searching for confirmation of what they already suspected about men and women. There is a clear tendency to find what one expects to find in empirical sex research.

In *The Psychology of Sex*, Eysenck (1979) used sociobiological concepts to explain an apparent greater acceptance among men for having many sexual partners. In regard to reproductive potential, Eysenck maintained that "males gain from having many mates, while females have nothing to gain from having multiple partners . . . hence they [men] compete for the opportunity to fertilize women" (p. 45). The implicit control of women is apparent as well in his view: "Men of course do invest parentally to some extent, and hence it is in their interest to protect themselves from cuck-

oldry, which would involve them in investing in the genes of other men"
(p. 45).

SOCIAL AND POLITICAL IMPLICATIONS

The reliance on sociobiological examples and biological models in
general is worrisome, not because biology or natural selection are irrelevant, but because the principles are poorly understood by those who ca-
sually rely on them to justify what are essentially political beliefs (and, yes,
beliefs about gender are political). For example, Newt Gingrich, former
Speaker of the U.S. House of Representatives, commented about women
in the military and their suitability for combat in a video course on American civilization at Reinhardt College in Georgia:

> females have biological problems staying in a ditch for thirty days be-
> cause they get infections, and they don't have upper body strength. I
> mean, some do, but they're relatively rare. On the other hand, men
> are basically little piglets, you drop them in a ditch, they roll around
> in it, doesn't matter, you know. These things are very real . . . because
> males are biologically driven to go out and hunt giraffes. (Romano &
> Welch, 1995)

Mr. Gingrich obviously had not rolled around in a battleground
trench of late, and one can only guess to what he attributes his resistance
to infection. More important, in one statement he both influenced directly
the perception of women in the military and defined the questions that
should be debated in this regard; that the dialogue should center on the
suitability of women for a specific if not unlikely military task, rather than
on their possible contribution to the defense of our nation. All this is
directed at students enrolled in college, in search of new impressions of
truth, ready to create truth for the next generation.

In another example, ABC News (Neufeld, 1995) aired a program on
the reality of sex differences, *Men, Women & the Sex Difference*, featuring
John Stossel, a special reporter for ABC News. The message of the program
was that men and women are "just biologically hard-wired to be different,"
and, accordingly, expectations of gender specific behaviors and attitudes
should be different as well. Stossel concluded that differences do not necessarily preclude equal opportunity, going on to point out that the historical
evidence clearly shows that equal opportunity did not exist for women and
minorities in the context of immutable biological differentiation before the
advent of political intervention. The implication of these pronouncements
is that the goals of equal opportunity are political overlays, whereas ineq-
uities are largely the result of natural biology.

The themes reflected by Gingrich and Stossel are unfortunately too common in the psychological interpretation of sexuality. No one can argue that meager gender differences in attitudes and behavior exist, but there is, and should be, considerable debate over the explanations for the origins of these differences, and certainly over the resultant social and economic stratifications.

It is difficult to dispel the misconceptions about natural sexuality in our culture when the myths of human sexual behavior are constantly reinforced, often by prominent psychologists and the media elite. How can the sexual double standard of male promiscuity and female coyness be dismantled when sociobiological theories are sensationalized in popular magazines? A *Time* cover article (Wright, 1994) reported that the "good news from evolutionary psychology . . . [is] that human beings are designed to fall in love . . . , " and "the bad news . . . [is] that they aren't designed to stay there" (p. 46). The article was a veritable sociobiological textbook explanation of male promiscuity. The themes apparent in the psychological interpretation of sexuality, as we have seen, are not immune from these neatly packaged views.

One disturbing feature of these misconceptions is that the natural biology of sexual reproduction is taken as a general template or justification for a wide range of stereotypic gender role behaviors, often producing prescriptions for behavior that limit individual opportunity and choice. In addition, stereotypes ostensibly supported by biological fact often are manifested in behavior that exploits or abuses women. It is especially disturbing when these erroneous views of sexuality and gender become the basis for repressive politics. According to the deterministic model, social reform designed to alter this dominance is an arbitrary overlay to human nature that can only hope to partially contain the more essential biology.

It is important to look at each of these points because socially constructed models of biology frequently are used in a post hoc fashion to justify intrusive social and political control in people's lives. The implementation of these political restrictions has tremendous implications for women's (and men's) lives. For example, the supposition of a single natural sexuality was one justification for Pope Paul VI's 1968 encyclical against birth control, seen by the Vatican as an unnatural act.

In another example of political applications, sodomy laws, targeting not sodomy but rather homosexuals, are justified in the public conscience because the act is unnatural and against Judeo-Christian law. Violence against homosexuals is rationalized partly on the basis that homosexuality is an offense to God, an offense because it doesn't adhere to the one, normal sexual script established by religions. This rationalization also is apparent in the rhetoric of hate groups, where often the connections are made between God, biology, and a repressive social order. Beyond concerns for frankly political uses of biological determinism, we are concerned that these politics impact personal experience, often causing distress, loneliness, and an impoverishment of spirit.

TOWARD A DECONSTRUCTIONIST VIEW OF SEXUALITY

There is an interactive link between culture and science, such that the frameworks adopted by science reflect cultural frameworks and the resultant findings of science are frequently the basis for bolstering those very frameworks. Four of these interlocking themes pervade the understanding of sexuality: sexual disorders as properties of individuals; sex as an energy system, manifested in normal and abnormal levels; progress through science; and a preoccupation with gender relations (Boyle, 1994). Part of what happens is that professionals construct public understanding by providing a language by which to organize thought and to communicate. The legitimated knowledge of science further defines what is normal and abnormal, what is appropriate and inappropriate (Boyle, 1994).

The construction of what is normal, typical, and therefore to be expected can be seen in observations regarding sexual permissiveness in men and cautiousness among women. Relative permissiveness in men has long been interpreted in terms of normal energy in men, whereas cautiousness among women has been viewed as part of normal femininity. The early work of Kinsey, initially viewed as quite daring and liberal, sanctioned these gender patterns as normal. For example, Kinsey, Pomeroy, and Martin (1948) described the lack of sexual activity in some men as abnormal. These "pruderies," as the authors called them, are most apparent in those who are "dull sexually as well as mentally" (p. 206). They further differentiated male and female arousal, noting that "younger females and, for that matter, a certain portion of the older and married female population, may engage in such specifically sexual activities as petting and even intercourse, without discernible erotic reaction" (p. 157).

These frameworks, which often reflect political structures of power and privilege associated with gender and are not specific to sexuality at all, become internalized as part of the implicit expectations individuals hold about how they should feel. Therefore, even sexual experience and identity that are typically viewed as most private, internal, and individual can be developed, evoked, and sustained by a cultural and political context.

In the next chapter, Mary Beth Oliver and Janet Hyde discuss their meta-analysis of the research on sexuality from the 1960s through the 1980s. The study illustrates how culture and science influence the views of even those who would be impacted most by the biases that are created. Consistent with Oliver and Hyde's predictions regarding the major theoretical perspectives on gender differences in sexuality, men had a greater number of sexual partners and more permissive attitudes toward casual sex than women. Remarkably they found little support for the sexual double standard, the idea that female premarital sexual activity is less acceptable than male premarital sexual activity. The support that was found was on the part of women. Women showed a higher level of acceptance for the sexual double standard than did men themselves.

Psychology as a discipline has the responsibility to recognize the misunderstandings of popular culture, to provide alternative visions for those who will follow, and to create a better world for both men and women to live in. Awareness of the issues raised in this chapter is of vital importance in understanding our past and creating our future. If reality is truly malleable and constructed, then we have the opportunity to contribute to the molding and creation of a fair and tolerant one.

We are hopeful about the possibility of expanding the scope of theory and research on sexuality, and the deconstruction of sexual myth. Nonsexist guidelines to research are a good place to begin (McHugh, Koeste, & Frieze, 1986). First, McHugh, Koeste, and Frieze suggest avoiding excessive confidence in traditional methods. This involves identifying underlying values, such as the pre-experimental belief in differential permissiveness. Alternative methods should also be used when possible. Few empirical researchers offer qualitative findings in tandem with quantitative ones. Second, explanatory models should be used with care. Special care must be taken to avoid unsubstantiated causal relationships between biology and behavior. Third, bias in interpretations should be avoided. The context of research should be examined, including the influences of researchers, confederates, and unbalanced sexual composition of groups. One particularly relevant suggestion concerns the nature of topics researched. Sexual permissiveness may be an important topic for men, but a more appropriate focus for women may be a discourse of desire.

We argue, along with other authors in this volume, that sexuality is a dynamic phenomenon that emerges in context. The context includes the relative status and power of the interacting individuals, implicit expectations held by individuals about what they should feel, rewards and costs associated with particular behaviors, and the social structure that may facilitate or depress certain features of sexual identity and experience. The focus on neuroanatomy, hormone physiology, and natural selection that has characterized much of the scholarly literature on human sexuality simply is inadequate to capture the intricacy of sexuality.

REFERENCES

Arnold, A. P. (1975). The effect of castration and androgen replacement on song, courtship, and aggression in zebra finches. *Journal of Experimental Zoology, 191*, 309–326.

Barash, D. P. (1982). *Sociobiology and behavior* (2nd ed.). New York: Elsevier.

Barinaga, M. (1991). Is homosexuality biological? *Science, 253*, 956–957.

Bateman, A. J. (1948). Intra-sexual selection in Drosophila. *Heredity, 2*, 349–368.

Begley, S., & Gelman, D. (1991). What causes people to be homosexual? *Newsweek, 118(11)*, 52.

Boyle, M. (1994). Gender, science and sexual dysfunction. In T. R. Sarbin, & J. I. Kitsuse (Eds.), *Constructing the social* (pp. 101–118). Thousand Oaks, CA: Sage.

Buss, D. M. (1989). Sex differences in human mate preferences: Evolutionary hypotheses tested in 37 cultures. *Behavioral and Brain Sciences, 12*, 1–49.

Byne, W. (1994). The biological evidence challenged. *Scientific American, 270(5)*, 50–55.

Cherfas, J. (1991). Sex and the single gene. *Science, 252*, 782.

Crabb, C. (1991). Are some men born to be homosexual? *U.S. News and World Report, 111(11)*, 58.

Crews, D. (1992). Diversity of hormone-behavior relations in reproductive behavior. In J. B. Becker, S. M. Breedlove, & D. Crews (Eds.), *Behavioral endocrinology* (pp. 143–186). Cambridge, MA: Bradford.

Daly, M., & Wilson, M. (1978). *Sex, evolution, and behavior.* North Scituate, MA: Duxbury.

Dawkins, R. (1976). *The selfish gene.* New York: Oxford University Press.

de Lacoste-Utamsing, C., & Holloway, R. L. (1982). Sexual dimorphism in the human corpus callosum. *Science, 216*, 1431–1432.

Demski, L. S. (1987). Diversity in reproductive patterns and behavior in teleost fishes. In D. Crews (Ed.), *Psychobiology of reproductive behavior* (pp. 2–27). Englewood Cliffs, NJ: Prentice Hall.

Dessi-Fulgheri, F., Lupo di Prisco, C., & Verdarelli, P. (1976). Effects of two kinds of social deprivation on testosterone and estradiol-17b plasma levels in the male rat. *Experientia, 32*, 114–115.

Donovan, B. T. (1967). The effect of light upon reproductive mechanisms, as illustrated by the ferret. In G. E. W. Wolstenhome & M. O'Conner (Eds.), *Effects of external stimuli on reproduction* (pp. 43–52). Boston: Little, Brown and Co.

Dunbar, R. I. M. (1982). Adaptation, fitness and the evolutionary tautology. In King's College Sociobiology Group (Ed.), *Current problems in sociobiology* (pp. 9–28). Cambridge: Cambridge University Press.

Eysenck, H. J. (1979). *The psychology of sex.* London: J. M. Dent.

Ezzell, C. (1991). Brain feature linked to sexual orientation. *Science News, 140*, 134.

Fausto-Sterling, A. (1985). *Myths of gender: Biological theories about women and men.* New York: Basic Books.

Fox, R. (1972). Alliance and constraint: Sexual selection in the evolution of human kinship systems. In B. Campbell (Ed.), *Sexual selection and the descent of man 1871–1971* (pp. 281–331). Chicago: Aldine Publishing Co.

Gelman, D., & Foote, D. (1992). Born or bred? *Newsweek, 119(8)*, 46–53.

Gibbons, A. (1991). The brain as sexual organ. *Science, 253*, 957–959.

Gladue, B. A., Green, R., & Hellman, R. E. (1984). Neuroendocrine response to estrogen and sexual orientation. *Science, 225*, 1496–1499.

Gorman, C. (1991). Are gay men born that way? *Time, 138(10)*, 60–61.

Gorman, C. (1992). Sizing up the sexes. *Time, 139(3)*, 42–51.

Gould, S. J. (1976). Biological potential vs. biological determinism. *Natural History, 85(5)*, 12–22.

Gould, S. J., & Lewontin, R. C. (1979). The spandrels of San Marco and the panglossian paradigm: A critique of the adaptationist programme. *Proceedings of the Royal Society of London, B, 205*, 581–598.

Grady, D. (1992). The brains of gay men. *Discover, 13(1)*, 29.

Holden, C. (1991a). Is the gender gap narrowing? *Science, 253*, 959–960.

Holden, C. (1991b). Touring the brain. *Science, 253*, 964.

Hubbard, R., Henifin, M. S., & Fried, B. (1979). *Women look at biology looking at women: A collection of feminist critiques*. Boston: G. K. Hall & Co.

Hubbard, R. (1990). *The politics of women's biology*. New Brunswick, NJ: Rutgers University Press.

Jean-Faucher, Ch., Berger, M., De Turkheim, M., Veyssiere, G., & Jean, Cl. (1978). The effect of early social deprivation and lack of sexual experience on sexual maturation of male mice. *Physiology and Behavior, 21(4)*, 491–496.

Kinsey, A. C., Pomeroy, W. B., & Martin, C. E. (1948). *Sexual behavior in the human male*. Philadelphia: Saunders.

Kinsey, A. C., Pomeroy, W. B., Martin, C. E., & Gebhard, P. H. (1953). *Sexual behavior in the human female*. Philadelphia: Saunders.

Kitcher, P. (1987). Precis of vaulting ambition: Sociobiology and the quest for human nature. *Behavioral and Brain Sciences, 10*, 61–100.

Kohn, M. (1992). Sex and the brain. *New Statesman and Society, 5(230)*, 31–32.

Latour, B., & Woolgar, S. (1979). *Laboratory life: The construction of scientific facts*. Princeton, NJ: Princeton University Press.

LeVay, S. (1991). A difference in hypothalamic structure between heterosexual and homosexual men. *Science, 253*, 1034–1037.

LeVay, S. (1993). *The sexual brain*. Cambridge: Bradford.

LeVay, S., & Hamer, D. H. (1994). Evidence for a biological influence in male homosexuality. *Scientific American, 270(5)*, 44–49.

Lewontin, R. C. (1979). Sociobiology as an adaptationist program. *Behavioral Sciences, 24*, 4–14.

Livingston, K. (1993). Other books of interest: The sexual brain. *Science, 261*, 30.

Lloyd, H. G. (1967). Variations in fecundity in wild rabbit populations. In G. E.

W. Wolstenhome, & M. O'Conner (Eds.), *Effects of external stimuli on repro-duction* (pp. 81–86). Boston: Little, Brown and Co.

Lumsden, C. J., & Wilson, E. O. (1981). *Genes, mind, and culture*. Cambridge, MA: Harvard University Press.

Maddox, J. (1991). Is homosexuality hard-wired? *Nature, 353,* 13.

Marshall, E. (1992). Sex on the brain. *Science, 257,* 620–621.

Mazur, A. (1976). Effects of testosterone on status in small groups. *Folia Primatol, 26,* 214–226.

Mazur, A., & Lamb, T. A. (1980). Testosterone, status, and mood in human males. *Hormones and Behavior, 14,* 236–246.

McHugh, M. C., Koeste, R. D., & Frieze, I. H. (1986). Issues to consider in con-ducting nonsexist psychological research. *American Psychologist, 41(8),* 879–890.

Money, J., Hampson, J. G., & Hampson, J. L. (1955). An examination of some basic sexual concepts: The evidence of human hermaphroditism. *Bulletin of the Johns Hopkins Hospital, 97,* 301–319.

Morris, D. (1967). *The naked ape*. New York: McGraw-Hill.

Neufeld, V. (Executive Producer). (1995, February 2). *Men, women & the sex dif-ference*. Washington, DC: American Broadcasting Company.

Nimmons, D. (1994). Sex and the brain. *Discover, 15(3),* 64–71.

Romano, L., & Welch, M. A. (1995, January 18). The reliable source: Gingrich: Big strong men on campus. *The Washington Post,* p. B3.

Rose, R., Bernstein, I., & Gordon, T. (1975). Consequences of social conflict on plasma testosterone levels in rhesus monkeys. *Psychosomatic Medicine, 37,* 50–61.

Rushton, V. P., & Bogaert, A. F. (1987). Race differences in sexual behavior: Testing an evolutionary hypothesis. *Journal of Research in Personality, 21,* 529–551.

Simpson, G. G. (1972). The evolutionary concept of man. In B. Campbell (Ed.), *Sexual selection and the descent of man 1871–1971* (pp. 17–39). Chicago: Al-dine Publishing Co.

Swaab, D. F., & Fliers, E. (1985). A sexual dimorphic nucleus in the human brain. *Science, 228,* 1112–1114.

Travis, C. B., & Yeager, C. P. (1991). Sexual selection, parental investment, and sexism. *Journal of Social Issues, 47(3),* 117–129.

Trivers, R. L. (1972). Parental investment and sexual selection. In B. Campbell (Ed.), *Sexual selection and the descent of man, 1871–1971* (pp. 136–179). Chi-cago: Aldine.

Wheeler, D. L. (1991). A researcher's claim of finding a biological basis for ho-mosexuality rekindles debate over link between brain morphology and be-havior. *The Chronicle of Higher Education, 38(2),* A9–A15.

Wilson, E. O. (1975). *Sociobiology: The new synthesis*. Cambridge, MA: Harvard University Press.

Wilson, E. O. (1978). *On human nature*. Cambridge, MA: Harvard University Press.

Wright, R. (1994). Our cheating hearts. *Time, 144(7)*, 45–52.

Zondek, B., & Tamari, I. (1967). Effects of auditory stimuli on reproduction. In G. E. W. Wolstenhome & M. O'Conner (Eds.), *Effects of external stimuli on reproduction* (pp. 4–16). Boston: Little, Brown and Co.

3

GENDER DIFFERENCES IN SEXUALITY: RESULTS FROM META-ANALYSIS

JANET SHIBLEY HYDE AND MARY BETH OLIVER

Feminist legal scholar Catharine MacKinnon wrote, "Sexuality is to feminism what work is to marxism: that which is most one's own, yet most taken away" (1982, p. 1). Feminists have long identified sexuality as a key issue for women. For example, many birth control advocates in the early 1900s, such as Margaret Sanger and Ezara Heywood, argued that women's control of their reproductive functions was instrumental to their economic and intellectual freedom (Gordon, 1977). The Declaration of Sentiments, delivered at Seneca Falls in 1848, denounced, among other things, the sexual double standard (Donovan, 1985). Implicit in these feminist analyses is a belief that there are gender differences in patterns of sexuality, although not all or even most of these gender differences are attributed to biological factors.

In this chapter we first review a number of theories that either directly address the issue of gender differences in sexuality or postulate a set of processes that readily lend themselves to predictions regarding gender differences in sexuality. Specifically, we review the perspectives of the neoanalytic theorist Chodorow, sociobiology and evolutionary psychology, social learning theory, social role theory and script theory, and feminist theory.

Next, we summarize the results of a major meta-analysis that we conducted on gender differences in sexual attitudes and behaviors. Following that, we consider several behaviors that were not part of our meta-analysis, including mate selection, fantasy, and sexual jealousy. Finally, we summarize the main conclusions that we think can be drawn from research on gender differences in sexuality.

THEORETICAL PERSPECTIVES ON GENDER DIFFERENCES IN SEXUALITY

Neoanalytic Theory: Chodorow

The neoanalytic theorist Chodorow (1978) sees herself as fusing psychoanalytic theory, sociological theory, and feminist theory, and views the causes of psychological gender differences as being rooted in the early family experiences of boys and girls. The core of her argument is that because childcare is done exclusively or mostly by women, as they grow up, boys have vastly different gender-related experiences than girls.

Chodorow begins with the observation that infants start life in a state of total dependency and that their dependency needs are satisfied almost exclusively by the mother, given the division of labor in most families. In addition, infants are narcissistic, and because mothers generally do such a good job of meeting their needs, infants blissfully assume that the mother has no other interests.

Chodorow contends that this early, intense attachment to the mother leads to different developmental progressions for boys and girls. To develop a masculine identity, boys must destroy or repress the intense attachment to the mother. Masculinity, according to Chodorow, involves denying feminine maternal attachment. Masculine identity is defined in terms of individuation and independence and involves rejection and devaluation of the feminine.

Girls do not need to sever the attachment to the mother to develop a feminine identity; rather, they need to maintain it. Therefore, girls never come to see themselves as separate in the way that boys do; rather, they define their identity in relational terms.

In regard to sexuality, the theory at first glance seems to predict a stereotyped outcome: Women should be far more oriented to the quality of the relationship and emotional intimacy, whereas men should be more oriented toward body-centered sexuality (Reiss, 1960) that denies attachment and intimacy. However, Chodorow views the matter in a more complex way (1978, pp. 192, 196). She sees women emerging from the oedipus complex oriented toward the father, and more generally, toward men, as erotic objects, but men do not necessarily satisfy women's emotional needs.

Men are taught to repress affect and keep relationships impersonal in the public sphere, leading them to seek satisfaction of their affective and relational needs in the privacy of a relationship with a woman.

The feminist component of Chodorow's theory focuses not on the consequences of the child's attachment to the mother, but on the male dominance in society. For example, Chodorow used women's economic dependence on men to explain social psychologists' research showing that men fall in love romantically, whereas women fall in love sensibly and rationally. Women's displays of romanticism, then, may actually be a way of making sure that they and their offspring are provided for, a theme that is echoed in the theorizing of evolutionary psychologists.

What does Chodorow's theory predict about outcomes of empirical studies of gender differences in sexual attitudes and behaviors? Parts of the theory lead to an apparent contradiction. The analytic portion led Chodorow to conclude that women are oriented toward men as erotic objects but that women could not find sufficient emotional satisfaction from men. This would lead to the prediction that women would feel comfortable with uncommitted sexual relationships with men (i.e., that women would be approving of casual sex). However, the feminist part of the theory, which stresses male dominance and women's economic dependence, predicts that women will approve of sex only in committed relationships such as marriage, hoping to win economic security. Moreover, the key focus of the theory is that women are relational and men are individuated and independent. This leads to a clear prediction that women will stress the quality of relationship in sexual interactions more than men will. If we follow the feminist and relational parts of Chodorow's reasoning, the theory predicts that women will be relatively disapproving of, and less likely to engage in, sex in casual relationships.

Chodorow's theory has been criticized by some feminists. Two of the criticisms are particularly relevant here. First, the theory has a heterosexist bias. It explains in detail why children grow up heterosexual, and seems to assume that all of them will, and makes no attempt to understand lesbian development (Rich, 1980). Second, the theory has been criticized for focusing exclusively on the impact of gender and ignoring the powerful influences of race and social class (Spelman, 1988).

Sociobiology and Evolutionary Psychology

Sociobiologists apply evolutionary biology to understanding the causes of human social behavior. The sociobiological approach to human sexuality has been articulated particularly by Symons (1979, 1987; see also Barash, 1977; Buss & Schmitt, 1993). The bottom line in understanding any social behavior, according to sociobiologists, is reproductive success, that is maximizing the number of genes one passes on to the next generations. Therefore, patterns of human sexual behavior should be powerfully shaped by their implications for reproductive success.

Sociobiologists have proposed two reasons for the existence of the double standard—society's permissive attitudes toward male promiscuity and intolerance for female promiscuity. First, they point out that sperm are plentiful (the human male manufactures millions per day), whereas the egg is comparatively rare (only one egg is produced per month) and is therefore precious. Thus, it makes evolutionary sense for the male to inseminate many females but for the female to be selective about which genes are paired with hers in the rare egg. Second, they point out that the woman commits nine months of her body's energy to gestation. Therefore, at birth her parental investment exceeds the man's considerably (Trivers, 1972). Greater parental investment fosters greater parental investment. Having already invested more, it is to the woman's advantage to continue caring for the young once they are born so that they survive into adulthood and pass on her genes to the next generation. She is also likely to prefer a mate who is willing and able to provide resources that will ensure that the offspring will be adequately cared for (Buss, 1989).

The predictions from sociobiology regarding gender differences in sexual behavior, then, are clear: Men should be more interested in and approving of casual sex and should have a larger number of different sexual partners, whereas women should be less interested in and approving of casual sex and should have a smaller number of different partners.

More recently, a second generation of sociobiologists, preferring to call themselves evolutionary psychologists, has emerged (e.g., Buss & Schmitt, 1993). In response to the criticism that much of sociobiology consists of post hoc explanations of phenomena, evolutionary psychologists have made efforts to frame hypotheses in advance and then test them with data.

Buss and Schmitt's (1993) sexual strategies theory is an example. They make a distinction between short-term mating strategies (e.g., casual sex) and long-term mating strategies (e.g., marriage). They argue that men and women have different sexual strategies (i.e., strategies to maximize reproductive success) in these two different contexts. Buss and Schmitt then frame a number of hypotheses based on this analysis, including the following:

1. Because of differences between women and men in parental investment, men devote a larger proportion of their total matings to short-term matings than women do.
2. Men's short-term mating strategies are influenced by a need to identify which women are fertile. Men generally use youth and physical attractiveness as indicators.
3. Women's long-term mating strategies are influenced by a

need to identify men who have both the ability and willingness to invest resources in her and her children on a long-term basis.

Thus Buss and Schmitt arrive at the same predictions as the older sociobiologists, namely that men are more interested in and approving of casual sex than women. Their theorizing also leads to specific predictions about mate selection, which we discuss in a later section.

Feminist criticisms of sociobiology are numerous (see, e.g., Hrdy, 1981; Janson-Smith, 1980; Travis & Yeager, 1991; Weisstein, 1982). Feminists are concerned that sociobiology can become a rationale for the status quo. If men have been selected for greater aggressiveness, for example, one might conclude that woman battering is genetically based and cannot be changed. Moreover, sociobiology has been criticized for resting on an outmoded version of evolutionary theory that modern biologists consider naive (Gould, 1987). For example, sociobiology has focused mainly on the individual's struggle to survive and pass on genes to the next generation, whereas modern biologists focus on more complex issues such as the survival of the group and the species, and the evolution of a successful adaptation between the species and its environment.

Social Learning Theory

Although Bandura's original writings on social learning theory did not address the issue of sexuality (e.g., Bandura, 1977; Bandura & Walters, 1963), Mischel (1966) applied principles of social learning theory to understanding gender roles and gender differences in behavior.

According to Mischel, gender differences are shaped by positive reinforcements for gender-role-consistent behavior, whereas role-inconsistent behavior is ignored or perhaps even punished and thereby becomes less frequent. At the same time, according to the theory, children imitate same-gender adults more than other-gender adults, so that the gender-role behavior of the previous generation perpetuates itself in the next generation. The media and other sources present additional models for imitation.

What predictions does social learning theory make for gender differences in sexuality? To the extent that the double standard is in force (Sprecher, McKinney, & Orbuch, 1987), substantial gender differences in attitudes and behaviors can be expected. In social learning terms, the double standard means that women are punished for sexual activities such as having numerous partners or engaging in casual sex, whereas men are less likely to be punished, or perhaps are positively reinforced (through admiration or increased social status), for such behaviors. Therefore, social learning theory predicts a lower average number of sexual partners for women than for men. It also predicts that women will hold more negative attitudes about casual sex than men. Finally, there will be a gender difference in sexual permissiveness: Women will be less permissive than men.

To what extent can social learning theory account for racial and ethnic group variations in patterns of gender differences in sexuality? On the superficial level, it can explain these variations in terms of differing patterns of reinforcements and punishments in different ethnic groups. If, for example, women with multiple sex partners are viewed considerably more negatively in Group X than in Group Y, women and girls living in Group X receive, or anticipate receiving, stronger punishments for having multiple partners than women living in Group Y. Assuming that norms for men are the same in both groups, Group X will evidence larger gender differences in the number of sexual partners than Group Y. This analysis, however, begs the question of why reinforcement contingencies are different in Groups X and Y.

Social Role Theory and Script Theory

Eagly has articulated social role theory and its application to gender roles and gender differences (e.g., Eagly, 1987; Eagly & Crowley, 1986). Here we will extend these applications to gender differences in sexual behaviors and attitudes.

Sexual behaviors are governed by roles; at the same time, sexuality is an important component of gender roles. Heterosexuality is a part of both the male role and the female role (Bem, 1981). Men who are described as having feminine qualities are assessed as having a higher probability of being gay (.40) than are men described as having masculine qualities (.20; Deaux & Lewis, 1984). That is, if a man is described as a male-role violator (has feminine qualities), he is assumed to violate the heterosexual part of the male role as well. A woman described as having masculine qualities is given a lower probability (.27) of being a lesbian than is a man with feminine qualities of being gay (.40). This suggests that the sexual aspects of gender roles are more rigid for males than females, with males' violations of these roles seen as more serious than females' violations. Social role theory, then, predicts that male homosexuality will be viewed as a more serious violation of roles than female homosexuality, resulting in differences in attitudes toward homosexuality depending on whether the target being rated is a man or a woman.

The sexual double standard, discussed earlier (e.g., Sprecher et al., 1987), is critical in defining male and female roles in the realm of sexuality. Evidence indicates that the old double standard of several decades ago, in which sexual intercourse outside marriage was acceptable for men but not for women (Reiss, 1960), has been replaced by a new, conditional double standard, in which sex outside marriage is tolerated for both men and women, but under more restrictive circumstances—such as love or engagement—for women (Sprecher et al., 1987).

What is the impact of the new double standard on role-related behaviors and attitudes? Social role theory predicts that women should have fewer premarital sexual partners than men and that women should hold more negative attitudes about casual premarital sex. The theory predicts that currently there should be no gender differences in attitudes about premarital sex in the context of a relationship such as engagement.

A closely related theory is script theory, originally applied to sexuality by Gagnon and Simon (1973). They used the term *script* in two ways. One deals with the interpersonal, in which the script organizes the mutually shared conventions that allow two people to participate in a complex sexual act involving mutual interaction. The other deals with internal states and motivations in which the individual has certain scripts that produce arousal and predispose to sexual activity. Gagnon and Simon addressed the issue of gender differences in sexuality. They traced much of the origin of these differences to the period of early adolescence, just after puberty. During this period, they argued, the boy's sexuality is focused on masturbation. He is likely to engage in a great deal of sexual activity at this time, but because it is centered on masturbation, it is typically done alone and secretly. Girls, in contrast, are far less likely to engage in masturbation during this period, which is relatively asexual for them. Instead, they focus, traditionally, on preparation for the adult female role, or at least on attracting male interest. The girl's earliest experiences with sexuality occur somewhat later than the boy's and are typically heterosexual, and therefore in a relational context. Indeed, many females see the existence of a committed relationship as the prerequisite for sexual expression.

Script theory emphasizes the symbolic meaning of behaviors. Following the arguments above, Gagnon and Simon concluded that the meaning of sexuality is tied far more to individual pleasure for men and to the quality of relationship for women. The implication is that men should be more interested in and approving of casual sex than women.

Mosher and Tomkins (1988) have extended script theory in their writings about the macho man and the macho personality constellation in men—which consists of callous sexual attitudes and a belief that violence is manly. Not all men, of course, become macho men, but the existence of the script in the culture means that it influences all men, some to a lesser extent and some to a greater extent. The macho man's sense of entitlement to callous sex means that he will have a large number of different sexual partners and that he will hold approving attitudes toward casual sex.

Social role theory and script theory easily accommodate a consideration of the role of ethnicity in shaping patterns of gender differences in sexuality. Different racial and ethnic groups have different norms or scripts regarding sexual behavior, and particularly regarding gendered norms or scripts for sexual behavior (e.g., Frayser, 1985; Gregersen, 1983). Essentially, the female role or script contains different expectations for sexual behavior in different cultures, as does the male role or script. Social role theory and script theory also are quite compatible with the social constructionist perspective that is part of feminist theory.

Feminist Theory and Social Constructionism

Feminist theory is multifaceted and diverse (see, e.g., Tong, 1989). It is beyond the scope of this chapter to provide a comprehensive review. Many feminist theorists focus on gender roles and socialization, using role theory and script theory, discussed earlier. Here we will focus on another important aspect of feminist theory, power.

The concept of power is key to feminist analysis (Yoder & Kahn, 1992). According to feminist theory, there is massive inequality of power between women and men. These inequalities of power occur at multiple levels of analysis, including interpersonal interactions, organizations, and national government. Men express power over women in interpersonal interactions in many ways, including interrupting women in conversations (e.g., West & Zimmerman, 1983) or sexually harassing women at work. At the organizational or institutional level, men have power over women. One example is the preponderance of medical school faculty who are men and wield enormous power over female medical students. A second example is women's underrepresentation as managers and supervisors. Among Fortune 1000 companies, 37% of all employees are women, but only 17% of all managers are women, and only 7% of executives are women (U.S. Department of Labor, 1992). Decisions having an impact on female workers are therefore made primarily by men, with the typical scenario featuring a female worker supervised by a male boss (i.e., a man having power over a woman). At the level of government, men again exercise power and control over women. Decisions regarding women's right to choose abortion are made by a Supreme Court that includes only two women.

One theme in this chapter is that men hold enormous economic power over women and that this has important consequences for sexuality. One factor contributing to men's economic power is the wage gap. Women earn only 75 cents for every dollar earned by men (U.S. Department of Labor, 1993), making many women economically dependent on their higher-earning husbands. The glass ceiling (Morrison, White, & VanVelsor, 1992) contributes as well; subtle barriers keep women from rising as far in organizations as their qualifications warrant. This holds back women's wages further. It is no surprise that the feminization of poverty has occurred. The bottom line, though, is that women lack economic power, and that men have economic power over women. In the sections that follow, we will examine how this leads to theoretical predictions regarding gender differences in sexuality.

Before leaving this discussion of feminist theories, it is important to note that many feminist theorists address issues of epistemology, that is, the origin and nature of knowledge. Many feminist theorists adopt an epistemology of social constructionism. In particular, they view gender not as a biologically created reality, but rather as a socially constructed phenomenon (Beall, 1993; Hare-Mustin & Marecek, 1988). The basic proposition of constructionism is that people—including scientists—do not discover reality; rather, they construct or invent it (Gergen, 1985; Watzlawick, 1984). According to social constructionism, we actively construct meanings for events in the environment based on our own experiences in our culture.

The extent to which we socially construct gender becomes clear if we view the issues through the lenses of other cultures. In European American cultures it is perfectly obvious—a clear reality—that there are two genders, males and females. However, among some Native Americans, such as the Sioux, Cheyenne, and Zuni, there is a third category, the two-spirit (also termed *berdache*): people who dress as and completely take on the role of the other gender. Some of these tribes consider the two-spirit to be a third gender, and it is perfectly clear in their culture that there are three genders (Beall, 1993; Kessler & McKenna, 1985). What seems like an obvious reality to European Americans, that there are only two genders, turns out to be a social construction.

This perspective of social constructionism should be borne in mind when reading the sections that follow, reporting on empirical studies of gender differences in sexual attitudes and behaviors. From a feminist point of view, these gender differences should not be regarded as real differences rooted in biology, but rather as differences that arise from gender roles, socialization, inequality of power—particularly economic power—between women and men, and the ways in which gender is socially constructed in dominant American culture.

Summary

The theories reviewed here, although operating under considerably different assumptions, actually make predictions that are more similar than different. All predict, for example, that women will be more disapproving of casual sex than men. The theories differ greatly in their understanding of some key constructs, particularly the sexual double standard. Evolutionary theorists see the sexual double standard as a product of evolution. Social learning theorists view the double standard as creating considerably different reinforcement contingencies for men's and women's sexual behaviors. Social role theorists view the double standard as creating different norms for women's and men's sexual behavior. Feminist theorists view the double standard as another instance of gender-based inequality, and as a means by which men exert power and control over women.

A META-ANALYSIS OF STUDIES OF GENDER DIFFERENCES IN SEXUALITY

Although there has been much theorizing about gender differences in sexuality, and many scattered empirical studies, there was a need to integrate this theorizing and research in a systematic manner. To meet this need, we conducted a meta-analysis of studies reporting data on gender differences in sexual behaviors and attitudes (Oliver & Hyde, 1993).

We were able to locate 177 usable studies that reported data on gender differences in 21 different sexual attitudes and behaviors: attitudes about premarital intercourse (general); attitudes about premarital intercourse in a casual relationship; attitudes about premarital intercourse in a committed relationship; attitudes about premarital intercourse when the couple are engaged but not married; attitudes toward homosexuality[1]; attitudes about civil liberties for homosexuals; attitudes about extramarital sex; general sexual permissiveness; anxiety, fear, or guilt about sexuality; sexual satisfaction; double standard attitudes (i.e., beliefs that sexual activity is more acceptable for males than for females); attitudes about masturbation; incidence of kissing; incidence of petting; incidence of intercourse; age at first intercourse; number of sexual partners; frequency of intercourse; incidence of masturbation; incidence of homosexual behavior; and incidence of oral sex. (See Oliver & Hyde, 1993, for details on methods of identifying and coding studies.) The studies represented, altogether, the testing of 128,363 respondents (58,553 males and 69,810 females).

For each study, we computed an effect size, to measure the magnitude of the gender difference. We used the formula

$$d = \frac{M_M - M_F}{s}$$

where M_M is equal to the mean for males, M_F is equal to the mean for females, and s is the average within-gender standard deviation. The d statistic essentially measures how far apart the male and female means are, in standard deviation units. A positive value of d therefore indicates that males scored higher than females, whereas a negative value indicates that

---

[1]We agree with APA style in the use of the terms *gay men* and *lesbians*. However, most of the research reviewed in the meta-analysis used the terms *homosexuality* or *homosexuals* in the questions given to respondents. We therefore use those terms in order to reflect the content of the actual research questions.

females scored higher. When means and standard deviations were not available, we used other formulas provided by Hedges and Becker (1986). Effect sizes for a given attitude or behavior were then averaged over studies following methods detailed by Hedges and Becker (1986). In interpreting the magnitude of effect sizes, we generally follow the guidelines stated by Cohen (1969): a d value of .20 is small, .50 is moderate, and .80 is large.

The resulting effect sizes for the 21 sexual attitudes and behaviors are shown in Table 1. Most striking are the two largest gender differences. One is the incidence of masturbation ($d = 0.96$). Kinsey found that 92% of males, compared with 58% of females, masturbate to orgasm at least once in their lives (Kinsey, Pomeroy, Martin, & Gebhard, 1953). Despite massive changes in patterns of sexual behaviors in the 50 years since Kinsey collected his data, this marked gender difference remains. Relevant data are found in the recent, well-sampled national survey of sexual behavior conducted by the National Opinion Research Center (NORC) (Laumann, Gagnon, Michael, & Michaels, 1994). Although they did not compute lifetime incidence statistics, they did inquire about incidence in the past year. The results indicated that 42% of women, compared with 63% of men, masturbated in the last year. This pattern, however, varies as a function of ethnicity. The large gender gap was found for Whites (67% of men,

TABLE 1
Magnitude of Gender Differences as a Function of Sexuality Measure

Measure	k	d	95% confidence interval for d
Premarital attitudes	46	0.37	0.35 to 0.40
Intercourse: casual	10	0.81	0.75 to 0.87
Intercourse: committed	10	0.49	0.44 to 0.53
Intercourse: engaged	5	0.43	0.32 to 0.54
Homosexuality attitudes	28	−0.01	−0.04 to 0.02
Homosexual civil liberties	14	−0.00	−0.03 to 0.02
Extramarital attitudes	17	0.29	0.26 to 0.32
Sexual permissiveness	39	0.57	0.55 to 0.60
Anxiety/fear/guilt	11	−0.35	−0.44 to −0.26
Sexual satisfaction	15	−0.06	−0.09 to −0.03
Double standard	7	−0.29	−0.37 to −0.21
Masturbation attitudes	12	0.09	0.04 to 0.14
Kissing incidence	15	−0.05	−0.10 to 0.01
Petting incidence	28	0.11	0.07 to 0.15
Intercourse incidence	135	0.33	0.32 to 0.35
Age at first intercourse	8	0.38	0.30 to 0.45
Number of sexual partners	12	0.25	0.19 to 0.32
Frequency of intercourse	11	0.31	0.27 to 0.36
Masturbation incidence	26	0.96	0.92 to 1.00
Homosexual incidence	19	0.33	0.30 to 0.37
Oral sex incidence	21	0.10	0.05 to 0.15

Note. k represents the number of effect sizes that contributed to the mean effect size, d.

44% of women) and Hispanics (67% of men and 34% of women) but was smaller for Blacks (40% of men and 32% of women).

The other large gender difference was in attitudes about premarital sex in a casual relationship ($d = 0.81$). Males were considerably more approving than females were, as predicted by all the theories reviewed earlier. This gender difference is illustrated by the findings of an innovative study by Clark and Hatfield (1989). An attractive man or woman confederate approached strangers of the other gender on a college campus and posed one of the following three questions: "I have been noticing you around campus. I find you very attractive. (a) Would you go out with me tonight? (b) Would you come over to my apartment tonight? (c) Would you go to bed with me tonight?" Of those approached for a date, roughly 50% of women accepted, as did 50% of men (i.e., there was no gender difference). The question of interest here, though, is the invitation for casual sex; 75% of men agreed to it, compared with only 6% of women. Men evidenced considerably more interest in casual sex. An alternative interpretation of these results is that women responded negatively to the invitation for casual sex because of personal safety issues, namely that it carries with it a potential for rape. These two interpretations are not mutually exclusive, of course; both factors may play a role.

Many other gender differences were moderate in magnitude, according to the meta-analysis (Oliver & Hyde, 1993). Males were more sexually permissive ($d = 0.57$), and females reported more anxiety, fear, and guilt about sex ($d = -0.35$).

Still other behaviors showed no gender difference. We advocate interpreting d values of 0.10 or less (in absolute value) as indicating no difference. Using this guideline, there were no gender differences in attitudes about civil liberties for homosexuals (-0.00), sexual satisfaction (-0.06), or attitudes about masturbation (0.09).

One of our findings of no gender difference was later contested. We found $d = -0.01$ for attitudes toward homosexuality (Oliver & Hyde, 1993). Whitley and Kite (1995) located a number of additional studies of gender differences in attitudes toward homosexuality, which we had not located for our original meta-analysis. With the addition of these studies, they found $d = 0.26$; that is males hold more negative attitudes. The magnitude of this difference is larger than the near-zero value we found, but it is still small. We were concerned that most of the studies added by Whitley and Kite were based on convenience samples of college students, whereas our original set of studies had contained well-sampled studies of the general population (Oliver & Hyde, 1995). The effect size found by Whitley and Kite may tell us more about college students than anything else. In addition, Whitley and Kite had a number of inflated computations of effect sizes. We concluded that the existence and magnitude of gender differences in general attitudes toward homosexuality is an open question, but is almost certainly small (Oliver & Hyde, 1995).

Whitley and Kite (1995) noted that gender differences in attitudes toward homosexuality may vary as a function of the gender of the person being rated (i.e., whether the study measures attitudes toward lesbians or attitudes toward gay men). Supporting this view, they found $d = 0.51$ for ratings of gay men, -0.03 for ratings of lesbians, and 0.35 for ratings with gender unspecified. Men hold considerably more negative attitudes about gay men than women do, whereas men and women do not differ in their attitudes about lesbians. This is an illustration of the complex ways in which gender and sexual orientation interact.

We turn now to a consideration of gender differences in some sexual practices that were not reviewed by Oliver and Hyde (1993).

OTHER SEXUAL PRACTICES

Mate Selection

Recent theorizing and research, particularly among evolutionary psychologists, has focused a great deal on mate selection (i.e., on the features that most influence men and women in their choice of sexual partners and marriage partners).

Much of social psychologists' research on mate selection preferences has been conducted in the laboratory using samples of college students. One exception is a study by Sprecher, Sullivan, and Hatfield (1994), which used data from a well-sampled survey, the National Survey of Families and Households. Among the questions on the survey was a set of items listing 12 possible assets or liabilities in a marriage partner; respondents were asked to indicate their willingness to marry someone possessing each of the traits. All respondents were age 35 or younger and were never married. Sprecher et al.'s findings were quite similar to those of studies using more limited samples. Specifically, they found that men rated physical attractiveness and youth as more important in a partner, whereas women gave higher ratings to earning potential.

In general, this pattern of gender differences in characteristics considered important in mate selection was consistent for Whites and for Blacks. There was one exception, however, for the item "not likely to hold a steady job." White men were more willing than Black men to marry a woman who did not have a steady job. Both Black and White women were less willing to marry a man who did not hold a steady job, but Black women were somewhat more willing than White women. It seems likely that this reflects the realities of unemployment for Black men.

As noted earlier, this is precisely the pattern of gender differences in mate preferences that one would predict based on theories in evolutionary psychology. It also is the pattern one would predict based on sociocultural factors (Howard, Blumstein, & Schwartz, 1987; Sprecher et al., 1994). Given the gender gap in wages—women in the United States currently earn only 75 cents for every dollar men earn (U.S. Department of Labor, 1993)—it is not surprising that women look for a spouse who is a steady earner. The emphasis on men's earning potential also is consistent with the importance of the good provider role for men (Bernard, 1981; Pleck, 1981). In addition, cultural norms dictate romantic pairings of young women with older men, but never of young men with older women.

Howard, Blumstein, and Schwartz (1987) noted another limitation in past research on gender differences in mate preferences: The research has assumed heterosexual pairings. Howard et al. investigated whether the typical patterns of mate preference also would be found among gay and lesbian couples, based on a nonrandom, volunteer sample of 4,314 heterosexual married and cohabiting couples, 969 gay male couples, and 788 lesbian couples. Theoretical predictions were made difficult because, on the one hand, evolutionary psychologists may argue that females have been selected for certain patterns of mate preferences, regardless of sexual orientation. On the other hand, because same-gender pairings have no reproductive intent or outcome, evolutionary selection may be irrelevant, and therefore the typical patterns of mate preference would not be found among gays and lesbians.

The pattern of results was quite similar to previous research. Specifically, men (whether heterosexual or homosexual) rated attractiveness of a partner as more important in mate selection than did women (whether heterosexual or homosexual) (Howard et al., 1987). Women (regardless of sexual orientation) rated ambitiousness in a mate as more important than did men (regardless of sexual orientation); however, the gap between heterosexual men and women was larger and the gap between lesbians and gay men was smaller. In general, sexual orientation did not have substantial effects on partner preferences.

Sexual Fantasies

Sexual fantasies were not reviewed by Oliver and Hyde (1993). This was due in large part to the fact that many studies focus on the content of males' and females' fantasies, while at the same time there is no standard method of categorizing sexual fantasies, making it difficult if not impossible to cumulate findings across studies.

Leitenberg and Henning (1995) reviewed research on sexual fantasies and included a particular focus on gender differences and similarities in sexual fantasy. They concluded that the incidence of fantasy during masturbation is higher for men than for women, with an average of about 86%

of men reporting such fantasizing, compared with 69% of women. (These statistics are computed just for those who masturbate, so the large gender difference in the incidence of masturbation does not influence the results.) Despite the gender difference in the incidence of fantasies, the majority of women (69%) do have fantasies during masturbation. Leitenberg and Henning also concluded that there was no gender difference in the incidence of fantasy during sexual intercourse. It is frustrating that the only study to report data separately for Blacks and Whites was based on a convenience sample of college students, severely limiting any conclusions that could be reached from it.

Many of the studies reviewed by Leitenberg and Henning were old (e.g., Kinsey et al., 1953) or based on convenience samples. The recent well-sampled NORC study found that 54% of men, compared with 19% of women, had sexual thoughts frequently, defined as every day or more (Laumann et al., 1994).

In one interesting study, college student participants used a diary method and recorded sexual fantasies as they occurred throughout the day (Jones & Barlow, 1990). The sexual fantasies were recorded according to whether they were provoked by an external stimulus (e.g., something they saw or read), were internally generated, or occurred during masturbation. On the average, men reported about 4.5 externally triggered sexual fantasies per day, about 2.7 internally generated fantasies per day, and less than 1 masturbatory fantasy per day. Women reported, on the average, about 2 externally triggered fantasies, 2.5 internally generated fantasies, and less than 1 masturbatory fantasy per day. Men and women, then, do not appear to differ in the incidence of internally generated fantasies or masturbatory fantasies. Men are considerably more likely than women, though, to experience externally triggered sexual fantasies. This gender difference may be the result of a number of factors, including men's greater exposure to and interest in sexually explicit materials, or men's greater responsiveness to sexually arousing visual stimuli.

Sociobiologists have especially emphasized the visual stimuli factor, arguing that responsiveness to a wide variety of sexual stimuli confers a reproductive advantage for men (e.g., Ellis & Symons, 1990). Sociocultural explanations, however, based on role theory and script theory, can just as readily explain these findings. As noted earlier, women and men are socialized considerably differently in regard to sexuality. Central to the message conveyed to girls and women is that sex for them is legitimate only in the context of a committed relationship, whereas men are allowed more sexual freedom (Sprecher et al., 1987). Sexual fantasy in response to a sexually explicit magazine is in essence a type of sexual expression where no relationship is involved; it may therefore be much more comfortable for males than for females.

Sexual Jealousy

Evolutionary psychologists have framed predictions about differing patterns of sexual jealousy in men compared with women (Buss & Schmitt, 1993). The argument is that men must solve the problem of uncertainty of paternity. That is, it is not to their evolutionary advantage to invest in offspring who are not theirs. Therefore, men should be more distressed (jealous) than women by sexual infidelity. Women, in contrast, are certain whether an offspring is theirs. Their evolutionary strategy is maximized, according to the theory, by being confident of their mate's continued commitment and investment. That is, women should be more distressed than men by emotional infidelity.

To test this prediction, respondents were asked to do the following: "Imagine that you discover that the person with whom you've been seriously involved became interested in someone else. What would distress or upset you more (please circle one only): (A) Imagining your partner forming a deep emotional attachment to that person. (B) Imagining your partner enjoying passionate sexual intercourse with that other person" (Buss, Larsen, Westen, & Semmelroth, 1992, p. 252). The former can be termed emotional infidelity and the latter sexual infidelity. The results, both measured by self-reported ratings and by physiological measures, indicated that men were most distressed by sexual infidelity, whereas women were most distressed by emotional infidelity.

These findings are consistent with the predictions of evolutionary psychology. Again, though, the results would have been equally predictable based on an analysis of sociocultural factors. There is a long history of ridiculing a man who is a cuckold. It is interesting to note that Webster's dictionary defines *cuckold* in gendered terms: a man whose wife has committed adultery. A woman cannot be cuckolded. Men, in short, have been told that they are undone if their spouse engages in sex with someone else. Again, women's economic dependence caused by the wage gap is a reasonable explanation for why they feel distressed about emotional infidelity, insofar as it signals potential desertion by the man and loss of economic support.

In cross-cultural research, respondents from 37 different societies around the world rated the importance of chastity in a marriage partner (Buss & Schmitt, 1993). The prediction from evolutionary psychology is that men should rate chastity as more important in a partner than women should. This hypothesis was supported by findings of a significant gender difference in 23 of the 37 samples; the remaining 14 societies showed no gender difference. Men's greater emphasis on chastity in a partner is scarcely a universal, according to these data.

CONCLUSION

In this chapter we reviewed the results of a meta-analysis of gender differences in sexuality, which indicated that there are large gender differences in the incidence of masturbation (with males having the higher incidence) and in attitudes toward casual sex (males hold more permissive attitudes). The meta-analysis also found evidence of no gender differences in some areas, including attitudes about civil liberties for homosexuals and sexual satisfaction.

We also reviewed evidence regarding gender differences in patterns of mate selection. These studies generally find that men place a high priority on youth and physical attractiveness in choosing a mate, whereas women place more emphasis on earning potential.

Sociobiologists and evolutionary psychologists have developed theoretical frameworks that "predict" many of the gender differences reported here, in particular the gender difference in attitudes toward casual sex and the gender difference in patterns of mate selection. Without pausing for breath, though, we must go on to say that these phenomena are equally well predicted by sociocultural factors, in particular by social role theory and feminist theory. For example, women's economic inequality is a very reasonable explanation for women's emphasis on a potential mate's earning potential.

The bottom line is that the theories reviewed here do not make strong differential predictions regarding patterns of gender differences in sexuality. Rather, they yield similar if not identical predictions. An important advance in this area of research will occur when the theories are sufficiently refined to specify differential predictions for different theories.

The magnitude of some of the gender differences reported here—particularly in the incidence of masturbation and attitudes about casual sex—is enormous compared with the magnitude of gender differences in other areas of psychology that have received much publicity and research. For example, overall, the magnitude of gender differences in mathematics performance in samples of the general population is $d = -0.05$ (Hyde, Fennema, & Lamon, 1990). The magnitude of gender differences in verbal ability, overall, is $d = -0.11$ (Hyde & Linn, 1988). We contend that researchers who have been searching for substantial gender differences in the realm of abilities have been looking in the wrong place. Multiple theoretical perspectives converge on predictions of large gender differences in some aspects of sexuality. Many of these differences seem to derive from the very different roles that men and women play in the reproductive aspects of sexuality.

In reviewing research published since our 1993 meta-analysis (Oliver & Hyde, 1993), it became clear that a few topics have come to the forefront, particularly mate preference, fantasy, and sexual jealousy. These are all domains in which evolutionary psychologists predict that there should be substantial gender differences. In short, evolutionary psychologists are setting the agenda for research on gender differences in sexuality. Feminist researchers must consider how to recapture the research agenda. It is clear, for example, that not much is known about gender differences in masturbation—particularly about how masturbation plays different roles in sexual development for women compared with men. An understanding of such basic research questions may in turn have implications for sex therapy with women. At the same time, feminist researchers should pursue avenues of research on women and sexuality other than gender differences. These include women's experience of sexuality during and after menopause, women's experience of sexuality during pregnancy and postpartum (see chapter 5, this volume, by Hyde & DeLamater), and patterns of sexuality that enhance women's sexual pleasure.

REFERENCES

Bandura, A. J. (1977). *Social learning theory.* Engelwood Cliffs, NJ: Prentice-Hall.

Bandura, A., & Walters, R. H. (1963). *Social learning and personality development.* New York: Holt.

Barash, D. P. (1977). *Sociobiology and behavior.* New York: Elsevier.

Beall, A. E. (1993). A social constructionist view of gender. In A. E. Beall & R. J. Sternberg (Eds.), *The psychology of gender* (pp. 127–147). New York: Guilford.

Bem, S. (1981). Gender schema theory: A cognitive account of sex-typing. *Psychological Review, 88,* 354–364.

Bernard, J. (1981). The good-provider role: Its rise and fall. *American Psychologist, 36,* 1–12.

Buss, D. M. (1989). Sex differences in human mate preferences: Evolutionary hypotheses tested in 37 cultures. *Behavioral and Brain Sciences, 12,* 1–49.

Buss, D. M., Larsen, R. J., Westen, D., & Semmelroth, J. (1992). Sex differences in jealousy: Evolution, physiology, and psychology. *Psychological Science, 3,* 251–255.

Buss, D. M., & Schmitt, D. P. (1993). Sexual strategies theory: A contextual evolutionary analysis of human mating. *Psychological Review, 100,* 204–232.

Chodorow, N. (1978). *The reproduction of mothering.* Berkeley: University of California Press.

Clark, R. D., & Hatfield, E. (1989). Gender differences in receptivity to sexual offers. *Journal of Psychology and Human Sexuality, 2,* 39–55.

Cohen, J. (1969). *Statistical power analysis for the behavioral sciences.* New York: Academic Press.

Deaux, K., & Lewis, L. L. (1984). Structure of gender stereotypes: Interrelationships among components and gender label. *Journal of Personality and Social Psychology, 46,* 991–1004.

Donovan, J. (1985). *Feminist theory: The intellectual traditions of American feminism.* New York: Frederick Ungar Publishing Co.

Eagly, A. H. (1987). *Sex differences in social behavior: A social role interpretation.* Hillsdale, NJ: Erlbaum.

Eagly, A. H., & Crowley, M. (1986). Gender and helping behavior: A meta-analytic review of the social psychological literature. *Psychological Bulletin, 100,* 283–308.

Ellis, B. J., & Symons, D. O. (1990). Sex differences in sexual fantasy: An evolutionary psychological approach. *Journal of Sex Research, 27,* 527–555.

Frayser, S. G. (1985). *Varieties of sexual experience: An anthropological perspective on human sexuality.* New Haven, CT: Human Relations Area Files Press.

Gagnon, J. H., & Simon, W. (1973). *Sexual conduct: The social origins of human sexuality.* Chicago: Aldine Publishing Co.

Gergen, K. (1985). The social constructionist movement in modern psychology. *American Psychologist, 40,* 266–275.

Gordon, L. (1977). *Woman's body, woman's right: A social history of birth control in America.* New York: Penguin Books.

Gould, S. J. (1987). *An urchin in the storm.* New York: Norton.

Gregersen, E. (1983). *Sexual practices: The story of human sexuality.* New York: Franklin Watts.

Hare-Mustin, R. T., & Marecek, J. (1988). The meaning of difference: Gender theory, postmodernism and psychology. *American Psychologist, 43,* 455–464.

Hedges, L. V., & Becker, B. J. (1986). Statistical methods in the meta-analysis of research on gender differences. In J. S. Hyde & M. C. Linn (Eds.), *The psychology of gender: Advances through meta-analysis* (pp. 14–50). Baltimore: Johns Hopkins University Press.

Howard, J. A., Blumstein, P., & Schwartz, P. (1987). Social or evolutionary theories? Some observations on preferences in human mate selection. *Journal of Personality and Social Psychology, 53,* 194–200.

Hrdy, S. B. (1981). *The woman that never evolved.* Cambridge: Harvard University Press.

Hyde, J. S., Fennema, E., & Lamon, S. J. (1990). Gender differences in mathematics performance: A meta-analysis. *Psychological Bulletin, 107,* 139–155.

Hyde, J. S., & Linn, M. C. (1988). Gender differences in verbal ability: A meta-analysis. *Psychological Bulletin, 104,* 53–69.

Janson-Smith, D. (1980). Sociobiology: So what? In Brighton Women & Science Group, *Alice through the microscope.* London: Virago.

Jones, J. C., & Barlow, D. H. (1990). Self-reported frequency of sexual urges, fantasies, and masturbatory fantasies in heterosexual males and females. *Archives of Sexual Behavior, 19,* 269–279.

Kessler, S. J., & McKenna, W. (1985). *Gender: An ethnomethodological approach.* Chicago: University of Chicago Press.

Kinsey, A. C., Pomeroy, W. B., Martin, C. E., & Gebhard, P. H. (1953). *Sexual behavior in the human female.* Philadelphia: Saunders.

Laumann, E. W., Gagnon, J. H., Michael, R. T., & Michaels, S. (1994). *The social organization of sexuality: Sexual practices in the United States.* Chicago: University of Chicago Press.

Leitenberg, H., & Henning, K. (1995). Sexual fantasy. *Psychological Bulletin, 117,* 469–496.

MacKinnon, C. A. (1982). Feminism, Marxism, method, and the state: An agenda for theory. In N. O. Keohane et al. (Eds.), *Feminist theory* (pp. 1–30). Chicago: University of Chicago Press.

Mischel, W. (1966). A social-learning view of sex differences in behavior. In E. E. Maccoby (Ed.), *The development of sex differences.* Stanford, CA: Stanford University Press.

Morrison, A. M., White, R. P., & VanVelsor, E. (1992). *Breaking the glass ceiling: Can women reach the top of America's largest corporations?* (Updated ed.). Reading, MA: Addison-Wesley.

Mosher, D. L., & Tomkins, S. S. (1988). Scripting the macho man: Hypermasculine socialization and enculturation. *Journal of Sex Research, 25,* 60–84.

Oliver, M. B., & Hyde, J. S. (1993). Gender differences in sexuality: A meta-analysis. *Psychological Bulletin, 114,* 29–51.

Oliver, M. B., & Hyde, J. S. (1995). Gender differences in attitudes toward homosexuality: A reply to Whitley and Kite. *Psychological Bulletin, 117,* 155–158.

Pleck, J. (1981). *The myth of masculinity.* Cambridge, MA: MIT Press.

Reiss, I. L. (1960). *Premarital sexual standards in America.* New York: Free Press.

Rich, A. (1980). Compulsory heterosexuality and lesbian existence. *Signs, 5,* 631–660.

Spelman, E. V. (1988). *Inessential woman: Problems of exclusion in feminist thought.* Boston: Beacon Press.

Sprecher, S., McKinney, K., & Orbuch, T. L. (1987). Has the double standard disappeared? An experimental test. *Social Psychology Quarterly, 50,* 24–31.

Sprecher, S., Sullivan, Q., & Hatfield, E. (1994). Mate selection preferences: Gender differences examined in a national sample. *Journal of Personality and Social Psychology, 66,* 1074–1080.

Symons, D. (1979). *The evolution of human sexuality.* New York: Oxford University Press.

Symons, D. (1987). An evolutionary approach: Can Darwin's view of life shed light on human sexuality. In J. H. Geer & W. T. O'Donohue (Eds.), *Theories of human sexuality* (pp. 91–126). New York: Plenum.

Tong, R. (1989). *Feminist thought: A comprehensive introduction.* Boulder, CO: Westview Press.

Travis, C. B., & Yeager, C. P. (1991). Sexual selection, parental investment, and sexism. *Journal of Social Issues, 47(3),* 117–130.

Trivers, R. L. (1972). Parental investment and sexual selection. In B. Campbell (Ed.), *Sexual selection and the descent of man.* Chicago: Aldine Publishing Co.

U.S. Department of Labor (1992). *Pipelines of progress: A status report on the glass ceiling.* Washington, DC: U.S. Government Printing Office.

U.S. Department of Labor (1993, June). *Employment and earnings.* Washington, DC: U.S. Department of Labor.

Watzlawick, P. (Ed.) (1984). *The invented reality: Contributions to constructivism.* New York: Norton.

Weisstein, N. (1982, November). Tired of arguing about biological inferiority? *Ms.,* 41–46.

West, C., & Zimmerman, D. H. (1983). Small insults: A study of interruptions in cross-sex conversations between unacquainted persons. In B. Thorne, C. Kramarae, & N. Henley (Eds.), *Language, gender, and society* (pp. 102–117). Rowley, MA: Newbury House.

Whitley, B. E., & Kite, M. E. (1995). Sex differences in attitudes toward homosexuality: A comment on Oliver and Hyde (1993). *Psychological Bulletin, 117,* 146–154.

Yoder, J. D., & Kahn, A. S. (1992). Toward a feminist understanding of women and power. *Psychology of Women Quarterly, 16,* 381–388.

4

THE SOCIAL CONSTRUCTION AND SOCIAL EFFECTS OF SEX RESEARCH: THE SEXOLOGICAL MODEL OF SEXUALITY

LEONORE TIEFER

> Ideology works precisely by making us believe that what is socially created, and therefore subject to change, is really natural, and therefore immutable. (Weeks, 1995, p. 34)

> The guiding metaphor of scientific nativism, that the body and its natural processes provide a "base" or "foundation" which determines the superstructure of social relations, in fundamental ways misrepresents the relationships between bodies and social processes. (Connell & Dowsett, 1992, p. 54)

What do we know about sexuality and how do we know it? In our[1] time, most people turn for answers to sex experts, who, they assume, rely

---

[1]I am assuming in my frequent use of the term *our* that both reader and writer come from the industrialized world, probably North America or Europe. Since situatedness is central to the argument of this chapter, it is important that both writer and reader acknowledge their own situatedness. I will refer to the idea of global culture as a new trend at some point, but a completely globalized culture is still some time away (although Coca-Cola and Elvis Presley seem to be everywhere already).

on contemporary prime sources of authority: science and professional training. People assume that experts know and draw on valid and reliable contemporary sex research methods such as surveys, laboratory research, and outcome studies in the clinical arena. Earlier sex research was primarily based on individual case studies, but they have gone out of favor. The contemporary public believes that experts' answers to questions about sexuality are professional, which means completely neutral with regard to sexual values, or on the side of sexual health. Who could argue with that?

In this chapter I will propose, by contrast, that viewing sex experts as having no particular ax to grind is as naive and inaccurate as believing Congressional investigative committees have no ax to grind or that journalists present just the facts. Rather, I will argue that professionals and anointed sex experts in the 20th century are neither neutral nor atheoretical in their research and formulations, but that they actively promote particular constructions of sexuality depending on their primary discipline and its frame of reference. Although the study of sexuality is multidisciplinary, there are certain core ideas I will label the "sexological model of sexuality."

This sexological model of sexuality is not simply a mirror held up to nature, but is a distinct perspective[2] on sexual life that privileges biological and psychological factors while making universal claims about sexuality. These emphases come through in the discussion of purposes for sexuality (procreation, pleasure, intimacy, health, and tension release), causes of sexuality (evolution, physiological factors, and early-life psychology), types of sexuality (normal and abnormal forms of arousal and sexual activity), and experts on sexuality (medical and other professionals). This perspective de-emphasizes or ignores sexuality as a means of fulfilling multiple and diverse motivations, the role of culture in determining sexual roles and enactment scripts, the effects of real-world power on lived sexualities, and the role of commercial factors in shaping current sexualities. Yet, we are so familiar with this psychobiological model and take it so for granted that it is difficult to acknowledge that alternate perspectives exist or are dealing with equally or more important variables.

In this chapter I will argue that the sexological model is not well suited to women's experiences of sexuality because of the realities of gender politics. The sexological model has neglected diversity among women in theory, and has neglected methods that take women's various social situations into account. Women need models that emphasize cultural and political realities and how they affect bodily and psychological experience.

Part of the obstacle to a feminist (or any alternative) model is that proponents of the sexological model dominate the field and define the

---

[2]A lengthier elaboration of these ideas would identify multiple sexological models arising from the various multidisciplinary perspectives. However, in this chapter I can only allude to such subtleties as it paints a picture of a framework that sorely needs feminist interrogation.

proper theoretical terms and research methods. Feminists wishing to replace the sexological model will have to "destabilize the plausibility of [its] strategies of explanation" (Haraway, 1986, p. 115) before they can expect any interest in their revised language and models of research.

SEXUAL AUTHORITY AND SOCIAL CONSTRUCTION

Authority, then, refers to the probability that particular definitions of reality and judgments of meaning and value will prevail as valid and true. (Starr, 1982, p. 13)

Authority on sexual matters within dominant culture has been increasingly conferred by mass media and the public on experts with medical or health perspectives. Sexuality is not alone in this, insofar as health seems to be the dominant ideology and source of morality in our time (Barsky, 1988; Lupton, 1994; Wright, 1994). Although the study of sexuality remains beholden to the ideology of healthism, feminists' attempts to reframe sexuality in light of history, ethics, and humanistic rather than health perspectives will seem incorrect and limited.

Scholars in the new interdisciplinary spheres of women's and cultural studies, building on the last two decades' work in social and cultural history, have recently begun to examine centuries of sexual authority from the perspective of the sociology of knowledge (e.g., Laqueur, 1990; Oudshoorn, 1994; Porter & Teich, 1994). Past histories of sexuality seemed to assume in their reviews that sexual conduct (e.g., the prevalence of masturbation, kissing, or same-sex activities) might vary among societies or historical periods, but they seemed to assume that sexual experience (e.g., what people experience when they masturbate or kiss) and maybe even sexual motives (e.g., why people masturbate or kiss) were probably pretty much the same. Moreover, there was no attention to the specifics of sexual conduct (what do people do when they kiss or masturbate).

That is, past histories of sexuality ignored issues of how sexual experience is constructed by social trends, meanings, and values apparently because they hadn't viewed sexuality as constructed at all. Expressions of sexuality were thought to be influenced by culture, but detailed study of those influences was often lacking, and the assumption remained that aspects of sexuality such as identities, drive, and the conduct of intercourse were essentially universal human phenomena.

Some recent histories of sexuality, by contrast, have been based on a "social contructionist perspective which moves the focus of concern from the sexual actions of specific bodies to the cultural and social contexts in which sexuality occurs" (Gagnon & Parker, 1995, p. 12). The social contructionist model rejects sexuality as a universal human phenomenon or natural force in favor of the view that no behavior or identity is intrinsically sexual, and that any aspect of social life or identity can be sexualized (or desexualized) through definition and regulation (Weeks, 1991). The focus is on the specifics of social location and how they define sexuality and establish the expectations and opportunities that will produce sexual experience.

The social constructionist model differs from the sexological model I describe below. Social constructionism specifically directs our attention to how sexual authorities and their claims and depictions create our expectations. It moves us away from a preoccupation with the direct influence of biological or psychological variables.

> How and why is marriage sexualized in some cultures, but not others? Why do some cultures identify adolescence as the most sexual time, while others select later or earlier periods? How is sexual identity defined on the Internet, the marriage license, and the research survey? How do cultures sexualize men and women differently? Under what social conditions has sexuality been seen as a matter of "health" and how have people's expectations changed in accordance?

That is, social constructionism directs our attention explicitly toward identifying forces of regulation and how they establish sexual expectations and norms.

THE SEXOLOGICAL MODEL OF SEXUALITY

A bird's-eye view of sexuality theories, research programs, and sex education in the 20th century industrialized world highlights certain themes and assumptions I call "the sexological model of sexuality." Ten of its most obvious tenets are:

1. Sex is a universal natural force, a product of evolution. This encourages the researcher to identify universal variables and cause and effect relationships.
2. Sex is "a material phenomenon which involves an extended series of physical, physiologic and psychologic changes [which] could be subjected to precise instrumental measurement if objectivity among scientists and public respect for scientific research allowed such laboratory investigation" (Kinsey, Pomeroy, & Martin, 1948, p. 157).
3. Biological factors such as hormones are a major source of sexual desire and explain changes at the time of puberty and changes in sexual desire with age and in response to illness.
4. There are important and natural differences between the

sexual interests and experiences of women and men, but the desire for sexual arousal and orgasm is built into everyone.

5. Heterosexual impulses are the norm, including desire for coitus, as a result of evolution.
6. Everyone has a sexual identity—heterosexual, homosexual, or bisexual, and a gender identity—girl/woman/female or boy/man/male.
7. Sexuality exists in individuals (i.e., is a factor or quality of individual experience and development).
8. Sexual attitudes, interests, and problems are significantly shaped by early-life events.
9. Sexuality is an important component of maturity and mental health. Boundaries can be drawn between healthy or normal and abnormal or pathological manifestations.
10. There are cultural differences in how sexuality is expressed.

The themes of this model stress that sexuality is a universal aspect of individual life and culture, that it makes sense to talk about it in terms of normality and abnormality, that as a bodily based phenomenon it is best understood in terms of acts, experiences, and identities based on physicality, that biological factors selected during evolution determine[3] sexuality, and that men and women experience some similarities and some differences in their sexuality. Boiling it down further, we may say that the themes are universality, health, salience, body, biology, and sex differences. You will not, however, find the sexological model listed or discussed in sexology texts, although it provides the backdrop for modern sex research.

WHAT IS SEX RESEARCH?

Sex research is what is recognized and acknowledged as sex research by those who write textbooks, publish journals, award research money, hire and quote experts, and so forth. In terms of cultural authority, who does the research, who publishes and disseminates it and to whom, who does the teaching, where and to whom—these are all important questions. When I first taught an undergraduate course in human sexuality in 1972 there were no textbooks available[4] and only one dedicated journal (*Journal*

---

[3]The recent growth of evolutionary psychology with its heavy reiteration of the falseness of the nature–nurture dichotomy and its insistence on interaction makes the use of a word like *determined* seem old-fashioned (e.g., Allgeier & Wiederman, 1994). Yet the prevailing sexological model does view biological variables as deterministic, and I am not yet persuaded that evolutionary psychology is not just window-dressing for biological determinism (Lewontin, 1992).

[4]The first college textbook I know of was by James L. McCary in 1963. *Human Sexuality*, (McCary, 1976). He was a long-term psychologist member of the American Association of Marriage and Family Counselors (founded in 1942).

of Sex Research). Therefore, what sex research did exist was within disciplines where each discipline had its own methodological standards and favorite themes. Very few people read outside their own field; thus, sociologists had one view of sex, public health specialists another, psychoanalysts another, literary critics another, criminologists yet another, and so forth. There was little discussion of sex research in the mass media, although much had been written throughout the century in terms of analysis of changing norms.

Thematic Affinities

By the late 1970s, sexology had become a recognized professional field with many textbooks and several journals and professional organizations. How had disciplinary diversity fared? In a handbook of sexology, Geer and O'Donohue (1987) presented 14 theoretical perspectives on sexuality identified with particular academic disciplines: psychology, physiology, theology, anthropology, and so forth. They propose that "each discipline involved in the study of sex can be uniquely characterized by a particular set of questions about sex it is concerned with, and by particular methodologies it uses to investigate these questions" (p. 3). In other words, standards for sex research are still related primarily to particular disciplines. This model of peaceful coexistence presumably works because each discipline investigates "such different questions" (p. 4).

In fact, whereas Geer and O'Donohue (1987) do describe considerable diversity, there are some important common thematic elements among their chapters that alert us to a possible sexological model. They conclude that "the two most obvious repeated themes [across chapters] are (a) the relative contribution of biological vs. experiential variables, and (b) the nature and source of sex differences" (p. 17). Also, although these points may have been too obvious to acknowledge, all the chapters except the feminist and sociological ones emphasize sex as genital activity, and omit any discussion of power, script, or commercial factors. The emphases on genital activity, sex differences, and the role of biological variables are central to the sexological model of sexuality.

Favored Methods

Central to the sexological model is an insistence on proper methods. How did they become established? Such questions are not unique to sex research, of course, and the recent work in the social studies of science (e.g., Knorr-Cetina & Mulkay, 1983), including psychology (Morawski, 1989), directs our attention to the role of the culture of science in setting traditions and norms (Dear, 1995). Questionnaire, survey, and experimental studies, for example, which make up the bulk of psychological sex research, can be seen as traditions that developed as psychologists differentiated themselves from philosophers around the turn of the century in Europe, England, and the United States. The new social studies of science show that social factors are an intrinsic part of the development of scientific knowledge (Gillespie, 1989), although scientific knowledge cannot be reduced solely to the political locations and beliefs of its generators. We can further contextualize the development of research traditions that have contributed to and are part of the sexological model of sexuality.

Objective, Scientific, Taxonomic

When Alfred Kinsey and his colleagues, authors of the most significant and trend-setting sex survey in 20th century America, discussed sexuality knowledge in the introductory chapter of their first research volume (Kinsey et al., 1948, pp. 21–34), they indicated that "a sex library . . . would have to cover materials drawn from practically all of the following fields" (p. 22) (see Table 1). Not all work in such a library would have equal value, however, if the goal is a true understanding of sexuality. Kinsey felt that most of the "inexhaustible" literature about sexuality failed to present an "objective, scientific approach" (p. 21), and that most could not pass the crucial test of valid generalizability. "Thousands of individual sex histories . . . contributed materially . . . but none of the authors of the older studies . . . had even an approximate knowledge of what average people do sexually" (p. 34). Kinsey and his colleagues proposed that their "fact-finding survey . . . to discover what people do sexually" (p. 3) would provide valid, generalizable answers because it would be "a taxonomic study of the frequencies and sources of sexual outlet among American males[5]" (p. 23).

Kinsey, a zoologist, viewed the taxonomic method as the gold standard of validity, and devoted four and a half pages (1948, pp. 16–21) to describing its value. Asserting that "problems in social fields involve the understanding of a whole species" (p. 18), he claimed that

> modern taxonomy is statistical in its approach. . . . It is, precisely, the function of a population analysis to help in the understanding of particular individuals by showing their relation to the remainder of the group. Given the range of variation, the mode, the mean, the median, [etc.], the clinician can determine the averageness or uniqueness of any particular person. (p. 20)

Thus, although Kinsey was aware of the tremendous quantity of knowledge on sexuality emanating from the diverse points of view represented in Table 1, he affirmed the value of only a few previous studies

---

[5]A subsequent volume used the same methods to study American women.

TABLE 1
Contents of Kinsey's Hypothetical Complete Sex Library

Biology
  Anatomy
  Embryology
  Physiology
  Endocrinology
  Genetics
  Taxonomic method
  Human evolution
  Biostatistics
Psychology
  General
  Experimental
  Clinical
  Abnormal
  Social
  Child and adolescent
  Comparative (anthropoids & lower
    mammals)
Sociology
  General
  Criminology
  Penology
  Special problems
  Marriage and the family
Anthropology
  Cultural
  Physical
  Ethnography
  Archeology
  Classical
Medicine
  Obstetrics
  Gynecology
  Pediatrics
  Clinical endocrinology
  Urology
  Fertility and sterility
  Contraception
  Pharmacology
  Public health
  Hygiene
  Social hygiene
  Psychiatry
  Psychoanalysis
Marriage Counseling
  Modern marriage manuals
  Classic manuals

Child Development
Personnel Programs
Public Opinion Surveying
Radio Programs
Philosophy
Ethics
Religion
Creeds
  Moral philosophy
  Sex cults
  History of religions
Education
  Child development
  Sex education
History
Law
  Legal procedure
  Criminal law
  Marriage law
  Paternity law
  History of law
Law Enforcement
  Police
  Parole and probation
  Censorship
  Military law
  Institutional management
Literature
  Fiction
  Essays
  Poetry
  Classical, of all cultures
  Biographies
  Travel
  Drama
  Journalistic, newspapers & maga-
    zines
  Propaganda
  Songs and ballads
  Folklore
  Linguistics
  Slangs and argots

TABLE 1 (*Continued*)

Art
  Graphic
  Sculpture
  Photography
  Moving pictures
  Music
  Dance
  Stage
Erotica, of Modern, Medieval, Classic, & Ancient Cultures
  Nude art
  Sculpture
  Art models
  Photographic materials
  Amateur drawings, stories, etc.
  Diaries
  Cartoons
  Moving pictures
  China & pottery
  Utensils
  Household implements
  Architectural designs
  Symbolism
  Music

Songs and ballads
Limericks
Wall inscriptions
Vocabularies
Literature
  Heterosexual
  Homosexual
  Flagellation, sadism, masochism
  Torture
  Religious persecution
  Corporal punishment
  Pseudo-psychologic
  Pseudo-anthropologic
  Love story magazines
  Physical culture magazines
  Nudist magazines
  Scandal sheets
  Advertising materials
Fetishistic objects
Materials on sex cults

Note. From Kinsey, Pomeroy, & Martin, 1948, pp. 22–23.

which are (1) scientific, (2) based on more or less complete case histories, (3), based on series of at least some size, (4) involving a systematic coverage of approximately the same items on each subject, and (5) statistical in treatment. (1948, p. 23)

The preference for statistical (quantitative), controlled, objective, and operationally rigorous studies, whether taxonomic or not, was hardly unique to sex research methodology. Their value is proclaimed throughout psychology and other areas of social and natural science, and they make important assumptions, which I will discuss later. Just for the moment, think about the familiar phrase in point (4) above—"the same items on each subject," and think about all that is packed into the term *same.* Yet there is a special attraction for these methods within sex research because of the peculiar political problems related to the subject matter.

Pre-Kinsey Sex Research

Bullough (1994a) describes pre-Kinsey American sex research on people as taking two forms: "moralistic" research and "fact-finding" research. In the first category he puts proponents as well as opponents of the movements for legal, educational, and public health reform who sought information about sexual practices (especially socially disapproved practices such as contact with prostitutes or masturbation) to support their political positions. By contrast, Bullough praises the development of quantitative survey studies because they are "increasingly free of the type of moralizing present in the earlier ones" (1994a, p. 318). This is an important element in the preference for so called rigorous methods by sex researchers.

But even virtuous aims couldn't prevent an aura of disrepute from surrounding sex research. There was a moral pollution associated with public writing about sex that is hard for us at the end of this century to fully appreciate, but that dates from the same ultraprudish period that saw naked piano legs covered up, advised that female physical examinations be conducted underneath a woman's skirts without exposing her body, or raided and censored stage productions and all kinds of publications with abandon.

Sex research in the United States had very low status throughout most of the 20th century (Corner, 1961). The sting of this disrespect, and its legacy of poor funding, little mainstreaming, and low academic status is felt and bemoaned to the present day (Abramson & Pinkerton, 1995). In consequence, until Kinsey, sex research flourished only in laboratory studies on animals, especially rodents, as well as in fieldwork in anthropology on "primitive" cultures with "exotic" (i.e., different from ours) sexual norms. The distance from the subject matter afforded by difficulties of intercultural and interspecies communication allowed decontamination of the subject matter and contributed the impersonality and universalness of the sexological model.

Legacy of Animal Sex Research

Laboratory sex research with animals affected sex research methods later used with people in important ways. Carolyn Wood Sherif (1979) described how specialty areas with lower prestige seek to improve their status "by adopting the perspectives, theories, and methodologies as high on the [status] hierarchy as possible" (p. 98). Prevented by public opinion, practical obstacles, and professional peer pressure from studying human sexuality, prior to the 1960s many sex researchers focused on animal mating behavior but insisted that they were studying principles applicable to the human situation. Moreover, they were at pains to use the most prestigious methods as they pursued their otherwise lurid subject matter, and they went to great lengths to justify how animal models permitted helpful simplification and better control of variables. Although animal studies could not address the human situation precisely (this caveat was always present in one form or another), they presumably permitted insight into relevant concepts, mechanisms, and patterns (e.g., Beach, 1977).

Whether or not animal sex research has taught us anything of value in understanding human sexuality, decades of studying mechanisms and patterns of animal mating have left their mark on the sexological model of human sexuality. It is easy, now, to assume without reflection that sexuality is something animals and people have in common, and that concepts like sexual attraction or inhibition, categories like heterosexual or male, or physiological mechanisms such as hormones or brain sites mean something similar in the sex lives of animals and human beings, even if the details vary widely. Most sex research meetings and journals contain reports both on animals and on people, and it's all called sexuality without reflection or analysis. This is a very important legacy of the sexological model of sexuality.

To point out these traditions is not to say that sex research is the only category in psychology in which animal studies have provided foundational input. However, the unique stigma associated with human sex research may have resulted in greater reliance on animal models than in other fields. Moreover, feminists may want to argue that particularly little insight has been provided by animal models toward understanding women's sociosexual situations and the relationships between gender and sexuality.

The need for legitimacy encouraged the scientism of animal sex research, the fact-finding focus of the taxonomic approach, and continues to affect contemporary human sex research. Of all subfields in psychology, sex research may be among the most fanatic in insisting its methods are above reproach. In terms of the constant stress on methodological objectivity and in terms also of the conceptual legacies of decades of animal research, contemporary sex research is thus still partly hostage to the moralistic heritage of sexuality in American culture that seems so long gone from other segments of society.

ORIGINS OF THE SEXOLOGICAL MODEL

The sexological model is distinctively Western and 20th century, and we have already seen many of its seeds in the political realities of the decades of animal sex research. The emphasis on evolution is a modernism marker, as is the importance of sexual and gender identity issues, and the relationship between sexuality and such modern concerns as maturity and mental health. The claim that sexuality is an extremely important part of an individual's life and personality is recognizably post-Freudian. More subtly, perhaps, the implication that sexuality is an individual quality or factor of personality is a hallmark of modern psychological thinking.

We have seen how the development of sex research methods was influenced by the stigma associated with public talk about sexuality, and the need for compensatory scientific orthodoxy. Tracking specific stages in the development of the sexological model is difficult because histories of sex research are themselves so selective. Historians of sexology have generally ignored animal sex research and neglected its implications for human studies. Histories of sex research have usually emphasized how 20th-century political reformers, eager to challenge authoritarian sexual norms, joined forces with Freudians, biologists, and students of human instinct to inaugurate a professional literature on human sexuality (Weeks, 1981). Such histories have sometimes recognized how sex research contributes to the construction of sexuality—but just as often histories have adopted a nativist view of sexuality as really being out there, just waiting for researchers to come and uncover the facts.

Robinson (1976) provides one of the few analyses of how sex research helped construct a particular model of sexuality. He argues that 20th-century sex research, from Havelock Ellis through Alfred Kinsey and William Masters and Virginia Johnson, created a modern sexuality: positive, physical, healthy, and ambivalent about romanticism, in reaction to the sexual repressions of Anglo-American Victorianism. Robinson's history, appearing before the advent of self-conscious social constructionism, exemplifies that approach in a brief text that has withstood the test of time.

Brecher's (1969) history, written earlier, provided a larger view of sex research, highlighting Robinson's foursome while also describing the research contribution of Europeans (Richard von Krafft-Ebing, Sigmund Freud, and Theodor H. van de Velde), women, students of gender and gender-identity, and researchers of love. Brecher, however, offered little theoretical analysis, suggesting that most of the contributors were drawn by the ideals of science (truth, objectivity, etc.) and the desire to counteract the lies and repressions of the Victorian era. Brecher's text describes events (and people) in a chronological fashion, ignoring reasons behind the success or failure of particular lines of thought or research. This type of uncritical history, written largely to praise the courage and usefulness of sex researchers, disguises its own role in promoting a nativist view of sexuality.

We can illustrate nativistic versus socially constructed histories with an example from Brecher (1969) and feminist Margaret Jackson (1994). Brecher (1969) describes Elizabeth Blackwell (1821–1910) as having made a limited contribution to sexology, and furthermore suggests that she was a somewhat misguided feminist (she was the first woman physician to be licensed to practice in England or the United States—she practiced both places). While praising her recognition of women's orgasm and her defense of a single standard, Brecher felt Blackwell wrongly overemphasized the mental and spiritual elements of sex, and did not differ from her time in condemning the evils and abuses of masturbation, prostitution, and fornication (defined as "the attempt to divorce the moral and physical elements of human nature," (Brecher, 1969, quoting Blackwell, 1969, p. 149).

Jackson (1994), by contrast, writes explicitly to identify the destructive impact of sexology on women's lives. Although Jackson acknowledges that Blackwell had limited impact on sexuality theory or public attitudes, she revives Blackwell's ideas and condemns those who call her a sexual Puritan. Jackson sees Blackwell's model of sexuality as feminist and anti-patriarchal in its challenge to naturalism as well as to the double standard, and because of its claim that physical passion can become "either an ennobling or a degrading force for both individual and society" (p. 65). Making naturalism central in the sexological model is considered by Jackson to be antifeminist, a theme we will return to later. Throughout several British books and articles in *Women's Studies International Forum*, Jackson argued that "sexology represented the appropriation of the sexual by male scientific 'experts,' who overturned more than half a century of feminist struggle to politicize sexuality and promote female sexual autonomy" (p. 183). Her feminist history specifically asserts that sexuality is malleable, and that experts contribute to its social construction.

In his history of 20th century American sex research, Bullough (1994b) discusses theoretical and clinical work deriving from Freudian themes, university-based laboratory studies of animal endocrinology and mating behavior supported by Rockefeller research money, survey research, contraceptive research, and anthropological studies in non-Western cultures. He also describes the beginnings of sex research with nonheterosexual populations, and how that stream of studies challenged traditional psychiatric positions. But, as with other traditional histories, Bullough (1994b) doesn't acknowledge the political role or aim of sex research, arguing that in line with societal sexuality in general, sex research expanded and sexuality was viewed more positively as the century wore on. He doesn't discern a particular line taken in the research, and he may disagree that there was a particular sexological model of sexuality promoted in these works or that sexuality is socially constructed. Bullough's point of view is most visible when he explicitly disapproves of sex researcher "members of special-interest groups" who "were more interested in propagandizing than in research findings" and bemoans how "the interested public found it difficult to distinguish between legitimate research and wishful thinking" (Bullough, 1994b, p. 274). I will return to the question of how to evaluate sex research quality, and the complications of special interests and propaganda.

By contrast, a history of British sex research begins with a blunt embrace of constructionism:

> There has been deep and animated debate of late regarding the constitution of the sexual and its history. . . . We entirely accept . . . that sex is not a natural datum awaiting discovery by doctors, scientists, and others . . . Rather, . . . the sexual is such a complex and contested domain, mightily charged with associations and emotions, norms and values, that the terms in which it is posited determine the entity itself. (Porter & Hall, 1995, pp. 7–8)

Although Porter and Hall (1995) do not describe a specific sexological model emerging in 20th century texts, they propose the larger thesis that throughout the past several hundred years, "sexual discourse has aimed to *limit* and create closures in sexual identity" (p. 11) by demarcating good from bad in terms of gender and erotics.

Irvine (1990) presents the most complete feminist and critical analysis of American sexology after the 1940s. She traces the preoccupation of sex researchers with biological variables and positivist research strategies to their quest for professional legitimacy and their naive political belief that these tactics will best aid sexual progress for women and homosexuals. She sympathizes with feminists like Margaret Jackson who argue that sexologists' focus on women's sexual pleasure was ultimately directed toward promoting heterosexual conformism, and that sexologists deliberately neglected (political) topics of interest to feminists such as sexual violence, rape, sexual abuse, negative impact of pornography, sexual harassment, and the negative aspects of prostitution. Although some of Irvine's points are overstated, her text is essential for feminists interested in the sexological model, and stands together with Robinson's (1976) as an example of social constructionist history of sex research written in the United States.

SPECIAL INTERESTS OF THE SEXOLOGICAL MODEL

One of the most important reasons to identify and name the sexological model is to reveal patterns of inclusion and exclusion in its research design and concepts. If the sexological model has promoted research paths of limited usefulness to women or has actively devalued paths important for women, then feminists must become committed to developing a successor model to better serve women's interests.

Basic, Universal Mechanisms of Sexuality

Within the positivist model of studying the true nature of sexuality and looking for variables with the greatest explanatory power, the sexological model of sex research has focused on identifying basic mechanisms of sexuality presumed to be universal to the human species. The scientific paradigm led sexologists to assume that once general laws were established, factors influencing individual and group variation would be identified and sexuality would be thoroughly mapped. Whether the sexual phenomenon of interest was choice of partner, premarital pregnancy, frequency of masturbation, or sexual desire, the work proceeded through surveys or laboratory research so as first to identify the most universal and significant variables.

With this focus, it is not surprising that *biological factors* and *group differences* have dominated sexological research. Issues such as the influence of prenatal hormones on sex differentiation in the brain have been studied in innumerable animal species and the results generalized into mammalian laws (van den Wijngaard, 1991). With gender differences in humans the outcome variable, a biological mechanism would be proposed by animal studies, years of research would be dedicated to working out specific details, individual differences would be ignored by group averaging, and any inquiry into cultural factors would be postponed indefinitely. The presumed existence of general mammalian laws gave validity to animal research, and the endless parametric studies (specificities of hormones, time periods, behaviors, etc.), although actually dealing with the details of particular species and research conditions, were expected to generalize someday and somehow to the vicissitudes of human lives.

Beginning in the 1940s, feminists pointed out that much of what was discovered in animal sex research was anthropomorphic, and that cultural gender relations were being projected onto observations of animals (Haraway, 1989; Herschberger, 1970 [1948]). Such projections distorted the observations of animal lives; in addition, but when the results were generalized back to humans, stereotypic sex differences were falsely said to be scientifically proven (Fedigan, 1992). An immense amount of such research on general animal mating patterns (now often within the sociobiological framework) still continues, providing endless repetitive newspaper columns that shore up the public's support for the sexological model (Fausto-Sterling, 1992).

Assumptions about universality are communicated by the pervasive use of context-free technical definitions in contemporary sexological model sex research (Connell & Dowsett, 1992). Homosexuality is defined as sexual activity between persons of the same sex. Masturbation is defined as self-stimulation of the genitals to orgasm. Erection is defined as hardness of the penis. The fact that these phenomena and experiences may be very different for people of different cultures, centuries, ages, genders, and social locations is considered unimportant (when it's even considered at all)—the operational definition is the real one, and everything else is merely a modification.

To put it another way, the sexological model assumes that socio-historico-cultural context is background, and that something meaningfully called basic principles are foreground in terms of understanding sexuality. Either generality is assumed (as with college student populations participating in every type of sexuality study), or group results are compared (as when surveys of safe sex behavior in San Francisco are compared with Brazil) so basic patterns can be identified by eliminating the effect of region, religion, age, marital status, and so on.

Research Ignores Social Context of Researcher and Research Participant

Another way to describe the search for universals is that the social-cultural-historical contexts of both researcher and research participant are ignored by the sexological model. The fact that a questionnaire is completed in a classroom, a home, or a bar is not considered relevant to the facts that are produced. Sexual laws and social norms of the research location are ignored. The fact that people who may be sexually interested in one another (or sexually fearful or sexually threatened) are together during a research study is ignored. The fact that people of different backgrounds completing identical questionnaires may have very unequal experience openly discussing the questionnaire topics is ignored. These contextual details are considered matters of minor, endless detail, and not interesting to study.

Assumptions about researchers' objectivity mask any impact of researchers' social specificity, except, as with Bullough's (1994a) comments about moralistic vs. fact-finding research in the pre-Kinsey era, researcher attitude is related to overall approval or disapproval. A current example of this debate occurs over the work of feminist social science researcher Shere Hite (Tiefer, 1995). Her sampling, questionnaire, interview, and selective-quotes publication methods have been loudly and strongly criticized as biased and therefore not objective or scientific in much the same way as Bullough and Kinsey drew lines between ways of knowing they regarded as more and less worthy in the past. Because Hite has written from a feminist point of view, phrasing questions and recruiting research participants to bring out neglected aspects of women's sexual and romantic experiences, it is easier to see the political nature of her work and thus the political nature of the criticism.

In fact, knowing Hite's politics (i.e., Hite's context) makes it easier to comprehend her particular methods and results. It requires historical excavation (e.g., Robinson, 1976) to detect the political goals of less candid sexologists. In recent decades, there have been widespread criticisms of the rhetoric of scientific objectivity (Guba, 1990), yet sexological research is still held to that standard. Much writing about sexuality is now in gender studies, cultural studies, and gay and lesbian studies. These multidisciplines, influenced by humanities' standards, are clearly affecting social science researchers (like me). But the rhetoric of objectivity still pervades mainstream social science and the science and health media, where much sexological material appears.

I have written elsewhere about the extraordinarily selective and intrusive nature of Masters and Johnson's 1966 research on the physiology of sexual response, identifying how the researchers selected participants who would comply with a predefined type of sexual response, and then actually coached participants when their performance didn't comply completely (Tiefer, 1991). Both researchers and research-consumers ignored the evidence and influence of such selection and coaching because they believed Masters and Johnson were studying universal patterns of behavior in which context was largely irrelevant. This is a very significant consequence of the focus on basic and universal mechanisms—whom you study or how or where all become invisible because they're unimportant to universal generalizations.

There are many ways in which sex researchers deliberately (although apparently without realizing the meaning of their actions) strip away the particularities of context by getting research participants to regard sexuality the same way they do. In questionnaire research, for example, researchers either define terms in the questionnaires for participants, or just assume the meanings of the terms are self-evident. Only as a result of debriefing or explicit interviews do they occasionally find out, for example, that questions about "frequency of intercourse" or "frequency of masturbation" are interpreted differently by people who count acts as intercourse or masturbation only if orgasm is involved versus those whose definition of the act doesn't require orgasm (Wellings, 1994). The assumptions researchers make in interpreting the results of their questionnaires is an important example of context-stripping in the service of looking for generalizations.

The meaning and significance of sexual acts is generally ignored in contemporary sex surveys, since such information is very difficult if not impossible to gather in questionnaire form. For example, some people have reasons and feelings about whether they define an act as masturbation if their partner is present. The researcher providing a technical definition ("masturbation means self-stimulation of the genitals whether a partner is present or not") avoids and neglects such differences of meaning. Thus, the largest amount of sexuality information we have is quantitative information about frequencies of different forms of genital activity. The almost complete reliance on counting implies that the context of such acts is at best of secondary importance, and that behavioral sex acts are comparable or identical.

Thus the belief in universal mechanisms produces methods that render individual differences invisible, which in turn results in conclusions and interpretations supporting the assumptions about universal mechanisms. How this cycle may actually become self-fulfilling in terms of its impact on real people's sexual lives will be discussed below in the section on the social impact of the sexological model.

Pre-Eminence of Biological Variables

Biology is considered fundamental and bedrock according to the reigning sexological model, both in terms of distal (prenatal and early life) and proximal (at the time of the sexual event or experience) control over sexuality. Sociobiologists and others insist that genetics and prenatal endocrinology create brain structures which determine aspects of sexuality such as sexual orientation, monogamousness, and any and all differences between men and women (LeVay, 1993). In puberty, changing sex hormone levels are said to initiate and stimulate sexual interests and activities. In adulthood, hormones are said to be mandatory for any sexual desire or arousal, although the research is often inconsistent as to which hormones cause which effects at which points in time (Fausto-Sterling, 1992; Vines, 1994). Biological alterations related to menstrual cycling, pregnancy, aging, diseases, and medications are said to exert profound influences on sexuality through direct effects on physical function, response, and desire.

A pervasive influence of biology within the sexological model has to do with the definitions of sex as a specific activity, penile-vaginal intercourse, (as in a question which may appear in a survey, "How many times did you have sex in the last month?"). If sex is assumed to be the act of heterosexual reproduction, unless otherwise specified (as, e.g., oral sex), then an unfortunate universality derived from biology is ascendant. Don't forget that it was the physical experience and bodily changes during some acts of sexual intercourse that was called "*the* human sexual response" by Masters and Johnson (1966). This particular physical experience of desire, arousal, and orgasm, again assumed to be transcultural and transhistorical, became the essence of sexual normalcy in the American Psychiatric Association's (APA) (1994) official manual of mental disorders.

Actually, the preeminence of biology in the sexological model is demonstrated by the listing of sexual dysfunctions that first appeared in the 1980 edition of the Diagnostic and Statistical Manual of Mental Disorders (APA, 1980), and has continued, with very minor modification, into the 1987 and 1994 editions (Tiefer, 1992). The dysfunctions all have to do with impairments in the performance of intercourse, and specify the necessity of physiological arousal (genital vasocongestion), orgasm (not too soon and not too delayed), sexual desire (no genital aversion), no genital pain, and no vaginal impediment to intercourse. One important consequence of the accentuation of genital function as the focal point of normal and disordered sexuality in the sexological model of sexuality is that the medicalization of sexuality has become a major industry and domain of basic research, with mixed benefits (Tiefer, 1987, 1995).

How is the commitment to this bodies-first position communicated by sexology? A statement such as, "The activities and physiological responses of the body are the central element in sexuality, and are universally defined and experienced," would not be found in a sexuality textbook. Rather, the primacy of biology guides the conceptualization of sexuality implicitly rather than explicitly. Initial chapters in sexuality textbooks typically describe the biological basis for sexuality—introducing the reader to endocrinology, neuroanatomy, and genital physiology at great length. Once this basis has been described, the text can go on to dozens of human sexual topics (e.g., attraction and flirting, sexuality according to different religions, sexual problems and treatments, sexual abuse and its consequences), which never again mention any biological variables. Yet the primacy of biology (basic and bedrock), the implication that universal biological standards set the parameters, has been established by the book's order of contents. Biology is presented as determined by genetics, embryology, or developmental biology. Absent is a discussion of how biological reactions can be learned, or that they may be expressed or experienced differently in different cultures. The model of biology that prevails is of a preexisting, evolution-dictated imperative. In a sense, the sexological model of sexuality has promulgated that old cliche, "anatomy is destiny."

Fragmented Components

Perhaps it is inevitable, given this biological framework, that universalized physical subsystems would become significant in themselves. Especially in the clinical literature on causes and treatments of sexual dysfunctions, sexuality becomes the successful performance of fragments in two different ways. First, there is the definition that having adequate performance components of desire, arousal, and orgasm is necessary for normal sexuality, and given an appropriate partner (these are defined in the section on sexual disorders in DSM-IV), performing these components is sufficient for normal sexual functioning.

Second, certain bodily fragments (i.e., parts of the genitalia) are specifically mentioned in the sexual dysfunction section of the DSM-IV—penile erection, vaginal lubrication, and so on. Proper function of these bodily components within the performance sequence qualify a person for adequate sexual function, given the appropriate choice of object or partner. Defining sexuality in this way omits whole-body, sensual, or subjective visions for sexual normalcy, which, as I suggest below, may work against women's interests.

Sexuality Exists in a Person

Sex research focuses on the conduct (mostly) and subjective experience (somewhat) of individuals, whether revealed through survey, questionnaire, interview, observation, or measurement. This is an exceptionally important element of the sexological model that is invisible, never discussed, completely taken for granted, and can be considered an aspect of our psychological century's focus on (some may say construction of) the individual (Giddens, 1991). Sexuality has come to be construed as an aspect of an individual, like intelligence. That is not to say that a culture's sexuality cannot be described, or that a couple's sexuality cannot be described, but most sex research assumes that an individual has sexuality that can be studied and theorized.

This individual quality, sexuality, can be aroused, satisfied, weak or strong, normal or abnormal, expressed or inhibited. Various behavioral and psychological phenomena are linked into a person's sexuality by biologists and psychoanalysts. Activities having to do with the genitalia or breasts, for example, are thought to be psychologically connected together (possibly through dependency or preverbal symbolism) into important components of sexuality. Likewise, one's psychological sense of self as a man or woman comes through sexuality in terms of preferences for activities, roles, or partners.

The dangers of such psychological generalizations can be shown by a brief discussion of kissing (Tiefer, 1995). Kissing can be extremely erotic in some cultures, especially European and North American cultures, which have produced much sexological research and theory. The desire for and enjoyment of erotic kissing has been generalized to all humans, and attributed to sequelae of important early experiences with breast-feeding together with the rich neurological innervation of the mouth and tongue. But, it turns out, erotic kissing is unknown in many cultures, and, what's more, kissing is regarded as a dirty (germ-transmitting) act in many others. Thus, what seems like a statement about sexuality based on presumably universal psychobiological processes can be a cultural expression mistakenly generalized.

Ultimately, the emphasis of the sexological model on the individual is its core element and the proof of its essential modernity. The 20th century invention of sexuality as a quality of personality, as "something each of us 'has,'" something "endowed with vast causal processes" (Giddens, 1992, pp. 15, 21), paves the way for all other contemporary developments, including political sexual identity rights movements, media and commercial sexuality elaboration and exploitation, and the consolidation of a research focus on sexuality within psychology.

Although this sexual individualism is often traced to Sigmund Freud, viewing sexuality as an individual quality must be seen as part of the development of the modern idea of the self, which itself is a consequence of the industrial revolution, late capitalism, a technological society, and the transformation of family life (e.g., D'Emilio, 1983). Throughout the 19th and 20th centuries, as goods formerly made in the home could increasingly be purchased, the family, losing the functions that had held it together as an economic unity, became transformed into an emotional entity for the nurture of children and the personal satisfactions of its members. Children were no longer needed for economic reasons, birth rates declined steadily, and procreation was replaced as a prime motive in sexual life. The growth of cities, travel, literacy, urban amusements, and media created a social context in which a new kind of personal life could develop. These irreversible social transformations created a space for new social constructions of sexuality as elements of the self. Sex researchers and psychologists have intentionally or unwittingly played an active role in fashioning such constructions.

SOCIAL IMPACT OF THE SEXOLOGICAL MODEL

What has been the impact of the sexological model? The primary influence has been on the parameters of sex research—what's been included and what's been excluded. The elements of the model provided the assumptions and norms that shaped sexology. Issues for sexology were those suggested by the model: working out the various elements of biology that contributed to sexual arousal, looking for differences between men and women in a million elements of sexual activity and attitude, looking for correlates of heterosexual and homosexual identity, classifying sexual behaviors around the world, and so forth. Among issues sexology ignored were those that focused on cultural and commercial construction of sexual meanings and expectations, how these played out in the lives of people with and without social and economic privilege, the view of sexuality not as a property of individuals, but as a cocreation of interaction, and the subjective elaboration of sexual experience over a lifetime.

Widely read professional publications published since 1965 such as *The Journal of Sex Research*, *Archives of Sexual Behavior*, and *The Journal of Sex and Marital Therapy*, as well as several lesser-known sexology outlets, are full of measurement-oriented empirical studies not unlike those found in other psychology journals. There is very little theory. A British journal, *Sexualities*, appeared in 1998 with a focus on theory. There is no feminist sexology journal.

IMPACT OF SEXOLOGICAL MODEL ON REAL
PEOPLE'S SEXUALITY

Davidson and Layder (1994) propose that "on the one hand, popular beliefs about sex are shaped by the findings of [sex] research, on the other, research into sexuality is powerfully influenced by the moral and normative values of the society in which it is undertaken" (p. xi). This circular relationship will make it extremely difficult to determine the impact of the sexological model on real people's lives and sexualities. From clinical work and sexuality teaching over the past two decades, it is my impression that the sexological model of sexuality has become the infrastructure of most people's everyday ideas about sexuality. It is the sexual Weltanschauung.

Despite differences in age, ethnicity, religion, sexual orientation, or social class, most people appear to accept the 10 points of the sexological model listed earlier and place the narrative of their own sexual life within its framework (Plummer, 1995). The sexological model pervades our thinking and rationalizes and justifies our choices so completely that it is only with extreme difficulty that we even contemplate alternatives.

Health and science media are largely responsible for promulgating the themes of the sexological model of sexuality as they comment on the sexual developments of the day, and as they advertise (selectively) new research results and treatment approaches. The tabloids and the serious news outlets, for example, are partial to sexologic ideas that emphasize pharmacologic and other medical breakthroughs, biological bases of sex differences, sex as a matter of health, the importance of sexual and gender identity, and the central role of evolution in establishing our sexual patterns and preferences (Coward, 1985; D'Emilio & Freedman, 1988; Fausto-Sterling, 1992; Vance, 1984).

One of the most obvious challenges for feminist sex research in the future is to demonstrate the actual impact of sex research and the sexological model on women's sexual lives and expectations. To do this, sex research will have to turn to models offered by academic traditions that have taken as their subject mass culture and its influences on behavior and imagination. Many recent analyses of women-oriented mass media such as popular music, soap operas, romance novels and magazines, prime-time television, and film have analyzed these media's messages about gender (e.g., Brown, 1990; Cantor, 1987; Modleski, 1984). Although such analyses have noted in passing the pervasive sexual double standard, women's difficulties with sexual assertiveness and pleasure, and the ubiquitousness of sexual danger, there are far more studies of how media construct gender than how they construct sexuality. Studies of sexual scripts (e.g., how sexual activities are initiated, how scripts are determined, what are participants' expectations and evaluations) have been dominated by a focus on gender differences rather than any examination of cultural, subcultural, or media sources for the scripts (e.g., Cupach & Metts, 1991).

There are few attempts to show how the sexological model has wormed its way into individuals' sexual consciousnesses. Plummer (1995), among others, has described how sexological literature shaped attitudes and expectations in the pre-sexual-liberation era for gay and lesbian people. He also quotes from numerous autobiographies of transsexuals showing how the sexological model of one, fixed gender identity informed their self-examinations and life decisions, as have many others writing about transsexuals (e.g., Hausman, 1995).

My work in urology departments over 13 years has showed how the development and promotion of medically fixable erections influences men's expectations for a perfectable penis (Tiefer, 1995). Also, I was often surprised in my (separately conducted) clinical interviews with men and their sexual parners (usually, but not always, wives) as to how much they regarded sexuality as a matter wholly of individual desire and satisfaction, and how much they thought it was determined by biological factors. Ehrenreich, Hess, and Jacobs (1986) provided only one feminist voice of many to celebrate the impact of the research of Masters and Johnson on women's sexual entitlements and orgasmic potential. Their statement "here was a body of objective, and by most standards, respectably scientific findings on which to rest the case for a radically new, feminist interpretation of sexuality (p. 69)," is an indication of the type of impact they believed this work to have had.

FEMINIST CHALLENGES TO THE SEXOLOGICAL MODEL

The last quote about the thrillingly positive impact of Masters' and Johnson's research on women alerts us to the importance of seeing sex research in the context of its time as we analyze its impact on women's sexual experiences and ideas. In our fast-changing world, so many things seem old-fashioned that may have been new and liberating for many at an earlier point in time, but that take on an entirely different aspect as circumstances change or unpredicted consequences become known. Let us not make the same mistake we criticize others for and forget to acknowledge the role of context as we examine some implications of the sexological model for women.

What sex research has benefitted women? And which women have benefitted? These questions can only be answered in retrospect and deserve a serious project of their own to answer. Studies that effectively puncture prevailing assumptions are generally in women's interest because prevailing assumptions generally stereotype and misrepresent women's lives—this is a prime assumption of academic feminism.

Beyond Universalism in Theory and Quantitation in Method

A prime challenge to the sexological model lies in taking on how its penchant for looking for universal principles has led us to ignore how sexual lives are different depending on social circumstances. Variables affecting sexual values and scripts such as class, age, socio-economic situation, religion, ethnicity, and assimilation are not prominent in most sex research, usually because the samples are too homogeneous and the variables are not thought interesting when universal principles were presumably under study. Relegating qualitative information to non-science, as in Kinsey's affirmation of statistical methods and disdain for the sexuality materials in Table 1, has further hobbled our efforts to understand the experiences of people in different social circumstances.

In outcome research on sexual dysfunction treatment, for example, researchers exclude couples who have complicating problems of health or employment difficulties in order to be able to draw valid conclusions about the actual impact of one type of treatment or another. If the sample were large enough (which it rarely is or realistically can be), couples with such problems would be included, and the impact of such factors on treatment outcome could be quantitatively assessed. But, looking more deeply, what would be the sex researcher's goal in such research? Probably it would be to ascertain the best possible method. But is that logical in terms of sexuality? Are such universalizations appropriate for couples, for sexuality, for service delivery realities, and so forth? It seems that positivistic assumptions about how the world is organized have pervaded all aspects of sex research, in ways we are only beginning to think about.

Gender and Sex Research

Gender has come to mean a great deal in the last three decades of feminist theory and scholarship, yet the sociopolitical realities of gendered lives and gendered sexualities are invisible in most research dictated by the sexological model. It's not just that men and women are different, and researchers have to document and analyze sex and gender differences in masturbation, jealousy, and so on. It's that men and women are different in a million ways having to do with the consequences of differences in social power, and that men and women in different sociocultural locations experience and manifest all kinds of variations of this social power difference having to do with sexuality. This is a mouthful, but it is the heart of the feminist critique. As feminists such as Jackson (1994) have recognized, the rhetoric of naturalism is the screen behind which hides perpetuation of the social status quo. The silence of the sexological model on the subject of power in sexuality is its major shortcoming from a feminist point of view.

A prime manifestation of this silence, of course, is that too often in the sexological model of sexuality the normative standard has been men's sexual experience, or perhaps more accurately, stereotypes pertaining to men's sexual experience. The idea that heterosexual impulses are the norm, that sexuality exists in individuals, that biological factors are the prime source of desire, that the best way to see sex is as a material series of physical changes in specific activities—assumptions in the sexological model—seem more in accordance with men's experience (or maybe we should say with the phallocentric experience) (see McCormick, 1994, for an overview of feminist writings about women's sexuality). The way such norms worked themselves into the diagnostic manual (APA, 1994) is only one example of the far-reaching consequences of the sexological model's sexism. Others have been noted throughout this chapter.

CONCLUSION

Who conducts sex research? Who publishes and disseminates it, where, and to whom? Sex research, like other contemporary academic areas of research, has been profoundly influenced, and I would say limited, by the pressure and structure of academic demands for publication, and the needs of professional journals (more all the time), generally put out by profit-oriented companies. Also, as I have shown, the sexological model that dominates sex research remains beholden to a specific history of choices made because of the political nature of sexuality in the United States. The quest for respectability and prestige has, ironically, left sexology with a legacy of positivist assumptions, concepts, and methods ill-suited to understanding a subject so thoroughly saturated with culture.

However, the explosion of sexual issues and opportunities in mass culture, the new sexual texts,[6] the explosion of media attention to gender and sexuality that has taken place in the last three decades—these offer sex research a new lease on life. If feminists, provoked by the limitations of the reigning sexological model, can seize the opportunity offered by new sexual stories to develop new ways of studying, analyzing, and reporting them, they may yet salvage and transform sex research.

In her 1973 presidential address to the American Psychological Association, Leona Tyler drew attention to how the choice of research projects had come to depend on "such things as the availability of a new technique or instrument, the recognition of an unanswered question in a report of previous research, a suggestion from a friend or advisor or just the fact that a federal program has made grant funds available" (p. 1025). Perhaps our feminist commitment to research because of its potential contributions to human liberation can direct us toward a new paradigm for sexology.

REFERENCES

Abramson, P. R., & Pinkerton, S. D. (1995). Preface. In P. R. Abramson & S. D. Pinkerton (Eds.), *Sexual nature/sexual culture* (pp. ix–xvii). Chicago: University of Chicago Press.

---

[6]By *texts* is meant not just textbooks that are studied in schools, but all forms of representation and discourse about sexuality, such as laws, novels, films, news articles, magazine features, advertising, art, popular music, hymnals, sermons, advice books, television, and so forth. Different types of sexual discourse, of course, will have significance for different audiences, and the more fragmented the culture the less uniform the sexual authority.

Allgeier, E. R., & Wiederman, M. W. (1994). How useful is evolutionary psychology for understanding contemporary human sexual behaviour? *Annual Review of Sex Research, 5,* 218–256.

American Psychiatric Association. (1980). *Diagnostic and statistical manual of mental disorders* (3rd ed.). Washington, DC: Author.

American Psychiatric Association. (1994). *Diagnostic and statistical manual of mental disorders* (4th ed.). Washington, DC: Author.

Barsky, A. J. (1988). *Worried sick: Our troubled quest for wellness.* Boston: Little, Brown.

Beach, F. A. (1977). Cross-species comparisons and the human heritage. In F. A. Beach (Ed.), *Human sexuality in four perspectives* (pp. 296–316). Baltimore, MD: Johns Hopkins University Press.

Brecher, E. M. (1969). *The sex researchers.* Boston: Little, Brown.

Brown, M. E. (Ed.). (1990). *Television and women's culture: The politics of the popular.* Newbury Park, CA: Sage.

Bullough, V. L. (1994a). The development of sexology in the USA in the early twentieth century. In R. Porter & M. Teich (Eds.), *Sexual knowledge, sexual science: The history of attitudes to sexuality* (pp. 303–322). New York: Cambridge University Press.

Bullough, V. L. (1994b). *Science in the bedroom: A history of sex research.* New York: Basic Books.

Cantor, M. G. (1987). Popular culture and the portrayal of women: Content and control. In B. B. Hess & M. M. Ferree (Eds.), *Analyzing gender: A handbook of social science research* (pp. 190–214). Newbury Park, CA: Sage.

Connell, R. W., & Dowsett, G. W. (1992). The unclean motion of the 'generative parts': Frameworks in western thought on sexuality. In R. W. Connell & G. W. Dowsett (Eds.), *Rethinking sex: Social theory and sexuality research* (pp. 49–75). Melbourne, Australia: Melbourne University Press.

Corner, G. W. (1961). In W. C. Young (Ed.), *Sex and internal secretions,* (Vol. 1, 3rd ed. pp. ix–xii). Baltimore, MD: Williams and Wilkins.

Coward, R. (1985). *Female desires: How they are sought, bought, and packaged.* New York: Grove Press.

Cupach, W. R., & Metts, S. (1991). Sexuality and communication in close relationships. In K. McKinney & S. Sprecher (Eds.). *Sexuality in close relationships* (pp. 93–110). Hillsdale, NJ: Erlbaum.

Davidson, J. O., & Layder, D. (1994). *Methods, sex, and madness.* London: Routledge.

Dear, P. (1995). Cultural history of science: An overview with reflections. *Science, Technology and Human Values, 20,* 150–170.

D'Emilio, J. (1983). Capitalism and gay identity. In A. Snitow, C. Stansell, & S. Thompson (Eds.), *Powers of desire: The politics of sexuality* (pp. 100–113). New York: Monthly Review Press.

D'Emilio, J., & Freedman, E. B. (1988). *Intimate matters: A history of sexuality in America*. New York: Harper & Row.

Ehrenreich, B., Hess, E., & Jacobs, G. (1986). *Re-making love: The feminization of sex*. Garden City, NY: Anchor Press.

Fausto-Sterling, A. (1992). *Myths of gender: Biological theories about women and men* (Rev. ed.). New York: Basic Books.

Fedigan, L. M. (1992). *Primate paradigms: Sex roles and social bonds*. Chicago: University of Chicago Press.

Gagnon, J. H., & Parker, R. G. (1995). Conceiving sexuality. In R. G. Parker & J. H. Gagnon (Eds.), *Conceiving sexuality: Approaches to sex research in a postmodern world* (pp. 3–16). New York: Routledge.

Geer, J. H., & O'Donohue, W. T. (Eds.). (1987). *Theories of human sexuality*. New York: Plenum Press.

Giddens, A. (1991). *Modernity and self-identity: Self and society in the late modern age*. Stanford, CA: Stanford University Press.

Giddens, A. (1992). *The Transformation of intimacy: Sexuality, love, and eroticism in modern societies*. Stanford, CA: Stanford University Press.

Gillespie, R. (1989). The Hawthorne experiments and the politics of experimentation. In J. G. Morawski (Ed.), *The rise of experimentation in American psychology*, (pp. 114–137). New Haven, CT: Yale University Press.

Guba, E. G. (Ed.). (1990). *The paradigm dialog*. Newbury Park, CA: Sage.

Haraway, D. (1986). Primatology is politics by other means. In R. Bleier (Ed.), *Feminist approaches to science* (pp. 77–118). New York: Pergamon.

Haraway, D. (1989). *Primate visions: Gender, race, and nature in the world of modern science*. New York: Routledge.

Hausman, B. L. (1995). *Changing sex: Transsexualism, technology, and the idea of gender*. Durham, NC: Duke University Press.

Herschberger, R. 1970 [1948]. *Adam's rib*. New York: Harper & Row.

Irvine, J. (1990). *Disorders of desire: Sex and gender in modern American sexology*. Philadelphia, PA: Temple University Press.

Jackson, M. (1994). *The real facts of life: Feminism and the politics of sexuality (1850–1940)*. London: Taylor & Francis.

Kinsey, A. C., Pomeroy, W. B., & Martin, C. E. (1948). *Sexual behavior in the human male*. Philadelphia, PA: W. B. Saunders.

Knorr-Cetina, K. D., & Mulkay, M. (Eds.). (1983). *Science observed: Perspectives on the social study of science*. Beverly Hills, CA: Sage.

Laqueur, T. (1990). *Making sex: Body and gender from the Greeks to Freud*. Cambridge, MA: Harvard University Press.

LeVay, S. (1993). *The sexual brain*. Cambridge, MA: MIT Press.

Lewontin, R. C. (1992). *Biology as ideology: The doctine of DNA*. New York: HarperCollins.

Lupton, D. (1994). *The imperative of health: Public health and the regulated body.* Newbury Park, CA: Sage.

Masters, W. H., & Johnson, V. E. (1966). *Human sexual response.* Boston: Little, Brown.

McCary, J. L. (1963). *Human sexuality.* Princeton, NJ: Van Nostrand.

McCormick, N. B. (1994). *Sexual salvation: Affirming women's sexual rights and pleasures.* New York: Praeger.

Modleski, T. (1984). *Loving with a vengeance: Mass-produced fantasies for women.* London: Methuen.

Morawski, J. G. (Ed.). (1989). *The rise of experimentation in American psychology.* New Haven, CT: Yale University Press.

Oudshoorn, N. (1994). *Beyond the natural body: An archeology of sex hormones.* London: Routledge.

Plummer, K. (1995). *Telling sexual stories: Power, change and social worlds.* London: Routledge.

Porter, R., & Hall, L. (1995). *The facts of life: The creation of sexual knowledge in Britain, 1650–1950.* New Haven, CT: Yale University Press.

Porter, R., & Teich, M. (Eds.). (1994). *Sexual knowledge, sexual science: The history of attitudes to sexuality.* Cambridge, England: Cambridge University Press.

Robinson, P. (1976). *The modernization of sex.* New York: Harper & Row.

Sherif, C. W. (1979). Bias in psychology. In J. A. Sherman & E. T. Beck (Eds.), *The prism of sex: Essays in the sociology of knowledge* (pp. 93–133). Madison, WI: University of Wisconsin Press.

Starr, P. (1982). *The social transformation of American medicine.* New York: Basic Books.

Tiefer, L. (1987). Social constructionism and the study of human sexuality. In P. Shaver & C. Hendricks (Eds.), *Sex and gender* (pp. 70–94). Newbury Park, CA: Sage.

Tiefer, L. (1991). Historical, scientific, clinical and feminist criticisms of "The human sexual response cycle." *Annual Review of Sex Research, 2,* 1–23.

Tiefer, L. (1992). Critique of the *DSM-III-R* nosology of sexual dysfunctions. *Psychiatric Medicine, 10,* 227–245.

Tiefer, L. (1995). *Sex is not a natural act and other essays.* Boulder, CO: Westview.

Tyler, L. (1973). Design for a hopeful psychology. *American Psychologist, 28,* 1021–1029.

Vance, C. S. (Ed.). (1984). *Pleasure and danger: Exploring female sexuality.* London: Routledge & Kegan Paul.

van den Wijngaard, M. (1991). *Reinventing the sexes: Feminism and biomedical construction of femininity and masculinity: 1959–1985.* Unpublished doctoral dissertation, University of Amsterdam, The Netherlands.

Vines, G. (1994). *Raging hormones: Do they rule our lives?* Berkeley: University of California Press.

Weeks, J. (1981). *Sex, politics and society: The regulation of sexuality since 1800.* London: Longman.

Weeks, J. (1991). *Against nature: Essays on history, sexuality and identity.* London: Rivers Oram Press.

Weeks, J. (1995). History, desire, and identities. In R. G. Parker & J. H. Gagnon (Eds.), *Conceiving sexuality: Approaches to sex research in a postmodern world* (pp. 33–50). London: Routledge & Kegan Paul.

Wellings, K. (1994). Sexual behaviour in Britain. Paper presented at the annual conference of the International Academy of Sex Research, Edinburgh, Scotland.

Wright, W. (1994). *The social logic of health.* Hanover, NH: Wesleyan University Press.

II

LIFE COURSE
DEVELOPMENT

5

A NORMATIVE PERSPECTIVE OF ADOLESCENT GIRLS' DEVELOPING SEXUALITY

DEBORAH P. WELSH, SHARON S. ROSTOSKY AND
MYRA CHRISTEN KAWAGUCHI

Adolescent girls' sexuality is of great interest and concern to developmental researchers, theorists, policymakers, educators, health care providers, parents, and adolescents themselves. One reason for this interest is that adolescence is a crucial time when many biological, psychological, and social changes occur. These changes, and their interaction within a cultural context, have important ramifications for girls' developing sense of sexuality. For example, puberty, the biological hallmark of adolescence, represents the greatest physical change since birth. The attainment of reproductive maturity has numerous social, cultural, and psychological meanings that, reflexively, impact on the experience of puberty and provide the link between reproductive maturity and sexuality for adolescent girls (Brooks-Gunn & Reiter, 1990; Buchanan, Eccles, & Becker, 1992). Another change is adolescents' newly acquired cognitive ability, formal operational thought,

This study was supported by a National Institute of Mental Health B/START award and a
University of Tennessee Professional Development Award to Deborah Welsh.

which permits girls to think abstractly and to take others' perspectives (Piaget & Inhelder, 1958; Selman, 1980). These new cognitive skills allow for more complex interpersonal relationships and facilitate the development of intimacy and identity (Erikson, 1968; Sullivan, 1953). These changes occur within a cultural context that imbues them with meaning and significance. One aspect of this context is the mass media, which targets adolescent consumers through soap operas, television sitcoms, movies, videos, song lyrics, and teen romance novels, both reflecting and constructing adolescence as a particularly meaningful time for the development and exploration of sexuality.

A second reason for the growth in interest in adolescent girls' sexuality stems from the cultural constructions of womens' sexuality. Womens' sexuality has historically been the target of cultural and political concern (Foucault, 1978). Over the past 25 years in the United States, however, women's sexuality during the adolescent period of life in particular has served as the target of research interest. This interest has primarily centered on the most visible aspect of girls' sexuality, pregnancy. Popular notions of adolescent pregnancy, and therefore sexuality, as an epidemic, sweeping the country, and endangering future generations, have sparked an avalanche of studies and programs designed to illuminate and eradicate the "problem".

This problem-oriented approach has largely ignored developmental theory regarding sexuality. As a result, attempts to understand sexuality have led researchers down a path quite divergent from theory. Developmental theorists have consistently defined sexuality as a fundamental aspect of personal identity, the formation of which is posited to be one of the most important developmental tasks of adolescence (Erikson, 1968; Josselson, 1987; Marcia, Waterman, Matteson, Archer, & Orlofsky, 1993). Sexuality is construed as a multifaceted component of identity that includes behavioral, affective, and cognitive features. Empirical researchers, however, have sought to understand adolescent sexuality by focusing almost exclusively on behaviors, primarily sexual intercourse and contraceptive practices (see Katchadourian, 1990; Miller & Moore, 1990, for reviews) through an epidemiological or problem-oriented approach, the aim of which is to prevent undesirable sequelae of these behaviors.

In this chapter, we address some of the results of this divergence of research from theory. Specifically, we first "unpack" some of the underlying assumptions that have guided research on adolescent girls' sexual behavior, and describe the existing framework for understanding adolescent girls' sexuality that has been based on these assumptions. We then present a framework for understanding the development of girls' sexuality from a normative perspective that is based on developmental theory. We take the position that sexuality includes both the sexual behaviors and the feelings of adolescent girls, as well as the developing sense of oneself as a sexual being. This new framework focuses on the subjective meaning of sexual behaviors and of girls' developing sense of themselves as sexual beings. We posit that any analysis of the meaning of adolescent sexuality can only be understood within a context that examines the role of ecological variables and personal characteristics of adolescents. We then present a selection of personal and ecological variables, discuss how they have been studied within the existing framework, and pose questions or make suggestions regarding the role of these variables in the new framework. Finally, we discuss implications of this normative framework.

ASSUMPTIONS UNDERLYING THE EMPIRICAL STUDY OF ADOLESCENT GIRLS' SEXUALITY IN AN HISTORICAL AND POLITICAL CONTEXT

There are three major assumptions that underlie the majority of empirical research on adolescent sexuality and shape the nature of the questions researchers ask, the design of the studies, and, thus, the state of our knowledge base about adolescent sexuality. We feel it is important to examine these assumptions and their implications for our literature base regarding adolescent girls' sexuality.

Girls' Sexuality as a Psychological and Social Problem

One underlying assumption that has guided the vast majority of empirical and political discourse on adolescent girls' sexuality over the past 30 years is that sexuality in girls is a dangerous social problem indicative of pathology and in need of prevention or at least control. This approach, which views adolescent girls' sexuality as a social problem, is constructed in the context of a climate of national panic from both the political left and right.

The politically liberal position is invested in the maintenance of this pathology perspective to advance an agenda of intervention programs, and has thus focused discourse and research on the negative consequences of sexual activity including teenage pregnancy, sexually transmitted diseases, poverty, and, most recently, AIDS. The political right has similarly emphasized the social problem of adolescent girls' sexuality, although in efforts to advance an agenda emphasizing the immorality of premarital sexuality. This agenda is typified by recent "Just Say No" campaigns and other programs aimed at abstinence education for adolescents. As a result of these two forces stemming from vastly divergent motivations, the body of research on adolescent girls' sexuality has focused on questions aimed at identifying when girls begin to engage in sexual behaviors, specifically sexual intercourse, and what factors precipitate or put an adolescent girl at risk for engaging in sexual intercourse (Irvine, 1994). The ultimate purpose of this path of research is to prevent, or at least control, adolescent girls' expressions of sexuality (Foucoult, 1978; Irvine, 1994; Nathanson, 1991).

Constance Nathanson (1991) provides a fascinating sociohistorical analysis of the emergence of adolescent girls' sexuality as a social problem. Although adolescent pregnancy, the most visible aspect of girls' sexuality, has emerged as one of the most controversial and politicized topics currently on our national table of social issues, it has only been on that table since about the mid-1970s. Although the sexual transgressions of adolescent girls have been problematic in this country for about 150 years, prior to the past two decades they were considered individual problems of individual girls rather than a national social problem. Something has happened over the past two decades that has suddenly made adolescent girls' sexuality a national emergency and put it at the top of our list of national social problems.

Nathanson (1991) provides compelling data to support her contention that the current construction of adolescent girls' sexuality as a social problem is not related to the magnitude of the problem but is rather a result of a variety of political forces advancing several moral and philosophical agendas. For example, adolescent pregnancy did not emerge as a national concern until almost a decade *after* the birth rate (the number of births per 1,000 women) for teenage girls had declined rapidly. Nathanson argues that the problem of adolescent girls' sexuality has been largely constructed over the past 25 years as a consequence of a variety of social forces.

Historically, adolescent girls' sexual transgressions were considered within the domain of morality and, addressing it was the property of religion. With the relatively recent invention of the birth control pill and later, legalized abortion, the sexuality of women in general became increasingly redistributed from the domain of the church to the medical community. Almost overnight, sexuality was transformed from a moral problem to a health problem that carried with it serious economic implications to women and society at large.

In the 1960s the birth control movement, led by Planned Parenthood, became prominent and powerful in setting national policy. The mission of this movement focused on providing birth control services to poor married adult women. The population explosion and need for population control was a prominent national agenda item at that time. The political left advanced the argument that poor married minority women were kept in a cycle of poverty by not having access to control their fertility and having child after child. The polical right was concerned with the economic cost to the country in social welfare programs. Thus, both the political left and right were invested in providing birth control to poor, primarily African American, adult women.

By the 1970s, the birth control movement had pretty much accomplished its goal, the birth rate had dropped to replacement level. In addition, there was widespread publicity surrounding the forced sterilizations of minority women that occurred in state-funded birth control clinics. The success of the movement, along with the political incorrectness of the eugenic implications highlighted by the sterilization incidents which were too distasteful to the politically liberal members of the Planned Parenthood, resulted in a redefining of the mission of this powerful and large organization. Specifically, the problem of women's sexuality was redefined on the basis of age rather than socioeconomic status. The racist undertones of focusing on controlling the fertility of primarily African American adult women were not as distasteful as controlling the fertility of still primarily African American adolescent girls.

The transformation of the problem from poor women's fertility to adolescent girls' fertility also came in the context of several other forces including the decreased tendency for adolescent mothers to be married, the public's perceived fear of youth generated by the counterculture movement of the late 1960s, and, more recently, the political power in the voice of the conservative religious right. Together, this hodge podge of diverse forces propelled the issue of adolescent girls' sexuality into the forefront of social, political, and academic discourse (see Nathanson, 1991, for more comprehensive analysis of these forces).

The public conception of adolescent girls' sexuality as an area of social concern, and as medically pathological and in need of treatment (or better, prevention), also served as the context for empirical investigators and funding agencies. No research occurs in a vacuum. Thus, as researchers are part of the culture in which they live, the conception of adolescent sexuality as pathological also forms the metaphor for the nature of the questions that scholars ask and agencies fund. For example, if one perceived adolescent girls' sexuality as an illness, one may wonder about the ways in which people with this illness differ from those who do not have it. Or, one may wonder whether this illness relates in meaningful ways to other illnesses. Indeed, researchers have found differences between adolescent girls who engage in sexual intercourse (the most prominent symptom of the illness) compared with adolescent girls who have never had sexual intercourse (see Katchadourian, 1990; Miller & Moore, 1990, for reviews). Additionally, researchers have found engaging in sexual intercourse to be associated with a constellation of problem behaviors including smoking, drinking alcohol, and using drugs (Donovan & Jessor, 1985; Elliott & Morse, 1989; Jessor, Costa, Jessor, & Donovan, 1983; Jessor & Jessor, 1975; Mott & Haurin, 1988; Rodgers & Rowe, 1990).

As with the early psychological research on ethnic minority groups in this country, these types of questions operate from a deficit model. That is, they assume that sexually active adolescent girls have a deficit (or illness), and they document this deficit by comparing them with girls without the deficit. This model does not capture the diversity within the construct being examined (e.g., sexuality or ethnicity). Thus, it may be that sexual intercourse in some adolescent girls may reflect some underlying psychological disturbance, but not in others.

Shedler and Block (1990), in an extremely important publication that won awards for its policy implications, applied this questioning to another controversial domain of adolescent behavior: drug usage. Numerous previous studies operating from the prevailing cultural assumptions regarding the pathology of adolescent drug usage had found drug use to be associated with many deleterious qualities in adolescents. Shedler and Block, however, differentiated different patterns of drug usage in adolescents, and found that adolescents who experimented with drugs but did not abuse them in fact were the psychologically most healthy, even compared with adolescents who did not use drugs. The authors believed that the same behavior, drug usage, might have very different meanings and serve different functions for different adolescents. In this instance, the willingness of these developmental researchers to move beyond deficit, illness models, to asking questions that can capture the diversity of our psychological constructs was fruitful. Researchers interested in adolescent sexuality are only beginning to take this step.

The assumption that adolescent girls' sexuality is pathological has implications for the empirical literature base on adolescent sexuality by influencing the *targets of research interest*. In most developmental domains (e.g., cognitive development, ego development, moral development, social development) the pioneering studies investigating the developmental phenomena were conducted with middle-class, European American male adolescents. The field of psychology in general has historically meant the psychology of middle-class, European American men. However, most research on adolescents' sexuality has focused on the sexuality of adolescent girls, and most often, economically disadvantaged, ethnic minority girls. Although this observation may initially seem peculiar, it makes sense in the context of understanding adolescent sexuality as pathology rather than as a normal developmental process, and given our cultural notions about gender and sexuality. When normal developmental processes are studied, it is the majority (White), powerful (male) population who is the standard (Bleier, 1986; Crawford & Marecek, 1989; Jacklin, 1981). When pathology or social problems are studied, it is the minority populations who are examined. That the overwhelming majority of empirical research on adolescent sexuality is being focused on girls, primarily poor minority girls, implies that only their sexuality is problematic and necessitates study (Tolman, 1994).

By their lack of attention to men, empirical investigators reinforce the cultural belief that male sexuality is biologically determined and uncontrollable. Therefore, to socially control adolescent sexuality, emphasis must be placed on the control of the female adolescent. This biological double standard is based on cultural scripts that designate the female as gatekeeper or final arbitrator of sexual behavior (Strouse & Fabes, 1987). That is, men are to pursue and women are to resist sexual behavior. It follows that contraception, pregnancy, and childbearing are the concerns of the woman (Chilman, 1990). One result is a large body of literature on adolescent girls' sexual behavior in regard to contraception, pregnancy, and intercourse with little or no empirical work on girls' sexual desire, sexual feelings, or sense of self as a sexual being or on any aspect of boys' sexuality.

Equation of Sexuality With Intercourse

A second assumption of empirical discourse on adolescent sexuality is that sexual behavior is synonymous with the act of heterosexual intercourse. The empirical literature casts an ahistorical, static portrait of adolescent sexuality that begins with intercourse and ends in pregnancy (Weddle, McKenry, & Leigh, 1988). This orientation stems, in part, from viewing adolescent girls' sexuality in terms of reproductive and health risks and also is consistent with a number of psychological theories. Many theoretical frameworks have viewed sexual intercourse as a crucial developmental step for adolescents. In psychodynamic theory, for instance, first intercourse is assumed to be a pivotal behavior that results in irreversible change in status in relationship to parents (Chodorow, 1978; Freud, 1933, 1953). This view is reminiscent of deeply entrenched Western cultural narratives concerning the significance of virginity, which is loaded with expectations and symbolic meaning (Thompson, 1984).

According to social exchange theory (Homans, 1974; Thibaut & Kelley, 1978), sexual intercourse is considered to be of great significance particularly for women in Western, patriarchial cultures because it involves many costs (e.g., pain, guilt, fear, potential pregnancy) (Strouse & Fabes, 1987). In fact, research does suggest that first intercourse is associated with more negative feelings and is more problematic for women than men (Eastman, 1972; Koch, 1988; Schofield, 1973; Sorensen, 1973; Waterman & Nevid, 1977), although women's reactions have become less negative than they once were (Christensen & Gregg, 1970; Weis, 1983).

Feminist theory has noted that the focus on intercourse is evidence of the male perspective that continues to dominate research in this area (Koedt, 1994). From this perspective, there is no sexuality prior to first intercourse. Feminists also have pointed out that sexuality research has traditionally assumed that male dominance is normal. One of the only studies of adolescent dating couples found the extent a couple engaged in affectionate sexual behaviors (e.g., holding hands and kissing) was associated with their commitment to their partner and to the relationship while commitment was not related to whether the couple was having sexual intercourse (Rostosky, Welsh, Kawaguchi, & Vickerman, 1999). The emphasis on intercourse, of course, also comes out of the context of a society that is not only male dominated, but also heterosexual dominated. The behavior of intercourse does not have the same salience to a lesbian couple that is does to a heterosexual couple.

Thus, adolescent sexuality takes place in the context of institutionalized heterosexuality, gendered power relations, and male sexual values, such as the primacy of intercourse and its biological imperative. Evidence of this narrow view of sexuality is found in the manner in which terms such as *sexual exploration, sexual activity*, and *sexual behavior* are used interchangeably to designate the act of sexual intercourse (DiBlasio & Benda, 1992; Foshee & Bauman, 1992). One consequence of this assumption is the almost complete lack of attention to the myriad of other sexual behaviors and feelings that adolescent girls experience.

Sexuality Is an Individual Property

A third underlying assumption of empirical investigations of adolescent sexuality is that the construct of sexuality is completely a property of the individual. Empirical investigations have not examined the adolescent couple as a unit of analysis. This is surprising in light of the fact that the girls' sexual behaviors, which are of such great concern to both researchers and policymakers, are occurring primarily in the context of dyadic relationships with boys. Yet researchers focus their attention exclusively on the personal characteristics (e.g., pubertal developmental status, values, self-esteem, sexual attitudes) or environments of adolescent girls (e.g., girls' parental marital status, socioeconomic status (SES), family size, sexual behaviors of friends) that are associated with their decisions regarding sexual intercourse and contraception. Sexual behaviors are typically occurring in romantic relationships for adolescent girls, who, in general, tend to require emotional involvement and commitment prior to having sexual intercourse (Carroll, Volk, & Hyde, 1985; Christopher & Cate, 1985; Coles & Stokes, 1985). Thus, this context serves as the initial context in which girls make meaning of the sexual behaviors in which they are engaging. The communication (verbal and nonverbal) between the couple or the relationship between the couple are not explored by researchers in attempts to understand adolescent sexuality. This may relate to the individualistic orientation of Western culture in general, or, as we discussed earlier, in our designation of females as gatekeepers of sexual behavior.

In summary, these three assumptions: (a) that adolescent girls' sexuality is problematic; (b) that sexuality is synonymous with sexual intercourse; and (c) that sexuality is the property of the individual independent of the relationship in which it is expressed, have provided the basis of the existing framework for the study of adolescent girls' sexuality. These assumptions have, for the most part, determined the questions that researchers have asked. These questions have focused on establishing which girls are at risk, and how sexual exploration can be prevented or controlled so that the unwanted outcomes, such as pregnancy and childbearing, can be avoided. This pathology oriented perspective prevents an understanding of adolescent girls' developing sexuality as normal and healthy. The perspective presented in this chapter is based on developmental theory and views sexuality as an integral part of identity in girls and women. Signs of a shift toward a more normative perspective have begun to appear.

Recent Shifts in Investigations of Adolescent Girls' Sexuality

Current cultural and theoretical perspectives of the meaning of sexuality to female *adults* have transitioned from an emphasis on reproduction to a view of sexuality as a healthy component of adult functioning and personal identity (D'Emilio & Freedman, 1988; Foucault, 1978; Irvine, 1994; Weeks, 1981). This view has only recently been adopted as a lens for investigating adolescent sexuality.

Two recent professional forums exemplify this transition (Feldman & Paikoff, 1994; Irvine, 1994). Janice Irvine's (1994) recent edited book, *Sexual Cultures and the Construction of Adolescent Identities*, presents a collection of articles that view adolescent sexuality from a normative perspective and posits that "sexual meanings, sexual practices, and adolescents' sexual bodies are complicated social artifacts mediated by such influences as race, ethnicity, gender, sexual identity, class, and physical ability" (p. vii). The authors of the articles take a social constructionist stance and argue that adolescent sexualities cannot be understood outside the context of cultural analysis.

In addition, at the 1994 meeting of the Society for Research on Adolescence, the primary mainstream arena for communication about research pertaining to adolescents in this country, 4 hours (twice the typical time allotment) were devoted to a symposium exploring "new perspectives on adolescent sexuality." Three major points were emphasized at this symposium: researchers and others interested in adolescent sexuality need to (a) promote greater understanding of adolescent sexuality in a normative context; (b) promote enhanced theoretical understanding of adolescent sexuality; and (c) understand individual differences in the meaning and experience of adolescent sexuality, particularly the influences of gender, ethnicity, SES, peer cultures, and media exposure. Thus, in the past 2 years, researchers' construction of adolescent sexuality has begun to change.

A FRAMEWORK FOR UNDERSTANDING ADOLESCENT GIRLS' SEXUALITY

Contemporary investigations of adolescent sexuality can be enhanced by using a framework that views adolescent sexuality from a normative developmental perspective. We present one such framework that focuses on girls' developing sense of themselves as sexual beings and the subjective meanings of their sexual behaviors. We argue that analysis of the meaning of adolescent sexuality must be understood within a context that examines the role of ecological and personal characteristics of adolescents. Ecological characteristics such as culture, ethnic community, family environment, peer environment, romantic relationship environment, organized religion, and the media influence the meanings that adolescents ascribe to their sexual behaviors and feelings and to their sense of themselves as sexual beings. Similarly, personal characteristics of adolescents including temperament, sexual orientation, physical characteristics, personal values, spirituality, and psychosocial, biological, and cognitive development also play a role in adolescents' developing sexuality. This framework allows empirical investigations to capture the complexity and diversity of adolescent girls' sexual development. In the rest of this chapter we consider the three central aspects of this framework (a normative stance, an emphasis on meaning, and inclusion of contextual variables), we examine studies that illustrate portions of the framework, and we pose new questions for future investigators guided by this framework.

A Normative Stance

Although sexuality in adults is considered to be an integral component of healthy functioning, researchers of adolescents have ignored the obvious developmental trajectory to this crucial aspect of healthy adult functioning. Instead, as we have discussed, previous research on adolescent girls' sexuality has operated from a framework that views adolescent sexuality as pathological. This pathological orientation recognizes that the sexual behavior of adolescent girls can be associated with dangerous, even deadly, consequences ranging from undesirable social reputations to unwanted pregnancies to sexual violence to sexually transmitted diseases including AIDS. We do not propose that researchers should ignore the potential dangerous sequelae of adolescent girls' sexuality or the possibility that some girls may experience their sexuality in unhealthful, even pathological ways. However, we contend that researchers should not neglect the healthful, developmentally appropriate spectrum of girls' sexuality.

Some recent preliminary findings from an ongoing project being conducted by Joseph Allen and his associates at the University of Virginia highlight the importance of examining girls' levels of responsibility in their sexual behaviors. Preliminary findings from this project indicate that sexually active adolescents are not less competent than adolescents who abstain from intercourse and that adolescents who engage in more responsible sexual activity feel more competent themselves and are perceived as more competent by others than adolescents who engage in more risky sexual

995). Studies such as this one support the
on a developmental continuum and that it
he adolescents for whom sexual behavior is
disturbance from those for whom sexual be-
hy, developmentally appropriate exploration.
lect of the normative development of ado-
tal theorists have considered sexuality as a
evelopment (Erikson, 1968; Sullivan, 1953).
y development is the primary developmental
others who have expanded on his work (Jos-
onsider the integration of sexuality into one's
the social world views her as a major aspect
of identity. Sullivan's interpersonal theory considers the development of
intimacy and the capacity to integrate sexuality into intimate relationships
to be the primary task of adolescence. These developmental theories, in
spite of the pathological orientation of most empirical research, make intuitive sense in a developmental perspective.

At least in the context of heterosexual adult married relationships
(the current holders of power in this country), there is little argument that
sexuality is a healthy aspect of these adults' lives. In fact, there is a fairly
large field of therapists who specialize in treating couples experiencing sexual difficulties, and the failure to express sexuality in the context of marriage is considered problematic by the general society. Yet, unlike almost
all other developmental processes (e.g., ego development, moral development, social development, cognitive development, physical development),
we do not understand how sexuality develops. It clearly is not something
that suddenly, almost miraculously, appears after marriage and was not experienced in any prior capacity.

We need a framework for viewing sexuality as a normal developmental process that would allow us to ask questions about developmental differences in the experience of sexuality. For example, do early adolescents
experience sexuality in different ways than middle or late adolescents or
adults? One may suspect that sexuality serves different purposes at different
life stages. For example, early adolescents may experience their sexuality
as a means of becoming closer and establishing power among their same
gender, platonic friendships; whereas, sexuality may be a means for older
adolescents to experience connection with their romantic partners. These
type of questions can only be addressed with a normative framework for
understanding adolescent sexuality. Additionally, and ironically, working
from a normative framework allows greater light to be shed on the pathology of sexuality. For example, asking how one differentiates between
adolescents whose sexual behaviors are expressions of normal, healthy exploration and those whose expressions of sexuality are symptomatic of severe psychological turmoil is an important empirical question that would be

of great use to many. We cannot ask this question unless we operate from a normative model that assumes sexuality can be healthy in adolescents.

The Importance of Meaning

As we have discussed, the majority of research on adolescent girls' sexuality has focused on describing the sexual behaviors of adolescent girls and determining which factors affect whether or not girls engage in various sexual behaviors or the age at which girls first engage in them. Few studies examine what sexual behaviors or sexual feelings mean to adolescent girls or the function these feelings and behaviors serve in their lives. Two recent reviews of adolescent sexuality research mention no studies that address the meaning of sexuality to adolescents or consider the different functions it may serve for different adolescents (Katchadourian, 1990; Miller & Moore, 1990). In fact, one of these reviews explicitly mentioned that the research "neglects the subjective dimension, the thoughts and feelings of adolescents themselves" because the social science perspective has focused almost exclusively on adolescent behavior (Katchadourian, 1990, p. 331).

Jerome Kagan wisely wrote, "the effects of most experiences are not fixed but depend upon the child's interpretation" (1984, p. 240). Kagan's assertion regarding the salience of meaning is echoed by social constructionists (Gergen, 1988). It is not enough for researchers to ask girls only about the sexual behaviors in which they engage and then correlate their behavior with a variety of variables measuring psychological functioning (or dysfunctioning). To understand the development of sexuality and the impact of sexuality on adolescent girls' lives, researchers must ask about their subjective understanding of their behavior and their feelings.

Consider Betsy, a 17-year-old adolescent girl who has always had strained relationships with her family, has not experienced success in academic or athletic settings, has abused drugs and alcohol, is sexually active with her new boyfriend, and rarely uses any form of contraception. Contrast Betsy with Denise, who is also 17 and has a strong attachment to her family, is functioning well in her academic and peer settings, is also sexually active, and uses contraception regularly with her boyfriend of 6 months. Betsy's understanding of sexuality may be that it gives her a high, that it serves as a temporary pleasure to escape her problems, that it allows her to retain her boyfriend, or that it is the only domain in which she experiences a sense of competence or esteem. Sex for Denise may represent a physical expression of her intimacy with her boyfriend, a way of experimenting or discovering how to physically pleasure another and be pleasured, or a way of rebelling against her parents. The information that both of these 17-year-old girls are sexually active captures little of the diverse experiences these two have of their sexuality or, potentially, of the impact their sexualities may have on their development.

important information necessary for understanding the phenomenon being studied.

Research on adolescent sexuality, previously behaviorally oriented, also benefits from including adolescents' own subjective understandings of their behaviors and feelings. For example, Miller, Christensen, and Olson (1987) found the relationship between sexual behavior and adolescents' self-esteem was moderated by adolescents' attitudes toward sex. Specifically, adolescents engaging in intercourse who felt that premarital sexual intercourse was acceptable had high self-esteem. Adolescents engaging in intercourse who felt that premarital intercourse was wrong had lower self-esteem. This finding suggests that these adolescents may be ascribing different meanings to their sexual behaviors, and, potentially, that these different meanings, rather than the sexual behavior itself, impact adolescents differentially.

A few research teams have recently begun to explicitly investigate the meaning and functions of sexuality to adolescents. For example, Rebecca Turner and S. Shirley Feldman are in the process of conducting an interview study aimed at understanding the functions that sex serves for late adolescents. In some preliminary qualitative analyses of 60 participants of varying cultural and ethnic backgrounds, they emphasize the important role sexuality plays in adolescents' development of autonomy and in their affect regulation (Turner & Feldman, 1994). The adolescents with whom they spoke talked about their ability to differentiate their own needs as sexual people in sexual relationships from the needs of their partners and how they struggled to negotiate these sometimes conflicting agendas. In many ways, the process adolescents described in their intimate peer relationships is similar to the individuation process adolescents are simultaneously negotiating in their family relationships. Trying to understand the links between adolescents' experience of their sexual relationship contexts and their family contexts is a fascinating area in need of investigation.

A second theme that frequently surfaced in Turner and Felman's study was how adolescents' sexuality was reflexively connected to their emotional well-being. They used sex to control their affect, to cope with life's difficulties, and also in response to their affect. They talked about how sex made them feel wonderful, how sex made them feel terrible, how sex made them feel out of control, and how sex gave them control. Turner and Feldman (1994) interviewed both men and women and did not try to examine gender differentially in this initial analysis. It will be interesting to see the ways in which these late adolescent men and women experience their sexuality similarly and the ways in which their experiences differ.

In another qualitative interview study, Deborah Tolman (1994) explored adolescent girls' experience of sexual desire. She found, in contrast to our cultural myth that girls only have sex in order to get emotional intimacy (i.e., sex in exchange for love from men), that 60% of the girls she interviewed reported experiencing sexual desire, while only 3 out of 30 (10%) denied experiencing sexual desire. The girls who discussed experiencing sexual feelings talked about their sexuality as a feature of a relationship. However, Tolman discerned,

> these girls make a key distinction between their sexual desire and their wish for a relationship. While their feelings of sexual desire most often arise in the context of relationships, they are not the same as or a substitute for wanting relationships. Rather, these girls say that sexual desire is a specific "feeling," a powerful feeling of wanting that the majority of these girls experience and describe as having to do with sex and with their bodies, a feeling to which they respond in the context of the many relationships that constitute their lives. (Tolman, 1994, p. 255)

A recent study conducted by Susan and Clyde Hendrick (1994) used both quantitative and qualitative methodologies to investigate the role of gender in adolescents' perspectives of their sexuality. Interestingly, they found different results from the different methodologies. When they asked participants about their sexuality using a questionnaire measure, they found gender differences in participants' attitudes toward sexuality. Specifically, they found men to have more of a recreational orientation toward sex, whereas women were more inclined to take a relational orientation toward sexuality. The Hendricks then conducted a qualitative study in which they asked men and women to describe their sexual relationships. When they used this qualitative methodology, they found few differences in the descriptions provided. Both viewed their sexual relationships as relational and highlighted both companionate and passionate aspects of their relationships.

Taken together, these studies of adolescent girls' sexuality exemplify a recent shift in research focus. They begin to identify areas in need of further clarification. Specifically, they emphasize the need to clarify the role of gender, relationship, and methodology in understanding the mean-

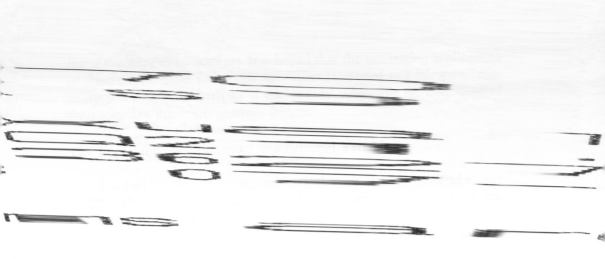

ical environment in which individuals live (see
processes that culminate in developmental outcomes. Researchers must
consider all components of this model—person variables, context variables, and process—to understand any developmental phenomenon. In the
context of understanding adolescent girls' sexuality, this model implies that
personal characteristics (e.g., temperament, sexual orientation, physical
characteristics, values, religiosity, self-esteem, and psychosocial, biological,
and cognitive development) and ecological characteristics (e.g., culture,
ethnicity, family environment, peer environment, organized religion, and
the media) of girls will influence processes that impact on their sexual
behaviors and feelings, the subjective meanings that they ascribe to their
behaviors and feelings, and their sense of themselves as sexual beings.

Much of the research on adolescent girls' sexuality has focused on
personal and ecological characteristics of girls that predict their sexual behaviors. The purpose for the large volume of literature dedicated to this
line of inquiry is to understand the factors associated with whether girls
engage in intercourse and contracepting behaviors in order to develop intervention programs for preventing intercourse or encouraging contraceptive behavior. Although, for the purposes of this chapter we are interested
in normative development, these pathology oriented studies can tell us
something about the personal and ecological factors that may influence
girls' developing sense of sexuality. We focus now on three personal variables (pubertal development, ego development, and sexual orientation) and
three ecological variables (family context, cultural context, and romantic
relationship context) as examples of how these factors may be related to
adolescent girls' sexuality in a normative framework.

Puberty—Biological Developmental Level

Girls who experience menarche earlier than their peers have been
found to engage in sexual intercourse sooner than their on-time and late
maturing peers (Morris, Mallin, & Udry, 1982; Zabin, Smith, Hirsch, &

Hardy, 1986). However, the impact of sex hormones on the sexual behavior of girls seems to depend on their social context. Specifically, although increased androgens are associated with increased interest in sex in adolescent girls, they are only associated with greater degrees of sexual behavior in girls with permissive attitudes and more sexually active friends (Udry & Billy, 1987). In addition, a variety of social factors are known to influence girls' pubertal development and, thus, hormone levels. For example, girls who are emotionally closer to their parents prior to puberty experience menarche later than those who do not have as close an emotional bond with their parents (Steinberg, 1988). Girls in father-absent homes also tend to physically mature earlier than girls in two-parent families (Surbey, 1990). Thus, the complex and recursive interaction between biology and environment clearly plays a role in understanding girls' sexuality and merits further study. From a normative perspective, physical maturation should be more broadly conceptualized than menarche, or hormone levels. The way that girls understand the changes in their bodies, what feelings they have regarding these changes, and the meanings that they attribute to these changes are all important aspects of puberty that merit further study. Evidence from existing research suggests that an adolescent girl experiences puberty in a context of family and peer relationships. These relationships influence the meaning of puberty to the individual adolescent girl. The processes by which this influence occurs are still largely unknown.

Developmental Level—Ego Development

Loevinger (1976) describes the ego as a search for meaning, a frame of reference, and a process of creating a coherent orientation toward the world. According to Loevinger, ego development is a normal sequence of stages involving an increasingly articulated view of the self and others. Each stage is characterized by how the individual copes with impulses, the nature of their interpersonal relationships, their conscious preoccupations, and their cognitive style. Ego development, then, not only influences how the adolescent makes decisions about sexual behaviors, but also influences the meaning that the adolescent attaches to these behaviors and her feelings about them. Ego development also may influence adolescents' interpretation of parental, peer, and media messages about sexuality, as well as how they negotiate whether or not to have sexual intercourse and whether or not to use contraception.

Studies of ego development and adolescent sexuality, like most of the research on adolescent sexuality, has focused on the relationship of the adolescent's ego development stage to a limited number of behaviors, grouping participants according to these behaviors or their outcomes, for instance, pregnant or parenting adolescents vs. non-pregnant or non-parenting adolescents (McIntyre & Saudargas, 1993; Oz, Tari, & Fine,

1992; Protinsky, Sporakowski, & Atkins, 1982; Romig & Bakken, 1990), or contracepting adolescents vs. those who fail to contracept (Hart & Hilton, 1988; Hernandez & Diclemente, 1992; Resnick & Blum, 1985).

Results concerning the differentiation of pregnant and parenting adolescents from adolescents not pregnant or parenting based on ego development are conflictual. Some studies have found pregnant adolescents to be functioning at lower levels of ego development than their peers (McIntyre & Saudargas, 1993; Protinsky, Sporakowski, & Atkins, 1982), whereas others have found no relationship between ego development and pregnancy or childbearing in adolescent girls (Romig & Bakken, 1990), and still others have found that parenting adolescent girls had higher levels of ego development than their non-parenting peers (Oz, Tari, & Fine, 1992). Results from studies examining adolescent girls' contraceptive behavior are less confusing. For the most part, these studies find that adolescent girls who have confronted and accepted their own sexuality and consistently use birth control to avoid unwanted pregnancies demonstrate higher levels of ego development than any other category of adolescent assessed, including those who abstain from sexual activity (Hart & Hilton, 1988; Resnick & Blum, 1985). These findings defy the current conceptualization of sexuality in adolescence as pathological. Both the sexually active, non-contracepting adolescent and the abstaining adolescent demonstrate lower ego development than sexually active, contracepting adolescents. The methodology and design of the studies, which group adolescents by their sexual behavior and do not take the meaning of the behavior into account, do not permit investigation of the potential mechanisms mediating the relationship between ego development and sexuality.

A normative framework for the study of adolescent sexuality aims to discover the processes by which various sexual behaviors, feelings, and their corresponding subjective meanings are derived in adolescence. Ego development, as one of several developmental trajectories, can serve as a frame of reference for the study of sexuality as a developmental phenomenon. For example, girls can be grouped by their level of ego development and followed longitudinally to see how their developmental level influences their subjective understanding of aspects of their sexuality.

Sexual Orientation

There is a striking lack of empirical investigations of lesbian adolescents' sexuality. This is not very surprising since sexual development has not been the focus of research on girls' sexuality. In other words, since lesbian adolescents do not become pregnant as a result of their sexual behavior nor does their sexual behavior put them at high risk for diseases such as AIDS, they have not been targeted by researchers as participants in research on sexuality. Additionally, since lesbian adolescents are not engaging in sexual intercourse, they are not considered sexual by typical research standards, given the assumption that sexuality necessarily means sexual intercourse. Lesbian adolescents experience additional obstacles to overcome in the development of a healthy sense of sexuality, including a lack of socialized role models, lack of social and cultural support, and restrictions in partner selection (Kurdek, 1991). There is some evidence that the average age of coming out has decreased over the last few decades from late adolescence to mid-adolescence. Herdt (1989) maintains that this transition constitutes a life crisis as the lesbian moves from the lifestyle and value systems of her heterosexual role-model parents to the lifestyle of the adult lesbian community. This transition occurs in the larger context of a homophobic society that provides little support and plenty of negative messages and even violence toward the adolescent for her desire for sexual relationships with women. Lesbian adolescents, even in geographic regions with large lesbian communities, experience cognitive, social, and emotional isolation (Martin & Hetrick, 1988). This sense of isolation may have profound ramifications for their developing sense of themselves as sexual beings. Studies of adult lesbians have found lesbians engage in sex less frequently than heterosexual or gay male couples (Bell & Weinberg, 1978; Blumstein & Schwartz, 1983; Kurdek, 1991). These researchers have speculated that this finding may relate to the restrictive societal context in which girls learn to internalize negative messages about their sexuality. Although research is greatly needed to understand more about the development of lesbian girls' sexuality, caution should be exercised in the essentialist dichotomization of lesbian vs. heterosexual status. Most self-defined lesbians have had heterosexual relationships and many self-defined heterosexual females have had same-gender sexual relationships (Ponse, 1978). Within a normative framework, developmental trajectories for lesbian girls' sexuality has yet to be charted. They, perhaps more forcefully than any other group, make apparent the inadequacies of a universal application of developmental standards based on European American men.

Family Context

Adolescent girls' family environments serve as important contexts for learning about sexuality and for providing secure foundations from which adolescents can explore their sexuality. In addition, adolescent girls' developing sexuality impacts the functioning of their family and the ways in which family members relate to them (Hill, 1988; Holmbeck & Hill, 1991). Girls' development into more noticeably sexual beings signifies a transition that impacts their families' stories about their understanding of themselves. These family understandings or narratives influence adolescents' sense of identity and behaviors (Anderson, 1993; Gergen, 1991; White & Epston, 1990). Sometimes family members, particularly parents, have difficulty adjusting to their daughters' sexuality. It is perhaps not surprising that the incidence of many psychological disorders with strong family components such as eating disorders and depression increase for girls at about the time their bodies begin puberty and their sexual feelings increase (Burke, Burke, Rae, & Reiger, 1991).

Research has consistently found relationships between measures related to the family context and adolescent sexual behavior. For example, daughters from single-parent families have consistently been found to have sexual intercourse earlier than daughters from two-parent families (Forste & Heaton, 1988; Hayes, 1987; Miller & Bingham, 1989; Newcomer & Udry, 1987; Zelnick & Kantner, 1980). The mechanism mediating this relationship, however, has not been thoroughly examined. Sexuality may have different meanings to daughters in single-parent families. For example, they may see their own mothers dating and, thus, may see sexuality as more healthy, normal, or acceptable.

Parenting behavior and family relationships also have been associated with girls' sexuality. Interestingly, parental discipline is curvilinearly related to adolescents' sexual attitudes and behaviors. Sexual activity is lowest among adolescents who perceive their parents to be moderately strict. Home environments that are either very liberal or very conservative are associated with greater adolescent sexual experience (Miller, McCoy, Olson, & Wallace, 1986). Although better mother-daughter communication has been associated with more responsible sexual behavior in daughters in some studies (Fox & Inazu, 1980; Furstenberg, Moore, & Peterson, 1985), other studies have not found mother-daughter communication to be related to the sexual behavior of daughters (Moore, Simms, & Betsey, 1986; Newcomer & Udry, 1984, 1985). One explanation for these inconsistent findings is that the impact of parent-daughter communication on girls' sexuality may be moderated by the content of the communication (Dyk, Christopherson, & Miller, 1991). There is some evidence to support this hypothesis. Girls who communicate more with their mothers and have liberal mothers tend to engage in more sexual activity (Fisher, 1989), whereas daughters of parents who hold traditional values and communicate with their daughters about sex are less likely to have had sexual intercourse (Moore, Peterson, & Furstenberg, 1986). Another finding that further corroborates the assertion that mothers are an important component in understanding the development of their daughters' sexuality is the strong relationship that has been identified between mothers' sexual experiences as teenagers and their adolescent daughters' sexual behavior (Newcomer & Udry, 1984). Although these studies suggest the importance of the family in adolescents' sexual behavior, they do not begin to examine the processes or mechanisms mediating the associations nor do they explore the nature of how adolescent girls' sexual identity is influenced by their family experiences.

Cultural Context

"Cultures infuse sexuality with meaning" (Irvine, 1994, p. 8). Sexual feelings, behaviors, and motivations are only given meaning, and thus, experiential significance, by the cultures in which the adolescent has been socialized. There are a variety of dimensions that define the cultural communities that are important in influencing adolescents, including race, ethnicity, neighborhood, and the mainstream culture of the country in which the adolescent lives. Ethnicity will be considered in greater depth here.

Statistics indicate large ethnic differences in the sexual behaviors of adolescent girls. For example, almost 40% of African American girls have had sexual intercourse by the time they are 17 years old, whereas only 25% of European American and 24% of Latina girls have had intercourse by age 17 (Hayes, 1987). The rates for Asian American girls are even lower, as only about 30% report having intercourse prior to marriage (Moore & Erickson, 1985). Differences also have been noted in the progression of sexual behaviors. Whereas European American adolescents tend to engage in a consistent progression of sexual behaviors beginning with kissing, followed by fondling, and then intercourse, African American adolescents tend to move more quickly to intercourse, and spend less time, skip altogether, or engage in the foreplay activities after intercourse rather than before (Smith & Udry, 1985). African American adolescent girls report more romantic and soap opera fantasies about their sexual experiences than European American girls (Muram, Rosenthal, Tolley, Peeler, & Dorko, 1992). The African American community also tends to be more tolerant of sex outside of marriage, considers marriage to be less important, and perceives greater tolerance of out-of-wedlock births than European American cultures (Moore, Nord, & Peterson, 1989; Moore, Simms, & Betsey, 1986). One study found that African Americans in an all-Black high school were more likely to report having sexual intercourse than were similar African Americans in an integrated school system (Furstenberg, Morgan, Moore, & Peterson, 1987). These studies do not assess the meaning that adolescents from different cultural communities ascribe to sexual intercourse, but it is reasonable to hypothesize that the vast differences in these statistics reflect different cultural meanings, values, and beliefs about sexuality and the conditions under which it should be expressed.

Romantic Relationship Context

Few studies have taken a dyadic approach to investigating adolescent sexuality. This is surprising as dyadic relationships form the principal context in which girls express their sexuality and the initial context in which they make meaning of their sexual behavior. As we discussed earlier, this may relate to a Western tendency toward viewing individualness rather than relatedness as important (Gilligan, 1982) or to a cultural tendency toward viewing women as the gatekeepers of sexual behavior (Strouse & Fabes, 1987).

The dating relationship has been found to have a strong impact on the initiation and frequency of sexual intercourse (Jorgensen, King, & Torrey, 1980; Leigh, Weddle, & Loewen, 1988; Miller, McCoy, & Olson, 1986; Zelnick & Shah, 1983). In one retrospective study, college students reflected on their first sexual partners. Students who reported having sex prior to the age of sixteen reported less commitment to their partners (Faulkenberry, Vincent, James, & Johnson, 1987), implying that sex may have different meanings for couples of different developmental levels. Two research teams working with college samples developed typologies of dating couples and related the different types of couples to their sexual behavior (Christopher & Cate, 1985; Peplau, Rubin, & Hill, 1977). The two studies found similar types of couples and found that couples used sex in different ways. For example, both research teams identified a type of couple who reported engaging in sexual behaviors primarily for erotic, physically pleasurable motivations. Commitment, although described by these couples as desirable, was not a crucial requisite for choosing to engage in sexual intercourse. Another type of couple described in these studies reported that they engaged in sexual intercourse for emotional reasons. These couples tended to view commitment as an important ingredient to their sexual behaviors. Both research teams also identified a type of couple who decided not to engage in intercourse in spite of a strong commitment. These couples saw love as an insufficient reason to decide to engage in sexual intercourse. Thus, the function of sexual intercourse and commitment varied for different couples.

We are currently in the process of conducting an observational study of the relationship between adolescent couples' interactional processes and their sexual behavior. A key component of this study involves obtaining each member's subjective understanding of their interaction with their romantic partner. One goal of this project is to describe the processes that occur in adolescent romantic relationships and to relate these processes to adolescents' sexual behaviors. Another goal is to understand the meaning of these sexual behaviors to each member and to determine the degree to which these meanings are shared and negotiated by the couple. Some preliminary analyses suggest that adolescent dating partners differ in their perceptions of their communications with each other, especially their views of men's communications. Specifically, adolescent girls reported being more aware of communications that reflected a dimension of power in their male dating partner's interactions with them (Welsh, Galliher, Kawaguchi, & Rostosky, in press). Certainly, future research needs to examine the impact of this important context for the development of adolescent sexuality.

CONCLUSION

Research on adolescent girls' sexuality, although plentiful over the past two decades, has focused on identifying factors associated with when girls engage in intercourse, whether they use contraception, or how to intervene to prevent intercourse or promote the use of contraception. We have discussed the cultural context and the underlying assumptions that have created a context which facilitated this voluminous, but narrow perspective on the development of girls' sexuality. Recently, a small movement within the research community has begun that uses a wider lens with which to view this developmental phenomenon. In this chapter, we have articulated a framework with which researchers can attempt to understand adolescent girls' developing sexuality. Key components of this framework include (a) viewing the development of girls' sexuality as a normative, developmental process; (b) examining girls' subjective understanding of their sexual feelings, behaviors, and their sense of themselves as sexual beings; and (c) understanding the development of sexuality in context, including both personal characteristics and ecological variables. In addition, we encourage a broadening of our construction of sexuality beyond merely examining sexual intercourse. Our view of sexuality needs to encompass a wide variety of sexual behaviors and sexual feelings and the subjective meaning that adolescents ascribe to these feelings and behaviors. We also must broaden our construction of sexuality to include the possibility of a relational component rather than viewing it exclusively as the property of the individual girl.

A shift in perspective from viewing adolescent girls' sexuality as a social problem to viewing adolescent girls' sexuality as an integral part of normal development has broad implications. Perhaps the most important ramification of this evolving perspective is that it highlights the critical need for research that examines the developmental trajectories of adolescent girls' sexuality. This examination must be sensitive to the complex interrelationships between girls' developing sense of their sexuality and their personal characteristics and ecological contexts. In other words, researchers need to ask how early adolescent girls experience their sexuality, how this experience changes for young women over the course of their adolescence, and how their personal characteristics and their ecological contexts impact on their sexual behaviors, feelings, and their understanding of themselves as sexual beings.

Once we have a sense of the different developmental pathways that girls take in the development of their sexualities, policies and programs can be developed to facilitate healthy sexual development. These policies and programs aimed at fostering healthy sexual development would complement our current policies and programs that are aimed exclusively at preventing or controlling the undesired sequelae of adolescent girls' sexual behaviors. The facilitation of healthy exploration may require policymakers and care providers to focus on creating safe environments for adolescents to explore and discuss their sense of themselves as sexual beings. These environments need to be sensitive to individual and cultural differences and must include the people who are most meaningful to adolescent girls such as their parents, clergy, teachers, counselors, and extended family. Adolescents benefit from the availability of appropriate role models with whom they can explore their feelings. Fear, generated by the existing problem-oriented approach, inhibits this sort of exploration by making adults afraid to talk about sexuality with adolescents. Healthy exploration must extend beyond public programs and into the lives of adolescent girls, involving family members and other culturally significant people, and incorporate an appreciation for diverse cultures and contexts.

A normative perspective that views sexuality as a developmental process rather than exclusively a pathological symptom allows for researchers, policymakers, clinicians, teachers, and others concerned about adolescents, including adolescents themselves, to begin dialogues about the development of healthy sexuality. Such discourses in the professional literature and with adolescents themselves will facilitate healthier sexual development by not automatically pathologizing important aspects of girls' identity and experience. Ultimately and ironically, this shift in focus and the resulting healthier developmental trajectories that may follow may also reduce the prevalence of negative outcomes associated with the girls' expression of their sexuality, which are too commonly experienced by adolescent girls today.

REFERENCES

Anderson, H. (1993). On a roller coaster: A collaborative language systems approach to therapy. In S. Friedman (Ed.), *The new language of change: Constructive collaboration in psychotherapy.* New York: Guilford Press.

Bell, A. P., & Weinberg, M. S. (1978). *Homosexualities: A study of diversity among men and women.* New York: Simon & Schuster.

Bleier, R. (1986). Sex differences research: Science or belief? In R. Bleier (Ed.), *Feminist approaches to science* (pp. 147–164). New York: Pergamon.

Blumstein, P., & Schwartz, P. (1983). *American couples.* New York: Morrow.

Bronfenbrenner, U. (1979). *The ecology of human development: Experiments by nature and design.* Cambridge, MA: Harvard University Press.

Bronfenbrenner, U. (1986). Ecology of the family as a context for human development. *Developmental Psychology, 22,* 723–742.

Brooks-Gunn, J., & Reiter, E. O. (1990). The role of pubertal processes. In S. S. Feldman & G. R. Elliot (Eds.), *At the threshold: The developing adolescent* (pp. 16–53). Cambridge, MA: Harvard University Press.

Buchanan, C. M., Eccles, J. S., & Becker, J. B. (1992). Are adolescents the victims of raging hormones: Evidence for activational effects of hormones on moods and behavior at adolescence. *Psychological Bulletin, 111*, 62–107.

Burke, K. C., Burke, J. D., Rae, D. S., & Reiger, D. A. (1991). Comparing age at onset of major depression and other psychiatric disorders by birth cohorts in five U.S. community populations. *Archives of General Psychiatry, 48*, 789–795.

Callan, V. J., & Noller, P. (1986). Perceptions of communicative relationships in families with adolescents. *Journal of Marriage and the Family, 48*, 813–820.

Carroll, J. L., Volk, K. D., & Hyde, J. S. (1985). Differences between males and females in motives for engaging in sexual intercourse. *Archives of Sexual Behavior, 14*, 131–139.

Chilman, C. (1990). Promoting healthy adolescent sexuality. *Family Relations: Journal of Applied Family and Child Studies, 39(2)*, 123–131.

Chodorow, N. (1978). *The reproduction of mothering: Psychoanalysis and the sociology of gender.* Berkeley: University of California Press.

Christensen, H., & Gregg, C. (1970). Changing sex norms in America and Scandinavia. *Journal of Marriage and the Family, 40*, 721–732.

Christopher, F. S., & Cate, R. M. (1985). Premarital sexual pathways and relationship development. *Journal of Social and Personal Relationships, 2*, 271–288.

Coles, R., & Stokes, G. (1985). *Sex and the American teenager.* New York: Harper & Row.

Crawford, M., & Marecek, J. (1989). Psychology reconstructs the female, 1968–1988. *Psychology of Women Quarterly, 13*, 147–165.

Cullen, M., & Boykin, K. A. (1995, April). *Beyond abstinence: Levels of adolescent sexual maturity and social competence.* Paper presented at the biennial meeting of the Society for Research in Child Development, Indianapolis, IN.

D'Emilio, J., & Freedman, E. (1988). *Intimate matters: A history of sexuality in America.* New York: Harper & Row.

DiBlasio, F. A., & Benda, B. B. (1992). Gender differences in theories of adolescent sexual activity. *Sex Roles, 27*, 221–239.

Dyk, P. H., Christopherson, C. R., & Miller, B. C. (1991). Adolescent sexuality. In S. J. Bahr (Ed.), *Family research: A sixty-year review, 1930–1990* (Vol. 1, pp. 25–64). Lexington, MA: Lexington Books.

Donovan, J. E., & Jessor, R. (1985). Structure of problem behavior in adolescence and young adulthood. *Journal of Consulting and Clinical Psychology, 53*, 890–904.

Eastman, W. (1972). First intercourse. *Sexual Behavior, 2*, 22–27.

Elliott, D. S., & Morse, B. J. (1989). Delinquency and drug use as risk factors in teenage sexual activity. *Youth and Society, 21*, 32–60.

Erikson, E. H. (1968). *Identity: Youth and crisis.* New York: W. W. Norton.

Faulkenberry, J. R., Vincent, M., James, A., & Johnson, W. (1987). Coital behaviors, attitudes, and knowledge of students who experience early coitus. *Adolescence, 22,* 321–332.

Feldman, S. S., & Paikoff, R. (1994, Feb.). *New perspectives on adolescent sexuality.* Study group presented at Society for Research on Adolescence biennial meeting, San Diego, CA.

Fisher, T. (1989). An extension of the findings of Moore, Peterson, and Furstenberg (1986) regarding family sexual communication and adolescent sexual behavior. *Journal of Marriage and the Family, 51,* 637–639.

Forste, R. T., & Heaton, T. B. (1988). Initiation of sexual activity among female adolescents. *Youth and Society, 19,* 250–268.

Foshee, V., & Bauman, K. (1992). Gender stereotyping and adolescent sexual behavior: A test of temporal order. *Journal of Applied Social Psychology, 22,* 1561–1579.

Foucault, M. (1978). *The history of sexuality* (Vol. 1). New York: Pantheon.

Fox, G. L., & Inazu, J. K. (1980). Patterns and outcomes of mother-daughter communication about sexuality. *Journal of Social Issues, 36,* 7–29.

Freud, S. (1933). The psychology of women. In *New Introductory Lectures on Psychoanalyses* (pp. 153–185). New York: Norton.

Freud, S. (1953). Three essays on the theory of sexuality. In J. Strachey (Ed. and Trans.), *The standard edition of the complete psychological works of Sigmund Freud* (Vol. 7). London: Hogarth Press.

Furstenberg, F. F., Moore, K. A., & Peterson, J. L. (1985). Sex education and sexual experience among adolescents. *American Journal of Public Health, 75,* 1331–1332.

Furstenberg, F. F., Morgan, S. P., Moore, K. A., & Peterson, J. L. (1987). Race differences in the timing of first intercourse. *American Sociological Review, 52,* 511–518.

Gergen, K. J. (1991). *The saturated self.* New York: Basic Books.

Gergen, M. M. (Ed.). (1988). *Feminist thought and the structure of knowledge.* New York: New York University Press.

Gilligan, C. (1982). *In a different voice.* Cambridge, MA: Harvard University Press.

Gottman, J. M., Notarius, C., Markman, H., Bank, S., Yoppi, B., & Rubin, M. E. (1976). Behavior exchange theory and marital decision making. *Journal of Personality and Social Psychology, 34,* 14–34.

Hart, B., & Hilton, I. (1988). Dimensions of personality organization as predictors of teenage pregnancy risk. *Journal of Personality Assessment, 52,* 116–132.

Hayes, C. (Ed.). (1987). *Risking the future: Adolescent sexuality, pregnancy, and childbearing* (Vol. 1). Washington, DC: National Academy Press.

Hendrick, S. S., & Hendrick, C. (1994, February). Gender, sexuality, and close relationships. In R. Turner (Chair), *Sexuality and interpersonal relationships.* Symposium conducted at the biennial meeting of the Society for Research on Adolescence, San Diego, CA.

Herdt, G. (1989). Introduction: Gay and lesbian youth, emergent identities, and cultural scenes at home and abroad. *Journal of Homosexuality, 17,* 1–42.

Hernandez, J. T., & Diclemente, R. J. (1992). Self-control and ego identity development as predictors of unprotected sex in late adolescent males. *Journal of Adolescence, 15,* 437–447.

Hill, J. P. (1988). Adapting to menarche: Familial control and conflict. In M. R. Gunnar and W. A. Collins (Eds.), *Minnesota symposia on child psychology: Development during the transition to adolescence* (pp. 43–77). Hillsdale, NJ: Erlbaum.

Holmbeck, G. N., & Hill, J. P. (1991). Conflictive engagement, positive affect, and menarche in families with seventh-grade girls. *Child Development, 62,* 1030–1048.

Homans, G. (1974). *Social behavior: Its elementary forms.* New York: Harcourt, Brace, Jovanovich.

Irvine, J. M. (1994). *Sexual cultures and the construction of adolescent identities.* Philadelphia, PA: Temple University Press.

Jacklin, C. N. (1981). Methodological issues in the study of sex-related differences. *Developmental Review, 1,* 266–273.

Jessor, R., Costa, F., & Jessor, S., & Donovan, J. E. (1983). Time of first intercourse: A prospective study. *Journal of Personality and Social Psychology, 44,* 608–626.

Jessor, S. L., & Jessor, R. (1975). Transition from virginity to nonvirginity among youth: A social-psychological study over time. *Developmental Psychology, 11,* 473–484.

Jorgensen, S. R., King, S. L., & Torrey, B. A. (1980). Dyadic and social network influences on adolescent exposure to pregnancy risk. *Journal of Marriage and the Family, 42,* 141–155.

Josselson, R. (1987). *Finding herself: Pathways to identity development in women.* San Francisco: Jossey-Bass.

Josselson, R. (1994). The empirical study of ego identity. In H. A. Bosma, T. L. G. Graafsma, H. D. Grotevant, & D. J. de Levita (Eds.), *Identity and development: An interdisciplinary approach* (pp. 67–80). Thousand Oaks, CA: Sage.

Kagan, J. (1984). *The nature of the child.* New York: Basic Books.

Katchadourian, H. (1990). Sexuality. In S. S. Feldman & G. R. Elliott (Eds.), *At the threshold: The developing adolescent* (pp. 330–351). Cambridge, MA: Harvard University Press.

Koch, P. B. (1988). The relationship of first intercourse to later sexual functioning concerns of adolescents. *Journal of Adolescent Research, 3,* 345–362.

Koedt, A. (1994). The myth of the vaginal orgasm. In A. M. Jaggar (Ed.), *Living with contradictions: Controversies in feminist social ethics* (pp. 481–487). Boulder, CO: Westview Press.

Kurdek, L. A. (1991). Sexuality in homosexual and heterosexual couples. In K. McKinney and S. Sprecher (Eds.), *Sexuality in close relationships* (pp. 177–205). Hillsdale, NJ: Erlbaum.

Leigh, G. K., Weddle, K. D., & Loewen, I. R. (1988). Analysis of the timing of transition to sexual intercourse for black adolescent females. *Journal of Adolescent Research, 3*, 333–344.

Loevinger, J. (1976). *Ego development.* San Francisco: Jossey-Bass.

Levenson, R. W., & Gottman, J. M. (1983). Marital interaction: Physiological linkage and affective exchange. *Journal of Personality and Social Psychology, 49*, 85–94.

Marcia, J. E., Waterman, A. S., Matteson, D. M., Archer, S. L., & Orlofsky, J. (1993). *Ego identity: A handbook for psychosocial research.* New York: Springer Verlag.

Marcia, J. (1994). The empirical study of ego identity. In H. A. Bosma, T. L. G. Graafsma, H. D. Grotevant, & D. J. de Levita (Eds.), *Identity and development: An interdisciplinary approach,* (pp. 67–80). Thousand Oaks, CA: Sage.

Markman, H. J. (1979). Application of a behavioral model of marriage in predicting relationship satisfaction of couples planning marriage. *Journal of Consulting and Clinical Psychology, 47*, 743–749.

Markman, H. J. (1981). Prediction of marital distress: A 5 year follow-up. *Journal of Consulting and Clinical Psychology, 49*, 760–762.

Martin, A. D., & Hetrick, E. S. (1988). The stigmatization of the gay and lesbian adolescent. *Journal of Homosexuality, 15*, 163–183.

McIntyre, A., & Saudargas, R. A. (1993, March). *Psychological immaturity among teenage mothers: Applied and theoretical implications.* Paper presented at the biennial meeting of the Society for Research in Child Development, New Orleans, LA.

Miller, B. C., & Bingham, C. R. (1989). Family configuration in relation to the sexual behavior of female adolescents. *Journal of Marriage and the Family, 51*(2), 499–506.

Miller, B. C., Christensen, R. B., & Olson, T. D. (1987). Adolescent self-esteem in relation to sexual attitudes and behavior. *Youth and Society, 19*, 93–111.

Miller, B. C., McCoy, J. K., & Olson, T. D. (1986). Dating age and stage as correlates of adolescent sexual attitudes and behavior. *Journal of Adolescent Research, 1*, 361–371.

Miller, B. C., McCoy, J. K., Olson, T. D., & Wallace, C. M. (1986). Parental discipline and control attempts in relation to adolescent sexual attitudes and behavior. *Journal of Marriage and the Family, 48*, 503–512.

Miller, B. C., & Moore, K. A. (1990). Adolescent sexual behavior, pregnancy, and parenting: Research through the 1980s. *Journal of Marriage and the Family, 52*, 1025–1044.

Moore, D. S., & Erikson, P. I. (1985). Age, gender, and ethnic differences in sexual and contraceptive knowledge, attitudes, and behavior. *Family and Community Health, 8*, 38–51.

Moore, K., Nord, C. W., & Peterson, J. (1989). Nonvoluntary sexual activity among adolescents. *Family Planning Perspectives, 21*, 110–114.

Moore, K., Peterson, J., & Furstenberg, F. (1986). Parental attitudes and the occurrence of early sexual activity. *Journal of Marriage and the Family, 48*, 777–782.

Moore, K., Simms, M. C., & Betsey, C. L. (1986). *Choice and circumstance*. New Brunswick, NJ: Transaction Books.

Morris, N. M., Mallin, K., & Udry, J. R. (1982, November 17). *Pubertal development and current sexual intercourse among teenagers*. Paper presented at the annual meeting of the American Public Health Association, Montreal.

Mott, F. L., & Haurin, R. J. (1988). Linkages between sexual activity and alcohol and drug use among American adolescents. *Family Planning Perspectives, 20*, 129–136.

Muram, D., Rosenthal, T. L., Tolley, E. A., Peeler, M. M., & Dorko, B. (1992). Race and personality traits affect high school senior girls' sexual reports. *Journal of Sex Education & Therapy, 17*, 231–243.

Nathanson, C. A. (1991). *Dangerous passage: The social control of sexuality in women's adolescence*. Philadelphia, PA: Temple University Press.

Newcomer, S. F., & Udry, J. R. (1984). Mothers' influence on the sexual behavior of their teenage children. *Journal of Marriage and the Family, 46*, 477–485.

Newcomer, S. F., & Udry, J. R. (1985). Parent-child communication and adolescent sexual behavior. *Family Planning Perspectives, 17*, 169–174.

Newcomer, S., & Udry, J. R. (1987). Parental marital status effects on adolescent sexual behavior. *Journal of Marriage and the Family, 49*, 235–240.

Oz, S., Tari, A., & Fine, M. (1992). A comparison of the psychological profiles of teenage mothers and their nonmother peers: I. Ego development. *Adolescence, 27*, 193–202.

Peplau, L. A., Rubin, Z., & Hill, C. T. (1977). Sexual intimacy in dating relationships. *Journal of Social Issues, 33*, 86–109.

Piaget, J., & Inhelder, B. (1958). *The growth of logical thinking from childhood to adolescence*. New York: Basic Books.

Ponse, B. (1978). *Identities in the lesbian world: The social construction of self*. Westport, CT: Greenwood Press.

Powers, S. I., & Welsh, D. P. (1998). Mother-daughter interactions and adolescent girls' depression. In M. Cox and J. Brooks-Gunn (Eds.), *Conflict and cohesion in families: Causes and consequences* (pp. 243–281). Hillside, NJ: Erlbaum.

Powers, S. I., Welsh, D. P., & Wright, V. (1994). Adolescents' affective experience of family behaviors: The role of subjective understanding. *Journal of Research on Adolescence, 4*, 585–600.

Protinsky, H., Sporakowski, M., & Atkins, P. (1982). Identity formation: Pregnant and non-pregnant adolescents. *Adolescence, 17*, 73–80.

Resnick, M. D., & Blum, R. W. (1985). Developmental and personalogical correlates of adolescent sexual behavior and outcome. *International Journal of Adolescent Medicine and Health, 1*, 293–313.

Rodgers, J. L., & Rowe, D. C. (1990). Adolescent sexuality and mildly deviant behavior: Sibling and friendship effects. *Journal of Family Issues, 11*, 274–293.

Romig, C. A., & Bakken, L. (1990). Teens at risk for pregnancy: The role of ego development and family processes. *Journal of Adolescence, 13,* 195–199.

Rostosky, S., Welsh, D. P., Kawaguchi, M. C., & Vickerman, R. C. (1999). Commitment and sexual behaviors in adolescent dating couples. In J. Adams, & W. Jones (Eds.), *Handbook of interpersonal commitment and relationship stability* (pp. 323–338). New York: Plenum Press.

Selman, R. L. (1980). *The growth of interpersonal understanding.* New York: Academic Press.

Shedler, J., & Block, J. (1990). Adolescent drug use and psychological health: A longitudinal inquiry. *American Psychologist, 45,* 612–630.

Schofield, M. (1973). *The sexual behavior of young adults.* Boston, MA: Little, Brown.

Smith, E., & Udry, J. (1985). Coital and noncoital sexual behaviors of white and black adolescents. *American Journal of Public Health, 75,* 1200–1203.

Sorensen, R. (1973). *The Sorensen report: Adolescent sexuality in contemporary America.* New York: World Publishing.

Steinberg, L. (1988). Reciprocal relation between parent-child distance and pubertal maturation. *Developmental Psychology, 24,* 122–128.

Strouse, J. S., & Fabes, R. A. (1987). A conceptualization of transition to nonvirginity in adolescent females. *Journal of Adolescent Research, 2,* 331–348.

Sullivan, H. S. (1953). *The interpersonal theory of psychiatry.* New York: Norton.

Surbey, M. (1990). Family composition, stress, and human menarche. In F. Bercovitch and T. Zeigler (Eds.), *The socioendocrinology of primate reproduction.* New York: Alan R. Liss.

Thibaut, N., & Kelley, H. (1978). *Interpersonal relations; A theory of interdependence.* New York: Wiley.

Thompson, S. (1984). Search for tomorrow: On Feminism and the reconstruction of teen romance. In C. S. Vance (Ed.), *Pleasure and danger: Exploring female sexuality* (pp. 350–384). London: Routledge & Kegan Paul.

Tolman, D. (1994). Daring to desire: Culture and the bodies of adolescent girls. In J. M. Irvine (Ed.), *Sexual cultures and the construction of adolescent identities.* Philadelphia, PA: Temple University Press.

Turner, R., & Feldman, S. S. (1994, February). *The functions of sex in everyday life.* Paper presented at the biennial meeting of the Society for Research on Adolescence, San Diego, CA.

Udry, J. R., & Billy, J. (1987). Initiation of coitus in early adolescence. *American Sociological Review, 52,* 841–855.

Waterman, C., & Nevid, J. (1977). Sex differences in the resolution of the identity crisis. *Journal of Youth and Adolescence, 6,* 337–342.

Weddle, K. D., McKenry, P. C., & Leigh, G. K. (1988). Adolescent sexual behavior: Trends and issues in research. Special issue: Adolescent sexual behavior. *Journal of Adolescent Research, 3,* 245–257.

Weeks, J. (1981). *Sex, politics, and society: The regulation of sexuality since 1800.* New York: Longman.

Weis, D. (1983). Affective reactions of women to their initial experience of coitus. *The Journal of Sex Research, 19*, 209–237.

Welsh, D. P., Galliher, R. V., Kawaguchi, M., & Rostosky, S. (in press). Discrepancies in adolescent romantic couples' and observers' perceptions of couple interaction and their relationship to mental health. *Journal of Youth and Adolescence.*

Welsh, D. P., Galliher, R. V., & Powers, S. I. (1998). Divergent realities and perceived inequalities: Adolescents', mothers', and observers' perceptions of family interactions and adolescent psychological functioning. *Journal of Adolescent Research, 13*, 377–402.

White, M., & Epston, D. (1990). *Narrative means to therapeutic ends.* New York: Norton.

Zabin, L. S., Smith, E. A., Hirsch, M. B., & Hardy, J. B. (1986). Ages of physical maturation and first intercourse in black teenage males and females. *Demography, 23*, 595–605.

Zelnick, M., & Kantner, J. (1980). Sexual activity, contraceptive use and pregnancy among metropolitan area teenagers: 1971–1979. *Family Planning Perspectives, 12*, 230–237.

Zelnick, M., & Shah, F. K. (1983). First intercourse among young Americans. *Family Planning Perspectives, 15*, 64–67.

6

SEXUAL ROLES OF GIRLS AND WOMEN: AN ETHNOCULTURAL LIFESPAN PERSPECTIVE

PAMELA TROTMAN REID AND VANESSA M. BING

"Are you a girl or a mother?" This question was posed to me (first author) by an 8-year-old boy many years ago on my first day in a summer job as assistant playground supervisor. As a teenage college student, neither description was apt, but I understood that the child was asking about my role in relationship to him using the only categories he knew for women.

The sexual personae of girls and women comprise a complex matrix of roles and attitudes prescribed and determined by ethnocultural socialization. However, the predominant views of women held in the United States and elsewhere appear to be not much more complex than the basic classifications we developed as children. Indeed, we still rely heavily on stereotypes in our attempts to define female roles (Castaneda, Ortiz, Allen, & Garcia, 1996; Loxley, 1996). Women have been represented on one polarity as asexual madonnas, and at the other end as highly sexual, alluring sirens. We have developed cultural icons of virtue, such as the woman who is chaste and pure—symbolic of the Virgin Mary, while also holding onto images of seductresses, like Eve and Delilah. In this chapter we will examine these socially constructed images and the roles that girls and women are (mis)led to adopt. Given our assumption that neither the sexual images nor roles for girls and women rely to any great extent on actual biological factors, we will necessarily focus on social factors and expectations.

Traditional expectations about the manner in which girls and women should behave impose themselves in every arena, both public and private. Beliefs about appropriate responses extend themselves into every social class, into all professions regardless of level of training, and across families of all backgrounds and ethnicities. Although the specifics of our expectations may vary widely, most observers agree that girls and women are universally cast in secondary roles and hold lower status than their male counterparts.

In the United States the notion of sexuality is most often considered to be specific to behaviors related to seduction and sexually intimate activities. These can, of course, be discussed in terms of level or degree. Thus, colloquially, one says a woman is more or less sexual, referring to the degree of sexual appeal or allure she possesses. At almost every age and every stage in women's lives, the promise or specter of sexual appeal looms as a factor in social exchanges. It leads us to conscientiously cover the immature breasts of prepubescent females—not only school-age girls, but also female toddlers and infants. It led in the not too distant past to restricting the work and even public appearances (i.e., going out in public) of pregnant women. And, it has led aging women to outfit themselves in fashions intended for the young.

The belief in the power of women's sexual allure is also used to explain and excuse men's antisocial behavior toward women. Ironically, although women are perceived as less able in many arenas, with respect to sexuality, it is acceptable to consider them in control of themselves and of most situations. Thus, activities as obnoxious as sexual harassment, sexual abuse, and sexual assault may be attributed to the personal characteristics and attractiveness of the victim, rather than to defects in the male perpetrator. According to society's demands, it is the woman who should be perceptive enough to understand the course of current and future behavior. Her youth or other forms of incapacitation (e.g., drugs, mental disability) often are not considered sufficient to remove her culpability in the opinion of many. A much-publicized example was the Glen Ridge, New Jersey, case (Houppert, 1993; Kantrowitz, 1993) in which a mentally retarded young woman was sexually assaulted by neighborhood boys. Another instance was a case in the Midwest in which a woman was raped while unconscious from alcohol. In both instances, the accused men argued their innocence by placing the blame on the women who were clearly not capable of giving consent.

Society holds some explicit notions about the relationship of sexual roles and sexuality; however, psychology has been more circumspect and most often focused on gender roles. Gender roles are defined as sets of behaviors assigned to an individual as a result of being a woman or man in a particular culture (Unger, 1991). The internalized sense of femaleness or maleness is referred to as gender identity (Money & Tucker, 1976). Neither gender roles nor gender identity have been conceptually related to sexuality (Lips, 1992). In fact, it is not clear if we are able to distinguish sexual roles from other gender-typed behavior. One may ask, what makes a role sexual? Or a more cynical question may be: Are there gender roles that are not sexual? Anderson (1993) noted the irony that our society appears excessively conscious of sex (through advertising and popular culture) while simultaneously adopting a repressive and proscriptive agenda for sexuality (Durham, 1998; Freedman & Thorne, 1984).

In this chapter we will adopt a broad definition of gender roles and examine those that are related or directly connected to the biological functioning of girls and women as sexual beings. This is in keeping with the current acceptance of gender as a social construction and sex as a biological fact (Riger, 1992). Obviously there will be considerable blurring of distinctions across definitions since there are many instances when biological function leads to social construction, but this is unavoidable. Indeed, Caulfield (1985, p. 356) indicated that it is "the culturalization of sex," that is, our ability to transform a biological function into a social activity with rules, expectations, and socialized demands, that render it a function of human nature.

The universal acceptance of the confluence of female gender roles and sexual roles has greatly contributed to psychology's tendency to ignore differences among girls and women. The belief that seems predominant in psychology is this: There is an essential experience of women, so we do not need to examine the variety of social conditions in which girls and women find themselves. Because psychology cannot easily disentangle the biological from the social, the need to separate contexts from one another has been left unattended. The narrowness of vision and oversights are particularly glaring with respect to issues of ethnicity and social class (Reid, 1993; Reid & Kelly, 1994). Still we have managed to identify a number of widely held images of women, some of which transcend group boundaries and many of which are defined within them.

STEREOTYPES: THE GOOD AND THE BAD

In the research literature and in popular culture, women have been typically categorized according to their sexuality. The classic archetypes represent women in terms of both biological and psychological characteristics. They are either good or evil. The good woman will be represented biologically as virginal (i.e., pure, innocent, and naive) and psychologically as a self-effacing, self-denying earth mother. The evil woman is seen as a whore; she is a scheming, ambitious, and a clever seductress.

Embedded in the distinctions about good women and evil women is an assumption of "cultural equivalency" (i.e., the view that the expectations, judgments, and behavioral assessments about good and bad will be similar across all groups) (Strong & DeVault, 1994). However, even the early investigators in the area of sexuality noted that normality must be defined by the cultural group (Kinsey, Pomeroy, & Martin, 1948). Strong and DeVault (1994) are unequivocal in their statement of this principle. "Sexuality cannot be fully understood," they maintain, "without considering ethnic variation" (p. 78). However, in psychology the research on sex and ethnicity has been slow to emerge. The scant attention in the literature was underscored in an article cowritten by Pamela Reid and Elizabeth Kelly (Reid & Kelly, 1994). This review of gender-related topics revealed that research on women of color is at best sparse. Perhaps even worse than no research has been the tendency to problematize sex research on ethnic minorities. This is particularly the case for African American women and Latinas. Since these women are often among the poor, the politics of sex allows society to justify the use of class and ethnic biases through the assertion that these poor ethnic women are promiscuous and in need of state control (Anderson, 1993; Reid, 1993); hence, the push for legislation to regulate payment to mothers receiving public assistance and to deny poor women access to free abortions.

Variations on sexual stereotoypes based on ethnicity have been noted by a number of social scientists. We are not surprised that most are dominated by phallocentric thinking (i.e., "the assumption that women's primary sexual orientation is naturally directed toward men"; Anderson, 1993, p. 81). For example, Reid (1988) reviewed the literature on African American women and reported the historic promotion of an image of Black women as licentious and promiscuous. Within the majority culture, roles for African American women were limited to "mammy, welfare cheat, Jezebel, period" (Painter, 1992, p. 210). Such a uniform perspective consistently fails to recognize the variety of social class experiences, religious orientations, and family or cultural backgrounds found among African American people.

Among all ethnic groups we can identify the diversity of cultures experienced. This is particularly true among Latina and Asian American women, yet they also have been depicted in formulaic ways. Latinas, for example, are categorized as hot-tempered and sensuous or virtuous and naive; this dichotomy leaves little room for individual expression (Espin, 1984). There also persist images of Asian American women as passive and willing to submit their will to men, thereby justifying their commodification as mail-order brides. More often, however, Asian women are left out of public view. Taylor and Stern (1997) note a trend toward depicting Asian women solely as workers and ignoring their human side and their personal relationships.

A few researchers, such as LaFromboise, Heyle, & Ozer (1990), have observed and disclosed the nature of gender roles among Native American communities. It is more likely, however, to find majority-held stereotypes of Native American women in popular films and literature. In the popular renditions of Native American women, for example, they are either silent domestics or loyal followers of the men who have claimed them, whether Indian or White. Tuan (1984) noted that attempts also have been made to portray Native American women as sexually uninhibited and wild. Stereotypic representations of women as naturally wild or animalistic also provide a rationale for control (i.e., taming the uncontrollable). Similarly, representations of women as puerile and simple-minded justify, for some, their treatment as chattel or children.

DEVELOPMENTAL THEORIES

Sexuality must be considered as an emergent process involving biological processes and social constructions that evolve on both the individual and group level to form each person's unique sexual identity (Anderson, 1993). Although the observations of cultural and experiential differences among women are noted in clinical and empirical literature, theories of gender role development typically are silent about these concerns. Psychological theories addressing sexual identity in girls and women appear to ignore individual circumstances and assume an essentialist position (i.e., the belief that there exists a basic female nature that remains relatively impervious to contextual factors).

Traditional psychoanalytic theorists proposed a universal explanation that tied gender-appropriate development to identification with the same-sex parent (Beal, 1994). It was proposed that girls had difficulty identifying with their mothers because they held sexual desires for their fathers. In light of current incidents of family sexual abuse and reexaminations of Freud's notes, researchers now give less credence to the notion of female gender emanating from penis envy or childhood feelings of female inferiority (Mason, 1984). Still, the connections to parents were established and are maintained as fundamental even in other theoretical approaches.

Social learning theorists suggested that children do more than observe parents. They found that children receive implicit and explicit incentives to adopt appropriate gender roles (Bussey & Bandura, 1984; Fagot & Hagan, 1991). Further, children are rewarded for imitating same-sex models and at times reprimanded for gender-inappropriate behavior. Interestingly, models may be found in the home (e.g., parents) (Bem, 1983; Block, 1983); or they may be teachers, friends (Carter, 1987; Wynn & Fletcher, 1987); or even characters on television (Lips, 1992). According to Beal (1994) the social learning theory does not explain variations among girls (e.g., why some girls are more feminine than others); it also does not explain why some discouraged behaviors are nevertheless exhibited or why some models are more salient than others.

Cognitive-developmental theorists also focus on components of gender role learning; however, they propose an active role for the child (Serbin, Powlishta, & Gulko, 1993). Theorists suggest that children create patterns or schemas to use in interpreting their world. These schemas, growing from repeated experience and observation, guide the child's decisions, choices, and behavior (Martin & Halverson, 1981).

Each of these major theoretical explanations of the development of gender-typed behavior leaves little room for understanding the roles of class, culture, or ethnicity (Reid, 1982). Whether we adopt a psychoanalytic perspective, a social learning, or a cognitive–developmental approach, the underlying assumptions of sexual identity are assumed to be based on traditional (i.e., White, middle-class lifestyles and expectations). Even recent versions of these standard explanations do little to dispel the notion that normal children are reared in a two-parent, heterosexual, nuclear family. Other assumptions appear to include: (a) a limited number of siblings, (b) few contacts during the first few years with adults outside of the primary caregiver, (c) parents who encourage early independence, and (d) family as the sole agent of socialization. It is beyond the scope of this chapter to deconstruct these myths; however, to examine them further one may see little basis for accepting such family universals.

PREADOLESCENT GIRLS: SOCIALIZATION OF GENDER

More than 20 years ago Anne Beuf (1974) questioned 3- and 4-year olds about their aspirations. She asked them what they wanted to be when they grew up. The intention of this and subsequent studies was to demonstrate the differences in sex-typed goals and aspirations. Such research also demonstrated the child's view of their adult options. In her investigation, Beuf found that both girls and boys responded with stereotypic occupations. For girls these included teacher, dancer, nurse, and mother. Beuf noted that no boys included father as a career goal, but it was common and accepted for girls to cite mother as an adult ambition. Although recent research demonstrates that today girls perceive more options available to them (Bobo, Hildreth, & Durodoye, 1998), most school-age girls still have gender stereotypic choices (e.g., teacher, nurse, and motherhood).

Indeed, it is no stretch of the imagination to interpret early girlhood experiences as painstaking preparation for gender-typed roles. Even the toys designated as appropriate for girls may be construed as preparing them for their dual roles as caregivers and as sexual ornaments, more than for careers. From baby dolls to Barbie dolls, little girls are encouraged to incorporate gender roles and sexuality into their play. Whereas baby dolls come with bottles, diapers, and strollers, Barbie and her friends bring glamorous clothes, lacy underwear, and the tools of seduction—a sports car, a town house, and a pool. In addition to reinforcing specific role expectations for girls, it has been suggested that the blond, blue-eyed, slender-hipped Barbie further reinforced the image of a standard form of beauty for American girls, an image that does not include women of color. Although a variety of Barbies are on the market including a career Barbie and a dark-skinned Barbie, the original blond remains the standard. Various print, film, and television media images also project a standard of femininity and feminine behavior. From fairy tales to *The Brady Bunch* to advertisement slogans, it is made clear to children in the United States that the epitome of female beauty is a blond woman who needs male approval and support.

Until recently few researchers examined the effects of such cultural assumptions and icons on girls. Although women of color seem to have resisted to some degree the limitations of the female role expectations with respect to career development, research (Bond & Cash, 1992) as well as personal narratives and fiction of women of color (Angelou, 1971; Bell-Scott, 1994; Washington, 1975) demonstrate the deleterious result of the White standard of beauty. Many African American women, for example, elaborate dreams of "turning white" or suddenly coming to terms with their hair and color. For girls who are outside the standards set by the majority, perceptions of attractiveness and femininity have been shaped by the often competing forces of the American culture and the culture of their ethnic or social class group.

Parental Influences

Parents, of course, are typically considered the major influence in the socialization of girls for their gender and sexual roles. Various background factors, including cultural norms, religious beliefs, and social class mores, result in differential expectations. Beginning with gender assignment at birth and the subsequent experience of growing up as a boy or girl, researchers note that social expectations are clearly as important as physical characteristics (Beal, 1994). For girls these expectations typically include their parents' belief that daughters are in need of extra protection, that they are also more fragile, easily frightened, and physically vulnerable (Kuebli & Krieger, 1991). These parental views lead to differential treatment, such as greater supervision and protectiveness. It is revealing that in spite of the limitations often placed on girls, many girls appear to recognize the disjunction between their capabilities and the social or parental restrictions. Boys, on the other hand, accept the limited activities of girls as due to capabilities (Smith & Russell, 1984). Although relative differences exist across ethnic, cultural, and class boundaries, in virtually all groups, women are more restricted and are treated with a different set of parental expectations. These gender-typed expectations become more explicit for girls as they approach puberty and adolescence, and the soon-to-be woman faces the demands and limitations of finding her place in the community.

Influences of Schools and Peers

Learning one's place in the community is an important function of the school experience. Along with reading and spelling, children are tutored (implicitly and explicitly) in gender roles and sexual mores. Investigators have demonstrated that social class determines how children are treated. For example, children from middle-class families receive more praise and are treated in a less arbitrary manner by teachers (Jackson, Clark, & Hemmons, 1991). Gender and ethnic background also influence school experiences, especially for girls. Kistner, Metzler, Gatlin, and Risi (1993) found that racial minority status for girls was particularly likely to result in peer rejection. Indeed, Carol Beal (1994) discusses the "hidden curriculum," that is, the formal and informal strategies occurring in schools to formally and informally lead children to behave in stereotyped ways.

The sexual socialization of girls is seriously impacted by their experiences at school and with peers. Most children are introduced to a regular association with same age children through school attendance. From preschool through adolescence, children maintain a number of gender-segregated activities (Maras & Archer, 1997; Sandberg & Meyer-Bahlburg, 1994). The choice of same sex playmates persists through grade school with girls and boys interacting on a rather sporadic basis. Thorne (1986) refers to the intermittent contact between boys' and girls' groups as "border work." He suggests that children create clear boundaries between girls and boys by acting as though contact with the other sex is forbidden and dangerous. The children can then create a type of excitement by raiding the enemy territory. Thorne suggests that these forays are preparatory for later adolescent romantic behavior and they operate in a way that minimizes prematurely extended contacts between the sexes.

Social Scripts and Sexuality

Ferguson and Crowley's (1997) findings of shame-proneness in women and guilt-proneness in men suggested that our society associates sex with shame and taboo and that children are socialized to have negative feelings about their gender roles. Young (1990) discussed the socialization of girls today and interpreted many changes as improvements. Many more girls and women are encouraged to engage in sports and physical activities. There is a relative lack of confinement of clothes (e.g., girls can wear pants) and other social practices (e.g., many women travel alone locally and internationally). Indeed, one may say that girls are freer to extend themselves socially, physically, and emotionally. Still observations of girls confirm Young's conclusion that "many girls and women still live a confined and inhibited experience of space and movement, which both expresses and reinforces a continuing confined and inhibited right to assert themselves in the social world" (p. 15).

Masters, Johnson, and Kolodny (1995) also have addressed the social influences on girls' sexual attitudes and behavior. They identified sexual *scripts* imposed by contemporary society that girls absorb and use. Two examples of these scripts are the *Don't Touch Yourself Down There* and the *Nice Girls Don't* scripts. The *Don't Touch Yourself Down There* script discourages girls from touching their genital region, making it a foreign entity that is dirty and never to be explored, The *Nice Girls Don't* script teaches girls that all forms of sex are dirty, sinful, and potentially dangerous. Sex, however, becomes miraculously transformed and is deemed acceptable and appropriate behavior when it is saved for marriage. Whether children accept the scripts described by Masters et al. or not, contemporary children are exposed to sexual choices and by adolescence must make decisions about their sexual lives.

SEXUAL ISSUES FOR ADOLESCENT GIRLS

"Like a virgin ... touched for the very first time"—Madonna, 1984
"I knew a girl named Nickie, I guess you could say she was a sex fiend. Met her in a hotel lobby masturbating to a magazine"—Prince, 1984
"Let's talk about sex baby, let's talk about you and me"—Salt-N-Pepa, 1990
"I can feel your body, pressed against my body, wrap yourself around me, love to feel your throbbin'"—Janet Jackson, 1993
"Flex ... it's time to have sex"—Mad Cobra, 1993

Adolescence is a time of passage characterized by change in every arena, biological, psychological, social, and sexual (Dougherty, 1993; Zaslow & Takanishi, 1993). Parents and educators across the nation debate how to assist adolescent adjustment, which today is jeopardized by demands leading to risks of homicide, suicide, sexually transmitted diseases (STDs), early unwed parenthood, school dropout, infection with the human immunodeficiency virus (HIV) that can lead to acquired immunodeficiency syndrome (AIDS), and substance abuse (Bearinger & Blum, 1987). Prevention advocates indicate that there are strategies for helping adolescents to manage their risks (Robinson, Ruch-Ross, & Watkins-Ferrell, 1993; e.g., through the accessibility of condoms and sexual education). Many parents fear exposing their children prematurely to graphic information about sex. In the MTV-music video generation adolescents not only have been exposed to the sounds and graphic lyrics about sexuality, but they also have visual images. Children no longer need to fantasize about how sexual behaviors and sexuality look. They can simply turn on their television and see with their own eyes the messages of sex. How young women and men interpret these messages is not clear. For adolescent girls who are incorporating these vivid images into the rapidly changing social milieu that includes their maturing bodies, we can only hypothesize that their confusion is magnified.

Critics of a number of popular music groups denounce the content of a number of current songs as both racist and sexist. They further insist that the words and video images promote violence against women. Although some content analyses support these contentions (Sommers-Flanagan, Sommers-Flanagan, & Davis, 1993), others are less judgmental (Tapper, Thorson, & Black, 1994; Zillman, Aust, Hoffman et al., 1995). Clearly, there are a variety of representations and images. The impact of music videos, particularly rap, was found to produce a negative view of African American women in one study (Gan, Zillmann, & Mitrook, 1997). Rap music, however, not only presents sexual messages; it also reflects the sexual world in which today's youths live. These messages are juxtaposed with those derived from other sources, such as parents, school, church, and the highly sexualized environment presented in many other media forums from newspapers to movies.

Although adolescents' sexual decisions reflect their individual psychological readiness, personal values, moral reasoning, fear of negative consequences, and involvement in romantic attachments (Masters, Johnson, & Kolodny, 1986), researchers note that the peer group provides a major source for understanding sexual roles among adolescents. Certain behaviors and conduct will vary along culture and class lines. Thus, what may be acceptable among middle-class youth may be derided in a working-class neighborhood, and vice versa. Similarly, practices common among White American adolescents may be unthinkable among Asian Americans or Latinos. In spite of these status and ethnic differences, we can identify crosscutting concerns for adolescent females. Among the issues that appear to crosscut ethnic boundaries in their importance to female sexuality are these: the issue of virginity, social messages and expectations, and the relationship with one's mother.

To Be or Not to Be—A Virgin

Adolescent women today remain preoccupied with the concept of virginity. In certain peer groups virginity results in embarrassment and indicates a level of unacceptable immaturity. Yet, in other circles, virginity is a badge of honor, signifying strength as well as purity. Anecdotal evidence of the stigma of purity imposed by some peer groups was obtained by the second author during the summer of 1994. Groups of 14- and 15-year-old inner-city African American and Latino boys and girls were brought together in New York City for an experimental job training and educational program. A sexuality component was included to heighten children's awareness of sexual responsibility, values, choices, and decisions related to sexual behavior. The hypothesis was that informed young people could make better decisions and life choices, such as delaying sexual activity or using contraceptives to prevent unwanted pregnancies.

The majority of the students involved in the summer activity represented themselves with a level of sophistication and street smarts that suggested an understanding and a personal knowledge of sexual practices. However, anonymous surveys indicated that the majority of adolescent girls in the program were not sexually active. Yet, most of the girls revealed major preoccupations concerning when they should lose their virginity, given that "everyone is doing it." In this group it was felt to be a greater shame to admit to sexual inactivity than to loss of virginity. Thus, even those who were not sexually active were required to present themselves as sexually knowledgeable and to adopt a sexual demeanor in order to protect the secret of their virginity from their peers.

The above report is confirmed by national data that the number of young adolescents engaging in sexual intercourse continues to be the minority. By late adolescence, however, the incidence of those reporting sexual activity increases greatly and has become a majority. There may, however, be misreading of the data on gender differences among ethnic groups. For example, the National Longitudinal Survey of Youth (U.S. Department of Labor, 1998) reported that by age 15, 12% of White boys had intercourse compared with 5% of girls; the rate for boys was more than double that for girls. In African American populations, 42% of boys compared with 10% of girls; the rate for boys was more than four times that of girls. Similarly, among Latino/a youth, 19% of Hispanic boys compared with 4% Hispanic girls had their first sexual experience. Data from the National Survey on Family Growth (Judkins, 1991) revealed that by Grade 9, 37% of high school girls have had sex as compared with 48.7% of boys; by Grade 10, 42.9% of girls vs. 52.5% of boys; by Grade 11, 52.7% of girls vs. 62.6% of boys, and by Grade 12, 66.6% of girls vs. 76.3% of boys. Broken down by ethnicity, this same study showed that 47% of White girls vs. 56.4% of White boys; 60% of Black girls vs. 87.8% of Black boys; and 45% of Hispanic girls vs. 63% of Hispanic boys have had sex. Although these figures reveal the consistency of the double standard in social expectations, they also suggest discrepancies across groups that are not explained by the data alone.

Sexy Virgins and Innocent Whores: Social Expectations for Girls

Adolescents receive a variety of messages about sexuality. Each cultural and ethnic group develops norms and proscriptions for behaviors for its adolescent population, which at certain times may appear to contradict the messages of mainstream culture. In the United States increasingly there has been a concern about sexualizing younger and younger girls. In the 1980s film *Pretty Baby*, Brooke Shields portrayed a sexually provocative child; similarly, Jodie Foster's role as a pre-teen hooker in the film *Taxi Driver* showed the seductive nature of the adolescent girl. Still, youth and sexuality sells. In the 1990s controversial advertisements for Calvin Klein underwear and jeans featured prepubescent teens in sexually suggestive poses, further perpetuating the connections of eroticism with youth.

Girls and young women receive the message that sexual allure is valuable and necessary to social success. They are provided with myths of romantic adventures that are powerful and rewarding. Ironically, the notion that being prepared for a romantic encounter (i.e., having a condom or diaphragm) is contradictory to the fable. The ideal appears to be that a woman should be overcome with passion, yet able to control the outcome; she should be innocent and pure, but still held responsible for resulting pregnancies. She may be taught by her family and other adults to abstain from sexual fulfillment (i.e., remain sexually immature) while her peers are pressuring her to grow up. Thus, negotiating adolescent years becomes a maze of contradictory sexual choices, values, and concerns, and unambiguous, sensitive guidance is often not available.

Mother–Daughter Relationships

The psychoanalytic literature informs us that women's identification with their mothers is essential for the development of the super ego, the fountain of moral development. Internalization of mothers' values is deemed fundamental to healthy development. Similarly, other theoretical perspectives have traditionally assumed the primacy of the mother–daughter bond through which girls learn what is expected and accepted by their social and class group. Ireland (1993, p. 102) further suggested that the essence of feminine identity is "self-in-relationship"—women rely on a mutuality with others, and this mutuality, according to Ireland, begins with the mother–daughter dyad. However, these assumptions are not always sustained. When the practices of a variety of cultural groups are examined, variations are revealed.

In West Indian families, for example mother–child relations are strong, but the stronger bond is considered to be that between mother and son (Gopaul-McNicol, 1993). This represents a deviation from the Western expectation about the mother–daughter attachment. The closeness in the mother–son relationship continues even after the son is married, such that the son's wife is expected to understand that her husband has to care for his mother in addition to his new family. There also remains the expectation that daughters are principal caregivers. Indeed, in the absence of her parents, the elder daughter becomes the "parental child" and shoulders more of the domestic responsibilities.

In today's complex society a variety of circumstances may dictate different mother–daughter attachments and relationships. Among immigrant families, for example, there may be a struggle between mother and daughter that is a function of the daughter's attempts to assimilate into the new culture. The child, in an attempt to fit into her peer group, seemingly rejects the values of her family. The mother holds onto the old-world values and customs while the daughter embraces the values of the new culture so that she may be accepted by her peers. Mothers may view their daughters as disrespectful, and daughters may view their mothers as useless in guiding their development (Flax, 1993).

Gender role expectations also may conflict during the process of acculturation. If a female child is expected to assume much of the responsibilities of the household when none of her peers are required to do so, this is likely to create tension and resentment. Through the movement toward the new culture and rejection of the old culture (instantiated by the rejection of their mothers and the old-world culture she represents), girls may be less able to connect with a primary source of their female identity development (Flax, 1993).

ETHNOCULTURAL VARIATIONS AMONG WOMEN'S SEXUAL ROLES

Sexual development and the influences of culture, class, and ethnicity are not completed in adolescence. The evolution of roles and the complexity of statuses continue into and across the adult years of womanhood. In the United States, there has been an assumption of marriage determining the lifestyle of a woman. However, even for heterosexual women who desire this experience, recent trends suggest that women are delaying this decision. (According to the U.S. Census Bureau statistics for 1970–1993, more than half of adults have never married. Those who do are on average older than they have been since 1890. The average age for women at first marriage in 1993 was 24.5 years and for men 26.5 years.) Thus, we have adults living for extended periods as singles.

Of course, many adults cohabitate without the sanction of marriage in both heterosexual and homosexual relationships. Although society has not fully formalized these extramarital arrangements, they are informally recognized and for the most part accepted. (In a recent *New York Times* announcement heralding the upcoming wedding of two socialites, the description of the couples' romantic history included the news that they had been living together for a year.) Most young adults believe that becoming sexually experienced as opposed to maintaining virginity is the precursor to selecting a life partner (Masters, Johnson, & Kolodny, 1986). Since they are not subject to the same types of pressures they faced during their adolescent years, young adults may decide on the type, number, and frequency of their sexual experiences. The increasing occurrence and acceptance of divorce is another consideration providing young adults with a reason to explore their sexuality further.

For young women particularly, this liberating period may present many challenges and conflicts. There is, on the one hand, the expectation that women will obtain sexual experience during their late adolescence and early adulthood (Masters, Johnson, & Kolodny, 1986). Nevertheless many women continue to be restrained by the images that have been internalized during adolescence. Issues of morality may impede the apparent sexual freedom of those raised in a strong religious family or in a cultural tradition that has frowned on women's expressions of sexuality. Thus, although the gender gap for premarital sex has narrowed significantly (Masters, Johnson, & Kolodny, 1995), in some areas the expectations and traditions have changed little. These competing messages can make it difficult for a woman to decide which role to take up (loyal daughter, faithful to religion and cultural tradition vs. contemporary woman with concomitant expectations). Today, women must juxtapose these choices with the growing risks associated with sexual activity (e.g., STDs and AIDS).

In examining the array of choices and roles from which modern women may select it continues to be difficult to disaggregate what have been defined as social roles from sexual roles. In fact, we determined that it may be a distortion of women's reality to attempt to do so. Thus, in an examination of roles that are important to women, it is important to consider the combined effects of social factors with sexual expectations. Among the social influences that are most pervasive and persistent with respect to sexual roles are those of religion. The sanctions and proscriptions are set firmly in history and tradition and they have been formalized in modern texts, religious sermons, and political discussions.

Jewish and Christian Women

Traditional Judaism firmly established the notion that women were possessions and that their primary role was to bring offspring into the world. Particularly among more fundamental Jewish groups women's bodies are considered unclean, and cleansing rituals are associated with menstruation and pregnancy (Rosen & Weltman, 1996). Similarly, the writings of Christianity saw women's basic sexual nature as a threat to the salvation of men since women distracted men with thoughts of sex rather than of God. Indeed, "good women" were not only *not* interested in sex, but did everything possible to keep men from viewing them as sexual partners (e.g., the practice of nuns fully covering their hair and bodies). By virtue of their seductress nature, women were deemed morally inferior to men. Thus, marriage was an accepted practice that sanctioned sexuality in women (to a limited degree). However, Christian doctrines made it very clear—true purity and holiness was associated with celibacy (Rushing, 1994).

Freudian writings in many ways supported the Judeo–Christian views. Implicit in Freud's psychosexual stages and other propositions was the notion that women are innately inferior to men and that their orientation to sexuality is around conception rather than sexual pleasure. These attitudes have become pervasive in our culture, and no ethnic group has been spared these views. Indeed, every cultural group has its own idealistic view of women that juxtaposes the two polarities of female sexuality.

Black Women

Comparisons of Black and White women are the focus of many studies. So primary is the cleavage in life experiences in the view of some psychologists (Drugger, 1988; Hatchett, 1991), that they often fail to recognize that Blacks are not a homogeneous group (Reid, 1993) and that their sexual experiences may vary widely based on various conditions and circumstances in their lives (Wyatt, 1990). Not only are there differences based on social class and educational statuses, but there are culturally distinct groups (e.g., Caribbean Islanders, those from the rural South, urbanites, and others).

The entertainment industry has typically limited the roles for Black women, casting them as asexual mammies (matriarchal types) or as sexually promiscuous and castrating women (Greene, 1990; McGoldrick, Garcia-Preto, Hines, & Lee, 1989). We recognize that cultural values and norms will affect a woman's sexual activities; however, the consistent findings that Blacks are more permissive than Whites—and that Latinos are less permissive than Anglos (Baldwin, Whitely, & Baldwin, 1992)—are simplistic and may distort realities.

Many studies of Black sexuality actually are self-reports of what constitutes acceptable practice. Analyses moving beyond measures of generalized tolerance for sexual variety demonstrate that single Black women have sex less often than single White women (Tanfer & Cubbins, 1992) and that Black adolescents are less sexually active and less sexually knowledgeable than they lead people to believe (Robinson, Ruch-Ross, & Watkins-Ferrell, 1993; Robinson & Calhoun, 1982). The apparent contradictions may be from a misreading of a Black woman's tolerance and sexual license for promiscuity. Spike Lee's early film *She's Gotta Have It* illustrates this sense of liberty. The main character, Nola Darling, is a Black woman who is actively involved with three men. The message of the movie, debatably controversial, represents a man's view of a liberated woman. It was viewed by some as the perpetuation of the stereotype of the licentious Black woman. Still, it struck a chord for women in that it portrayed a Black woman who makes her own choices about her sexuality and sexual expression.

Motherhood: A Central Role for Black Women

Motherhood is considered a position of high honor and status in the Black community. Linguists have often made much of the ritualized insult game, "Playing the dozens," yet few have observed that to talk about another's mother is considered the deepest of insults and the most likely way to lead to physical retaliation. The "mandate of motherhood," as Russo (1976) termed the societal demand that women become mothers, continues to intrigue feminist scholars. Nowhere is this fascination more clearly demonstrated than in Ireland's book on motherhood and female identity. In this analysis, Ireland (1993, p. 104) describes "femaleness (pre-Oedipal mother) as the central organizer of female identity, with biology and culture as contextualizing influences. Yet, regardless of whether maleness or femaleness is seen as the primary influence, maternity is still considered the equivalent of adult female development. There is no normative female identity for the woman who is not a mother." In Zinn and Eitzen's (1990) study of inner-city Blacks, they noted that in the Black community a girl "becomes a woman by becoming a mother." The high value placed on children in Black families appears to convey status and authority; the role of mother serves to protect the unmarried woman and to absolve her from stigma (Collins, 1991; Stack, 1974).

Although motherhood is considered to be the culmination of a woman's sexual experience, "mother" is ironically construed as asexual. Neither research nor folklore suggests that mother–child relationships are connected to erotic or physical pleasure. Young (1990) noted that there is a dichotomy of motherhood and sexuality that "maps onto a dichotomy of good/bad, pure/impure" and that has become translated into a repression of the body itself. The separation that has been enforced by patriarchal codes, according to Young, keeps women dependent on men for sexual pleasure. She suggests that "lesbian mothering may be the ultimate affront to patriarchy, for it involves a double displacement of an erotic relation of a woman to a man" (p. 198). Clearly, neither Young nor we recommend the social eroticising of motherhood. It does seem worth noting, however, that there is a significant degree of denial about the relationship of motherhood to sexuality.

Jamaican Women and Caribbean Women

In examining women of African descent, as with women of other backgrounds, the variability and variations of women must be asserted, while seeking common ground. There is no one African or Black community; differences require sensitivity and insight and should not be glossed over as trivial. Sexuality in Jamaican and other West Indian cultures represents a paradox. On the one hand, propriety is taught with West Indian women learning to sublimate or repress their sexual drives and to conceptualize sex as an obligation (Gopaul-McNicol, 1993). From birth, girls are taught to be modest, which typically causes a sense of embarrassment about their bodies. On a woman's wedding night she should not be concerned about receiving any sexual pleasure, as at the point of marriage she is expected to be ignorant about sex. Her only concern is to be a good mother and sexual partner to her spouse. This is particularly true of upper- and middle-class women (Gopaul-McNicol, 1993).

As in Black communities, although sexual propriety is regarded as important, premarital sex and children born out of wedlock is not uncommon and is not necessarily frowned on. How the family feels about a child born out of wedlock depends in large part on the role that the child's father assumes. If the father is without ambition or income, then he will be scorned and the unwed child will be regarded in a more negative light. Related to this, unwed pregnancies by older women who are mistresses to married men may be viewed either positively or negatively, depending again on the role of the father. Some people may find her to be morally lacking, whereas others may admire her ability to gain entry into the upper class by connecting with a financially capable man who is able to take care of her, his child, and his other family (Brice-Baker, 1994).

Marriage is important in West Indian culture, and the role of a woman is sharply defined by her marital status. Unmarried women are regarded as a source of embarrassment and are referred to as old maids and seen as barren if they are childless (Gopaul-McNicol, 1993). This stigma is not placed on an unmarried man, who may be seen as taking his time to choose a wife or may be called a "sweet man" because he has many ladies (Gopaul-McNicol, 1993).

Latina Women

In discussing the sexual expectations of Latina women, it is important to consider the diversity of the variety of Latin American groups (Durant, Pendergast, & Seymore, 1990; Vega, 1991), socioeconomic status (Bean & Tienda, 1987; Staples, 1988), and degree of acculturation to Anglo society (Pavich, 1986). In addition, across the various groups (e.g., Chicanas, Cubans, Puerto Ricans, and others) Catholic traditions are a major influence on a Latina woman's sexuality.

The Catholic church advocates premarital virginity and prohibits contraception and abortion. In Latino cultures, *marianismo*, the cultural counterpart to *machismo*, represents this view of the woman as chaste before marriage. Once married, the woman must conform to her husband's macho behavior. *Marianismo* is based on the Catholic cult of the Virgin Mary, which dictates that when women become mothers, then and only then do they attain the status of Madonna, and in so doing they are expected to deny themselves in favor of their children and husbands. The cult of the Virgin Mary considers women morally and spiritually superior to men and therefore capable of enduring all suffering inflicted by men (Reid, & Comas-Diaz, 1990; Salgado de Snyder, Cervantes, & Padilla, 1990). Indeed, the role of martyr is expected to be fulfilled by good Latina women.

Implicit in the concept of *marianismo* is women's repression or sublimation of sexual drives and consideration of sex as an obligation. Thus, if a Latina woman engages in premarital sex, she will lose face—she will lose the man's respect, a man will not marry her, and she will bring dishonor and disgrace on her family. Furthermore, she will be labeled a *puta* (whore) and will not receive the respectful title of *dona* given to married women that signifies she is a lady worthy of respect. Depending on the strength of their convictions, Latina women may experience guilt and confusion when using contraception (Pavich, 1986). Traditional Latina women were found to be more negative toward birth control and less likely to use it than more acculturated women (Ortiz & Casas, 1990). Among bicultural Latinos, there may be gender role conflict (Salgado de Snyder, Cervantes, & Padilla, 1990).

Indian Women

Cultural values and belief systems permeate the mind of an Indian woman's view of her place in the world. Life views are based primarily on an understanding of ones *dharma* and *karma*. Dharma, a Hindu concept, is defined as the traditional established order, including all individual, moral, social, and religious duties. Each person's dharma is determined by contextual factors such as stage of life cycle. For Indian women, identity is based on relationships—mother, daughter, niece, sister, pupil—and identities outside of these may seem inconceivable (Jayakar, 1994). Dharma, therefore, has profound implications on a woman's sexual identity.

In traditional Indian cultures, marriages are arranged. Women are chosen and must be observed by members of the prospective family so that they may make note of her physical attributes. Many brides and grooms do not see each other face to face until the wedding day, when the bride's face is unveiled in a romanticized ritual. To not marry is a source of embarrassment and humiliation for the woman's family. There is a stigma attached to remaining single, and families will pay hefty dowries to ensure that their daughters are married off. In the tradition of arranged marriages, implicit is the expectation that the bride-to-be is a virgin. Brides who are found to be sullied will be returned in disgrace to their family. This is illustrated in the following clinical example:

> K., a 36-year-old Indian woman entered treatment for posttraumatic stress disorder. While in India, K. was raped in her early 20s. K.'s family subsequently rushed to arrange a marriage for her as she was considered tainted, tarnished, and impure. K. struggled with issues around her self image as well as her role as a sexual being. She developed conversion symptoms whereby she was unable to "see" her body in a mirror, from her breast up. She was reluctant to engage with her husband sexually, but did so out of obligation, particularly since he was the man who allowed her honor to be saved. Although she entered treatment 15 years after the rape took place, she continued to feel dirty and spoiled, because her virtue was stripped away after the rape, and she brought embarrassment to her traditional Indian family. K., who has two preadolescent daughters, is very fearful for them and unwilling to speak of them in any sexual terms.

Jayakar (1994) notes that Indian women are treated like property and are valued according to their physical attributes. Jayakar notes that "stories of the wedding night experience highlight the blatant lack of attention given to the importance of sexual satisfaction for women, and sexual education in modern Indian culture for both men and women" (Jayakar, 1994, p. 170).

Asian Women

The development of a sexual identity in Asian culture is complicated by the fact that it is considered taboo to discuss sex, which is deemed a shameful topic (Chan, 1997). Wolf (1995) noted that the avoidance of sexual discussion made virtually impossible any true survey of sexual practices among most Asian groups. Indeed, any Asians who would respond to sexual surveys are likely to be particularly unrepresentative.

Asian women are reared in a culture where women assume subservient roles to men. Confucian precepts, which dominated many cultures of

China, Japan, and Korea and continue to do so today, are patriarchal. The "Three Obediences" for women according to Confucian precepts require respect to father at home; respect to husband after marriage; and respect to sons at old age. The "Four Virtues" of women are chastity, reticence, a pleasing manner, and domestic skills. Even Asian American women must struggle with the conflicting messages from their unique families and those promoted by the dominant U.S. society (Pfeifer & Sussman, 1991).

Recognizing the multiplicity of cultures, it is difficult to discuss Asian women or Asian American women as a group. Still, the stereotypes are pervasive. Asian American women have been presented as submissive, gentle, and quiet while also being portrayed as highly sexualized, erotic geisha, or "Suzie Wong" types (Chan, 1997; Oyserman & Sakamoto, 1997). Del Carmen (1990) confirmed that Asian Americans are less verbal and expressive in their interactions than White Americans. They appear to rely to a great degree on indirection and nonverbal communication, such as silence and the avoidance of eye contact as signs of respect. Japanese Americans, for example, value implicit, nonverbal, intuitive communication over explicit, verbal, and rational exchange of information. Whether these images and findings will carry across Chinese, Vietnamese, Korean, and all other Asian groups is a question still to be examined.

CONCLUSION

For girls and women sexuality evolves from simple stereotyping into a constellation of complex roles and challenges across the lifespan. Beginning in girlhood gender socialization involves the combination of socially constructed expectations, biological transformations, and individual adjustments. Girls and women continuously shape and reshape their sexual lives in an effort to understand and meet their personal needs and the expectations of society. Although there are sets of experiences, issues, and stereotypes that appear relevant to gender regardless of class, culture, or ethnic background, there are other domains impacting the daily lives of women of color that must be interpreted through the different lenses these women are forced to wear. Thus, an understanding of sexual roles cannot occur without the simultaneous examination of the various contexts in which they occur.

The critical issue that must be examined is whether we can continue to ignore the variations across and within groups of ethnic women. Clearly, there are points that all women have in common, but the differences arising from social class, religion, and cultural background require attention and explication. As researchers become more sophisticated in dealing with these distinctions, they will become more understanding of the sexual roles across the lifespan and the expectations these entail.

REFERENCES

Anderson, M. L. (1993). *Thinking about women: Sociological perspectives on sex and gender* (3rd ed.). New York: Macmillan.

Angelou, M. (1971). *I know why the caged bird sings.* New York: Bantam Books.

Baldwin, J. D., Whitely, S., & Baldwin, J. I. (1992). The effect of ethnic group on sexual activities related to contraception and STDs. *Journal of Sex Research, 29,* 189–206.

Beal, C. R. (1994). *Boys and girls: The development of gender roles.* New York: McGraw-Hill.

Bearinger, L., & Blum, R. W. (1987). Adolescent medicine and psychiatry: Trends, issues and needs. *Psychiatric Annals, 17,* 775–779.

Bell-Scott, P. (1994). *Life notes: Personal writings by contemporary Black women.* New York: Norton.

Bean, F., & Tienda, M. (1987). *The Hispanic population of the United States.* New York: Russell Sage Foundation.

Bem, S. L. (1983). Gender schema theory and its implications for child development: Raising gender-aschematic children in a gender schematic society. *Signs, 8,* 598–616.

Beuf, A. (1974). Doctor, lawyer, household drudge. *Journal of Communication, 24,* 142–145.

Block, J. (1983). Differential premises arising from differential socialization of the sexes: Some conjectures. *Child Development, 54,* 1335–1354.

Bobo, M., Hildreth, B. L., & Durodoye, B. (1998). Changing patterns in career choices among African-American, Hispanic, and Anglo children. *Professional School Counseling, 1,* 37–42.

Bond, S., & Cash, T. F. (1992). Black beauty: Skin color and body images among African American college women. *Journal of Applied Social Psychology, 22,* 874–888.

Brice-Baker, J. R. (1994). West Indian women of color: The Jamaican women. In L. Comas-Diaz & B. Greene (Eds.), *Women of color* (pp. 139–160). New York: Guilford Press.

Bussey, K., & Bandura, A. (1984). Influence of gender constancy and social power on sex-linked modeling. *Journal of Personality and Social Psychology, 47,* 1292–1302.

Carter, D. B. (1987). *Current conceptions of sex roles and sex typing.* New York: Praeger.

Castaneda, X., Ortiz, V., Allen, B., & Garcia, C. (1996). Sex masks: The double life of female commercial sex workers in Mexico City. *Culture, Medicine & Psychiatry, 20,* 229–247.

Caulfield, M. D. (1985). Sexuality in human evolution: What is 'natural' in sex? *Feminist Studies, 11,* 343–364.

Chan, C. (1997). Attitudes toward sexuality and sexual behaviors of Asian-

American adolescents: Implications for risk of HIV infection. In R. D. Taylor & M. C. Wang (Eds.), *Social and emotional adjustment and family relations in ethnic minority families* (pp. 133–144). Hillside, NJ: Erlbaum.

Chin, J. L. (1993). *Transference and empathy in Asian American psychotherapy: Cultural values and treatment needs.* New York: Praeger.

Collins, P. H. (1991). The meaning of motherhood in Black culture. In R. Staples (Ed.), *The Black family* (4th ed.). Belmont, CA: Wadsworth.

Del Carmen, R. (1990). Assessment of Asian-Americans for family therapy. In F. Serafica et al. (Eds.), *Mental health of ethnic minorities* (pp. 139–166). New York: Praeger.

Dougherty, D. M. (1993). Adolescent health: Reflections on a report to the U.S. Congress. [Special issue]. *American Psychologist: Adolescence, 48,* 193–201.

Drugger, K. (1988). Social location and gender-role attitudes: A comparison of Black and White women. *Gender and Society, 2,* 425–448.

Durant, R., Pendergast, R., & Seymore, C. (1990). Contraceptive behavior among sexually active Hispanic adolescents. *Journal of Adolescent Health, 11,* 490–496.

Durham, M. G. (1998). Dilemmas of desire: Representations of adolescent sexuality in two teen magazines. *Youth & Society, 29,* 369–389.

Espin, O. M. (1984). Cultural and historical influences on sexuality in Hispanic/Latin women: Implications for psychotherapy. In C. Vance (Ed.), *Pleasure and danger* (pp. 149–164). London: Routledge & Kegan Paul.

Fagot, B. I., & Hagan, R. (1991). Observation of parent reactions to sex-stereotyped behaviors: Age and sex effects. *Child Development, 62,* 617–628.

Ferguson, T. J., & Crowley, S. L. (1997). Gender differences in the organization of guilt and shame. *Sex Roles, 37,* 19–44.

Flax, J. (1993). Mothers and daughters revisited. In J. van Mens-Verhulost, K. Schreurs, & L. Woertman (Eds.), *Daughtering and mothering: Female subjectivity reanalysed* (pp. 145–156). London: Routledge & Kegan Paul.

Freedman, E., & Thorne, B. (1984). Introduction to 'The feminist sexuality debates.' *Signs, 10,* 102–105.

Gan, S., Zillmann, D., & Mitrook, M. (1997). Stereotyping effect of Black women's sexual rap on White audiences. *Basic & Applied Social Psychology, 19,* 381–399.

Gopaul-McNicol, S. (1993). *Working with West Indian families.* New York: Guilford Press.

Greene, B. A. (1990). What has gone before: The legacy of racism and sexism in the lives of Black mothers and daughters [Special issue]. *Women & Therapy: Diversity and complexity in feminist therapy, 9,* 207–230.

Hatchett, S. J. (1991). Women and men. In J. S. Jackson (Ed.), *Life in Black America* (pp. 84–104). Newbury Park, CA: Sage.

Houppert, K. (1993, March/April). Glen Ridge rape trial: A question of consent. *MS,* 86–88.

Ireland, M. S. (1993). *Reconceiving women: Separating motherhood from female identity*. New York: Guilford Press.

Jackson, M. S., Clark, S. B., & Hemmons, W. (1991). Class, caste and the classroom: Effective public policy vs. effective public education. *Western Journal of Black Studies, 15,* 242–247.

Jayakar, K. (1994). Women of the Indian subcontinent. In L. Comas-Diaz & B. Greene (Eds.), *Women of color: Integrating ethnic and gender identities in psychotherapy* (pp. 161–181). New York: Guilford Press.

Judkins, D. R. (1991). *National survey of family growth: Design, estimation, and inference.* Washington, DC: U.S. Government Printing Office.

Kantrowitz, B. (1993, March 29). Verdict after a day of horror. *Newsweek, 127,* 27.

Kinsey, A., Pomeroy, W., & Martin, C. (1948). *Sexual behavior in the human male.* Philadelphia, PA: W. B. Saunders.

Kistner, J., Metzler, A., Gatlin, D., & Risi, S. (1993). Classroom racial proportions and children's peer relations: Race and gender effects. *Journal of Educational Psychology, 85,* 446–452.

Kuebli, J., & Krieger, E. (1991, April). *Emotion and gender in parent-child conversations about the past.* Paper presented at the biennial meeting of the Society for Research in Child Development, Seattle, WA.

LaFromboise, T. D., Heyle, A. M., & Ozer, E. J. (1990). *Gender and ethnicity: Perspectives on dual status* [Special issue]. *Sex Roles, 22,* 455–476.

Lips, H. (1992). *Sex and gender.* Mountain View, CA: Mayfield.

Loxley, W. (1996). "Sluts" or "sleazy little animals"? Young people's difficulties with carrying and using condoms. *Journal of Community & Applied Social Psychology, 6,* 293–298.

Maras, P., & Archer, L. (1997). "Tracy's in the home corner, Darren's playing Lego, or are they?" Gender issues and identity in education. *Feminism & Psychology, 7,* 264–274.

Martin, C. L., & Halverson, C. F. (1981). A schematic processing model of sex typing and stereotyping in children. *Child Development, 52,* 1119–1134.

Mason, A. A. (1984). Psychoanalytic concepts of depression and its treatment. *American Journal of Social Psychiatry, 4,* 29–37.

Masters, W. H., Johnson, V. E., & Kolodny, R. C. (1986). *Masters and Johnson on sex and human loving.* Boston: Little, Brown.

Masters, W. H., Johnson, V. E., & Kolodny, R. C. (1995). *Human sexuality* (5th ed.). New York: Harper & Row.

McGoldrick, M., Garcia-Preto, N., Hines, P. M., & Lee, E. (1989). Ethnicity and women. In M. McGoldrick, C. M. Anderson, & F. Walsh (Eds.), *Women in families: A framework for family therapy* (pp. 169–199). New York: Norton.

Money, J., & Tucker, P. (1976). *Sexual signatures: On being a man or a woman.* London: Harrap.

Ortiz, S., & Casas, J. M. (1990). Birth control and low-income Mexican American women: The impact of three values. *Hispanic Journal of the Behavioral Sciences*, 12, 83–92.

Oyserman, D., & Sakamoto, I. (1997). Being Asian American: Identity, cultural constructs, and stereotype perception. *Journal of Applied Behavioral Science*, 33, 435–453.

Painter, N. I. (1992). Hill, Thomas, and the use of racial stereotype. In T. Morrison (Ed.), *Race-ing justice, en-gendering power* (pp. 200–214). New York: Pantheon Books.

Pavich, E. G. (1986). A Chicana perspective on Mexican culture and sexuality. [Special issue]. *Journal of Social Work & Human Sexuality: Human Sexuality, Ethnoculture, and Social Work*, 4, 47–65.

Pfeifer, S. K., & Sussman, M. B. (Eds.). (1991). *Families: Intergenerational and generational connections*. New York: Haworth Press.

Reid, P. T. (1982). Socialization of black female children. In P. Berman & E. Ramey (Eds.), *Women: A developmental perspective* (pp. 137–155). Washington, DC: U.S. Government Printing Office.

Reid, P. T. (1988). Racism and sexism: Comparisons and conflicts. In P. A. Katz & D. Taylor (Eds.), *Eliminating racism* (pp. 203–221). New York: Plenum Press.

Reid, P. T. (1993). Poor women in psychological research: Shut up and shut out. *Psychology of Women Quarterly*, 17, 133–150.

Reid, P. T., & Comas-Diaz, L. (1990). Gender and ethnicity: Perspectives on dual status. *Sex Roles*, 22, 397–408.

Reid, P. T., & Kelly, E. (1994). Research on women of color: From ignorance to awareness. *Psychology of Women Quarterly*, 18, 477–486.

Riger, S. (1992). Epistemological debates, female voices. *American Psychologist*, 47, 730–740.

Robinson, W. L., & Calhoun, K. S. (1982). Sexual fantasies, attitudes and behavior as a function of race, gender and religiosity. *Imagination, Cognition & Personality*, 2, 281–290.

Robinson, W. L., Ruch-Ross, H. S., & Watkins-Ferrell, P. (1993). Risk behavior in adolescence: Prediction and prevention. *School Psychology Quarterly*, 8, 241–254.

Rosen, E. J., & Weltman, S. F. (1996). Jewish families: An overview. In M. McGoldrick, J. Giordano, & J. K. Pearce (Eds.), *Ethnicity and family therapy* (2nd ed., pp. 611–630). New York: Guilford Press.

Rushing, S. M. (1994). *The Magdalene legacy: Exploring the wounded icon of sexuality*. Westport, CT: Bergin & Garvey.

Russo, N. F. (1976). The motherhood mandate. *Journal of Social Issues*, 32, 143–153.

Salgado de Snyder, V. N., Cervantes, R., & Padilla, A. (1990). Gender and ethnic differences in psychosocial stress and genderalized distress among Hispanics. *Sex Roles*, 22, 441–453.

Sandberg, D. E., & Meyer-Bahlburg, H. F. L. (1994). Variability in middle childhood play behavior: Effects of gender, age and family background. *Archives of Sexual Behavior, 23,* 645–663.

Serbin, L. A., Powlishta, K. K., & Gulko, J. (1993). The development of sex typing in middle childhood. *Monographs of the Society for Research in Child Development, 58* (92, Serial No. 232).

Smith, J., & Russell, G. (1984). Why do males and females differ? Children's beliefs about sex differences. *Sex Roles, 11,* 1111–1120.

Sommers-Flanagan, R., Sommers-Flanagan, J., & Davis, B. (1993). What's happening on music television? A gender role content analysis. *Sex Roles, 28,* 745–753.

Stack, C. B. (1974). *All our kin: Strategies for survivial in a black community.* New York: Harper & Row.

Staples, R. (1988). The Black American family. In C. Mindel et al. (Eds.), *Ethnic families in America: Patterns and variations* (3rd ed.). Amsterdam: Elsevier.

Strong, B., & DeVault, C. (1994). *Human sexuality.* Mountain View, CA: Mayfield.

Tanfer, K., & Cubbins, L. A. (1992). Coital frequency among single women: Normative constraints and situational opportunities. *Journal of Sex Research, 29,* 221–250.

Tapper, J., Thorson, E., & Black, D. (1994). Variations in music videos as a function of their musical genre. *Journal of Broadcasting & Electronic Media, 38,* 103–113.

Taylor, C. R., & Stern, B. B. (1997). Asian-Americans: Television advertising and the "model minority" stereotypes. *Journal of Advertising, 26,* 47–61.

Thorne, B. (1986). Girls and boys together, but mostly apart. In W. W. Hartup & Z. Rubin (Eds.), *Relationships and development* (pp. 167–184). Hillsdale, NJ: Erlbaum.

Tuan, Y. (1984). *Dominance and affection: The making of pets.* New Haven, CT: Yale University Press.

Unger, R. K. (1991). Toward a redefinition of sex and gender. *American Psychologist, 34,* 1085–1094.

U.S. Department of Labor. (1998). *Labor market experiences and more: Studying men, women and children since 1966.* Washington, DC: Bureau of Labor Statistics.

Vasquez, M. J. (1994). Latinas. In L. Comas-Diaz & B. Greene (Eds.), *Women of color* (pp. 114–138). New York: Guilford Press.

Vega, W. (1991). Hispanic families. In A. Booth (Ed.), *Contemporary families: Looking forward, looking back.* Minneapolis, MN: National Council of Family Relations.

Washington, M. (1975). *Black-eyed Susans.* Garden City, NY: Anchor.

Wolf, A. P. (1995). *Sexual attraction and childhood association: A Chinese brief for Edward Westermarck.* Stanford, CA: Stanford University Press.

Wyatt, G. E. (1990). African American women's sexual satisfaction as a dimension of their sex roles. *Sex Roles, 22,* 509–524.

Wynn, R., & Fletcher, C. (1987). Sex role development and early educational experiences. In D. B. Carter (Ed.), *Current conceptions of sex roles and sex typing* (pp. 79–88). New York: Praeger.

Young, I. M. (1990). *Throwing like a girl and other essays in feminist philosophy and social theory*. Bloomington: Indiana University Press.

Zaslow, M. J., & Takanishi, R. (1993). Priorities for research on adolescent development. [Special issue]. *American Psychologist: Adolescence, 48,* 185–192.

Zillman, D., Aust, C. F., Hoffman, K. D., Love, C. C., Ordman, V. L., Pope, J. T., Seigler, P. D., & Gibson, R. J. (1995). Radical rap: Does it further ethnic division? *Basic & Applied Social Psychology, 16,* 1–25.

Zinn, M. B., & Eitzen, D. S. (1990). *Diversity in Families* (2nd ed.). New York: HarperCollins.

7

SEXUALITY DURING PREGNANCY AND THE YEAR POSTPARTUM

JANET SHIBLEY HYDE AND JOHN DeLAMATER

The topic of sexuality during pregnancy and the year postpartum is ripe for feminist analysis because it represents the combination of biological events that are unique and meaningful to women (pregnancy and childbirth) with a heavy layer of social constructions based on cultural beliefs about the proper roles of women and men and the appropriateness of sexual expression. In many ways there are parallels to issues in adolescent girls' sexuality, in the combination of biological events (puberty) with cultural constructions. Therefore, concepts from the chapter by Welsh, Rostosky, and Kawaguchi (chapter 5, this volume) on adolescent girls' sexuality also are relevant here.

In this chapter we review cultural beliefs about sexuality during preg-

This research was supported by the National Institute of Mental Health Grant No. MH44340 to Janet Hyde and Marilyn Essex, with Marjorie Klein and Roseanne Clark. Developmental phases of this work were funded by the University of Wisconsin Graduate School and the Wisconsin Psychiatric Research Institute. Special thanks are extended to project staff, Ashby Plant, Will Shattuck, Laura Haugen, Nancy Smider, and Francine Horton, and to the Wisconsin Survey Research Laboratory and its staff. Rosalind Barnett and Joseph Pleck were helpful consultants to the project in its early stages.

Portions of this article appeared previously in an article published in *The Journal of Sex Research* (Hyde, DeLamater, Plant, & Byrd, 1996). Reprinted material is used with permission.

nancy and the postpartum period; prior research on patterns of sexual expression during pregnancy and following childbirth; and our new research based on data from more than 500 women who were studied longitudinally from the fifth month of pregnancy through 1 year postpartum.

CULTURAL BELIEFS ABOUT SEXUALITY DURING PREGNANCY AND POSTPARTUM

Pregnancy taboos of various sorts are common in many cultures (Frayser, 1985). Most commonly, pregnant women are expected to restrict or change their diet in some ways, an adjustment that is expected in 38% of 45 cultures surveyed in one study (Frayser, 1985). Other taboos are unique to a particular culture. For example, the Aztecs believe that a pregnant woman who looks at the sky during an eclipse will have a child with a harelip. What all these taboos have in common is the belief that actions of a pregnant woman may in some way harm the child, and taboos help alleviate these anxieties. There also are some groups that believe that the actions of a pregnant woman's husband may affect the child. For example, the Eastern Pomo of central California have pregnancy restrictions that apply to both parents (Frayser, 1985).

In this context, it is not surprising that sexual taboos during pregnancy exist in many cultures, that the taboos are thought to prevent harm to the unborn child, and that the exact nature of the taboos varies substantially from one culture to another. At one end of the spectrum, the Goajiro believe that a pregnant couple should refrain completely from intercourse or the woman will have a prolonged delivery and the child will be sickly (Frayser, 1985). At the other end of the spectrum, Chamorro, Kurtatchi, Lepcha, and Pukapukans believe that intercourse may continue throughout pregnancy until childbirth begins, but men are warned not to allow too much weight to rest on their partner during the last few weeks of pregnancy (Ford & Beach, 1951). In many cultures, intercourse is considered acceptable during pregnancy except for the last few weeks before childbirth. The point of these taboos, as with other pregnancy taboos, is to prevent damage to the unborn child.

Some cultures have unique taboos. For example, the pregnant Tswana woman is warned that intercourse during pregnancy with any man other than the baby's father will result in illness and possibly death for both herself and her lover (Ford & Beach, 1951).

It is interesting to note that almost all societies that completely forbid intercourse during pregnancy are polygynous, and it is considered acceptable for the father to continue to have sexual intercourse with his other wives (Ford & Beach, 1951).

Societies generally also have a set of postpartum restrictions; these restrictions are thought to protect either the child or the child and the mother (Frayser, 1985). In one cross-societal survey, only 7% of 41 societies did not have a postpartum restriction on sexual relations (Frayser, 1985). The duration of the restriction varies widely from one society to another. A 1- to 5-month interval is most common, yet in 32% of societies the prohibition extends beyond 1 year.

From these cross-societal patterns, we can see that (a) sexual patterns during pregnancy and the postpartum period are deeply rooted in culture —that is, women's sexuality during pregnancy and postpartum is socially constructed; and (b) pregnancy and the postpartum period often are seen as delicate periods during which harm can be done to a child, and sexual intercourse may be seen as one of the potential sources of harm.

PRIOR RESEARCH ON SEXUALITY DURING PREGNANCY AND POSTPARTUM IN AMERICAN SOCIETY

Sexuality During Pregnancy

Studies of sexuality during pregnancy generally report a decrease in sexual desire and frequency of intercourse from the first to the third trimester (Alder, 1989; White & Reamy, 1982). In contrast, Masters and Johnson (1966), who studied 101 pregnant women, reported "a marked increase in eroticism and sexual performance" (p. 158) in the second trimester, but this finding has not been replicated.[1] Other studies report either no change in sexual activity from the first to the second trimester, or a slight decline. Most investigators, including Masters and Johnson, report a marked decline in frequency of coitus from the second to the third trimesters. A recent study of frequency of marital intercourse, using well-sampled data from the National Survey of Families and Households, reported that pregnancy is associated with a significant decrease in monthly frequency of intercourse (Call, Sprecher, & Schwartz, 1995).

A variety of reasons have been suggested for this decline in sexual desire and frequency of intercourse during pregnancy (Bogren, 1991). Reports of decreased desire early in pregnancy are related to the woman's fears about the pregnancy and possible miscarriage. Such reports during the third trimester are related to the woman's fears about the health of the child at birth, and to both mothers' and fathers' fears that the fetus may be harmed

---

[1]A number of Masters and Johnson's (1966) findings reported in this chapter are discordant with others' research. We believe that this is likely due to the problematic methods of sampling used by Masters and Johnson, which may yield a distorted view of female sexuality, as feminist critics have noted (Tiefer, 1991). In particular, participants in Masters and Johnson's research were required to be well-functioning sexually; for women, this was operationalized as having the capacity to have orgasms through vaginal intercourse, which may characterize only a minority of women in the United States.

by intercourse or orgasm. However, according to the authoritative medical textbook, *Williams Obstetrics*, "it has been generally accepted that in healthy pregnant women, sexual intercourse usually does no harm before the last four weeks or so of pregnancy" (Cunningham, MacDonald, Leveno, Gant, & Gilstrap, 1993, p. 263).

Other reasons that have been associated with the decline in frequency of intercourse include physical discomfort associated with intercourse, particularly in the man-on-top position, and loss of interest in sex. Also, some women report feeling less physically attractive and sexually desirable as pregnancy progresses.

Sexuality Following Childbirth

There is less agreement in the findings of research on the resumption of sexual activity following childbirth (Reamy & White, 1987). The inconsistency across studies is likely due to both variations in sampling methods, and variations in the number of weeks postpartum when respondents are interviewed. Kenny (1973), in a study of 33 women, found that at four weeks postpartum 75% reported that their sexual activity had returned to pre-pregnancy levels. Masters and Johnson (1966) reported that all 101 women they studied had resumed coitus 6 to 8 weeks after delivery. In most other studies, however, researchers have found a much slower return of sexual functioning following birth. For example, Grudzinskas and Atkinson (1984) interviewed 328 women at 5 to 7 weeks postpartum and reported that only 50% had resumed intercourse.

Kumar, Brant, and Robson (1981) reported results from the most intensive longitudinal study to date. They recruited 147 women who were in the first 14 weeks of pregnancy. The women were interviewed three times during the pregnancy, at 12, 24, and 36 weeks. They also were interviewed at about 1, 12, 26, and 52 weeks after delivery. During the pregnancy, frequency of intercourse declined slightly from 12 to 24 weeks, and more substantially from 24 to 36 weeks. In contrast, reported sexual pleasure increased from 12 to 24 weeks and then declined. Ninety-five percent of the women had resumed intercourse 12 weeks after delivery, but coitus was less frequent at one year postpartum than it was prior to the pregnancy. Reported level of enjoyment at 12 weeks postpartum was similar to levels reported at 12 weeks of pregnancy.

Numerous reasons have been suggested for delaying resumption of vaginal intercourse after childbirth (Reamy & White, 1987). The principal ones are pain and tenderness related to an episiotomy, vaginal bleeding and discharge, fatigue, and discomfort related to inadequate vaginal lubrication. According to *Williams Obstetrics*, "coitus should not be resumed prior to 2 weeks postpartum" in order to reduce the risk of hemorrhage, infection, and pain. Beyond 2 weeks, "coitus may be resumed *based upon the patient's desire and comfort*" (Cunningham et al., 1993, p. 470).

Several studies indicate that women's sexual patterns are influenced by breastfeeding. In a study of 91 women, Alder and Bancroft (1988) found that breast-feeding (BF) women (*n* = 60) were less likely to have resumed intercourse 3 months postpartum than non-breast-feeding (NBF) women, and BF women reported less sexual interest and enjoyment than before the pregnancy. By 6 months the differences between BF and NBF women had disappeared. Forster and colleagues studied 19 women before and after weaning; after weaning, an increase in frequency of intercourse occurred (Forster, Abraham, Taylor, & Llewellyn-Jones, 1994). In another study Alder (1989) found no relationship between breastfeeding and resumption of intercourse. As we noted elsewhere in this chapter, the Masters and Johnson research is an outlier; they reported that the 24 nursing mothers in their sample of 101 reported the highest level of sexual interest in the 3 months following delivery (Masters & Johnson, 1966).

Methodological Issues

Most studies on pregnancy, childbirth, and sexuality suffer from methodological problems. The studies are based on nonrandom convenience samples. The samples often are small. Some rely on retrospective reports about sexual behavior during pregnancy or about resumption of sexual activity after childbirth, introducing possible inaccuracies in memory. There has been little consistency across studies in the variables measured or in the definition of key variables, such as breastfeeding. These problems make it difficult to reconcile the conflicting results. Moreover, most studies have used single-gender designs, interviewing women only; this reflects an assumption that sexuality during pregnancy and postpartum is a only a women's issue and ignores the potential impact on husbands or partners.

From a feminist perspective, the most serious issue is the androcentric focus on penis-in-vagina intercourse as the only or primary sexual behavior of importance. Prior studies have not, for example, inquired about women's sexual expression through masturbation.

THE WISCONSIN MATERNITY LEAVE AND HEALTH PROJECT

The Wisconsin Maternity Leave and Health (WMLH) Project is a large-scale, longitudinal study of women and their families from pregnancy through one year postpartum (Hyde, Klein, Essex, & Clark, 1995). The focus of the WMLH Project is on women, work, maternity leave, and health (defined to include physical health, mental health, and the health of social relationships with husband or partner and child). The focus here is on data from a brief sex questionnaire that was administered during the interviews.

The data reported here have a number of substantial advantages over previous studies: (a) the respondents were not recruited for sex research, but rather for a study on a far less sensitive topic: maternity leave, work, and families; (b) the data include questions on behaviors other than intercourse (e.g., masturbation); (c) the data are longitudinal, following the same persons from pregnancy through 12 months postpartum; and (d) the data set includes reports from both mothers and fathers.

Method

A total of 570 pregnant women and 550 of their husbands or partners (all partners were men) were recruited for participation in the WMLH Project (for a more detailed description of recruiting procedures and characteristics of the sample, see Hyde et al., 1995). Attempts were made to recruit as diverse a sample as possible. Approximately 78% of the sample resided in the Milwaukee area, and 22% in the Madison, Wisconsin, area. To be included in the sample, female participants had to be over the age of 18, and married to or living with the baby's father at the time of entry into the study. The latter criterion was instituted because we did not want to make maternity leave just a women's issue, but wanted to include men fully in the study.

The average age of the mothers at the beginning of the study was 29 years, ranging between 20 and 43 years; 95% of the mothers were married to the father. Ninety-three percent of the mothers were White (not of Hispanic origin); 2.6% were Black (not of Hispanic origin); 1.8% were Hispanic; 1.9% were Native American; and 0.7% were Asian American. In regard to education, 1.8% had less than a high school education; 15.4% graduated from high school or had a GED; 9.6% received some technical training beyond high school; 19.8% had some college; 34.9% had earned a college degree; 7.5% received some education beyond the college degree; and 10.9% had completed a masters, doctoral, or professional degree.

At the time of the first interview, 81.5% of the women were employed. For 38% of the women this was their first child, and for the remaining 62% it was a second or later child.

Mothers were interviewed in their homes by a female interviewer on each of four occasions: (a) during the fifth month of pregnancy (Time 1); (b) 1 month after the birth (Time 2); (c) 4 months after the birth (Time 3); and (d) 12 months after the birth (Time 4). In addition, mothers completed mail-out questionnaires on their own in advance of the interview and returned them to the interviewer. Fathers were interviewed by telephone and completed a mail-out questionnaire on each of the same four occasions.[2]

One page of questions about sexual behavior was part of the mothers' home interview. About halfway through the interview, the page was handed to the woman, who filled it out in privacy, placed it in a sealed envelope, and returned it to the interviewer.[3] For fathers, the page of questions about sexual behavior was included in the mail-out questionnaire.

Patterns of Sexual Behavior

Descriptive data on sexual behaviors in the last month, as reported at Times 1, 2, 3, and 4, are shown in Table 1.

The percentage of couples who engage in intercourse in any given month is about 90%, except at Time 2, 1 month postpartum, when the majority have not yet resumed intercourse. The frequency of intercourse is estimated somewhat higher by women than by men, and is about 5 times per month on average during pregnancy and at 4 and 12 months postpartum; it is strikingly low, as expected, at 1 month postpartum.

The percentage of men who masturbate in a month holds relatively constant at about 43% at each time. The percentage for women is lower, and is especially low 1 month postpartum. The question on frequency of masturbation was asked only at Time 4; the frequency was considerably higher for men than for women. The incidence of cunnilingus is about 45% at Time 3 and 4, but is slightly lower at Time 1, and is especially low, about 7%, at 1 month postpartum. It should be noted that there is one potential health risk associated with cunnilingus during pregnancy. Some women enjoy having their partner blow air forcefully into the vagina. When used on a pregnant woman, this technique has been known to cause damage to the placenta, and embolism, apparently as a result of air getting into the uterine veins (Sadock & Sadock, 1976).

The incidence of fellatio shows close agreement in mothers' and fathers' reports, and is fairly constant at 45%, except that it drops to about 35% at 1 month postpartum.

---

[2]A different method was used for data collection with fathers (telephone interview) than with mothers (face-to-face interview in the home). In pilot testing, many fathers expressed an unwillingness to participate in the lengthy face-to-face interviews to which their wives or partners committed and expressed a strong preference for a telephone interview. In the interests of maintaining a high response rate from fathers, then, we opted for telephone interviews for them.

[3]In order to maintain privacy and encourage honesty, interviewers were instructed to conduct the interview with only the woman in the room. Occasionally someone walked through the room, as recorded by interviewers in their notes, but in no case was a husband, other adult, or child above preschool age present in the room during the interview. Moreover, the sex questions were not administered or responded to orally (they were recorded by the woman on paper and sealed in an envelope before handing to the interviewer), further ensuring that responses would not be influenced by the presence of another person in the room.

TABLE 1
Sexual Behaviors in the Last Month, Reported by Mothers and Fathers During Pregnancy and the Year Postpartum

Variable	Pregnancy 2nd trimester	Postpartum		
		1 mo.	4 mo.	12 mo.
Had intercourse				
Mothers	90%	19%	90%	92%
Fathers	85%	14%	87%	89%
Mean frequency of intercourse/month				
Mothers	5.47	.51	5.25	5.29
Fathers	4.29	.34	4.51	3.87
Masturbated				
Mothers	25%	11%	18%	20%
Fathers	41%	43%	44%	45%
Mean frequency of masturbation				
Mothers	NA	NA	NA	.58
Fathers	NA	NA	NA	2.30
Fellatio				
Mothers	45%	35%	46%	48%
Fathers	40%	32%	43%	42%
Cunnilingus				
Mothers	34%	8%	42%	48%
Fathers	30%	6%	43%	45%
Petting				
Mothers	93%	66%	91%	93%
Fathers	87%	60%	86%	89%
Satisfaction with sexual relationship				
Mothers	3.82	3.36	3.42	3.64
Fathers	3.49	3.12	3.37	3.42
Decreased sexual desire				
Mothers	1.71	1.65	1.19	.83

Note. NA = question not asked at that time. All questions were asked for a time frame of the last month. Satisfaction was rated on a scale from 1 (very dissatisfied) to 5 (very satisfied). Decreased sexual desire was rated on a scale from 0 (never) to 4 (almost always).

Although there is a slight dip in satisfaction with the sexual relationship at 1 month postpartum, both men and women, on the average, are moderately satisfied with their sexual relationship at all times.

The question regarding sexual desire was part of a different questionnaire administered to women only. The results indicate that the decreased sexual desire was fairly common both during the middle trimester of pregnancy and at 1 month postpartum, as expected. There were fewer reports of decreased desire at 4 months postpartum and still fewer at 12 months postpartum, when 56% of the women reported that they never experienced decreased sexual desire.

According to the women's retrospective reports at 12 months postpartum, couples resumed intercourse, on average, 7.33 weeks postpartum, but there was wide variability; 19% of the couples had resumed intercourse within the first month after birth, whereas 19% did not resume until 4 months after the birth or later.

Breast-Feeding and Sexuality

At Time 2, 1 month postpartum, we compared women who were currently breast-feeding (BF, n = 361, 68% of the sample) with those who were not (NBF, n = 169, 32% of the sample). Several differences were revealed (Table 2). NBF women were significantly more likely to have resumed intercourse (29%) than BF women (15%). Fathers' reports confirmed this result.

Several measures of sexual satisfaction showed differences between the BF and NBF groups. Although there were no differences between BF and NBF women on a single item assessing sexual satisfaction, husbands or partners of NBF women indicated significantly more sexual satisfaction than husbands or partners of BF women. Although there were no differences between BF and NBF women in their ratings of how physically affectionate their partners were, husbands or partners of NBF women rated them as significantly more physically affectionate than husbands or partners of BF women. Both NBF women and their husbands or partners rated their sexual relationship as significantly more rewarding than BF women and their husbands rated theirs.

At Time 3, 4 months postpartum, BF women (n = 233) were still less likely than NBF women (n = 296) to have resumed intercourse; 85% of BF women and 95% of NBF women had. Ratings of satisfaction show similar results to those at Time 2. Various measures showed more sexual satisfaction among NBF couples, particularly among the husbands of NBF women.

By Time 4, 12 months postpartum, few women were still breastfeeding and most of the differences between BF and NBF groups had disappeared. Retrospective reports at Time 4 indicated that NBF women resumed intercourse significantly earlier on average (6.9 weeks) than BF women (7.8 weeks).

DISCUSSION

The data from the WMLH Project indicate that sexual patterns are remarkably similar at the fifth month of pregnancy, 4 months postpartum, and 12 months postpartum, but that sexual expression is considerably reduced at 1 month postpartum, when the majority of couples have not resumed intercourse. On average, couples resumed intercourse at about 7 weeks postpartum.

TABLE 2
Comparison of Sexuality of Breast-Feeding (BF) and Non-Breast-Feeding (NBF) Couples
(Means, With Standard Deviations in Parentheses)

	Women			Men		
	BF	NBF	p	Wife BF	Wife NBF	p
1 Month Postpartum						
Sexual satisfaction	3.29 (1.08)	3.36 (1.25)	n.s.	2.95 (1.27)	3.46 (1.22)	.0001
Partner rewards:						
Physical affection	2.69 (0.89)	2.86 (0.87)	n.s.	2.57 (0.81)	2.78 (0.76)	.01
Sexual relationship	2.09 (0.88)	2.38 (0.95)	.001	2.16 (0.83)	2.46 (0.96)	.001
4 Months Postpartum						
Sexual satisfaction	3.37 (1.19)	3.45 (1.32)	n.s.	3.14 (1.34)	3.59 (1.29)	.0001
Partner rewards:						
Physical affection	2.64 (0.84)	2.89 (0.80)	.001	2.64 (0.83)	2.84 (0.75)	.01
Sexual relationship	2.35 (0.86)	2.63 (0.84)	.001	2.37 (0.79)	2.67 (0.79)	.0001

There were significant differences between breast-feeding and non-breast-feeding women, both at 1 month and 4 months postpartum. The sexual relationship looks more positive for non-breast-feeding couples than for breast-feeding couples, although husbands seem more sensitive to the differences than wives do. Our results are consistent with those of Alder and Bancroft (1988). However, our results are not consistent with the assertions of Masters and Johnson (1966), who reported that sexual responsiveness returns sooner after childbirth among women who breast-feed than among women who don't. Again, the Masters and Johnson results seem to be the outlier, probably because of their peculiar methods of sampling.

There are three possible explanations for decreased sexual activity and satisfaction among breast-feeding couples compared with non-breast-feeding couples. The first is biological. Estrogen production is suppressed during the period of lactation. Decreased levels of estrogen result in decreased vaginal lubrication, making intercourse uncomfortable. Physicians and therapists working with women during pregnancy or the postpartum period should discuss this issue with their clients. Generally women are reticent to bring up this topic, so practitioners need to be responsible for taking the initiative. Much of the difficulty can be overcome with the use of sterile lubricants.

The second possible explanation involves psychological factors. Masters and Johnson (1966) reported that breast-feeding is erotically satisfying to some women, and a few women are even stimulated to orgasm by it. It may be that breast-feeding mothers derive some erotic satisfaction, or at least have their needs for intimate touching met, by breast-feeding and therefore show less interest in sexual expression with their husband or partner. Men, in contrast, do not receive this satisfaction from the baby and continue to seek sexual intimacy with their wives or partners, who are less interested than usual. This leads husbands of BF women to report less sexual satisfaction than husbands of NBF women, whereas there are no differences in satisfaction between the two groups of women.

A third possibility is that BF women are more fatigued, which puts a damper on sexual desire. They may be more fatigued because they must do all the feeding and therefore may have fewer opportunities to sleep through the night. Greater fatigue also may result from the metabolic demands of breast-feeding. Support for the hypothesis of greater fatigue while breast-feeding comes from a study by Forster et al. (1994), which found that, after weaning, women reported a significant decrease in fatigue as well as an increase in sexual activity and sexual feelings.

The BF and NBF groups did not differ on some variables: incidence of masturbation, performing fellatio, and engaging in cunnilingus.

CONCLUSION

The data reported here show that women have similar patterns of sexuality—perhaps their ordinary pattern—during the fifth month of pregnancy and at 4 and 12 months postpartum. At 1 month postpartum, however, sexual expression is markedly reduced. This reduction occurs not only in vaginal intercourse, but in masturbation as well. The data also show a more positive sexual relationship for NBF women and their partners, compared with BF women.

Biological factors surely play a role in these phenomena. At 1 month postpartum, women may still be healing and sore and are likely to be fatigued, which may contribute to a lack of enthusiastic sexual expression. Breast-feeding women have reduced vaginal lubrication, making intercourse uncomfortable.

Earlier in this chapter we identified both pregnancy and postpartum sex taboos that are found in many cultures around the world, supporting the notion that women's sexuality during this time is socially constructed. Here we consider the nature of these social constructions in the United States, focusing on four factors: physicians' pronouncements, the invisibility of sexuality during pregnancy and postpartum, the incompatibility of motherhood and sexuality, and the impact of Masters and Johnson's (1966) research.

Pregnancy and childbirth have been medicalized in the United States. In that climate, advice from physicians constitutes an important component of the social construction of sexuality during this period. No doubt the comments given by individual physicians vary greatly and are not always completely consistent with the official position of *Williams Obstetrics*. The 6-week postpartum check-up is itself a kind of ritual. Traditionally, physicians have told couples not to engage in intercourse until after this check-up. In addition, even if some physicians do not prescribe such a taboo today, couples themselves may think that they must wait until the woman's health is certified by the check-up. It is probably not accidental that couples in our study resumed intercourse on average at 7 weeks postpartum, that is, in the week following the 6-week check-up.

Sexuality during pregnancy and the postpartum period has been largely invisible. When actress Demi Moore appeared nude and quite visibly pregnant on the cover of *Vanity Fair* magazine in August 1991, the event was claimed to be a first and there was much public discussion—and considerable disapproval. Thousands of women had posed nude on thousands of magazine covers prior to Demi Moore's disrobing, but none had been visibly pregnant. The combination of sexually suggestive nudity and pregnancy had apparently been unthinkable. Insofar as sexuality during pregnancy and the postpartum period is invisible, this time in a woman's life may be construed as asexual by the women herself and by others close to her.

There exists in the United States a cultural heritage of dichotomizing women into two groups, madonnas or whores. Virtuous motherhood and exuberant sexuality are seen as incompatible, an irony given that sexuality is precisely what causes motherhood. During pregnancy and the year following birth, a woman's status as mother is especially salient, perhaps making the expression of her sexuality seem inappropriate, both to her and to her husband or partner.

It is also worth considering the possibility that Masters and Johnson's (1966) well-known research and writings have created a cultural climate in regard to sexuality during pregnancy and the postpartum period. Masters and Johnson, for example, stated that intercourse is safe until the last few weeks before delivery, and the results from a number of studies show that couples engage in intercourse at fairly constant rates until the ninth month of pregnancy. Moreover, Masters and Johnson stated that sexual responsiveness returns earlier for BF women than for NBF women. Several physicians with whom we have shared the results of the WMLH study have expressed surprise about the results for BF women. They generally consider BF women to be more at ease with their bodies (and therefore sexier) and likely to be more sexually interested and satisfied. Physicians' views have been shaped by Masters and Johnson culture. This does a disservice to BF women, who would be better off with an explanation of why they don't produce much vaginal lubrication, and therefore may feel discomfort during sex, and with advice on how to use lubricants to ease the problem.

Pregnancy and childbirth are major reproductive events in a woman's life. They carry with them certain biological correlates, but also a thick overlay of cultural meaning and taboo. At this juncture in research and theorizing the field needs (a) an analysis of pregnancy and postpartum sex taboos—which have been fair game for study among non-European Americans—in the United States today; and (b) qualitative research designed to understand the symbolic meaning to the woman and her husband or partner of sexuality during pregnancy, as well as the reasons for and meanings of the reduction in sexual activity that couples experience in the month or more postpartum.

REFERENCES

Alder, E. M. (1989). Sexual behaviour in pregnancy, after childbrith and during breastfeeding. *Balliere's Clinical Obstetrics and Gynaecology, 3,* 805–821.

Alder, E. M., & Bancroft, J. (1988). The relationship between breastfeeding persistence, sexuality and mood in postpartum women. *Psychological Medicine, 18,* 389–396.

Bogren, L. (1991). Changes in sexuality in women and men during pregnancy. *Archives of Sexual Behavior, 20*, 35–45.

Call, V., Sprecher, S., & Schwartz, P. (1995). The incidence and frequency of marital sex in a national sample. *Journal of Marriage and the Family, 57*, 639–652.

Cunningham, F. G., MacDonald, P. C., Leveno, K. J., Gant, N. F., & Gilstrap, III, L. C. (1993). *Williams Obstetrics* (19th ed.). Norwalk, CT: Appleton and Lange.

Ford, C. S., & Beach, F. A. (1951). *Patterns of sexual behavior*. New York: Harper & Row.

Forster, C., Abraham, S., Taylor, A., & Llewellyn-Jones, D. (1994). Psychological and sexual changes after the cessation of breast-feeding. *Obstetrics & Gynecology, 84*, 872–876.

Frayser, S. G. (1985). *Varieties of sexual experience: An anthropological perspective on human sexuality*. New Haven, CT: Human Relations Area Files Press.

Grudzinskas, J. G., & Atkinson, L. (1984). Sexual function during the puerperium. *Archives of Sexual Behavior, 13*, 85–91.

Hyde, J. S., DeLamater, J. D., Plant, E. A., & Byrd, J. M. (1996). Sexuality during pregnancy and the year postpartum. *Journal of Sex Research, 33*, 143–151.

Hyde, J. S., Klein, M. H., Essex, M. J., & Clark, R. (1995). Maternity leave and women's mental health. *Psychology of Women Quarterly, 19*, 257–285.

Kenny, J. A. (1973). Sexuality of pregnant and breastfeeding women. *Archives of Sexual Behavior, 2*, 215–229.

Kumar, R., Brant, H. A., & Robson, K. M. (1981). Childbearing and maternal sexuality: A prospective survey of 119 Primiparae. *Journal of Psychosomatic Research, 25*, 373–383.

Masters, W. H., & Johnson, V. E. (1966). *Human sexual response*. Boston: Little, Brown.

Reamy, K. J., & White, S. E. (1987). Sexuality in the puerperium: A review. *Archives of Sexual Behavior, 16*, 165–186.

Sadock, B. J., & Sadock, V. A. (1976). Techniques of coitus. In B. J. Sadock et al. (Eds.), *The sexual experience*. Baltimore, MD: Williams & Wilkins.

Tiefer, L. (1991). Historical, scientific, clinical, and feminist criticisms of "The Human Sexual Response Cycle" model. *Annual Review of Sex Research, 2*, 1–24.

Welsh, D. P., Rostosky, S. S., & Kawaguchi, M. C. (2000). A normative perspective of adolescent girls' developing sexuality. In C. B. Travis & J. W. White (Eds.), *Sexuality, society, and feminism* (pp. 111–140). Washington, DC: American Psychological Association.

White, S. E., & Reamy, K. J. (1982). Sexuality and pregnancy: A review. *Archives of Sexual Behavior, 11*, 429–444.

8

MENOPAUSE AND SEXUALITY: AGEISM AND SEXISM UNITE

SHARON S. ROSTOSKY AND CHERYL BROWN TRAVIS

Images and stereotypes of women over 40 are overwhelmingly negative. The popular literature conveys a message, based on a medical model, that older women are sicker and more frail than younger women, and less optimal than the male norm. We discuss the implicit and not-so-implicit messages about women's sexuality in general and the sexuality of older women in particular. In this chapter, we delineate some serious methodological problems common to the medical literature that support these negative images, including such fundamental errors as failure to acquire baseline data, failure to establish dose-response relationships, and blatantly pejorative language. Finally, we consider feminist alternatives to biomedical conceptualizations that encompass the lived experiences of mid-life women.

As with other chapters in this volume, we have adopted a social constructionist perspective. Previous chapters in this volume have set the stage for this philosophical approach, which we use as the context for a feminist critique of both popular media images and scholarly writing on aging women, sexuality, and menopause. We argue that the basic picture of menopause and sexuality constructed both in the popular media and in published medical literature is replete with negative biases. Furthermore, we show that scientific conclusions in established medical journals are often based on flawed theory and slipshod methodology. Following this critique, we point to new, more positive research results that are beginning to make inroads into the literature. We also describe several new feminist models for research and health care. We conclude that getting beyond negative cultural views propagated by the medical model requires more than a careful adherence to reliable techniques or the use of more precise instruments. Instead, the collective view regarding older women and sexuality needs be reworked.

MAKING THE INVISIBLE VISIBLE: IMAGES OF AGING, SEX, AND MENOPAUSE

A basic tenet of social constructionist theory is that the distinction between the knower and the known is never as sharp as supposed by logical positivism. Culture infuses science and science infuses culture. The questions researchers think to ask in their scientific endeavors are influenced by an understanding of the basic nature of the phenomenon they wish to study. Understanding is heavily influenced by cultural precepts and worldviews that are invisible to those who operate within these frameworks. However, these invisible frameworks necessarily influence the approach to a field of inquiry. Views about aging women, sexuality, and menopause are therefore particularly relevant to deconstructing how these topics have been studied and understood.

Images of Aging

Images of old women in literature and myth are almost universally negative. The terms *crone* and *hag* continue to evoke powerful images when reading English literature. Fairy tales from a variety of cultures convey the idea of evil and dangerous old women (e.g., Hansel and Gretel, Sleeping Beauty, and Snow White). Indeed, witches in literature (most of whom are women) were regularly assigned the role of foiling the efforts of protagonists.

European and early American history also are replete with examples of harsh and often cruel treatment of older women. Until the turn of the 19th century, the life expectancy of most women was 45–50; therefore, a woman in her 30s or early 40s would have been considered old. If her husband died, his property, land, and the income from related enterprises were accorded to his male heir. Often, an American widow found herself relegated to a room in the farmhouse now managed by a son and his wife and children. Civil authority, abetted by the church, similarly mythologized the dangers of older women during the witch trials of Salem and surrounding New England communities.

Currently, there remains a general anxiety about aging in the dominant American culture. Americans speak frequently about mid-life crises, empty nests, and even, occasionally, male menopause. Products designed to disguise the physical signs of aging are a large part of a multimillion dollar cosmetic industry. Makeup in the form of concealers, rejuvenators, moisturizers, and exfoliants promises to delay or hide the fine lines of aging. Most hair color products for men and women are designed for the coverage of gray, including special products for men's moustaches. Cosmetic surgery continues as a booming trade (chemical facial peels, facelifts, and tummy tucks). Recent clothing developments include corsets that control a man's growing paunches and prosthetic inserts to create the illusion of muscular development in the otherwise flattened middle-aged buttocks.

Images of Sexuality

A content analysis of best-selling novels and films from 1959 to 1979 revealed the persistent message that sexual participants must be single, attractive, physically healthy, and young (i.e., the SAPHY constellation) (Abramson & Mechanic, 1983). Furthermore, Abramson and Mechanic found that, no matter the time, place, or circumstance portrayed in the media, common sexual occurrences such as sexual dysfunction or need for lubricants were absent. Contrasting this with the realities of sexuality in the clinical literature, the authors voiced their concern over unrealistic sexual scripts promulgated through the enormous appeal of popular fiction and movies. Have things changed in the last 20 years? The answer would seem to be both yes and no. A more recent example of these entrenched views is the successful novel and movie *The Bridges of Madison County*. In this story a mid-life farmer's wife has a 3-day affair with a roguish, itinerate photographer. The emphasis is on how attractive she still is, yet sexual awakening and fulfillment eludes her until the sexual prowess of the male protagonist magically and wordlessly provides the key. Her passivity is contrasted with the unending activity of the older, middle-aged man:

> He was an animal ... A graceful, hard, male animal who did nothing to dominate her yet dominated her completely, in the exact way she wanted that to happen at this moment ... But it was far beyond the physical, though the fact that he could make love for a long time without tiring was part of it ... she had whispered to him, "Robert, you're so powerful it's frightening" ... It was almost as if he had taken possession of her, in all of her dimensions ... But he simply took it away, all of it ... She who had ceased having orgasms years ago, had them in long sequences now with a half-man, half-something-else creature. She wondered about him and his endurance, and he told her he

could reach those places in his mind as well as physically. (Waller, 1992, pp. 105–107)

Despite this stereotypical portrayal of powerful male sexuality and passive female sexuality, we do note the progress shown in the film version of the novel where Meryl Streep, a female actress over 40 years of age, was actually cast in the lead role. Perhaps this would not have happened 20 years ago, although we might cynically argue that the purpose was to make the Clint Eastwood (an actor in his 60s) character more believable.

From the media come other messages. In a 1993 episode of CBS's *Picket Fences*, menopause was used as a defense against a murder charge (cited in Jessee, 1993). The controversial *Murphy Brown* became a single mom in one season and then regressed to fretting over her lover seeing her mid-life body in the next. Although blatantly sexual, Cybil Shepherd is the constant brunt of aging women jokes in her television show. Although mid-life women are becoming more visible in the media, the picture is still largely one of rewarding those who can pass (i.e., continue to meet cultural prescriptions for beauty) or who can relieve our anxiety by making mid-life funny.

Still another example of this emphasis on *looking* sexy (passive and unrealistic) rather than *being* sexy (active and realistic) can be seen in the October 16, 1995, issue of *People* magazine, which showcases a pictorial of women over 40 who met the "sexy criteria," that is, looking at least 10 years younger than their chronological age. In other words, the unrealistic standards of beauty foisted on the young are being extended to older and older women. Again, we ask who benefits from this construction? Certainly not women whose resources support the cosmetic, surgical, and fitness industries. When will we collectively say, "Enough is enough!"

These examples are particularly disconcerting in light of a recent study of 500 highly educated mid-life women. Sixty-five percent claimed to obtain their information on menopause from books and magazines, whereas only 16% listed their physician as a primary source of information. Although 75% of the women looked forward to the cessation of their menstrual periods, the majority had negative views and attitudes as they approached menopause (Mansfield & Voda, 1993). We contend that women lack a sense of achievement or freedom at mid-life partially because their primary sources of information are negative. Since so many people rely on the mass media for information, others have suggested that feminist sex researchers work to become influential through writing popular books, consulting with journalists and script writers, and participating on talk shows (McCormick, 1994).

Despite the plethora of negative examples, we are optimistic that changes toward more positive and diverse images are being fashioned. Powerful and highly visible mid-life women such as Lauren Hutton, Goldie

Hawn, and Meryl Streep are blazing new territory in Hollywood. Highly competent and successful television personalities now include women over 40, such as Oprah Winfrey, Connie Chung, and Cokie Roberts. Gloria Steinem, likewise, is continuing her feminist activism on behalf of women. It is our hope that we are experiencing the beginnings of a sea change that will produce changes in long-held cultural stereotypes regarding aging women and sexuality. Certainly, until more widespread changes in media portrayals occur, entrenched stereotypes of gender, aging, and sexuality will continue to proliferate.

Images of Menopause

As a physical and biological marker of aging, menopause is most often portrayed as a stressful, disruptive, and negative experience in women's lives. This creates a certain angst and feeling of impending loss when contemplating menopause, expressed by one woman thus: "I don't want to go through the rest of my life feeling that I lost my wallet with everything in it" (Sand, 1993).

Defined by a long list of symptoms, women are urged to combat menopause with hormone replacement therapy (Chrisler, Torrey, & Matthes, 1991). Even woman-friendly approaches present many negative images. Gail Sheehy (1991), for instance, describes her own experience of menopause with metaphors of destruction such as "a battle," "first bombshell," "a little grenade went off in my brain," and, "some powerful switch had been thrown" (p. 15). In a chapter on mid-life sexuality, Gayle Sand (1993) states, "Menopause has had a magical effect on our sex life. It made it disappear" (p. 151). Are these experiences typical of mid-life women? Are they induced or exacerbated by negative stereotypes that pervade American culture so that they become self-fulfilling prophecies? If so, who benefits from this social construction, and what does it cost us?

We propose that the images of menopause as a problem characterized by symptoms of decline and deficiency are both reflected in and perhaps partially derived from medical and scientific discourse. That is, medical literature and to a lesser extent social science and psychological literature, as sources of scholarly knowledge and officially sanctioned truth, have been influenced by cultural worldviews of women and aging and in turn have become bases for contemporary popular discourse. We contend that commonly held negative attitudes both heavily influence and are influenced by the received knowledge that endorses (that is, socially constructs) these negative views. This circular influence is problematic because it is likely to endorse popular beliefs that are inaccurate and harmful to women. To the extent that biased scholarly wisdom saturates and reinforces popular views, it is likely to affect the social identities of mid-life women and to color women's actual experiences of mid-life and aging. In the following section we examine traditional sexual scripts and their impact on mid-life sexuality research.

SEXUAL SCRIPTS AND SEXUAL SCIENCE

The sexual identity available to women in general is conflicted and constrained. Across the lifespan, narrow bands of identity are offered to women. For instance, adolescent girls' developing sexuality is considered problematic (see chapter 5, this volume, by Welsh, Rostosky, & Kawaguchi). According to traditional sex-role socialization, girls and young women should be virtually asexual until marriage. This view likely impacts the actual experiences of girls and young women. For example, self-report data indicate that girls typically discover masturbation later than boys. Unlike boys, girls' discoveries mostly occur in a context of privacy with less likelihood of comparing experiences and meanings with peers (Hyde, 1996; Oliver & Hyde, 1993). Another typical sexual script of adolescence centers on sexual initiation. It is not uncommon for girls' first erotic experiences to occur, not in early self-exploration and masturbation, but in dating relationships where male partners assume the initiative. Sexuality then evolves in a social context of negotiation, often covert in nature. Not surprisingly, the question of whose body it is and whose sexuality it is may become blurred for women.

In contrast, one may argue that boys and young men receive a message of acknowledgment of, if not affirmation and approval of, their sexuality. Although boys and young men may fairly infer that their sexuality is only tangentially derived from social negotiation and relationship, girls and young women typically are led to believe and perhaps to actually experience their sexuality as something that emerges only in close relationships. In fact, in chapter 10 in this volume Travis et al. suggest that women may come to experience erotic arousal largely as a function of their perceptions of themselves as desirable objects and their abilities to evoke desire in men.

We would be surprised if this theme of mixed messages and uncertainty did not also affect older women. We supposed that the research literature on older women and sexuality would in some way address these dilemmas and conflicts from the perspective of hindsight, if not mature wisdom. Instead we found a heavy emphasis on "Doing It." Goldstein and Teng (1991) note that major geriatric textbooks have companion chapters on sexuality and aging. The chapters on men discuss sexual function, whereas those on female sexuality discuss estrogen deficiency, reflecting the general tendency to avoid discussing the sexual functioning of older women. This emphasis on the frequency of sexual intercourse and the hormonal correlates of intercourse reinforces a reductionist view of sexuality as primarily a biological act involving penetration. As a result, there is a heavy emphasis on anatomy, especially dysfunctional anatomy (e.g., dyspareunia [pain during intercourse], atrophic vagina [vaginal dryness and thinning of vaginal walls], and vaginismus [constriction of the vagina]). In the next section we discuss the significance of this sort of research focus; in this section we summarize the general findings on frequency of intercourse and hormonal correlates of intercourse.

Frequency

Does sexual behavior increase or decrease with age? Since American society links sexuality to youth, beauty, and vigor, sexual behavior among the elderly is treated in the literature as a talking platypus phenomenon. That older individuals engage in sex at all is apparently worthy of comment. Several studies have remarked on the continued interest in and expression of sexual activity in the elderly (Hallstrom & Samuelsson, 1990; Hawton, Gath, & Day, 1994; Kobosa-Munro, 1977; Koster & Garde, 1993). Some have even suggested there might be enhanced sexuality in the elderly (Adams & Turner, 1985). However, most also note gradual decline in sexual interest or capacity with age, and clinic staff have been alerted to the presence of sex problems that should be diagnosed (Sarrel & Whitehead, 1985). In almost no study was there any concern about the meaning or function of sexuality for personal, interpersonal, or social identity.

A variety of reasons for the decline in sexual activity have been proposed. A well-known quote by Alex Comfort presents one analysis. "In our experiences old folks stop having sex for the same reason they stop riding a bicycle—general infirmity, thinking it looks ridiculous, no bicycle" (Comfort, 1974, p. 140). Ann McCracken (1988) has wisely added another possibility, namely, never having learned to ride a bicycle with confidence. It seems that barring illness or poor health, past sexual behavior is the best predictor of future sexual behavior (Bretschneider & McCoy, 1988). In some longitudinal studies, there may be a self-fulfilling prophecy at work; that is, respondents who anticipated a decline with age subsequently did experience this with menopause (Koster & Garde, 1993).

Such self-fulfilling prophecies based on traditional stereotypes and myths about sex interfere with our ability to answer any questions about sexuality at mid-life. In the traditional sexual script, the only sexual event of any significance is heterosexual intercourse. However, some researchers have begun to expand the script by introducing a bit more complexity into their questionnaires and interviews such as needs for physical affection, emotional intimacy, and social partnership (Kaplan, 1990; Malatesta, Chambless, Pollack, & Cantor, 1988). Researchers also have begun to separate measures of interest or motivation from behavioral activity (Nilsson, 1987).

An interesting finding is that men typically report more interest or activity, or both, than women and that when sexual intimacy is stopped it is most often the man's choice (Pfeiffer, Verwoerdt, & Wang, 1968). This seems to reemphasize the interpersonal and heterosexual understanding of sexuality. It also suggests that men may have more influence in the expression of sexual intimacy than do women, a pattern that may have begun in early dating negotiations about sexual intimacy. It also may mean that when men can no longer achieve the sexual script of their youth they may forgo sexual intimacy entirely, perhaps because it is so difficult to modify this culturally compelling script about male sexuality.

Hormonal Correlates

The enthusiasm for a hormonal direct-drive model for sexuality is reflected in many studies that imply benefits from estrogen replacement therapy (HRT). In biological models of menopause, sexual functioning should be closely associated with changes in reproductive hormones—estradiol (a form of estrogen), progestin, or androstenedione (a form of testosterone). Most, if not all, of the sanctioned scientific literature on menopause and sexuality mention the possible association between hormones, sexual interest, and sexual function. However, few actually collect empirical data on levels of circulating hormones that may confirm (or disconfirm) the supposition. Several published papers report a favorable association between estrogen replacement therapy and sexual function (Leiblum, 1990; Sarrel, 1990), but few actually present empirical data to confirm (or disconfirm) this hypothesis (Riley, 1991). Other articles promote the indirect value of estrogen replacement on sexual activity, because it can slow the progress of osteoporosis, which may discourage sexual activity (Reyniak, 1987).

Belief in the ubiquitous value of estrogen for women, despite inadequate data, is also reflected across cultures. For example, one Finnish author suggested that HRT could preserve brain and cognitive functions (Sourander, 1994), and a German author recommended that estrogen be prescribed for all women of menopausal age (Takacs, 1991). Alternatively, a Spanish language magazine, *Buenhogar* (good housekeeping), noted that if women had more frequent sex with their husbands, their natural estrogen levels would rise, providing benefits in the reduction of heart disease, maintain bone density, and reduce depression (Dennis, 1997).

In contrast to these claims, recent findings not only suggest that estrogen has little effect on sexual arousal or sexual activity (Lindgren, Berg, Hammar, & Zuccon, 1993; Nathorst-Boos, Wiklund, Mattsson, Sandin, & von Schoultz, 1993), but also implicate hormonal replacement therapy in increasing women's breast cancer risk (Colditz et al., 1995). Yet, despite all the unanswered questions and inadequate data, wholesale endorsements by medical authorities abound in the print media, as illustrated by the following two quotes from *The Detroit Free Press*: "For every one woman who dies of breast or uterine cancer that might have been associated with the use of estrogen, there are 35 to 50 women dying of complications due to hip fracture or heart disease that could have been prevented with hormone replacement." Another gynecologist is quoted in the same article querying, "Why would you want to live without a hormone that's so vitally important to your well-being and to the prevention of disease? ... Exercise and a good diet are a drop in the bucket compared to what estrogen does to the body" (Anstett, 1994). In contrast to these testimonial endorsements, research has found that benefits attributed to estrogen replacement, particularly protection against heart disease, instead may be due to the fact that women who take estrogen replacement therapy are initially more healthy than the cohort of women who do not. Women who opt for consistent and extended use of hormone replacement have initially better health than women who do not. Before beginning replacement therapy, users have better cholesterol profiles, triglyceride levels, and body mass index than non-users (Matthews, Kuller, Wing, & Jansen-McWilliams, 1997). Most of the studies of the benefits of estrogen replacement have been cohort studies of more or less self-selected women, and cohort studies simply cannot substitute for good clinical trials (Matthews et al., 1997).

Conjugated estrogen is the most prescribed drug in America. A two-page color advertisement that we recently spotted in *U.S. News and World Report* pictured a thin, conventionally attractive woman with long blonde hair blowing in the wind as she walks along the beach with her two huge golden retrievers. She's looking toward the camera and smiling. The lengthy text begins, "For more than 50 years, health care providers have prescribed Premarin. In fact, today more than 8,000,000 American women take Premarin." Does this imply it is safe? The last sentence reads, "Premarin, earning your confidence generation after generation." Then, on the reverse side of the ad, in minuscule print, is a daunting full-page list of dangers of estrogen, side effects, and risks. If one reads the fine print, it is less than confidence-inspiring.

In contrast to the emphasis on estrogen, the most consistent empirical data suggest that forms of androgen are more likely to underlie sexual interest or activity than estrogen (Bachmann & Leiblum, 1991; Sherwin & Gelfand, 1987). One may even surmise that a decline in estrogen in relation to testosterone may lead to increased sexual interest. However, some studies have suggested that the effects of androgens are related to sexual motivation rather than to sexual activity (Sherwin, Gelfand, & Brender, 1985), and other studies have reported no association at all (Bachmann, Leiblum, Kemmann, Colburn, Swartzman, & Shelden, 1984). One study by James Frock and John Money (1992) recruited 20 postmenopausal women and elicited responses to a short questionnaire but collected no physiological measures at all. The study nevertheless concluded, with egregious errors of logic, that androgen maintains sexual functioning and can be administered with good therapeutic effect. A more thorough review of the literature indicates that androgen may affect sexual functioning for surgically menopausal women, but perhaps does not affect naturally menopausal women (Walling, Andersen, & Johnson, 1990).

In conclusion, examining sanctioned and lay literature on mid-life sexuality leads us to again wonder what larger stakes are involved in continuing to define menopause as a deficiency disease to which estrogen provides the obligatory and necessary answer. Writing on the 1970–1980 estrogen debates between the pharmaceutical industry, the scientific community, the government, the media, and the medical profession, Patricia Kaufert and Sonja McKinlay (1985) delineated "how the production of medical knowledge is determined by ideological and sociopolitical factors among which women's own needs and interests have low priority (p. 113)." Certainly, there are economic incentives for having the majority of "menoboomers" on hormone replacement therapy for years of their lives. Although we acknowledge that there are women for whom hormone therapy is appropriate and beneficial, as of this time there is an inadequate scientific basis for unequivocal blanket endorsements.

So far, we have noted how popular and scientific literature negatively portray menopause and aging. We now take a closer look at the medical model of menopause. First, we present a broad survey of the field of published literature to acquaint the reader with the lay of the land. Then we present examples of the methodological and conceptual problems that infest it.

MEDICAL LITERATURE ON MENOPAUSE AND MID-LIFE WOMEN

In this section we present the publication patterns and topical focus of the medical and psychological literature on menopause and identify some pervasive methodological and conceptual problems. More extended discussion of particular details of this analysis is presented in Rostosky and Travis (1996). What the following figures reveal is that compared with the vast array of other topics and other journal articles, little has been published on women at mid-life, women's roles as a function of age and experience, or even women and menopause. What has been published is overwhelmingly colored by a medical, biological lens. A potential problem with such a biological emphasis is that women themselves may come to view their own lives and experiences as fundamentally characterized by illness that requires medical intervention in the form of pharmaceutical and surgical procedures.

A search of the Medline database was conducted for the years 1984–1994 to identify all articles on menopause. Medline cites about 300,000 articles each year from more than 3,200 journals. It encompasses all major medical journals, including those of interest to the general field, such as *Lancet* and the *New England Journal of Medicine* and journals specific to obstetrics and gynecology. Additionally, there is coverage of the major psychiatric journals such as the *American Journal of Psychiatry* and the *Archives of General Psychiatry*. Medline also includes some social, psychological, and interdisciplinary journals such as *The Journal of Clinical Psychology* and *Women and Health*.

The number of articles on menopause from all sources cited in Medline totaled 9,018, ranging from a low of 448 in 1994 to a high of 690 in 1992. Most of these articles focused on medical treatment rather than theory, and the most frequent topic was reproductive hormones and their replacement. Examples included articles such as, "Effect of oestrogen and testosterone implants on psychological disorder in the climacteric" (Montgomery et al., 1987) and "A prospective one-year study of estrogen and progestin in post menopausal women: Effects on clinical symptoms and lipoprotein lipids" (Sherwin & Gelfand, 1989). Articles that had a focus on social aspects of menopause made up only about 6% of all menopause articles. There were an additional 5,606 articles published that were on aging or mid-life women, but were not specifically about menopause. Nevertheless, these articles focused almost exclusively on disease conditions (e.g., cardiovascular disease).

We conducted a search of PsychLit using the same strategy. PsychLit cites approximately 40,000 articles per year from more than 1,300 journals. As did the Medline search, the search included articles on menopause in general, and then identified a subset of these that had a specifically psychosocial focus. Finally, the search was expanded to locate the articles that did not mention menopause but that did focus on women and middle age or aging.

Over the study years, 227 articles from PsychLit were on menopause, or about 16 articles each year. This body of work contained many studies that reflected the message of decline and deficiency (Facchinetti, Demyttenaere, Fioroni, Neri, & Genazzani, 1992; Gannon, 1988; Greendale & Judd, 1993). Most of these were medical in focus and only about 25% dealt with specifically psychosocial factors. Very few articles addressed any mid-life developmental issues.

Articles published in a selected subset of journals were reviewed to better characterize the publication trends for medical, psychiatric, and psychological journals. The medical journals, such as *New England Journal of Medicine*, were selected because we assumed they would be widely read and reported. During the study years of 1984–1994 these influential medical journals published 508 articles on menopause or women's middle age or women's aging; of these only 18 articles addressed psychosocial considerations. Psychiatric journals, such as *Archives of General Psychiatry*, and psychology journals, such as *Journal of Health and Social Behavior*, contained a total of 16 articles for the same decade. Most of these articles focused on depressive symptomatology. The three psychology-based studies addressed issues of roles for women at mid-life (Erdwins & Mellinger, 1984; Harris, Ellicott, & Holmes, 1986) and job stress (Abush & Burkhead, 1984).

Examination of a set of psychology journals focused specifically on women revealed only a nominally better record, with 31 articles focusing on middle age. Approximately one fourth of all these articles appeared in *Psychology of Women Quarterly*. Three of the articles focused on attitudes or perceptions of menopause (Cowan, Warren, & Young, 1985; Gannon & Ekstrom, 1993; Koff, Rierdan, & Stubbs, 1990). Two focused on depression and menopausal symptoms (Hagstad, 1988; Lennon, 1987). Three of four conceptual and theoretical papers discussed menopause and sexuality (Cole & Rothblum, 1990; Lieblum, 1990; Morokoff, 1988), and one reviewed the literature on exercise and menopausal symptomatology (Gannon, 1988).

Of the 22 psychological articles on mid-life that did not focus on menopause, 15 were empirical studies using self-report data on topics such as employment and career issues (Ackerman, 1990; Adelmann, Antonucci, Crohan, & Coleman, 1989, 1990; Waldron & Herold, 1986), physical activity (Dan, Wilbur, Hendricks, O'Connor, & Holm, 1990), cross-cultural comparisons (Friedman & Pines, 1992; Sanchez-Ayendez, 1988; Todd, Friedman, & Kariuki, 1990), generativity (Ryff & Migdal, 1984; Stewart & Gold-Steinberg, 1990; Vaillant & Vaillant, 1990), and sex roles (Frank, Towell, & Huyck, 1985; Tinsley, Sullivan-Guest, & McGuire, 1984). Conceptual or theoretical papers on mid-life that appeared in these women's psychology journals addressed topics such as aging and minority women (Padgett, 1988), mid-life childbearing (Mansfield, 1988), and psychological theory and aging (Gergen, 1990; Porcino, 1985).

In summary, there is a paucity of information on mid-life sexuality available. Although we were encouraged by some notable exceptions, mainly found in nursing journals and feminist-oriented journals, most of the available information remains negative and disease-focused. As we mentioned earlier, a potential danger of this pattern is that women may incorporate these negative images into their own identities. Furthermore, this one-sided view of menopause may become extended to views of women in general. Presently, these remain empirical questions in need of exploration. If these negative images do affect personal views, it is particularly disturbing that the scientific basis for a substantial portion of the published literature is irretrievably flawed, both methodologically and conceptually. The fact that it is nevertheless published as sanctioned (i.e., peer-reviewed) knowledge to be taken seriously and applied broadly demonstrates the operation of a social construction by which jury-rigged methods are used in the service of biased cultural beliefs. In the following section we briefly delineate some of these methodological and conceptual flaws that pervade the literature on menopause and subsequently are packaged as a basis for understanding women's lives.

METHODOLOGICAL AND CONCEPTUAL PROBLEMS

Methodological Problems

A host of methodological flaws form the backdrop of the published medical literature on menopause. Common flaws include: (a) vague or nonexistent operational definitions; (b) lack of baseline data; (c) problems in establishing dose-response relationships; (d) lack of control groups; (e) overgeneralization; (f) retrospective reporting; (g) use of biased symptom checklists; (h) lack of context; (i) pejorative language; and (j) neglect of issues of diversity. A brief discussion of some of these is provided below; more detailed commentary is presented elsewhere (Rostosky & Travis, 1996). These methodological flaws are the mechanisms by which details of a distorted science are constructed into established facts that form the basis for medical practice.

Even the most elemental aspects of established scientific methodology were missing. For example, studies vary greatly in the operational definitions applied, and they frequently consist of only the most casual specifications (e.g., a general age range without any reference to the status of individual women). Under such arrangements, a 55-year-old woman on hormone replacement therapy could be labeled menopausal, whereas a 35-year-old woman with a complete hysterectomy and no hormone replacement could be placed in a control group.

It is not uncommon for studies to include menopausal and perimenopausal women, implying that if a woman is not actually menopausal, she may soon become so; and also implying that women falling within a broad age range are potentially at risk for menopause symptoms. These studies may encompass 20 or more years of women's lifespan (e.g., 36–61 years; Huerta, Mena, Malacara, & Diaz-de-Leon, 1995) or 33–56 years (Cutler, Garcia, & McCoy, 1987). When menopausal and perimenopausal age ranges are combined with the premenstrual and perimenstrual phases, fully 30% of a woman's lifespan can be discounted as "under the influence" of some hormonal upheaval. Throughout, one finds terms reflecting decline, deficiency, and disease, for example *pelvic atrophy*, *ovarian dysfunction*, and *estrogen deprivation*. One study went so far as to refer to "these problem women" (Garnett, Studd, Henderson, Watson, Savvas, & Leather, 1990, p. 918).

Occasionally studies do code individual women with respect to key variables of interest, but these efforts often involve retrospective reporting. The respondent women may be asked to remember their daily fluctuations and physiological conditions from two years previously. To assist memory, researchers may present symptom checklists. However, these typically have an overwhelmingly negative slant (e.g., joint pain, nervousness, and short temper).

In any case, conditions and experiences with specific relevance to women are often strongly characterized by their biological correlates. Such language and focus imply that the experience is fundamentally determined by biology. It is constructed as a biological event rather than a social or political event. For example, Masters and Johnson (1966) noted a variety of physiological changes in menopause related to sexual response and attributed these to "steroid starvation," although they reported no data about levels of circulating hormones. Such characterization typically ignores important contextual variables and conveniently locates the problem in the individual woman.

We were particularly disturbed that many studies supposedly designed to assess the efficacy of a particular clinical practice would not logically allow such inferences because comparison baseline data was not available. In a related problem, many studies failed to include control groups. Thus, for example, although the responses of menopausal women to symptom checklists (e.g., joint pain, short temper) are seen as informative, these are never compared with responses of men in the same age groups. The lack of comparative or baseline data leaves a question about the nature and size of differences in the experiences of menopausal women and women with other hormonal statuses, or even in comparison with men, who may also experience such symptoms. This lack of baseline or reference data can render a general picture of menopause as a stressful experience plagued by numerous discomforts.

More troubling than the distortion of descriptions of menopause itself is the opportunity for the construction of claims regarding the curative powers of medical interventions, especially the use of hormone replacement to alleviate various conditions that may be secondary to menopause. For example, Lobo and colleagues reported that 75% of the women in the study experienced no dyspareunia following hormonal replacement therapy, but they never indicated what percentage had reported dyspareunia before treatment (Lobo, McCormick, Singer, & Roy, 1984). This kind of methodology is equivalent to the use of testimonials to prove the benefits of hormone replacement. If the same methods were used to advocate the merits of a health elixir, it would be recognized as merely advertising rather than promoted as science.

Conceptual Problems

These methodological flaws do not arise from the random oversights of different researchers, but reflect underlying conceptual biases. This bias revolves around a heavy biological reductionism that flavors views about all women. In this section we elaborate three assumptions that underlie this biological focus and lead to concepts of women as opposite from the male norm—deficient and diseased, and weak and powerless.

First, women are presented in the medical literature on menopause as fundamentally Other in comparison to the male norm. For example, hormonal changes known to take place in mid-life men are not routinely pathologized as they are in women. The underlying assumption is that women are disabled by their reproductive physiology (including menstruation, childbirth, and menopause) and require medical expertise for diagnosis and treatment. This results in women's health and sexuality being constructed and defined from a narrow and limiting perspective, and, in the case of menopause, one that pathologizes women's natural aging processes and ignores broader sociocultural contexts.

Not only are women seen as other, they also are presented as sicker. Menopause in Western society is constructed in the popular and scholarly discourse as a biological event entailing unique types of discomfort although even the most common symptom, the hot flash, has been documented in women of all ages (Neugarten & Kraines, 1965). There are more than 40 symptoms commonly listed as part of the menopausal syndrome, yet many of these (e.g., depression, headaches, irritability, dizziness, etc.) are unique neither to menopause nor to women. Even the "defining feature" of menopause, the cessation of menstruation, is not unique to menopause, but may indicate pregnancy, athletic training, malnutrition, or some disease process (Kaufert, 1982).

Finally, the traditional biomedical model of menopause leads to conceptualizing women as weak and powerless in relation to medical and scientific authority. That is, if menopause is essentially a medical problem, then medical solutions are needed, including gynecological specialists, gynecological procedures, and pharmaceuticals designed for gynecological applications. Others have noted the parallel between the expansion of the medical profession and the treatment of women as patients with little power (Kaufert, 1982). By defining a menopausal syndrome or symptom package, the medical profession determines what menopause is, and, perhaps most important, how it will be experienced.

With the establishment of a medical authority in women's lives, women themselves become disempowered. Evidence of the domination of the biomedical paradigm and the resulting construction of medical authority and expertise can be seen in qualitative studies of women's experience of menopause (see Dickson, 1990; Gergen, 1989; Jones, 1994). Findings suggest that most women identify their physicians as the primary source of knowledge about menopause, yet continue to feel uninformed and unknowledgeable. Although frustrated with this lack of information, they continue to turn their care over to their physicians.

Sanctioned medical interpretations become filters through which women interpret their own experience (Bowles, 1990). The personal impact of this has been substantiated by Gannon and Ekstrom (1993) in a study finding that women who had adopted an implicitly biomedical model reported more negative attitudes about menopause than did women who focused on menopause as a developmental transition.

We certainly acknowledge that some mid-life and older women do encounter problems during menopause. However, the context of these problems is typically ignored in the biomedical literature. Instead, problems of menopause are viewed as embedded in women's different, sick, and weak bodies while the psychosocial aspects of menopause, middle age, and aging are neglected. Despite this gloomy picture, there are signs of change as feminist researchers and health care specialists begin to challenge the traditional biomedical model and as women experience menopause in a changed historical context (i.e., longer lifespan and more power and privilege compared with past generations). It is to these changing conceptualizations and practices that we now look.

POSITIVE RESEARCH RESULTS

In contrast to the compendium of deficiency and disease literature, recent evidence suggests that menopause is not particularly problematic for most women (Avis & McKinlay, 1991; Ballinger, 1990; DeLorey, 1992; Greene & Cooke, 1980). Cross-cultural and lifespan developmental studies have been particularly useful in constructing alternatives to unidimensional biomedical paradigms.

Cross-cultural studies have found that menopausal symptoms are more a function of cultural attitudes than biology (Datan, 1986; Flint, 1982). Women in non-Western, nonindustrialized cultures, in which the mother-in-law role is associated with increased power and status, associate menopause with increased freedom, sexual satisfaction, and frank relief that childbearing is over (Beyene, 1986). However, we feel compelled to point out that in many instances the enhanced role of a mother-in-law pertains to increased authority over only the traditional household domains of women and often comes at the expense of the servitude of younger wives and daughters-in-law.

Many cross-cultural studies document that women do not associate menopause with physical or emotional symptomology. Some cultures even lack the supposed universal symptom of menopause—the hot flash (Beyene, 1986; Martin, Block, Sanchez, Arnand, & Beyene, 1993). Other studies of Japanese women (Lock, 1986, 1994), Mayan women (Beyene, 1986), African women (Todd, Friedman, & Kariuki, 1990; Udvardy, 1992), and Indian women (George, 1988) attest to the diversity of women's experience and the interaction of biology and culture. Many of these studies point out the existing cultural differences in diet, exercise, and attitudes toward this phase of the female life cycle. Similarly, Nancy Woods (1993) delineates many dimensions of health that universally are unaffected by menopausal status, such as well-being, functional status, adaptability. These dimensions are likely a product of personal and social resources, past health experiences, socialization for mid-life, past and current social demands and patterns of coping with them, and health-promoting and health-damaging behavior patterns.

The life-span developmental paradigms also have contributed models of adult development that are sensitive to the multifaceted ecological contexts in which women create and maintain their identities. These offer the potential for more comprehensive and accurate perspectives for understanding menopause (e.g., Helson, 1992; Peck, 1986; Ryff, 1985; Schlossberg, 1981). Beginning with a focus on healthy adaptation to transitions, these models hold potential for examining individual differences in coping with the challenges of the menopause transition. Similarly, qualitative methodologies that provide "thick description" of women's experiences with the menopause transition have contributed alternative voices to the biomedical discourse (see Dickson, 1990; Gergen, 1989; Jones, 1994). These compelling stories of personal struggle with and against pervasive negative images of the mature woman remind us of the (sometimes destructive) power of culturally assigned meanings. As always, the personal is political. It is not especially useful to limit our understanding to individual adaptation to the challenges of menopause. It is more productive to question those challenges and work toward removing them where they serve to build barriers to the growth and development of women (and men). That is, the institutionalized forms of ageism and sexism that make it difficult for women to thrive and prosper in their later years must be rigorously addressed through both research and public policy. We must work to break the myths about mid-life women and begin to value all the female cycles, not in terms of the body as machine, but as body, mind, and spirit interacting.

More holistic approaches that integrate biological, social, psychological, and cultural factors are currently under way. For example, the Massachusetts Women's Health Study (McKinlay, Brambilla, & Posner, 1992; McKinlay, McKinlay, & Brambilla, 1987) is a comprehensive, longitudinal study of more than 2,500 mid-life women that was undertaken in 1981 for the purpose of describing and understanding the normal menopause experience. Another notable example is The Healthy Women Study (Matthews, 1992; Matthews et al., 1990), which has followed more than 500 women from pre- to postmenopause, examining the relationships between their expectations, psychosocial stressors, and hormonal and physiological changes. It is our hope that these research programs and others will begin to counterbalance the predominant paradigm in ways that will contribute to the quality of life of mid-life women.

We challenge feminist researchers to construct a more balanced view, through increased interdisciplinary research and scholarship that are supportive of mid-life women. This is crucial for a complete understanding of the physical and symbolic nature of menopause. Certainly, alternate views of women and menopause will lead to different definitions and different questions. For example, if menopause is viewed as a developmental life phase (like adolescence), the focus of discussion may shift from technicalities about hormone levels to, for example, the changing status of the individual in personal, interpersonal, and social realms. New constructions will bring new perspectives on the training of health professionals and will educate the public in ways that will dispel current negative and unidimensional constructions of mid-life women.

We propose that the following research agenda will facilitate a move toward the goal of women's sexual empowerment. First, more studies should examine sexual attitudes and experience among women from diverse socioeconomic groups, sexual orientations, religious groups, health statuses, ages, occupations, and ethnicities. In addition, the within group differences that characterize women from the same demographic address must be documented. Qualitative methodologies will be particularly useful in this endeavor as feminists seek to redefine what constitutes sexual experience for women and what subjective meanings they attach to their experiences.

FEMINIST MODELS

Arguing that medical authorities have claimed a privileged and powerful position in constructing the predominant discourse of sexuality, Sue Sherwin (1992) challenges feminists to critically address biomedical ethics and excise prevailing practices that result in women's oppression. She points out that "physicians have been socially authorized to advise on sexual matters, although most of them have little training in the multidimensional aspects and varieties of human sexuality (and virtually no lessons on the politics of such studies). Many simply pass on their personal views about sexual matters under the guise of 'scientific experts'" (p. 216).

In contrast, feminist visions of holistic health care, if widely implemented, would revolutionize traditional constructions of medical care and the doctor-patient relationship. The nurse-practitioner model, for instance, values the consultant role rather than the patriarchal model of unquestioned authority and power over the diseased body part of the patient. In this model, the full context of women's lives—nutrition, exercise, work, relationships, stressors, personality strengths and weaknesses, and even spirituality—is assessed. This fuller picture, which takes much longer to form than the typical physician's office visit, allows for a collaborative relationship, better exchange of information, and more informed decision making for women.

Feminist notions of women's sexuality must counteract and correct the assumptions pervading the biologically based, partner-oriented, heterosexist, and patriarchal models that continue to dominate sex research. As Naomi McCormick (1994) points out, a feminist alternative should view sexuality as a whole mind and whole body experience. It is more than physiology (frequencies of orgasms, strength of vaginal contractions, and amount of lubrication). Relational dynamics and subjective meanings and motivations to understand female sexuality should be a central part of this picture. The power relationships that exist must similarly be addressed. Women must be free to explore, free to have pleasure, and free to be diverse. They must be free of the tyranny of traditional sex-role expectations that limit good sex to the young, the attractive, the healthy, and the middle and upper classes while obscuring a transforming vision of masculinity and femininity in the second half of the life cycle (Allgeier, 1983). Cross-cultural analyses have found that there are two universal aspects to sexuality: pleasure and self-disclosure (Reiss, 1986). Mid-life women (and men) can enjoy both; yet our concern about performance and technique leaves room for neither (Rubin, 1982).

Datan and Rodeheaver (1983) distinguish between the generative love of young adults that is about the task of procreation and nurture of children and the existential love of mid-life and old age that recognizes the finitude of life and cherishes the present moment. "The supreme triumph of our humanity over our biology is that we do not only make babies, we also make love ... [yet] we have not yet awakened to the potential for existential love between old women and old men, just as we are not yet prepared to recognize the pleasures of sexuality as natural to the life span, particularly to the postparental period" (pp. 286–287).

Conventional sexual scripts shortchange both men and women, creating pressures that contradict internal needs, particularly in the mandate that good sex equals intercourse equals orgasm. As McCormick states, "A feminist vision of sexual salvation would redefine lovemaking to include behaviors other than genital contact and orgasm" (p. 187). We must recognize that sexual intercourse is not necessarily a woman's favorite erotic activity. We must offer women at all stages of development more alternatives than those implied in the simplistic cultural messages to "Just Say No" before marriage and "Never Say No" after.

The "change" that is not addressed in current literatures is the change from sexual object to sexual being that mid-life women frequently report (e.g., Rountree, 1993). Holistic conceptualizations of women's sexuality at mid-life will value all the biological cycles, offering rituals and support for each. One nurse-practitioner questioned the extensive and long-term use of hormone replacement therapy, not necessarily because of its questionable safety, but because it potentially induces a developmental arrest (Kelsea, 1991). That is, the natural order is for women to become hormonally more like men as they age, and for men to become hormonally more like women. By preventing this natural order, are we preventing women from achieving certain psychological and spiritual benefits that are the reward of "the other side of menopause?"

Certainly, many women report that they are more assertive, autonomous, and authentic after the menopausal transition. Many view this as a time of blossoming spirituality, creativity, expressiveness, and passion. Many reflect, reorder, reevaluate, and reinvest, ultimately transforming and reconstituting the meaning of their lives. Words such as exploration, play, humor, and joy pepper the language of many mid-life women (Rountree, 1993). Ironically, at the very time that older adults begin to experience the physiological effects of aging, they also experience increased levels of sensuality and psychological integration (Allgeier, 1983). If sexuality were viewed as more than equipment malfunction, enriched sexuality and sexual expression would be the norm rather than the exception. In any case, we cannot know for sure until we disentangle from our pervasive cultural stereotypes of femininity, not a small struggle even for those with the courage, vision, and psychosocial resources to rebel. For these pioneers, a rich tapestry of sexual expression and involvement is available. For others, perhaps the greatest loss is not physiological functioning or the loss of a partner, but the loss of social acceptance of aging persons as sexual beings (Genevay, 1982).

Therefore, social constructions that have medicalized and pathologized sexuality and aging must be deconstructed. When sexuality at menopause becomes a medical problem in need of a medical solution, women lose control. Although benefitting some individual women, universal and routine medical intervention has iatrogenic consequences for women as a group.

Certainly, viewing mid-life and older women as sexual actors would disturb social and economic arrangements. As it is, lucrative industries surrounding HRT, penile implants, and traditional sex therapy benefit from propagating the myth of the coital imperative. Because sexual dysfunction diagnoses reflect stereotypically male sexual values (Rosen & Beck, 1988; Tiefer, 1995), a new interpretation of sexuality at mid-life carries the potential of disrupting current power relationships between men and women. Additionally, all patriarchal institutions that embody the ideology of "hetero-reality" benefit from constructions that serve to define all aspects of women's lives in relation to male priorities and needs (Raymond, 1986). Sexual autonomy, considered a male entitlement, if extended to women would strain the traditional patriarchal bargain (Nathanson, 1991).

In contrast, rare studies of women's subjective reports of their sexual experiences paint quite a different picture than the predominant diagnostic framework. Women most often list concerns such as an inability to relax, disinterest or being turned off, too little foreplay and too little afterplay, and annoyance at the partner for choosing inconvenient times to initiate lovemaking (McCormick, 1994). Reconstructing definitions of sexual dysfunction in terms of feminist values would radically depart from the current equipment failure and desire disorder diagnostics. The overriding goal of feminist sex research, political activity, and therapy must be empowerment. Models of pathology that conceptualize solutions as matters of individual change are too limiting. What is needed are new ideas, theories, and methods that value female sexual well-being as defined by women themselves. We must empower women with (a) self-esteem uncontingent on the cultural requisites of youth and narrowly defined beauty, (b) values that laud the accumulation of experience in loving rather than devaluing the physical changes that accompany such experience; and (c) encouragement to initiate sexual relationships that they find personally rewarding and meaningful and based on internal needs rather than external pressures (Genevay, 1982).

CONCLUSION

The current medicalization of menopause and of sexuality sustains social arrangements that are detrimental to women. It establishes a conceptual and explanatory framework based on biology and disguises the larger social and political nature of women's lives. Focus on the flawed and deficient individual as a basis for understanding implies that the issues and solutions are solely personal. The message is that women need to change who they are, or at least to disguise who they are in order to better please a larger society and to sustain their own happiness. Although this message reflects a received wisdom that is comfortable to most of society, it is costly to women. Women who may feel justified in speaking and acting on their acquired experience and wisdom are instead exhorted to spend their energy disguising their age. Because sexual activity in American society is believed to be so central to personal identity, older women (or any women for that matter) who do not attract the validation of a male sexual partner are seen as less than whole. It is hard to resist this view, and many older women themselves may feel diminished self-worth.

Messages about menopause and the lives of older women tend to reflect basic themes whereby power arrangements are camouflaged as biology, passivity is advanced in place of agency, and women are marginalized as Other. These themes are present in the discourse about menopause and women's sexuality in general. A general message is that the facts of women's sexuality are fundamentally biological and even evolutionary. Since these facts are thought to be objective and universal, there are no politics to any of this. Thus politics, power, status, authority over resources, viable choice, and access to alternatives are tacitly removed from the discussion.

A second theme is the notion of the body, and, in association, one's self-identity, as a passive attractant begins early and is carried throughout the life span; it is operational in various forms for much more than menopause. This theme is based on denying agency to women and is partly why feminists hold that women of all walks of life, ethnicities, and ages share certain common bonds. The determination of self-worth on the basis of being an object pleasing to men does not begin with menopause. A consequence of this that will be revisited in other chapters is that women do not truly own their sexuality. A third theme is that women are Other. As such, women are unknown, problematic, perhaps dangerous, and certainly deficient. In the realm of women's sexuality, arrangements are established whereby women's sexuality can be controlled and channeled in the service of a man's experience. Many of these arrangements are internalized by women themselves.

Feminist answers to these problems will involve resistance to received wisdom and the current social constructions of women's sexuality. Resistance means creating a dialogue that occurs outside as well as within normative bounds. Asking questions and giving voice are tactics that can validate women's experience and promote agency for women. Society will not thank women for engaging in such dialogue, nor will society make it easy.

REFERENCES

Abramson, P. R., & Mechanic, M. B. (1983). Sex and the media: Three decades of best-selling books and major motion pictures. *Archives of Sexual Behavior, 12*, 185–206.

Abush, R., & Burkhead, J. E. (1984). Job stress in midlife working women: Relationships among personality type, job characteristics, and job tension. *Journal of Counseling Psychology, 31*, 36–44.

Ackerman, R. J. (1990). Career developments and transitions of middle-aged women. Special issue: Women at midlife and beyond. *Psychology of Women Quarterly, 14*, 513–530.

Adams, C. G., & Turner, B. F. (1985). Reported change in sexuality from young adulthood to old age. *Journal of Sex Research, 21*, 126–141.

Adelmann, P. K., Antonucci, T. C., Crohan, S. E., & Coleman, L. M. (1989).

Empty nest, cohort, and employment in the well-being of midlife women. *Sex Roles, 20,* 173–189.

Adelmann, P. K., Antonucci, T. C., Crohan, S. E., & Coleman, L. M. (1990). A causal analysis of employment and health in midlife women. *Women and Health, 16,* 5–20.

Allgeier, A. R. (1983). Sexuality and gender roles in the second half of life. In E. R. Allgeier & N. B. McCormick (Eds.), *Changing boundaries: Gender roles and sexual behavior* (pp. 112–123). Palo Alto, CA: Mayfield Publishing Company.

Anstett, P. (1994, December 14). New study will help doctors give better advice on estrogen treatment. *Detroit Free Press,* 17.

Avis, N. E., & McKinlay, S. M. (1991). A longitudinal analysis of women's attitudes toward the menopause: Results from the Massachusetts women's health study. *Maturitas, 13,* 65–79.

Bachmann, G. A., & Leiblum, S. R. (1991). Sexuality in sexagenarian women. *Maturitas, 13,* 43–50.

Bachmann, G. A., Leiblum, S. R., Kemmann, E., Colburn, D. W., Swartzman, L., & Shelden, R. (1984). Sexual expression and its determinants in the postmenopausal woman. *Maturitas, 6,* 19–29.

Ballinger, C. B. (1990). Psychiatric aspects of the menopause. *British Journal of Psychiatry, 156,* 773–787.

Beyene, Y. (1986). Cultural significance and physiological manifestations of menopause: A biocultural analysis. Anthropological approaches to menopause: Questioning received wisdom. [Special issue] *Culture, Medicine, and Psychiatry, 10,* 47–71.

Bowles, C. (1990). The menopausal experience: Sociocultural influences and theoretical models. In R. Formanek (Ed.), *The meanings of menopause: Historical, medical, and clinical perspectives* (pp. 157–177). Hillsdale, NJ: Analytic Press.

Bretschneider, J. G., & McCoy, N. L. (1988). Sexual interest and behavior in healthy 80- to 102-year-olds. *Archives of Sexual Behavior, 17,* 109–129.

Chrisler, J. C., Torrey, J. W., & Matthes, M. M. (1991). Brittle bones and sagging breasts, loss of femininity and loss of sanity: The media describe the menopause. In A. M. Voda & R. Conover (Eds.), *Proceedings of the 8th conference of the Society for Menstrual Cycle Research* (pp. 23–35). Salt Lake City, UT: Society for Menstrual Cycle Research.

Colditz, G. A., Haninson, S. E., Hunter, D. J., Willitt, W. C., Manson, J. E., Stampfer, M. J., Hennekens, C., Rosner, B., & Speizer, F. E. (1995). The use of estrogens and progestins and the risk of breast cancer in postmenopausal women. *New England Journal of Medicine, 332,* 1589–1593.

Cole, E., & Rothblum, E. (1990). Commentary on "Sexuality and the midlife woman." Women at midlife and beyond. [Special Issue] *Psychology of Women Quarterly, 14,* 509–512.

Comfort, A. C. (1974). Sexuality in old age. *Journal of the American Geriatric Society, 22,* 440–442.

Cowan, G., Warren, L. W., & Young, J. L. (1985). Medical perceptions of menopausal symptoms. *Psychology of Women Quarterly, 1,* 3–14.

Cutler, W. B., Garcia, C. R., & McCoy, N. (1987). Perimenopausal sexuality. *Archives of Sexual Behavior, 16,* 225–234.

Dan, A. J., Wilbur, J., Hendricks, C., O'Connor, E., & Holm, K. (1990). Lifelong physical activity in midlife and older women. Women at midlife and beyond. [Special issue] *Psychology of Women Quarterly, 14,* 531–542.

Datan, N. (1986). Corpses, lepers, and menstruating women: Tradition, transition, and the sociology of knowledge. *Sex Roles, 14,* 693–702.

Datan, & Rodeheaver, D. (1983). Beyond generativity: Toward a sensuality of later life. In R. B. Weg (Ed.), *Sexuality in the later years: Roles and behavior* (pp. 279–288). New York: Academic Press.

DeLorey, C. (1992). Differing perspectives of menopause: An attribution theory approach. In A. J. Dan & Linda L. Lewis (Eds.), *Menstrual health in women's lives* (pp. 198–205). Chicago: University of Illinois Press.

Dennis, C. (1997, August). El secreto de las parejas que disfrutan el sexo. *Buenhogar, 328,* 80–82.

Dickson, G. L. (1990). A feminist poststructuralist analysis of the knowledge of menopause. *Advanced Nursing Science, 12(3),* 15–31.

Erdwins, C. J., & Mellinger, J. C. (1984). Mid-life women: Relationship of age and role to personality. *Journal of Personality and Social Psychology, 47,* 390–395.

Facchinetti, F., Demyttenaere, K., Fioroni, L., Neri, J., & Genazzani, A. R. (1992). Psychosomatic disorders related to gynecology. *Psychotherapy and Psychosomatic, 58,* 137–154.

Flint, M. (1982). Male and female menopause. In A. M. Voda, M. Dinnerstein, & S. R. O'Donnell (Eds.), *Changing perspectives on menopause* (pp. 363–375). Austin: University of Texas Press.

Frank, S. J., Towell, P. A., & Huyck, M. (1985). The effects of sex-role traits on three aspects of psychological well-being in a sample of middle-aged women. *Sex-Roles, 12,* 1073–1087.

Friedman, A., & Pines, A. M. (1992). Increase in Arab women's perceived power in the second half of life. *Sex-Roles, 26,* 1–9.

Frock, J., & Money, J. (1992). Sexuality and menopause. *Psychotherapy Psychosom, 57,* 29–33.

Gannon, L. (1988). The potential role of exercise in the alleviation of menstrual disorders and menopausal symptoms: A theoretical synthesis of recent research. *Women and Health, 14,* 105–127.

Gannon, L., & Ekstrom, B. (1993). Attitudes toward menopause: The influence of sociocultural paradigms. *Psychology of Women Quarterly, 17,* 275–288.

Garnett, T., Studd, J. W., Henderson, A., Watson, N., Savvas, M., & Leather, A. (1990). Hormone implants and tachyphylaxis. *British Journal of Obstetrics and Gynaecology, 97,* 917–921.

Genevay, B. (1982). In praise of older women. In M. Kirkpatrick (Ed.), *Women's sexual experience: Explorations of the dark continent* (pp. 87–101). New York: Plenum Press.

George, T. (1988). Menopause: Some interpretations of the results of a study among a non-western group. *Maturitas, 10,* 109–116.

Gergen, M. (1989). Talking about menopause: A dialogic analysis. In L. E. Thomas (Ed.), *Adulthood and Aging* (pp. 65–87). Albany: State University of New York Press.

Gergen, M. (1990). Finished at 40: Women's development within the patriarchy. Women at midlife and beyond. [Special issue] *Psychology of Women Quarterly, 14,* 471–493.

Gergen, M. (1994). Part I. Public documents as sources of social constructions: The social construction of personal histories: Gender lives in popular auto-biographies. In T. R. Sarbin & J. I. Kitsuse (Eds.), *Constructing the social* (pp. 19–43). Thousand Oaks, CA: Sage.

Goldstein, M. K., & Teng, N. N. H. (1991). Gynecologic factors in sexual dysfunction of the older women. *Geriatric Sexuality, 7,* 41–61.

Greendale, G. A., & Judd, H. L. (1993). The menopause: Health implications and clinical management. *Journal of the American Geriatrics Society, 41,* 426–436.

Greene, J. G., & Cooke, D. J. (1980). Life stress and symptoms at the climacterium. *British Journal of Psychiatry, 136,* 486–491.

Hagstad, A. (1988). Gynecology and sexuality in middle-aged women. *Women and Health, 13,* 57–79.

Hallstrom, T., & Samuelsson, S. (1990). Changes in women's sexual desire in middle life: The longitudinal study of women in gothenburg. *Archives of Sexual Behavior, 19,* 259–268.

Harris, R. L., Ellicott, A. M., & Holmes, D. S. (1986). The timing of psychosocial transitions and changes in women's lives: An examination of women aged 45–60. *Journal of Personality and Social Psychology, 51,* 409–416.

Hawton, K., Gath, D., & Day, A. (1994). Sexual function in a community sample of middle-aged women with partners: Effects of age, marital, socioeconomic, psychiatric, gynecological, and menopausal factors. *Archives of Sexual Behavior, 23,* 375–395.

Helson, R. (1992). Women's difficult times and the rewriting of the life story. *Psychology of Women Quarterly, 16,* 331–347.

Huerta, R., Mena, A., Malacara, J. M., & Diaz-de-Leon, J. (1995). Symptoms at perimenopausal period: Its association with attitudes toward sexuality, lifestyle, family function, and FSH levels. *Psychoneuroendocrinology, 20,* 135–148.

Hyde, J. (1996). *Half the human experience: The psychology of women* (5th ed.). Lexington, MA: DC Heath.

Jessee, J. (1993, December). The menopause myth. *Working Woman, 18,* 82–100.

Jones, J. (1994). Embodied meaning: Menopause and the change of life. *Social Work in Health Care, 19,* 43–65.

Kaplan, H. (1990). Sex, intimacy, and the aging process. *Journal of the American Academy of Psychoanalysis, 18,* 185–205.

Kaufert, P. (1982). Myth and the menopause. *Sociology of Health and Illness, 4*, 141–166.

Kaufert, P. A., & McKinlay, S. M. (1985). Estrogen-replacement therapy: The production of medical knowledge and the emergence of policy. In E. Lewin & V. Olesen (Eds.), *Women, health, and healing: Toward a new perspective* (pp. 113–138). London: Tavistock.

Kelsea, M. (1991). Beyond the stethoscope: A nurse practitioner looks at menopause and midlife. In D. Taylor & A. Sumrall (Eds.), *Women of the 14th moon: Writings on menopause* (pp. 268–279). Freedom, CA: The Crossing Press.

Kobosa-Munro, L. (1977). Sexuality in the aging woman. *Health and Social Work, 2*, 70–88.

Koff, E., Rierdan, J., & Stubbs, M. L. (1990). Conceptions and misconceptions of the menstrual cycle. *Women and Health, 16*, 119–136.

Koster, A., & Garde, K. (1993). Sexual desire and menopausal development: A prospective study of Danish women born in 1936. *Maturitas, 16*, 49–60.

Lennon, M. C. (1987). Is menopause depression? An investigation of three perspectives. *Sex Roles, 17*, 1–16.

Leiblum, S. R. (1990). Sexuality and the midlife woman. Women at Midlife and beyond. [Special issue] *Psychology of Women Quarterly, 14*, 495–508.

Lindgren, R., Berg, G., Hammar, M., & Zuccon, E. (1993). Hormonal replacement therapy and sexuality in a population of Swedish postmenopausal women. *Acta Obstetrica Gynecol. Scandinavia, 72*, 292–297.

Lobo, R. A., McCormick, W., Singer, F., & Roy, S. (1984). Depomedroxyprogesterone acetate compared with conjugated estrogens for the treatment of postmenopausal women. *Journal of the American College of Obstetrics and Gynecology, 127*, 572–180.

Lock, M. (1986). Ambiguities of aging: Japanese experience and perceptions of menopause. Anthropological approaches to menopause: Questioning received wisdom. [Special issue] *Culture, Medicine, and Psychiatry, 10*, 23–46.

Lock, M. (1994). Menopause in cultural context. *Experimental Gerontology, 29*, 307–317.

Malatesta, V. J., Chambless, D. L., Pollack, M., & Cantor, A. (1988). Widowhood, sexuality and aging: A life span analysis. *Journal of Sex & Marital Therapy, 14*, 49–62.

Mansfield, P. K. (1988). Midlife childbearing: Strategies for informed decision-making. Women's health: Our minds, our bodies. [Special issue] *Psychology of Women Quarterly, 12*, 445–460.

Mansfield, P. K., & Voda, A. M. (1993). From Edith Bunker to the 6:00 news: How and what midlife women learn about menopause. *Women and Therapy, 14*, 89–104.

Martin, M. C., Block, J. E., Sanchez, S. D., Arnaud, C. D., & Beyene, Y. (1993). Menopause without symptoms: The endocrinology of menopause among rural Mayan Indians. *American Journal of Obstetrics and Gynecology, 168*, 1839–1845.

Masters, W. H., & Johnson, V. E. (1966). *Human Sexual Response*. Boston: Little, Brown.

Matthews, K. A. (1992). Myths and realities of the menopause. *Psychosomatic Medicine, 54*, 1–9.

Matthews, K., Kuller, L., Wing, R., & Jansen-McWilliams, L. (1997, August). *Premenopausal characteristics of long term users of postmenopausal estrogen replacement therapy*. Paper presented at the annual meeting of the American Psychological Association, Chicago, IL.

Matthews, K., Wing, R., Kuller, L., Meilahn, E., Kelsey, S., Costello, E., & Caggiula, A. (1990). Influences of natural menopause on psychological characteristics and symptoms of middle-aged healthy women. *Journal of Consulting and Clinical Psychology, 58*, 345–351.

McCormick, N. B. (1994). *Sexual salvation: Affirming women's sexual rights and pleasures*. Wesport, CT: Praeger.

McCracken, A. L. (1988). Sexual practice by elders: The forgotten aspect of functional health. *Journal of Gerontological Nursing, 14*, 13–17.

McKinlay, S. M., Brambilla, D. J., & Posner, J. G. (1992). The normal menopause transition. *Maturitas, 14*, 103–115.

McKinlay, J., McKinlay, S., & Brambilla, D. (1987). Health status and utilization behavior associated with menopause. *American Journal of Epidemiology, 25*, 110–121.

Montgomery, J. C., Appleby, L., Brincat, M., Versi, E., Tapp, A., Fenwick, P. B. C., & Studd, J. W. W. (1987). Effect of oestrogen and testosterone implants on psychological disorder in the climacteric. *Lancet, 1*, 297–299.

Morokoff, P. (1988). Sexuality in perimenopausal and postmenopausal women. *Psychology of Women Quarterly, 12*, 489–511.

Nathanson, C. A. (1991). *Dangerous passage: The social control of sexuality in women's adolescence*. Philadelphia, PA: Temple University Press.

Nathorst-Boos, J., Wiklund, I., Mattsson, L. A., Sandin, K., & von Schoultz, B. (1993). Is sexual life influenced by transdermal estrogen therapy? A double blind placebo controlled study in postmenopausal women. *Acta Obstetrica Gynecol. Scandinavia, 72*, 656–660.

Neugarten, B., & Kraines, R. (1965). Menopausal symptoms in women of various ages. *Psychosomatic Medicine, 27*, 266–273.

Nilsson, L. (1987). Sexuality in the elderly. *Acta Obset. Gynecol. Scand Suppl., 140*, 52–58.

Oliver, M. B., & Hyde, J. S. (1993). Gender differences in sexuality: A meta-analysis. *Psychological Bulletin, 114*, 29–51.

Padgett, D. (1988). Aging minority women: Issues in research and health policy. *Women and Health, 14*, 213–225.

Peck, T. (1986). Women's self-definition in adulthood: From a different model? *Psychology of Women Quarterly, 10*, 274–284.

Pfeiffer, E., Verwoerdt, A., & Wang, H-S. (1968). Sexual behavior in aged men and women. *Archives of General Psychiatry, 19*, 753–758.

Porcino, J. (1985). Psychological aspects of aging in women. *Signs, 10*, 115–122.

Raymond, J. (1986). *A passion for friends: Toward a philosophy of female affection.* Boston: Beacon Press.

Reiss, I. L. (1986). *Journey into sexuality: An exploratory voyage.* Englewood Cliffs, NJ: Prentice Hall.

Reyniak, J. V. (1987). Sexual and other concerns of the women with osteoporosis. *Medical Aspects of Human Sexuality, 21*, 161–167.

Riley, A. J. (1991). Sexuality and menopause. *Sexual and Marital Therapy, 6*, 135–146.

Rosen, R. C., & Beck, J. G. (1988). *Patterns of sexual arousal: Psychophysiological processes and clinical applications.* New York: Guilford Press.

Rostosky S. S., & Travis, C. B. (1996). Menopause and the dominance of the biomedical model 1984–1994. *Psychology of Women Quarterly, 20*, 285–312.

Rountree, C. (1993). *On women turning fifty: Celebrating mid-life discoveries.* New York: Harper & Row.

Rubin, L. B. (1982). Sex and sexuality: Women at midlife. In M. Kirkpatrick (Ed.), *Women's sexual experience: Explorations of the dark continent* (pp. 61–82). New York: Plenum Press.

Ryff, C. (1985). The subjective experience of lifespan transitions. In A. Rossi (Ed.), *Gender and the life course* (pp. 97–113). Chicago, IL: Aldine.

Ryff, C. D., & Migdal, S. (1984). Intimacy and generativity: Self-perceived transitions. *Signs, 9*, 470–481.

Sanchez-Ayendez, M. (1988). Puerto Rican elderly women: The cultural dimension of social support networks. *Women and Health, 14*, 239–252.

Sand, G. (1993). *Is it hot in here or is it me? A personal look at the facts, fallacies, and feelings of menopause.* New York: HarperCollins.

Sarrel, P. M. (1990). Sexuality and menopause. *Obstetrics and Gynecology, 75*, 26s–35s.

Sarrel, P. M., & Whitehead, M. I. (1985). Sex and menopause: Defining the issues. *Maturitas, 7*, 217–224.

Schlossberg, N. (1981). A model for analyzing human adaptation to transition. *The Counseling Psychologist, 9*, 2–18.

Sheehy, G. (1991). *The silent passage.* New York: Random House.

Sherwin, B. B., & Gelfand, M. M. (1987). The role of androgen in the maintenance of sexual functioning in oophorectomized women. *Psychosomatic Medicine, 47*, 339–351.

Sherwin, B. B., & Gelfand, M. M. (1989). A prospective one-year study of estrogen and progestin in postmenopausal women: Effects on clinical symptoms and lipoprotein lipids. *Obstetrics & Gynecology, 73*, 759–766.

Sherwin, B. B., Gelfand, M. M., & Brender, W. (1985). Androgen enhances sexual motivation in females: A prospective, crossover study of sex steroid administration in surgical menopause. *Psychosomatic Medicine, 47,* 339–351.

Sherwin, S. (1992). *No longer patient: Feminist ethics and health care.* Philadelphia, PA: Temple University Press.

Sourander, L. B. (1994). Geriatric aspects of estrogen effects and sexuality. *Gerontology, 40* (supp. 3), 14–17.

Stewart, A. J., & Gold-Steinberg, S. (1990). Midlife women's political consciousness: Case studies of psychosocial development and political commitment. Women at midlife and beyond. [Special issue] *Psychology of Women Quarterly, 14,* 543–566.

Takacs, L. (1991). The therapy of menopausal depression with hormonal substitution. 14th Danube Symposium of Psychiatry (Budapest, Hungary). *Psychiatria Danubina, 3,* 287–289.

Tiefer, L. (1995). *Sex is not a natural act and other essays.* Boulder, CO: Westview Press.

Tinsley, E. G., Sullivan-Guest, S., & McGuire, J. (1984). Feminine sex-role and depression in middle-aged women. *Sex-Roles, 11,* 25–32.

Todd, J., Friedman, A., & Kariuki, P. W. (1990). Women growing stronger with age: The effect of status in the United States and Kenya. Women at midlife and beyond. [Special issue] *Psychology of Women Quarterly, 14,* 567–577.

Udvardy, M. (1992). The fertility of the post-fertile: Concepts of gender, aging, and reproductive health among the Giriama of Kenya. *Journal of Cross-Cultural Gerontology, 7,* 289–306.

Vaillant, G. E., & Vaillant, C. O. (1990). Determinants and consequences of creativity in a cohort of gifted women. Women at Midlife and Beyond. [Special issue] *Psychology of Women Quarterly, 14,* 607–616.

Waldron, I., & Herold, J. (1986). Employment, attitudes toward employment, and women's health. *Women and Health, 11,* 79–98.

Walling, M., Andersen, B. L., & Johnson, S. R. (1990). Hormonal replacement therapy for postmenopausal women: A review of sexual outcomes and related gynecologic effects. *Archives of Sexual Behavior, 19,* 119–137.

Waller, R. J. (1992). *The bridges of madison county.* New York: Warner Books.

Woods, N. F. (1993). Midlife women's health: There's more to it than menopause (pp. 164–196). Annual Review of Women's Health. National League of Nursing Publications.

III

MEANING AND FUNCTION

9

ONLY JOKING: HUMOR AND SEXUALITY

MARY CRAWFORD

In a California university, a professor circulates a memo to faculty proposing a faculty–student conference room outfitted with an inflatable Madonna doll and a waterbed, for innovative conferences with women students. When he is reprimanded by the university's faculty representative on sexual harassment, he calls her a "nasty, scheming, backstabbing bitch." The waterbed memo, he says, was only a joke (Wilson, 1995).

A 7-year-old boy comes home from summer day camp and eagerly tells his mother a farmer's daughter joke: the farmer "stuffs razor blades up her pussy to hurt these guys when they do it with her. The three guys are American, Indian, and Polish" (Arcana, 1994).

In describing the sexual humor of U.S. southern women, folklorist Rayna Green (1977) tells of the time her sister, observing their grandmother stepping out of the bathtub, commented that the hair on the older woman's privates was getting rather sparse. Granny retorted, "Grass don't grow on a racetrack" (p. 31).

What do these incidents have in common? Each could be described

Much of the content of this chapter appears in somewhat different form in my 1995 book *Talking Difference: On Gender and Language*. (London: Sage).

213

as "only joking." Whether you consider them funny or outrageous (indeed, whether you classify them as humor at all) depends on your interpretation of their meaning and the speakers' intentions—what you believe the speakers were trying to do.

People use humor every day in ways that have many implications for the social construction of sexuality. When they tell a dirty joke, use a flip remark as an assertion of sexual autonomy, or express sexual hostility with a smile and the disclaimer, "just kidding," people use humor to teach, recreate, and sometimes to subvert gender norms. A social constructionist approach tells us that to understand sexuality we must look to its creation in culture, including the most mundane, taken-for-granted aspects of culture. In this chapter I will explore how people talk about sexuality in everyday interaction. I will first review how a social constructionist approach to gender allows us to conceptualize gender as a system of social relations rather than an attribute of individuals. I will then focus on how people use humor in everyday life to negotiate sexual meanings and understandings.

A SOCIAL CONSTRUCTIONIST APPROACH TO SEXUALITY AND ITS REPRESENTATION IN HUMOR

The social constructionist views gender as a system of meaning that organizes interactions and governs access to power and resources. From this view, gender is not an attribute of individuals but a way of making sense of transactions. Gender exists not in persons but in transactions; it is conceptualized as a verb, not a noun. Feminist sociologists, starting with Candace West and Don Zimmerman (1987), speak of "doing gender," and feminist psychologists have adopted the term to designate how sex is a salient social and cognitive category through which information is filtered, selectively processed, and differentially acted on to produce self-fulfilling prophecies about women and men (Crawford & Unger, 1992, 2000).

The social constructionist approach may be contrasted with an essentialist approach. Essentialism views gender as a fundamental, essential part of the individual, a set of properties residing in one's personality, self-concept, or traits. Gender is something women and men *have* or *are*; it is a noun (Bohan, 1993). Essentialism does not necessarily imply biological determinism, or even necessarily stress the importance of biological underpinnings for gender-specific characteristics (although historically this has been a prevalent form of essentialism with respect to sex, sexuality, and gender). Rather, it is the location of characteristics within the individual and not their origins (socialized or biological) that defines essentialism. Essentialist models "portray gender in terms of fundamental attributes which are conceived as internal, persistent, and generally separate from the ongoing experience of interaction with the daily socio-political contexts of one's life" (Bohan, 1993, p. 7). These fundamental attributes, (which make up masculinity and femininity), are believed to determine gendered roles and actions.

Janis Bohan (1993, p. 7) illustrates the difference between essentialist and social constructionist modes of thought:

> [C]onsider the difference between describing an individual as friendly and describing a conversation as friendly. In the former case, "friendly" is construed as a trait of the person, an "essential" component to her or his personality. In the latter, "friendly" describes the nature of the interaction occurring between or among people. Friendly here has a particular meaning that is agreed upon by the participants, that is compatible with its meaning to their social reference groups, and that is reaffirmed by the process of engaging in this interaction. Although the essentialist view of gender sees it as analogous to the friendly person, the constructionist sees gender as analogous to the friendly conversation.
>
> If friendly were gendered, an essentialist position might argue that women are more friendly than men. Whether this quality came from biological imperatives, from socialization, or from a combination of both, it is now a trait of women. A constructionist position would argue that the gendering of friendly transactions is the product of social agreements about the appropriateness of certain behavior. The differential exposure of men and women to those contexts that elicit friendly behavior results in a linkage between sex and friendliness, and friendliness becomes gendered.

Gender-related processes influence behavior, thoughts, and feelings in individuals; they affect interactions among individuals; and they help determine the structure of social institutions. The processes by which differences are created and power is allocated can be understood by considering how gender is played out at three levels: societal, interpersonal, and individual.

All known societies recognize biological differentiation and use it as the basis for social distinctions. Although there is considerable variability in the genetic, hormonal, and anatomical factors that form the basis for the label male or female, they are treated for social purposes as dichotomous categories (Crawford & Unger, 1992, 2000). Gender is what culture makes out of the raw material of (already socially constructed) biological sex. The process of creating gendered human beings starts at birth. The newborn infant's vagina or penis represents sex—and, in middle-class Western society, if the genitals should be ambiguous, medical science is recruited to surgically eliminate the troublesome variability. The pink or blue blanket that soon enfolds the baby represents gender. The blanket serves as a cue that this infant is to be treated as boy or girl, not as a generic human, from the start.

The Social Structural Level: Gender as a System of Power Relations

Men have more public power in most societies, controlling government, law, public discourse, and academics. Alternative views of gender relations are culturally muted, and ideologies of gender can be represented and reproduced as "objective facts" (Fine, 1985). Conceptualizing women as a culturally muted group (cf. Kramarae, 1981) implies that researchers must make special efforts to uncover and understand their systems of meanings. Understanding gender at the structural level involves this sort of searching for suppressed meanings. It also involves analyzing the representation of women, men, and gender relations in the mass media.

It is easy to show that popular humor about the sexes reflects dominant cultural values of misogyny. Later in this chapter I will describe specific examples. It is less easy to see how academic disciplines maintain those values through the questions they ask, their modes of research, and their interpretations of results. Most psychologists are well trained in the methods of their discipline but not in analyzing its assumptions about nature and culture or how these assumptions lead to particular conceptions of evidence and truth.

Elsewhere, I have analyzed how psychological research on humor has represented the typical woman as a person who lacks the ability to appreciate humor and the wit to create it (Crawford, 1989; Crawford & Gressley, 1991). Much of this research functions to support dominant cultural representations of women as deficient or inferior to a male norm.

There has been little research on the social functions of humor. This area is particularly interesting from a feminist perspective because humor has the potential to infiltrate and disrupt dominant meanings. When messages are delivered in the form of humor, they can have an impact greater than that of more literal or serious talk. Although most humor probably functions to maintain the social order, I will show how its subversive potential has been recognized and used by women, including women who are doubly marginalized because they are lesbians or women of color, or both.

The Interpersonal Level: Gender as a Cue

Gender cues are used to tell us how to behave toward others in social interactions, although much of this sex-differential treatment happens outside awareness. The behavior of men and boys is often evaluated more positively than the behavior of women and girls. Even when a woman and a man behave in identical ways, their behavior may be interpreted differently (Crawford, 1988; Porter & Geis, 1981; Wallston & O'Leary, 1981; Wiley & Eskilson, 1982; Yarkin, Town, & Wallston, 1982).

Moreover, sexual categorization is not simply a way of seeing differences, but a way of creating differences. When men and women are treated differently in ordinary daily interactions, they may come to behave differently in return. Thus, gender can be conceived as a self-fulfilling prophecy —a set of processes by which gender difference is created, the observed differences are conflated with sex, and belief in sex difference is confirmed.

An example of self-fulfilling prophecies in conversational interaction comes from a laboratory social psychology experiment[1] (Snyder, Tanke, & Berscheid, 1977). Male college students were shown a photograph of a woman who was either conventionally attractive or unattractive, and they then had a short telephone conversation with her. The men were unaware that there was no relationship between the photograph they saw and the woman they talked to. The women, in turn, were unaware that their conversational partners had received any information about their heterosexual attractiveness. Nevertheless, judges who later heard only the women's part of the conversations rated those women who had been talked to as though they were attractive as more friendly, sociable, and likable than those who had been talked to as though they were unattractive.

By abstracting some features of social interaction from their normal context, the study shows how social actors can create their own social reality even in brief encounters. Presumably, men who thought they were interacting with attractive women spoke in ways that cued more socially engaged and friendly behaviors from their conversational partners, perhaps because they shared the widespread belief that "what is beautiful is good" (Dion, Berscheid, & Walster, 1972). The men produced the behaviors they expected through their talk and probably confirmed their belief in a link between attractiveness and positive personality traits in women. Yet the traits they believed in were produced by their own modes of social interaction.

At the interactional level, conversational humor about sex and heterosexual relationships can function to create and maintain gender relations, and, under some conditions, to subvert them. The key to understanding how these constructions of gender and sexuality are accomplished is that people use humor to convey messages that they can then deny, or develop further, depending on how the message is received. Because it is indirect and allusive, humor protects the joker from the consequences that his or her statement would have if conveyed more directly and seriously. For this reason, initial sexual overtures are often made in humorous ways—

---

[1]Feminists are critical of the construct of attractiveness as it has been used in social psychological research. It objectifies women and privileges heterosexuality. This study certainly exemplifies those limitations, as well as demonstrating the manipulation and deception of research participants. Although the experiment exemplifies many weaknesses of a positivist approach to knowledge generation, I cite it here as a compelling example of how self-fulfilling prophecies are created in social interaction. As I have argued elsewhere, it is one of the paradoxes we live with that static, decontextualized laboratory research can be useful in exposing dynamic, context-dependent social constructions (cf. Crawford & Unger, in press, chapter 3.)

a big part of flirting consists of joking comments that assess the potential partner's availability without committing either partner to follow up (Mulkay, 1988).

Other sensitive topics, too, are brought into conversation through humor. In medical settings, humor enables staff and patients to interact around the topics of fear, pain, and even death. Franca Pizzini (1991) analyzed humor generated in 100 observations of conversations surrounding childbirth in the maternity wards of five hospitals in Milan, Italy. Pizzini noted the topic of humor, its initiators and targets, and the social functions it served. She found that most humor in the childbirth setting functions to introduce the two taboo topics related to birth: pain and sex. Even as they work on the sexual parts of a woman's body, the staff are not permitted to openly connect what is happening to her with sexual activity. Nor are they taught to openly acknowledge her pain. Therefore, both topics are dealt with in the humor mode, where the talk "need not become part of the history of the encounter, nor need it be . . . built into the meaning of subsequent acts. Because humor officially does not count, persons are induced to risk sending messages that would be unacceptable if stated seriously" (Pizzini, 1991, p. 481).

In the birth episodes, there were jokes about the woman's vagina, with medical staff interpreting suturing of an episiotomy as "making it new again," or "tailoring." Pain was sexualized in remarks that encoded both taboo topics:

> A woman became taut with pain during post-partum cleaning and the nurse said with a smile: "Do you act this way when your husband touches you too?" The patient shook her head in disagreement. A nurse said: "Naughty girl, when her husband touches her she's all relaxed, but when we touch her she gets tense!" (Pizzini, 1991, p. 481)

People choose indirect speech styles in delicate situations. Indirectness can save face, minimize accountability for one's actions, and slip taboo topics into conversation. Humor is perhaps the most flexible and powerful of indirect modes, and sexually focused encounters perhaps the most complex of interpersonal situations. It is not surprising that people so often cope with sexual ambiguity, vulnerability, and danger by using humor. Nor is it surprising that gendered power plays in interaction are so often framed as humor: If the power move is challenged, the speaker's intent can readily be denied.

Christine Griffin (1989, p. 173) recorded a conversation on a train in which three women were discussing their work as reference librarians. The male companion of one interrupted with the following joke: "What's the difference between a feminist and a bin liner? A bin liner gets taken out once a week." The joke, which was totally unrelated to the women's topic, was greeted by silence, not laughter. Having interrupted the flow of conversation, the man then introduced a different, unrelated topic and took an active part in the conversation. In this case, the intrusive use of disparaging humor allowed the speaker to gain attention and conversational control.

The Individual Level: Gender as Masculinity and Femininity

Within the discourse of gender, certain traits, behaviors, and interests are associated with women, and others with men. Gender is assumed to be dichotomous—a person can be classified as either masculine or feminine but not both—and to reside within the individual. Moreover, the masculine pole of this constructed dichotomy is the more valued.

People develop their sense of self within prevailing discourses, including the discourse of gender (Shotter & Gergen, 1989). To a greater or lesser extent, women and men come to accept gender distinctions visible at the structural level and enacted at the interpersonal level as part of the self-concept. They become gender-typed, ascribing to themselves the traits, behaviors, and roles normative for people of their gender in their culture.

At the individual level, gender is re-created when women internalize their devaluation and subordination. Feminist theories of personality development (e.g., Miller, 1986) stress that feminine characteristics such as passivity, excessive concern with pleasing others, lack of initiative, and dependency are psychological consequences of subordination. Members of subordinate social groups who adopt such characteristics are considered well-adjusted, even though the characteristics would not be considered healthy for adult men. Those who do not adopt such characteristics are controlled by psychiatric diagnosis, violence, or the threat of violence, and social ostracism.

Gender, then, is a self-fulfilling prophecy (Crawford & Unger, 1992; 2000). Women *are* different from men. Yet, paradoxically, this is not because they are women (Bohan, 1993). Each of us behaves in gendered ways because we are placed in gendered social contexts. Women encounter different social contexts than men. Women and men face different expectations and norms even for what look like identical situations. If women try not to do gender, they confront the social consequences of violating these norms and expectations.

Keeping Sight of the System

I have conceptualized gender as a system operating at three levels in order to provide a heuristic for examining how sexuality is constructed in mundane interaction, and how the interactional level functions in conjunction with social structural and individual aspects of gender. I hope that this approach will foster thinking across disciplinary boundaries. Gender at the social structural level has traditionally been the province of sociolinguistics, sociology, anthropology, and mass communication studies, whereas the interactional level has been encompassed by social psychology and interpersonal communication studies, and the individual level by clinical, developmental, and personality psychology. In studying any aspect of gender, including sexuality, each researcher must focus on one level, but it is best to keep sight of the system as a whole. Moreover, I hope that conceptualizing gender as a social system will help researchers who focus on gender and sexuality recognize that they share conceptual and methodological concerns with those attempting to understand other systems of social classification, such as age, race, and class.

Ordinary talk is a powerful resource that is brought to bear in influencing other people, enlisting their help, offering them companionship, protecting ourselves from their demands, saving face, justifying our behavior, establishing important relationships, and presenting ourselves as having the qualities that they (and we) admire. The study of everyday talk and its functions is an example of analysis at the interactional level. However, when examining talk at this level, it is especially important to keep sight of the gender system as a whole. Talk makes use of a pre-existing set of rules for interaction that can be analyzed at the structural level. Talk creates self-fulfilling prophecies that become internalized at the individual level. All the levels of the gender system interact. The reality constructed through language forms the basis of social organization (Crawford, 1995; Heritage, 1984; Potter & Wetherell, 1987).

CONSTRUCTIONS: HOW SEXUAL HUMOR MAINTAINS A SEXIST SOCIAL ORDER

Sexual Humor and Male Dominance

Michael Mulkay (1988) has examined the representation of women in men's sexual humor by analyzing dirty jokes (collected by folklore researchers) and comic routines in British pubs (observed by ethnographers). The assumptions underlying men's sexual humor, and the ways in which it represents male–female relationships, may function both to express male dominance and to support and strengthen it. Mulkay outlined four basic themes in this sexual humor:

1. The primacy of intercourse—all men want is sex.
2. The availability of women—all women are sexually available to all men even when they pretend not to be.
3. The objectification of women—women exist to meet men's needs, and are, or should be, passive.

4. The subordination of women's discourse—women must be silenced.

It is easy to find examples of male sexual humor based on these four principles. Currently, a popular format for sexual humor is "beer is better than women" one-liners. To my knowledge, they first appeared on North American college campuses, and spread to T-shirts, bumper stickers, and formal publication. Examples from a book include "beer is better than women because

> beer doesn't expect an hour of foreplay before satisfying you.
> you can try dark beers and lite (sic) beers without upsetting your parents. (This line was illustrated with a caricature of an African American and a White woman.)
> a beer doesn't change its mind after you've taken off its top.
> a beer never wants to stay up afterwards talking about respect. (Brooks, Hanbery, Matz, Westover, & Westover, 1988)

In this humor, the male voice always triumphs over the female voice. "In men's dirty jokes, it is not only women's bodies and services that are at men's disposal, but also women's language" (Mulkay, 1988, p. 137).

The same principles operate in humor use as in representation. The mother whose young son came home from summer camp with the sexist joke described at the beginning of this chapter wrote about the issues it raised for her as a feminist parent.

> Fortunately, this happens on a day when I am so exhausted that I haven't the energy to get hysterical, so I behave calmly while I explain. This takes a long time, covering—as it must—not only women, sex, fathers and daughters, racism, profane/pornographic language, and the telling and hearing of such jokes by men and boys, but also an explanation of why, really, this "joke" isn't funny, even to him. Which he took in readily, having wondered what was funny about it, all the while laughing with a bunch of other little boys. That may be why he rushed in right off the camp bus and began to tell it to me, almost before saying hello. Maybe he was mystified by the story, by the experience. Am I always going to be there afterward? Will I continue to be willing to explain? At some point, certainly when he's older, I'm going to really resent this. I'm going to want him to be able to smell it coming like I do, to sense what's wrong, and not to laugh—even at cost to himself. I'm going to want him to do something about it, and maybe crack the glue of his male bond in the process. (Arcana, 1994, pp. 235–236)

This mother recognizes that in the telling and hearing of hostile, racist, and sexist humor, her son is being initiated into a dominant group, a group that has the privilege of using humor to silence women and negate their personhood.

Both the telling of set-piece jokes and the use of informal, spontaneous remarks can further these ends and maintain control of ongoing interaction. Michael Mulkay analyzes these uses of humor by drawing on James Spradley and Brenda Mann's classic ethnographic study of cocktail waitresses. In the bar under study, all the cocktail servers were women and all the bartenders were men. The bartenders had legitimate authority over the waitresses, but were also dependent on them. Men initiated and benefited from joking in this situation. They used it to reinforce their control over the women and deal with problems in maintaining their authority (for example, when they had made a mistake in an order). They made fun of the women's bodies with such remarks as, "It'd look better if you had some tits. Who wants to pull down a zipper just to see two fried eggs thrown against a wall?" (Mulkay, 1988, p. 148).

For women, humor was a source of frustration because it was asymmetrical—women had much less latitude in what they could say, and they knew it, as illustrated by the following reconstruction of a conversation among waitresses:

> Rob made some reference about my chest.
> Same here. But I don't know what we can do to get him back.
> Maybe we could all get together and try grabbing him.
> That's silly. We aren't strong enough and they would just make a joke about it.
> We could all ignore him, but that wouldn't work because he would just pick at us until we responded. If we ignore him, we're admitting defeat.
> There's no way we can get them back. We can't get on their level. The only way to get them back is to get on their level and you can't do that. You can't counter with some remark about the size of his penis or something without making yourself look really cheap. (Mulkay, 1988, p. 145)

Mulkay concludes from his analysis of bar talk that "men's informal humor constantly denigrates women's bodies and stresses their inferiority as social beings" (1988, p. 149). Lest we think that only bartenders do this sort of thing, it is worth noting that in a sex discrimination case against the Wall Street investment firm Goldman Sachs, an employee, Kristine Utley, testified that the office humor was a source of sexual harassment. Memos introducing new female employees were illustrated with nude *Playboy* magazine pinups, and other company memos contained "beer is better than women" jokes, for example, "because a beer always goes down easy" (Kocol, 1989). And the professor whose "humorous" memo about sex with women students opened this chapter provides another example.

In this sort of interaction, "I was only kidding! Can't you take a joke?" is a common and effective form of denial when the behavior is challenged. There is evidence that the perceived sexism of harassment incidents is related to their perceived humor—that is, sexist incidents that were seen as funny were also seen as more acceptable and less discriminatory (Bill & Naus, 1992). Perceiving and labeling an incident as humor takes it out of the serious realm and diminishes its perceived sexist impact.

Agency Within Constraints

If the discourse of sexist humor is an attempt to control women's meanings, are there effective strategies for reasserting control? Cocktail waitresses, students, and investment bankers alike can be effectively silenced when those who denigrate them have institutionalized power over them. But there are other situations in which power relations are less constraining. Street remarks from strangers, often a source of embarrassment and shame to women, serve to remind their targets that men control public spaces and that women's bodies are acceptable objects for public denigration (Gardner, 1980). But what if women respond not with shame but with counterattacks? Regina Barreca (1991) has argued that returning hostility with hostility is a legitimate form of self-defense. She suggests that when a construction worker yells, "I'd like to get into your pants, baby!" a woman should feel free to yell back, "No thanks, I've already got one asshole in there!" or "The bigger the mouth, the smaller the dick!"

Like the strategies women learn in physical self-defense classes, verbal strategies for self-defense turn the aggressor's energies back onto the aggressor. Like physical strategies, they are not natural but must be learned through practice (Russell & Fraser, 1999). Women who have internalized the myth of the humorless woman may believe that they lack creativity, a sense of humor, or the ability to take center stage in conversation, and that these deficiencies are uniquely theirs. It is important for women to recognize that what may seem like women's deficiencies actually reflect situations in which anyone, woman or man, may find it difficult to deliver a witty riposte.

When I was a graduate student, the area of psychology in which I then specialized (learning theory and animal behavior) was almost entirely sex-segregated and sex-stratified. In other words, there were far more men than women specializing in this area of research, and the higher up the academic hierarchy one looked, the fewer women were present. A substantial minority of graduate students in the field—but virtually no prominent researchers, journal editors, or senior faculty—were women.

As happens in any setting where women are but a token presence, there were many occasions on which I became the target of sexual verbal aggression. Specialized conferences in particular were troublesome because men were overrepresented by at least 10:1. At one such conference I found myself on an elevator with six men: four friends and colleagues and two strangers. I recognized one of the latter because, earlier in the day, I had attended his paper presentation on inducing tonic immobility (a response that can be seen in birds and some mammals in which they go limp, and "play dead" when attacked).

Turning to this man, I remarked that I had enjoyed his paper. He proceeded to go into a lengthy routine about how his technique worked with women, too: "Just grab them by the back of the neck and hold tight and they go glassy-eyed and stop resisting." It was an excruciating moment: between floors on an elevator, with no possibility of a dignified withdrawal, and surrounded by watching men. The effrontery of a man who publicly would make a joke of rape, and so totally without provocation (other than the presence of a lone woman), rendered me speechless. After an eternity, the elevator doors opened and we parted. My colleagues and I walked a few feet. I was red-faced and near tears with shame and humiliation. But when I finally looked up at my friends I saw that they too were red-faced and shamed. Unlike me, they had not been directly attacked, but they had been witnesses to clearly out-of-bounds behavior and had not spoken up. Finally, one mumbled, "You didn't do anything to deserve that." Like me, they had been unable to come up with a response—dignified, witty, or any other—in response to unwelcome, hostile, and aggressive humor.

In North American society, there is an implicit male norm of assertive speech that implies that normal people (a.k.a. White men) typically respond swiftly and assertively to infringements of their rights (Gervasio & Crawford, 1989). Elsewhere, I have reviewed research showing that such direct assertion is not nearly as prevalent as the standard implies (Crawford, 1995). Like the notion of universal male assertiveness, the idea that men have a universal ability to top insults or squelch another's verbal aggression is a myth. Women's alleged deficiencies in this regard are socially constructed in part by representing stereotypes of men's abilities as actualities to which women should aspire. Moreover, women and members of other subordinated groups live in different social worlds than White men of privilege. Other sites of subordination overlap with gender (color, sexual orientation, disability, age), and the assaults on subordinated people are much more frequent and intense. One can hardly imagine a situation comparable to rape jokes in an elevator that could be aimed at a White man as White man. If privileged men were presented with similar situations at a similar rate as other people, their limitations would become more evident—but, of course, if they were, they would no longer be privileged men.

RECONSTRUCTIONS: HOW HUMOR CAN SUBVERT THE SOCIAL ORDER AND CREATE NEW REALITIES

Humor in Women's Talk With Women

A few researchers have studied women's humor in all-female groups, and most have noted differences between it and the kind of humor that emerges in mixed-sex or all-male groups. The most extensive discussion of these differences is by Mercilee Jenkins (1986), who maintains that humor in all-female and all-male groups serves different functions. Women's humor supports a goal of intimacy by being supportive, compassionate, and healing, whereas men's humor supports performance goals: competition, maintaining hierarchies, and self-aggrandizement:

> Men in their groups seem to be saying, "I'm great." "I'm great, too." "Gee, we're a great bunch of guys." In contrast, women seem to be saying, "Did this ever happen to you?" "Yeah." "Oh, good, I'm not crazy." (p. 10)

Jenkins also noted a collaborative storytelling style. Instead of a single speaker holding the floor and leading up to the climax or punch line of a story in linear fashion, speakers told stories of their own experiences by first presenting the main point and then recounting the tale with the encouragement and participation of the other group members. Susan Kalcik (1975) observed a similar dynamic in women's rap groups. The kernel of a story would be told first so that hearers could participate in the telling, knowing the direction and point of the story all along in collaboration with the teller.

Women's reputation for telling jokes badly (forgetting punch lines, mixing up the sequence of the story, etc.) may reflect a male norm that does not recognize the value of cooperative storytelling (Jenkins, 1986). Although the collaborative style of storytelling is not unique to women, it may serve their interests better than more individualistic styles when they are in all-female groups.

However, we should be cautious in interpreting sex differences. Humor is a flexible speech strategy that may be used for many different conversational goals. Any approach that dichotomizes humor strategies and goals by sex is surely oversimplified. Moreover, the study of humor in women's and men's social groups creates an interpretive problem in itself. Many of the women's groups to which researchers have had access are support groups of one kind or another—rap groups, consciousness-raising groups, mothers' clubs. It is impossible to decide whether the cooperative, supportive speech styles observed occur because the participants are women or because the norms of support groups call for cooperation. In contrast, the men's groups studied have been larger and more public (e.g., pub gatherings), with different norms and goals. As so often happens in sex difference research, social context is confounded with speaker sex. One approach to the problem of separating sex from context is to study one's own social groups, where group norms and goals are understood from the inside by the researcher (Coates, 1996; Jenkins, 1986).

Because humor is so dependent on the social context, particularly shared group meanings, it is important that the humor of particular groups of women be studied by insiders to those groups. To date, there has been little systematic research on humor among lesbians, African American or other women of color, older women friends, and so on. However, several writers have speculated about the characteristic humor of some of these groups from an insider's perspective, and these speculations can provide useful starting points for future research.

Marsha Stanback (1985) has proposed that the communication style of middle-class Black women is characterized by a tendency toward equality with men. Black women have always worked outside the home, and self-reliance, strength, and autonomy for women have long been the norm within the Black community. Research on women's friendships across color lines also suggests that in pairs of Black and White friends, the Black women are typically more assertive and direct (McCullough, 1998). At the same time, Stanback argues, there is pressure toward more gender-differentiated styles due to the Black women's recognition that this is valued within White middle-class culture. The Black tradition of female outspokenness and the White ideal of femininity may present a unique set of contradictions for Black women. One way to look for the expression of these contradictions, I believe, is in the humor created by Black women in same-ethnicity and mixed-ethnicity groups.

The African American oral tradition of folktales and ballads also may provide a window into contemporary Black women's humor (Watkins, 1994). There have been many collections of these materials made by folklorists, but few capture the interactive nature of their telling. (An exception is Zora Neal Hurston's *Mules and Men*, 1978). These tales were typically recounted in ways that tailored the story to the immediate audience and incorporated a great deal of audience commentary and response. On the surface their function may have been amusement, but their underlying function was as "moral instructives and coded expressions of outrage at actual grievances" (Watkins, 1994, p. 444).

Mel Watkins (1994) in his comprehensive history of African American humor, maintains that the storytelling tradition, with its valuing of verbal acuity and spontaneous wit, still forms the basis of much Black humor. The decontextualized, set-piece joke, of White (male) culture "is rarely witnessed at black rap sessions or social gatherings." Instead, (humor) flows from the participants' commonly held satiric view of the world and themselves . . . it is derived from an acknowledgement of the shared ironic attitude underlying the quip (p. 472).

Creativity, spontaneity, and the ability to leave a personal stamp on the story are valued much more highly than the simple retelling of a joke. Watkins (1994) gives an example of the inventive use of a familiar story by describing a conversation between two men and a woman overheard at a New York bar:

The original folktale . . . concerned two men standing on a bridge and comparing the length of their penises while urinating; one says, "Damn, the water's cold," and his friend replies, "Yeah, and it's *deep*, too!" The response was put to an altogether different use in that Manhattan bar. After one of the men went on too long with a rap about how much money he had, the woman sarcastically snapped, "Fool, if money was air, you'd have to borrow an oxygen tank to breathe." Bent with laughter, the other man said, "Damn, home boy, that's cold." Without missing a beat, the woman quipped, "Yeah, and it's deep, too," which caused all three to break into spasms of laughter. Their spontaneous banter, which . . . inventively refocused the punchline from a traditional folktale with which they were all familiar (in this case heightening the original put-down, since the woman indirectly suggested that she was as much a man as her would-be admirer), was a perfect example of spontaneous reshaping of familiar folk wit. (p. 473)

This example underscores the importance of insiders' perspectives on humor. To an observer unfamiliar with the original tale, the meanings and functions of this humor would be obscure.

In a unique insider's account of humor in its social context, folklorist Rayna Green (1977) has described the sexual humor of U.S. southern women based on her own (White, lower-middle-class) family network. Most of the humor she describes occurred at family gatherings at which men congregate outdoors while women and children are in the kitchen. Many of the most outspoken of the bawdy humorists were old women. Like many traditional cultures, the U.S. South allows increasing license to old women, and Green notes that the women she observed took full advantage in presenting themselves as wicked—as in the retort by "Granny" quoted at the beginning of this chapter.

Green observed a great deal of sexual joking. Often the source of humor was men's boasts, failures, or sexual inadequacies—what one woman termed "comeuppance for lack of uppcomance." Preachers were the butt of many jokes, reflecting the rigid control of women's lives by evangelical Christian traditions. However, there was a marked absence of racism and hostility in humor about sexuality. Instead, these women engaged in creative word play, inventing comic names for genitals that mocked the euphemism expected of them. Thus, children were told to "wash up as far as possible, down as far as possible, and then wash possible." Women's pubic areas were affectionately called "Chore Girl" (after a bristly scrubbing pad) or "wooly booger"; male genitals were "tallywhackers."

The functions of humor were several. First, the storyteller gained respect and admiration as an inventive and entertaining user of language. "The ability to evoke laughter with bawdy material is important to these women's positive images of themselves" (Green, 1977, p. 33). Second, the humor was educational. Green suggests that the sexual information children gleaned from stories of lustful young married couples, cynical prosti-tutes, rowdy preachers, impotent drunks, and wicked old ladies was at least as accurate as a parental lecture on where babies come from, and much more creative and fun.

Perhaps most important, women's bawdy humor was subversive of the gender system. The bawdy tales functioned to break the cultural rules con-trolling women's sexuality. "The very telling defies the rules ... Women are not supposed to know or repeat such stuff. But they do and when they do, they speak ill of all that is sacred—men, the church, marriage, home, family, parents" (Green, 1977, p. 33). Green speculates that in their humor women vent their anger at men, offer alternative modes of understanding to their female hearers, and, by including the ever-present children in the circle of listeners, perform "tiny act(s) of revenge" on the men who have power over their lives.

Humor as a Feminist Strategy

Humor and Feminist Identity

In an early study of discourse in feminist consciousness-raising groups, Susan Kalcik (1975) noted that humor was used supportively to increase group cohesion. The women in these groups frequently mocked themselves. When one woman had difficulty expressing herself, she apologized with, "Well, you know how we women are; our hormones get up in our brains and fuck up our thinking." This self-mocking humor was also noted by Jenkins (1986) in her groups. However, it is only superficially a humor of self-denigration. By pointing out the stereotypes of women and their own failures to meet patriarchal standards, these women mock the norms and standards.

Mary Jo Neitz (1980) reports an impressionistic study of humorous interaction in a group she describes as radical feminists tending toward separatism who met on a college campus over a 2-year period (1971–1972). According to Neitz, set-piece jokes were rare; most humor consisted of spontaneous witticisms. The two most common themes for conversational humor were self-denigration and hostility toward men. Like Jenkins and Kalcik, Neitz speculates that apparently self-denigrating remarks (e.g., a group of women climbed into a car and the driver remarked, "Do you think you can be safe with a woman driver?") functioned to help women manage role incongruities and affirm group values in opposition to the dominant culture. Remarks denigrating women and their roles generated no laughter when they were contributed by outsiders. Hostile humor, much of which consisted of castration themes, functioned to overcome two taboos for women, sexuality and aggression. Moreover, "These jokes gloried in women's strength rather than colluding to hide it" (Neitz, 1980, p. 221).

The group used hostile humor in mixed-sex as well as same-sex settings, but used woman-denigrating humor only among themselves.

What values are expressed in feminist humor? How do feminists differentiate themselves as feminists in and through their humor? And what functions does humor serve in the creation of a feminist culture? To address these questions, Cindy White (1988) asked self-identified feminists to keep diaries of feminist humor in mundane settings over an 8-week period. From an analysis of three diaries, White concluded that the following values were expressed:

1. Generalized positive evaluation of women.
2. Celebration of women's experiences.
3. Affirmation of women's strengths and capabilities.
4. Autonomy and self-definition for women.
5. Valuing men by making a distinction between men as individuals and patriarchal culture.

One reported witticism that reflects some of these values is the following:

> At a staff meeting at a college health center, the clinic director told a story about Harvard University's struggle with their health fee. Men objected to paying the same fee as women, since they couldn't get a Pap smear. So Harvard went through all this rigamarole to figure out what part of the health fee was attributable to the Pap smear. Finally, Harvard notified the men that they could come pick up their 50-cent checks. K (a feminist and therapist) says quietly, "Pap smear envy." (pp. 82–83)

This example uses wordplay to ridicule the Freudian-based belief that women are more envious by nature than men due to penis envy. The feminists in the group were able to reverse the notion of penis envy to their own advantage. (Interestingly, the diary writer noted that the feminists were the only ones who laughed at this joke.) Moreover, the feminist speaker takes a routine gynecological test as the norm and celebrates it. The Pap smear becomes an enviable experience, one that men feel deprived of, and this explains their overreaction to differential health fees.

The value of sexual self-definition for feminists is suggested by the following diary entry quoting a woman who presented a paper on lesbian sexuality at a conference:

> Politically correct sex lasts at least three hours, since everyone knows we're process-oriented and not goal-oriented. If we do have orgasms, those orgasms must be simultaneous. And we must lie side by side. Now I know that some people think that orgasms are patriarchal. But I've given up many things for feminism, and this isn't going to be one of them. (White, 1988, p. 83)

White notes that just as feminist humor subverts the inflexible gender roles of the dominant culture it mocks inflexibility in feminism. In the orgasm example, a feminist jokes about how the notion of political correctness can be coercive for women and asserts her own autonomy, placing limits on the influence she will allow to feminist doctrine in constructing her own sexuality.

White argues on the basis of the humor diaries she analyzed that the most important role for humor in the creation of a feminist culture is the articulation of common meanings. Feminists differentiate themselves as feminists through humor not by adhering to a doctrinaire or monolithic notion of feminism, but by expressing shared, ingroup meanings. By creating and affirming their own meanings, feminists create a sense of community. When common meanings express ingroup and outgroup relationships, they help set the boundaries for feminist culture. These factors allow women to self-identify as feminists and re-create (enact) their feminism in everyday interaction.

Feminist Humor Goes Public

In recent years, feminist humorists have increasingly had a public voice, and this change has had radical implications. Kate Clinton (1982), a lesbian comedian, has described feminist humor as not just a string of jokes but a "deeply radical analysis of the world and our being in the world because it, like the erotic, demands a commitment to joy. Feminist humor is a radical analysis because we are saying that we have the right to be happy, that we will not settle for less" (p. 40).

Kate Clinton's words capture the subversive potential of women's humor, a potential that Naomi Weisstein (1973), a feminist psychologist and superb humorist, eloquently expressed more than 25 years ago:

> The women's movement is taking back what has been taken from us. We are reclaiming our autonomy and our history, our rights to self-expression and collective enjoyment. In this process, we are taking back our humor. The propitiating laughter, the fixed and charming smiles are over. When we laugh, things are going to be funny. And when we don't laugh, it's because we have a keen and clear sense of humor, and we know what's not funny ... we are constructing a women's culture with its own character, its fighting humor, its defiant celebration of our worth, a women's culture that will help get us through to that better world, that just and generous society. (1973, pp. 9–10)

Perhaps creating humor is culturally specified to be something that women cannot and must not do precisely because women's humor undermines the social order. And perhaps this danger is the source of the even more strongly made claim that feminists in particular lack a sense of humor.

When a charge is directed against a political and social movement, it is wise to examine the politics behind the charge (Weisstein, 1973).

Feminist humor is not just a reversal of misogynist humor, although it sometimes mocks the idea that women need men to fulfill their sexual and emotional needs and cannot survive without them. A 1970s feminist aphorism (later recycled in a pop song) is "A woman without a man is like a fish without a bicycle." A current example of feminist humor that pokes fun at women's presumed obsession with men is Nicole Hollander's two-panel cartoon seen on T-shirts and calendars. The first panel, titled "What men hope women are saying when they go to the washroom together," depicts two women bragging about the skill of their lovers. The second panel, "What they're really saying," shows the women's actual conversation: "Do you think cake is better than sex?" "What kind of cake?" (Hollander, 1994).

In an interview, Hollander noted that "men are frightened by women's humor because they think that when women are alone they're making fun of men. This is perfectly true, but they think we're making fun of their equipment when in fact there are so many more interesting things to make fun of—such as their value systems" (quoted in Barreca, 1991, p. 198).

A great deal of feminist humor can be thought of as the humor of a muted group. Although women's constructions of reality are obscured by the gender system, they emerge in self-aware women's humor. This humor may well acknowledge men's ability to define reality in ways that meet their needs. Yet, in making that acknowledgement public, it subverts men's reality by exposing its social construction. As Florynce Kennedy said, "If men could get pregnant, abortion would be a sacrament." Gloria Steinem's essay, "If Men Could Menstruate" (Steinem, 1983), describes how "menstruation would become an enviable, boast-worthy, masculine event" and "sanitary supplies would be federally funded and free." Women would, of course, suffer from acute cases of "menses envy." Revisionist humor on menopause is articulated on T-shirts that proclaim "I'm not having hot flashes, I'm having power surges."

Another much-reprinted feminist classic applies the blame-the-victim logic often used about rape victims to robbery victims. An exchange between the investigator and the robbery victim in "The Rape of Mr. Smith" illustrates the absurdity of the questions posed to victims of rape:

"Have you ever given money away?"
"Yes, of course—"
"And did you do so willingly?"
"What are you getting at?"
"Well, let's put it like this, Mr. Smith. You've given away money in the past—in fact, you have quite a reputation for philanthropy. How can we be sure that you weren't *contriving* to have your money taken

from you by force?"

"Listen, if I wanted—"

"Never mind . . . ."

And later:

"What were you wearing at the time, Mr. Smith?"

"Let's see. A suit. Yes, a suit."

"An *expensive* suit?"

"Well,—yes."

"In other words, Mr. Smith, you were walking around the streets late at night in a suit that practically *advertised* the fact that you might be a good target for some easy money, isn't that so? I mean, if we didn't know better, Mr. Smith, we might even think you were *asking* for this to happen, mightn't we?" (Unknown, 1990, pp. 283–284)

In the following joke, which was told to me in conversation, a man learns about the social construction of women's reality the hard way:

Joe used to spend many evenings at his neighborhood bar with his friends, having a beer and socializing. Then, inexplicably, he was absent for over a year. One evening, a beautiful woman came into the bar, sat down, and said, "Hello everybody. Do you remember me? I used to be Joe, but I had a sex change operation, and now I'm Debbie." His/her friends were astounded. They gathered around to hear the story.

"What was it like? Did you have to take hormones?"

"Yes, I took hormones for a year, but it wasn't too bad."

"Did you have to learn how to dress and walk like a woman? And wear high heels?"

"Yes, but that's okay, I liked it actually."

"But . . . the operation! You know . . . Wasn't it horrible? I mean, when they cut . . .

"Yes, I know what you mean. No, that part wasn't too bad, it was all done by medical experts."

"Well, then, what was the *worst part* about becoming a woman?"

Joe/Debbie replied slowly and thoughtfully, "I guess it was when I woke up from the operation and found out that they'd cut my paycheck by 40%."

With the reemergence of a feminist sensibility and culture since the late 1960s, there has been increasing attention given to feminist humor. Several anthologies have been published (Kaufman, 1991; Kaufman & Blakely, 1980; Stillman & Beatts, 1976). Researchers have measured appreciation of nonsexist and feminist jokes, cartoons, and slogans in women and men with difference degrees of allegiance to feminism (e.g., Stillion & White, 1987). To date, however, there have been few studies of the social functions of women's self-aware humor.

CONCLUSION

People construct the meaning of sexuality in many ways. Cultural critics and social science researchers have examined the assumptions of the medical model of sexuality, deconstructed the prescriptions of sex manuals, and explored the effects of religious codes on cultural constructions of womanhood (Altman, 1984; Espin, 1986; Tiefer, 1995). These are all important sources of sexual meaning. Analyzing them helps reveal the cultural discourse of sexuality that may otherwise be rendered invisible, and therefore made to seem natural and inevitable.

A truism of feminist analysis is that the more natural a belief or behavior seems, the more it should be analyzed as a social construction. In looking at mundane representations of sexuality in everyday talk, I have tried to make visible the taken-for-granted constructions of sexuality that occur within ongoing social transactions. When people make jokes about sexuality, they may be only kidding, but they are accomplishing serious social acts. The reality constructed in everyday talk forms the basis of social organization.

REFERENCES

Altman, M. (1984). Everything they always wanted you to know. In C. S. Vance (Ed.), *Pleasure and danger: Exploring female sexuality* (pp. 115–130). Boston: Routledge & Kegan Paul.

Arcana, J. (1994). The book of Daniel (an adaptation). In D. Taylor (Ed.), *Feminist parenting: Struggles, triumphs, and comic interludes* (pp. 233–242). Freedom, CA: Crossing Press.

Barreca, R. (1991). *They used to call me Snow White . . . But I drifted.* New York: Viking.

Bill, B., & Naus, P. (1992). The role of humor in the interpretation of sexist incidents. *Sex Roles, 27,* 645–664.

Bohan, J. (1993). Regarding gender: Essentialism, constructionism and feminist psychology. *Psychology of Women Quarterly, 17,* 5–22.

Brooks, M. L., Hanbery, D. E., Matz, I., Westover, T., & Westover, C. (1988). *Beer is better than women because . . .* Watertown, MA: Ivory Tower.

Clinton, K. (1982). Making light: Another dimension. *Trivia, 1,* 37–42.

Coates, J. (1996). *Women talk.* Oxford, England: Basil Blackwell.

Crawford, M. (1988). Gender, age, and the social evaluation of assertion. *Behavior Modification, 12,* 549–564.

Crawford, M. (1989). Humor in conversational context: Beyond biases in the study of gender and humor. In R. Unger (Ed.), *Representations* (pp. 155–166). New York: Baywood Publishing Company.

Crawford, M. (1995). *Talking difference*. London: Sage.

Crawford, M., & Gressley, D. (1991). Creativity, caring, and context: Women's and men's accounts of humor preferences and practices. *Psychology of Women Quarterly, 15*, 217–232.

Crawford, M., & Unger, R. (1992). Gender issues in psychology. In A. Colman (Ed.), *Companion encyclopedia of psychology* (Vol. 2, pp. 1007–1027). New York: Routledge.

Crawford, M., & Unger, R. K. (2000). *Women and gender: A feminist psychology* (3rd ed.). New York and Philadelphia: McGraw-Hill and Temple University Press.

Dion, K. K., Berscheid, E., & Walster, E. (1972). What is beautiful is good. *Journal of Personality and Social Psychology, 24*, 285–290.

Espin, O. M. (1986). Cultural and historical influences on sexuality in Hispanic/Latin women. In J. Cole (Ed.), *All American women: Lines that divide, ties that bind* (pp. 272–284). New York: Free Press (Macmillan).

Fine, M. (1985). Reflections on a feminist psychology of women: Paradoxes and prospects. *Psychology of Women Quarterly, 9*, 167–183.

Gardner, C. B. (1980). Passing by: Street remarks, address rights, and the urban female. *Language and Social Interaction, 50*, 328–356.

Gervasio, A. H., & Crawford, M. (1989). Social evaluations of assertiveness: A critique and speech act reformulation. *Psychology of Women Quarterly, 13*, 1–25.

Green, R. (1977). Magnolias grow in dirt: The bawdy lore of Southern women. *Southern Exposure, 4*, 29–33.

Griffin, C. (1989). "I'm not a women's libber but . . . ": Feminism, consciousness, and identity. In S. Skevington & D. Baker (Eds.), *The social identity of women* (pp. 173–193). London: Sage.

Heritage, J. (1984). *Garfinkel and ethnomethodology*. Cambridge, MA: Polity Press.

Hollander, N. (1994). T-shirt advertisement. *Funny Times, 9*, 22.

Hurston, Z. N. (1978). *Mules and men*. Bloomington: Indiana University Press.

Jenkins, M. (1986). What's so funny? Joking among women. In S. Bremner, N. Caskey, & B. Moonwomon (Eds.), *Proceedings of the first Berkeley women and language conference* (pp. 135–151). Berkeley, CA: Berkeley Women and Language Group.

Kalcik, S. (1975). " . . . like Ann's gynecologist or the time I was almost raped." Personal narratives in women's rap groups. *Journal of American Folklore, 88*, 3–11.

Kaufman, G. (1991). *In stitches: A patchwork of feminist humor and satire*. Indianapolis: Indiana University Press.

Kaufman, G., & Blakely, M. K. (1980). *Pulling our own strings*. Bloomington: Indiana University Press.

Kocol, C. (1989). Taking responsibility. *The Humanist, 49*, 33–34.

Kramarae, C. (1981). *Women and men speaking*. Rowley, MA: Newbury House.

McCullough, M. W. (1998). *Black and White women as friends: Building cross-race friendships*. Cresskill, NJ: Hampton.

Miller, J. B. (1986). *Toward a new psychology of women*. Boston: Beacon Press.

Mulkay, M. (1988). *On humor*. New York: Basil Blackwell.

Neitz, M. (1980). Humor, hierarchy, and the changing status of women. *Psychiatry, 43*, 211–223.

Pizzini, F. (1991). Communication hierarchies in humour: Gender differences in the obstetrical/gynaecological setting. *Discourse & Society, 2*, 477–488.

Porter, N., & Geis, F. (1981). Women and nonverbal leadership cues: When seeing is not believing. In C. Mayo & N. Henley (Eds.), *Gender and nonverbal behavior* (pp. 39–61). New York: Springer-Verlag.

Potter, J., & Wetherell, M. (1987). *Discourse and social psychology*. London: Sage.

Russell, G. M., & Fraser, K. L. (1999). Lessons from self-defense training. In S. N. Davis, M. Crawford, & J. Sebrechts (Eds.), *Coming into her own: Educational success in girls and women* (pp. 260–274). San Francisco, CA: Jossey-Bass.

Shotter, J., & Gergen, K. J. (Eds.). (1989). *Texts of identity*. London: Sage.

Snyder, M., Tanke, E. D., & Berscheid, E. (1977). Social perception and interpersonal behavior: On the self-fulfilling nature of social stereotypes. *Journal of Personality and Social Psychology, 35*, 656–666.

Stanback, M. H. (1985). Language and black women's place: Evidence from the black middle class. In P. A. Treichler, C. Kramarae, & B. Stafford (Eds.), *For alma mater: Theory and practice in feminist scholarship* (pp. 177–193). Urbana, IL: University of Illinois Press.

Steinem, G. (1983). *Outrageous acts and everyday rebellions*. New York: New American Library.

Stillion, J., & White, H. (1987). Feminist humor: Who appreciates it and why? *Psychology of Women Quarterly, 11*, 219–232.

Stillman, D., & Beatts, A. (1976). *Titters: The first collection of humor by women*. New York: Collier.

Tiefer, L. (1995). *Sex is not a natural act*. Boulder, CO: Westview.

Unknown. (1990). "The rape" of Mr. Smith (3rd ed.). In S. Ruth (Ed.), *Issues in feminism* (pp. 283–284). Mountain View, CA: Mayfield.

Wallston, B., & O'Leary, V. (1981). Sex makes a difference: Differential perceptions of women and men. In L. Wheeler (Ed.), *Review of personality and social psychology* (Vol. 2, pp. 9–41). Beverly Hills, CA: Sage.

Watkins, M. (1994). *On the real side*. New York: Simon & Schuster.

Weisstein, N. (1973). *Laugh? I nearly died*. Pittsburgh, PA: Know, Inc.

West, C., & Zimmerman, D. H. (1987). Doing gender. *Gender and Society, 1*, 125–151.

White, C. (1988). Liberating laughter: An inquiry into the nature, content, and functions of feminist humor. In B. Bate & A. Taylor (Eds.), *Women communicating: Studies of women's talk* (pp. 75–90). Norwood, NJ: Ablex.

Wiley, M., & Eskilson, A. (1982). Coping in the corporation: Sex role constraints. *Journal of Applied Social Psychology, 12,* 1–11.

Wilson, R. (1995, January 13). A "fractured" department. *The Chronicle of Higher Education,* A15–A16.

Yarkin, K., Town, J., & Wallston, B. (1982). Blacks and women must try harder: Stimulus persons' race and sex and attributions of causality. *Personality and Social Psychology Bulletin, 8,* 21–24.

10

BEAUTY, SEXUALITY, AND IDENTITY: THE SOCIAL CONTROL OF WOMEN

CHERYL BROWN TRAVIS, KAYCE L. MEGINNIS,
AND KRISTIN M. BARDARI

Beauty is considered to be a fundamental quality in women, as can be documented in the personal ads of any American newspaper. The never-ending pursuit of beauty occupies center stage for many women; the emphasis placed on appearance can be partially estimated by the millions of dollars spent annually on cosmetics and other beauty-enhancing efforts. Why this compulsory focus on beauty? What role does beauty play in the formation of individual identity? What are the social mechanisms that foster this phenomenon, and whose interests are being served in the process?

This chapter is based on the premise that beauty has become a key factor in defining and controlling women's sexuality. Socially constructed, narrow definitions of beauty and, thereby, sexuality are used as mechanisms to maintain social, political, and economic control by those who benefit from traditional patriarchal structures. We propose that the conflation of physical appearance and sexuality is detrimental to women on individual, interpersonal, and systemic levels and that it ultimately sustains gender-based oppression. In the first section of this chapter we elaborate on the social construction of sexuality as a means of sustaining the social control of women. In the second section we examine the social construction of beauty by documenting the arbitrary changes in beauty ideals over the course of the last century. Correlates to changing social roles and sexual expectations of women are explored. In the third section we identify the physical and emotional costs of the beauty sexuality equation. In the final section we offer some reformulations and suggestions for transforming the politics of sexuality and beauty.

THE SOCIAL CONSTRUCTION OF SEXUALITY AND THE SOCIAL CONTROL OF WOMEN

The social construction of reality shapes everyday forms of social exchange, the arrangement of work, family, and play, and the definitions of appropriate and acceptable behavior. It forms the basis for ideals and hopes, establishing what is normal and therefore understandable. Social, psychological, and political factors combine to form a social framework that constructs meaning. The social framework provides a way of understanding the world, each other, and ourselves. Because the social framework is ubiquitous and transparent, the exact mechanisms by which meaning gets constructed are often hidden and difficult to expose. We have used some of the standard tools for deconstructing any phenomenon to look at the connection between beauty and sexuality. We have looked for inconsistencies, apparent anomalies, and arbitrary features of everyday life; these are the equivalent of societal slips of the tongue that may reveal hidden structures or unacknowledged dynamics. What may seem at one point in time as something quite unremarkable or ordinary may be revealed as arbitrary and capricious when a more historical perspective is taken; thus we have included a retrospective on standards of beauty over several decades. We have examined variations and diversities in behavior and social arrangements as another way of clarifying the unspoken rules about what is considered normative. We also have explored the costs and ultimate consequences of the beauty sexuality connection as a way to question whose interests are served and to identify the political elements inherent in the social framework of women's beauty, sexuality, and identity.

Despite traditional notions that sexuality is based in anatomy and biology, we contend that sexuality is a socially constructed phenomenon; sexuality is negotiated between people and groups and emerges as a result of normative standards about what is both typical and desirable. The social framework of sexuality provides rules about who can be sexual and under what circumstances sexual behavior is appropriate. The social framework of sexuality even defines what counts as sex. Ultimately, individual experiences of being sexual and sexually aroused are determined, at least in part, by these socially constructed realities.

Although sexuality may be experienced as a personal and highly private aspect of the self, social and political frameworks fundamentally shape the ways in which we think about and experience sexuality. These frameworks encompass norms, expectations, labels, habits, customs, judgments, values, and social scripts of sexuality and sexual behavior. Socially constructed definitions assign meanings and determine whether behaviors are seen as flirtatious, titillating, provocative, salacious, or criminal. The experience of desire and the formulation of what even constitutes sexuality have developed within a social and political context.

Most important, the social framework determines who has the power to exercise choice and authority. Socially constructed definitions of sexuality do not occur randomly but derive from the interests of privileged groups. Those who are in power (political, economic, and social) have the most influence in establishing the social framework and are in positions to exert more influence over its design, usually for their own comfort. The sociopolitical context in most societies has consistently advantaged men at the expense of women. In particular, North American ideals of sexuality have functioned largely as a way of keeping women in their (subservient) place. Controlling women's sexuality, like controlling women's bodies in general, is a medium through which the oppression of women occurs.

The Beauty = Sex Equation

A primary mechanism used to monitor and control women's sexuality resides in the realm of beauty. For women, sexuality is inextricably linked to physical appearance. Sexuality is distorted as ornamental and observable rather than being viewed as a quality that emanates from the context of women's lives and relationships. Thus, the shape of a woman's body, the size of her breasts, and the color of her hair, are all features commonly used to assess her value as a sexual being.

Ideas about sexual appeal and beauty are not benign expressions of aesthetic preference, but are symbolically constructed systems of knowing and meaning. The social construction of women's sexuality as embedded in attractiveness constitutes a conflation between beauty and sexuality. This merger moves sexuality into the public realm, making it concrete and external, and thereby amenable to inspection, definition, social monitoring, and control. Equating physical appearance with sexuality facilitates a pervasive and ready monitoring of whether women are adhering to an appropriate sexual identity and, most important, an appropriate social role. Although standards of sexual conduct may vary across time and subcultures, the essential features of monitoring and control remain constant. As a consequence, women's sexuality has come to belong not to women themselves but to some other person or group.

By linking women's identity to observable markers and signs that are readily available for public monitoring, comment, and sanction, the social control of women is sustained. Under the framework, women whose identities are not centered on the display of sexuality through beauty and who instead may be focused on obtaining power through educational and economic pursuits are pejoratively labeled as unfeminine, asexual, or lesbian. Women who live in poverty or who are unable to effectively pursue normative standards of beauty are viewed as lazy and even mentally ill. Women routinely suffer humiliation, harassment, and even discrimination for failing—or refusing—to submit to the normative expectations of beauty, sexuality, and social role. The social construction of women's identity demands selflessness; healthy, good women attempt to meet the needs of others, specifically, the needs of men. A consequence of the internalization of the beauty-sexuality-identity equation is that normative standards and expectations that are destructive for women often are unseen and unchallenged.

By emulating beauty ideals and attracting and pleasing men, women are taught that sexuality is generated and made real by the responses of men. Sexuality is not promoted as a sensual benefit for women, but is defined as the capability to evoke sexual arousal in others. To be sexual, for women, means to be an object of desire. Thus, whether or not one is sexual is determined almost exclusively by the judgments and experiences of others. Others, then, largely define women's sense of identity and worth. There is an increased internal motivation to attract the attention and affirmation of others, and the preferences and needs of others become defining features of the self. Sexuality is construed in the flair of the nostril, the arch of the brow, the proportions of the waist and hips, the tone of the skin, ad infinitum. This formulation renders older women; larger, heavy women; and handicapped women asexual.

Despite the fact that women are able to periodically receive moderate rewards for upholding social constructions of beauty, sexuality, and identity, several noteworthy exceptions exist. Women who expend too much effort in the pursuit of beauty or the display of sexuality are punished. Women trying to emulate the ideal are often chastised by society for their wantonness and narcissism and are regarded as self-centered and neurotic. Women who are overly made-up are considered unattractive; there is a demand that the final effect must look natural and effortless. Women who are overly sexualized are considered to be unclean, immoral, and even pathological. The effort women put forth in attempting to elicit desire from men must fall within mainstream standards in order to be rewarded. Somehow, if women are too beautiful or too sexual, men's sense of pleasure—or power—is diminished.

It is important to note that the social construction of beauty, sexuality, and identity is most compulsory with respect to women; it doesn't operate in the same way for men. Despite the fact that there are normative appearance standards for men, they are not singularly used to perpetuate oppression and disempowerment. Men—and by this we mean Caucasian, heterosexual, middle-class, able-bodied men—are encouraged to develop their sense of identity and self-esteem through less destructive and self-denying means, such as occupational status and financial achievement. Additionally, although physical appearance is considered important for men, a wider variety of acceptable standards exist. Men of various proportions, features, and ages are considered attractive. Finally, the social and psychological consequences of failing to meet the ideal standard are not the same for men as they are for women. Few men would feel badly about themselves for not looking like Mr. Atlas, but women regularly feel inadequate and guilty because they do not look like Miss America.

Internalize False Dreams

Ultimately, women come to internalize these beliefs and standards, rendering the elements of social control even more transparent. Women themselves promote the value of breast enlargement surgery, the perfectly matched cosmetic set. Women themselves become members of the social police who monitor and judge other women for failing to embody the ideal. Women themselves equate personal success with the ability to attract attention from men. Women are proud when they have been able to teach their daughters to pursue similar success. The internalization process is multilayered and generated by social, occupational, economic, and legal policies that inherently support patriarchy (i.e., policies that benefit men, for example, in the areas of reproduction, prostitution, childcare, marriage and divorce, etc.). Internalization also is fostered by billion dollar advertising campaigns that prey on insecurities regarding identity and acceptance. Most important, internalization is crystallized through the administration of moderate rewards to women who cultivate their physical attractiveness in accordance with normative expectations.

Despite the fact that these rewards are often fleeting, women who are willing and able to elicit sexual desire from men through the use of beauty are often able to achieve a certain level of self-worth and validation. It may be painful, time-consuming, and expensive to embody the current beauty ideal, but nevertheless there are gains to be had for doing so. First, there is a general bias that what is beautiful is good, and attractive women tend to receive more favorable attention and social deference and have more social alternatives. Second, as long as women continue to occupy second-class status in educational, economical, and political pursuits, they are made vulnerable and in need of protection by a male partner. Sexuality and beauty are strategies for survival for women who face disadvantages of discrimination, harassment, and crime. It is a survival strategy, in that making themselves attractive to men is a way of (temporarily) acquiring status and protection. The degree to which a woman is successful at modeling herself after the popular beauty ideal often determines her ability to attract men and thereby an acceptable social identity. Undoubtedly, many women seek, and often receive, validation of their own identity by attracting the attention and approval of men. Unfortunately, to the extent that these constructions of beauty and sexuality are internalized, women will continue to experience ongoing anxiety regarding their identity and social standing, especially in times of financial crisis, divorce or death of spouse, and when the inherent promises of acceptance and safety are ultimately found to be flimsy and unfulfilling.

Our society reveres women as "keepers of the hearth" and as mothers of future leaders, but not as figures of financial or political authority in the public realm. Appropriate and acceptable identities for women are those that do not interfere with the status quo. The social construction of beauty, sexuality, and identity is based on the translation of sexuality into external features of appearance and style that may be monitored and controlled by men. Internalization of this process by women themselves enables the destructive elements to remain largely unchallenged. Ultimately, the standards of beauty and, thus, sexuality promote a system of oppression that is physically harmful, psychologically debilitating, economically draining, and spiritually demoralizing, but that is often unknown to women themselves. Factors that perpetuate this system include the unattainable, contradictory, and highly capricious standards of beauty that are consistently demanded but ever changing. We explore these standards in more detail in the next section.

THE CHANGING NATURE OF BEAUTY AND IDENTITY

One way of illustrating the social construction of beauty, sexuality, and identity is to document the standards of beauty and attractiveness over the course of the last century. These ever-changing ideals are not merely a matter of aesthetics, but are historically linked to social, economic, and political factors. Conceptualizations of beauty are generally considered fixed. A deconstruction of beauty ideals illuminates that expectations of beauty are related to the needs of the majority culture and that these ideals change over time. In general, as mainstream women have gained more freedom regarding identity and self-expression, constraints on beauty and sexuality have increased. Thus, what may appear during any given era to be a matter of individual taste or vanity is very much a societal phenomenon related to the roles and status of women at that time.

The development of an ideal beauty in North America throughout the 20th century has several unique features (Banta, 1987; Clark, 1980; Ford & Beach, 1951). A cultural myth has developed that the ideal is normative, and all women should be able to achieve it if only they put forth enough effort. Promised rewards of increased emotional security and social acceptance help promote this myth. Consequently, women over the past century have "painted, powdered, scented, dyed, corseted, slimmed, fattened, paled, tanned, and shaved" in hopes of emulating the ever-changing ideal (Baker, 1984, p. 11). The image of the ideal has been a source of anxiety for women and has been remarkably expensive to pursue (Stewart, 1977). The pursuit of this moving target imbues women with the chronic feelings of inferiority and unacceptability; thus, they remain hypervigilant for ever-changing trends.

In this section, we emphasize three points. First, standards of beauty are ever changing; second, ideas about beauty emerge in a social, political, and economic context; and third, physical appearance has become a defining factor in women's sexuality and, ultimately, in women's identities in general. The beauty phenomena reviewed here are undoubtedly determined by multiple factors and maintained by a variety of mechanisms. Regardless of what elicits or sustains them, however, they have implications for women's social, psychological, and sexual identities. The examples that follow are not meant to provide a comprehensive review or a complete chronology; they are intended, rather, to illustrate the beauty-sexuality-identity equation and its relation to sociocultural forces.

Turning the Century

The late 1800s and early 1900s saw dramatic changes in virtually all aspects of American life: family, industry, occupation, and social ideals. As conventional gender role arrangements and realities changed, individual identities became less fixed, precipitating a need for other avenues of control and regulation of women.

Dramatic industrial expansion during the turn of the century produced a general atmosphere of progressive social change. As cities bulged with workers from rural towns in search of paychecks, the labor movement and socialist ideals emerged with new propositions about economic justice and social class. The American Federation of Labor (AFL) developed under the direction of Samuel Gompers, and the International Workers of the World (Wobblies) organized strikes across the country. Women joined in efforts at general social reform, participating in the formation of the Parent Teachers Association (PTA) and the League of Women Voters (Schneider, 1993). Factory workers became part of a new social and economic class that included women as paid workers, especially in textile mills. Factory work involved long hours, low pay, and many safety and health risks. For the first time, young women were leaving farms and family households for paid employment, often living separate from the supervision and auspices of their families.

During the early 1900s, the nation's ideal was the Gibson Girl—a wholesome, healthy, athletic girl based on a series of drawings aimed at portraying a new kind of femininity (Banner, 1983). The Gibson Girl was tall and thin, but had a large bust and hips. During this time, dieting was common among women, although by present-day standards women were still plump (Banner, 1983). For example, the 1904 National Physique Contest winner, Emma Newkirk, weighed 136 pounds standing at 5 feet, 4 inches (Todd, 1987). Beauty during the early 20th century became equated with that which could be purchased (e.g., beauty parlor treatments and the products one was able to buy there). As women began to internalize the messages and ideas regarding cosmetic use, they began to view cosmetics as necessary for their own success and fulfillment (Peiss, 1990). Women began to purchase and use cosmetics, convinced that painting themselves not only was respectable but also had become a general requirement of womanhood (Peiss, 1990).

The implications for women's sexuality and identity were subtle but pervasive. The Gibson Girl was a highly feminine image highlighted by a soft body physique. The style was one of voluptuous dimensions combined with high collars, long sleeves, and deferential manners. For the first time, the ideal woman was to be both socially and morally acceptable and also —ever so subtly—sexual. Prior to this time, women were dichotomized as either virtuous and maternal, or sensual and pathological. The Gibson Girl ideal represented a shift toward expectations that every woman be both. Although women's sexuality during this time was to be private, constrained, and not publicly displayed, subtle evidence of their sexuality was now expected.

As women at the turn of the century moved into a variety of new roles, expectations of women's appearance and expression of sensuality became more demanding. Women were now supposed to embody all characteristics considered important: saintliness, athleticism, motherhood, sensuality, and so on. As women acquired new status and skills outside the home, even more was demanded of them in terms of social, moral, and occupational identity within the family. Changes in these expectations are captured in the ideal image of the Gibson Girl and illustrate the evolution of the contemporary superwoman phenomenon.

1910s and 1920s

Adding to the roiling mix of prosperity and social change of the early 1900s, World War I (1910–1914) further increased women's participation in public life and paid employment. More women began to work outside the home in an effort to replace the male workers that had been recruited for battle. The shirtwaist was exchanged for the chemise, and brash young women were known to smoke and drink alcohol. Industrial growth, the general shuffle of workers from farms to cities, and the demands for soldiers on foreign fronts contributed to changing ideas about gender and identity.

Women's right to vote was a pressing political debate, as Susan B. Anthony and other feminists stumped the country to energize the suffrage movement. Marches, oratory, arrests, and hunger strikes were part of the battle. It is noteworthy that imprisoned suffragettes resorting to hunger strikes as a form of political protest were often force-fed by their captors. Thus, the literal bodies of women became a battleground for political freedom. The necessary 36th vote by Tennessee to ratify the 19th amendment came in 1919.

Although the general tenor of the times promoted identities for women that were fun-loving, social, and perhaps even rebellious, women's bodies were nevertheless strictly controlled. Family and church patriarchs had initially managed the control of women's sexuality through contraception and birth control. However, as women moved into more public realms, these issues became matters of public policy. Through the late 1800s and early 1900s the Comstock Laws prohibited the mailing of lewd materials, especially anything that mentioned reproductive physiology or birth control. In 1914, Margaret Sanger began distributing a newsletter, *The Woman Rebel*, that advised women of birth control methods.

Sexual appeal increasingly became a matter of external appearance. The ideal body deflated and the look of the flapper came in vogue (Garland, 1957). Slender legs, narrow hips, and flat breasts were considered very important (Baker, 1984; Banner, 1983; Garland, 1957). Women's physical attractiveness was assessed primarily by the shape and size of their legs and "ideal" bodies became curveless and almost boy-like (Mazur, 1986). Women of the 1920s often bound their breasts to achieve the slender figure that was so popular (Banner, 1983). Illustrated figures used for fashion design reflected and confirmed the changing ideals of body shape. Whereas in 1918, the ideal figure is described as pear shaped, by 1929, the sexy figure was slim, flat, and youthful with a minimized bust and hip (Danielson, 1989, p. 37). Sex appeal was extended to include standards about body hair, and during this time, women's body hair became viewed as particularly undesirable. Methods for removing it were widely practiced. Women began shaving the hair under their arms and on their legs as changing fashions exposed more of their bodies, thereby making their arms and legs objects of scrutiny (Banner, 1983). Standards about body hair continue to be powerful, and many contemporary women who disdain cosmetics nevertheless remove much of their body hair. In fact, a woman's hairy armpits would be almost anathema to sex appeal.

During the 1910s and 1920s, women were breaking traditional images of domesticity and deference like never before. It is not accidental that women's right to vote was secured in a period of relative peace and prosperity, a time of hope and optimism when it was assumed there would be plenty for all. Despite these assumptions, constraints on beauty and sexuality continued to increase. Reproduction and birth control emerged as matters of public debate at exactly the time when women were otherwise moving toward autonomy and independence.

Following the war, and for the first time in history, population data revealed that the number of women exceeded the number of men (Broby-Johansen, 1968). This imbalance undoubtedly created greater competition among women and greater power and choice among men. Despite the freedoms that women were able to secure, personal style and glamour became even more difficult to embody, thus effectively maintaining control over women through sexual and social arenas.

1940s and 1950s

World War II impacted the lives of tens of thousands of military personnel and their families and created significant economic changes for the lower working classes. Women were part of the military endeavor as WACs, WAVES, and medical corps and were actively and intentionally mobilized for war (Rupp, 1978). The war also generated full employment, and a propaganda machine of the War Department focused on convincing women that Rosie the Riveter was a heroine (Honey, 1984). For many women, work as welders and ship fitters resulted in dramatically higher and more consistent income, although women continued to be paid less than men, and Black women were paid less than White women. The end of World War II also produced long-term economic benefits through various provisions of the GI (Government Issue) Bill, which included underwriting college education and home loans. The 1940s was an era of national optimism, upward mobility, and consumer products in a kind and number never before experienced.

After the war, defense industry jobs dried up and Rosie the Riveters were sent home to make room for returning veterans in the workplace. Instead of being encouraged to continue working outside the home, women were encouraged to make comfortable homes and have babies. Progress was measured by one's modern, labor-saving appliances, automobiles, and new homes (i.e., keeping up with the Jones's). It was a time when people's identity was linked to their houses, cars, and landscaped lawns, as well as their personal style.

During this time, there were two competing ideals of beauty: the slender and sophisticated woman, and the pinup girl with ample bust and hips (Banner, 1983; Mazur 1986). Both ideals were difficult to attain. Marilyn Monroe, who wore a size 12, represented the ideal body image of the general times. As the first woman to pose nude for *Playboy* magazine, she epitomized an opulent physique associated with femininity and sex appeal. During this time, breasts were in. Although the ideal breast size had been steadily increasing since the 1920s, it was not until after the end of World War II that "bosom mania" set in (Mazur, 1986). The culture became so focused on the size of women's breasts that Howard Hughes designed an entire film around Jane Russell's cantilevered bosom.

As the war ended, happiness for women was socially constructed in the role of wife and mother. The key mechanism for such happiness and true fulfillment was a husband who was a good provider and kind to his children, a concept explored by Jesse Bernard (1972). But first, the prospective wife had to be attractive and sexually appealing to men. Thus, sexual attractiveness and availability to men served a gatekeeping function for women's access to the roles (wife and mother) women believed most important to their personal identity and happiness. These decades were tailor-made for a conflation of beauty and sexiness and for the internalization of these standards by women. Self-worth was again linked to the capacity to be attractive to others.

1960s and 1970s

The 1960s saw the beginnings of the civil rights movement as well as the antiwar movement surrounding Vietnam. Both movements produced a general atmosphere that boundaries could be broken and assumptions about traditional politics could be challenged openly. Women were active in both movements, reflecting the longstanding tradition of feminist women's commitment to social change and equality in general. For example, Rosa Parks's refusal to sit in the back of the bus provided a catalytic spark that is timeless, and Angela Davis's outspoken criticism of the war was front page news across the nation. Like the antislavery movement, temperance movement, and labor movements of earlier decades, the activism of the 1960s and 1970s set the contemporary stage for women to dispute traditional sex role boundaries and to rediscover the ideals of feminism (Lakoff & Scherr, 1984). One would think that with all this growing political consciousness and social activism, the acceptable range of appearance would be similarly expanded. However, there probably was as much, or more, emphasis on women's physical appeal to men.

It was also a time when go-go dancers, topless bars, and all-nude dancing became commonplace. Breast enlargement was an essential part of the female entertainment industry, with some women gaining notoriety and publicity by virtue of having hugely enlarged breasts as part of their topless shows. Makeup and body physique continued to be narrowly defined. Heavy eye makeup was favored with an Egyptian style; iridescent eye shadow and polished lipstick were derigueur.

Women's sexuality and social roles were more openly debated during the 1960s and 1970s than in the previous generation, and a second wave feminism flourished. This period saw the publication of Betty Friedan's *The Feminine Mystique* (1963), viewed by many as the official beginning of the second wave of feminism, and the 1966 founding of the National Organization for Women (NOW). Truly radical statements were promoted with Kate Millet's *Sexual Politics* (1970), Shulamith Firestone's *The Dialectic of Sex* (1970), and Ellen Frankfort's *Vaginal Politics* (1972). Unfortunately, these social movements took place in the context of a good deal of self-indulgence and narcissism. Drugs and free love were also part of these decades. Embedded in these movements were contradictory messages for women's sexuality and social roles.

Development of a birth control pill in the early 1960s provided a technological underpinning for rejection of traditional standards for sexuality. Although the early high dosage pill carried significant risks (see reviews by Barbara Seaman, 1969), women welcomed it as a way of finessing the much trickier issues of negotiating birth control with their male partners. Breaking traditional roles meant first and foremost breaking sexual rules. Women were supposed to be sexually liberated. However, this message was popularly translated in the dominant culture as being available to men without expecting a long-term, relational commitment.

Beauty ideals went through further transformation. In the 1960s, the larger, fleshy, busty woman began to decline in popularity and was replaced by a woman with a trim lower torso; thus began the "trend toward slenderization" (Mazur, 1986). Women, more than ever, began to be evaluated primarily on their figures. Twiggy became one of the first international super models, primarily because of her skeletal thinness. This trend toward slenderization is documented by Silverstein, Peterson, and Perdue (1986) who analyzed the ratios between bust, waist, and hip measurements of women depicted in photographs of two popular magazines from 1902 to 1982 and correlated them with acutely thin, college-aged women during this era.

The popular conception of women's liberation during the 1960s revealed underlying views of women; namely, that sexual and reproductive status was the most salient aspect of women's identities. While the pill gave women some control, the basic issues of sexual equality in and out of the bedroom were only partially addressed. Thus, the ideal for women's personal identity as liberated women was constructed—as it was before—in ways that privileged male interests. As Pat Minardi (1971) noted, there is a big difference between the terms "liberated women" and "women's liberation."

During the 1960s and 1970s, women who were vigorously opposed to traditional work and family roles for women were often labeled as lesbians, especially if they refused to display the standards of beauty and style in vogue. Feminists were regularly viewed as physically unattractive (Goldberg, Gottesdiener, & Abramson, 1975). The underlying belief was that feminists simply could not attract a man and that the angry rhetoric was a disguised form of sour grapes. The public mindset of the time demonstrates the close connection between beauty ideals and sexual politics. Thus, despite the progressiveness of the time, cultural expectations for women and their identities remained fixed. Women who embodied the ideal pursuits—ideal in that they benefited men—were considered attractive and appropriately sexual. In contrast, the rewards of social acceptance were withheld from women who resisted standard social-political roles. Their protests were dismissed as a product of their own failure to achieve a traditional role, a failure due to their own lack of physical appeal.

Contemporary Ideals

The 1990s have been an odd mix of prosperity and economic uncertainty. Although unemployment rates have been low, many Americans are worried about their jobs and future well-being. Recent years have been associated with corporate growth and low interest rates, but downsizing has typically followed mergers. As a result, large numbers of well-educated, middle-class people worry about their financial stability. In addition, international trade agreements like NAFTA (North American Free Trade Agreement) have made it easier for corporations to move production facilities, and jobs, out of the country. Added to the economic uncertainty experienced by many individuals is the fact that the U.S. population is aging, and there are serious concerns about the future of Social Security and health care.

During uncertain financial periods, political sanctions often increase against marginal groups that have made demands for a greater share of economic resources. It is ironic that during a time when an increasing percentage of the work force is composed of women and more women with children are working, there is vigorous political rhetoric about family values. Family values are a topic of news coverage and are played out in political arenas. For example, Susan Molinari, a New York Republican and member of the House of Representatives resigned her position to take a job in television, partly to enable her to spend more time with her infant daughter. In response to her resignation, a conservative commentator, David Frum, noted that one could not have a high-powered career and "be a conscientious mother" (Young, 1998). The rhetoric of family values has powerful appeal and gets votes. For example, the election of GOP gubernatorial candidate James S. Gilmore III of Virginia was attributed in exit polls to his strong stance on family values (Morin, 1997).

The issues of how to balance family, relationships, career, and equality have again become matters of personal struggle in the lives of individual women rather than an impetus for change in the larger system. The idea that women could have it all has come under serious scrutiny (Morical,

1984; Spain, 1996). Book titles emphasize hard choices, dilemmas, balancing acts, and compromise (e.g. *Choice and Compromise: A Woman's Guide to Balancing Family and Career*, Douglas, 1983; *Hard Choices: How Women Decide About Work, Career, and Motherhood*, Gerson, 1985; and *Dilemmas of a Double Life: Women Balancing Careers and Relationships*, Kaltreider, 1997). Considerable attention also is given to the idea of essential sex differences. John Gray's 1992 bestseller, *Men Are From Mars, Women Are From Venus*, is just one of many examples. It appears that economic uncertainty has been teamed with the concept of family values, resulting in a view that makes traditional women's roles—and the women who occupy them—especially valorous and laudable.

Beauty ideals of today reflect increasingly unrealistic images for women, images made omnipresent by mass media. Media images not only work to establish normative reference points for gender behavior and appearance, but they also confer subtle messages about status and entitlement. Television commercials and print advertisements create idealized and unrealistic portrayals of women's beauty and continue to perpetuate the piecemeal objectification of women's bodies (Kilbourne, 1994). Fashion magazines promote the possibility of beauty through illusion, as models' stretch marks and other skin imperfections are airbrushed away and their body shapes distorted by the tricks of photography and computer-generated images (Lakoff & Scherr, 1984).

One of the most critical elements of the contemporary ideal beauty has been the continuing trend toward slenderization. In fact, for women to be seen as acceptable, they need to be "painfully thin" (Kilbourne, 1994). More recently, fitness has become a crucial factor in maintaining this ideal body shape. More and more women participate in aerobics, jogging, and bodybuilding. This trend is seen in the declining body measurements of Miss America beauty pageant contestants and *Playboy* centerfolds over the past 20 years, who have averaged 10–15% below the average weight for women of equal heights (Garner, Garfinkel, Schwartz, & Thompson, 1980). Fashion models may weigh as much as 23% less than the average American woman (Kilbourne, 1979). One speculates that if store mannequins were alive, they would be too thin to menstruate. Thus, although only 5% of American women have the body type of a tall, thin, long-legged physique, those characteristics make up the majority of images that are portrayed in the media (Kilbourne, 1994). This leaves 95% of us to wonder what is wrong with our bodies! The pursuit of thinness carries with it an economic component. The marketers of diet books, diet programs, health spas, and celebrity exercise videos all profit from women trying to achieve the ideal body (Travis, 1988). The economy virtually relies on women being obsessed with thinness and forever unsuccessfully attempting to achieve it. This phenomenon is illustrated by the 33 billion dollar diet industry that is unproven in its success (Kilbourne, 1994). A casual perusal of magazine headlines confirms that the demand for thinness continues as a ubiquitous message for women.

In addition to the increased demands of thinness and perfection, sexuality in the 1990s has been constructed as even more external to women than in previous eras. The centrality of lingerie to women's sexuality and sex appeal has thrust Victoria's Secret and Frederick's of Hollywood into multimillion dollar status. In order to be considered sexual, women must not only have the ideal body, but they must also adorn themselves in expensive—and often uncomfortable—g-strings, push-up bras, and corsets. There is a mass marketing of women's lingerie catalogs that have defined, at least in part, what it means to be sexual. In the 1990s, women's sexuality and, thus, their identity is inextricably linked to mass marketing and capitalistic pursuits.

Youthful pursuits also have become central in defining beauty and identity for women. Entire cosmetic lines are geared toward reversing the effects of aging, and facial scrubs, moisturizers, and acids are promoted as critical regimes for women over the age of 30. Although the market-appeal of aging baby boomers certainly drives this movement, one cannot help but speculate on the additional factors that motivate such attention to aging. Although young women have been the primary targets of beauty-(identity) enhancing efforts with promises of social rewards including eligibility for marriage, older women have been infused with anxiety about divorce. Since men have more socially allowable options for younger partners, older women are given the message that they must compete with younger women. It is only acceptable to be older if the woman continues to look 30. If you are 50 with wrinkles and sags, the prevailing message is that your husband may leave you for having the nerve to focus on viable aspects of your life such as children, career, friends, and activities instead of continuing to orient your identity and life toward pleasing him.

Feminists have viewed these developments as evidence that social change toward equality has been an illusion all along (Hewlett, 1986), or that these voices of authority represent a backlash against equality. Naomi Wolf (1991) has argued that along with the increasing resistance to feminism and equality there has been a redefinition of sex as beauty. The message is that a woman must be beautiful in order to feel sexual. She surmised the phenomenon succinctly: "Sexuality follows fashion, which follows politics" (p. 133). Wolf (1991) argues, as does Faludi (1991), that changes in the way beauty and sexuality are conceptualized occur as a reaction to women's imminent sexual and political freedom.

As women have continued to move into the public world of employment and politics, another set of demands for perfection has intensified. There has been increasing rhetoric about family values, in which the implicit image of family is a heterosexual couple in a nuclear grouping with children. There is a great deal of emphasis on the instruction of children in moral values and an emphasis on parental supervision of children. These images of family and what it takes to have a healthy family imply that women will be present to ready children for school, take them to team practice, and supervise them in household duties. In the rhetoric of family values, the role of mom is a full-time job. The idea of a family where mom is the emotional nurturer has great appeal. For example, when young women who will soon be college graduates "talk," it is rare for them to envision their future caretaking of children in terms of economic provisioning (Travis, personal observation). In counterbalance to this image of full-time mom, it is important to remember that most women work because of economic necessity. Government poverty standards indicate that providing even the basic necessities for a family of four requires an annual income of at least $30,000. The fact is that women must work, but they are made to feel guilty and inadequate about it.

We suggest that the image of an ideal family and full-time domesticity for women represents an increased pressure on women to restrict their educational and career aspirations to those endeavors that can be managed as secondary to husband and children. This image of full-time mom also carries the hidden message that somewhere there will be a man who takes care of the financial worries while mom provides emotional caretaking. It requires that young women spend a good deal of their time attracting, nurturing, and pleasing a good provider. At some level the young woman must be sexually desirable to a man.

Beauty and Identity in African American Women

Racism also is evident in beauty ideals and body politics; beauty standards tend to demand "whiteness" (Trepagnier, 1994). Ethnic women have had difficulty approximating the Caucasian ideal with differences in skin color, eye color, hair, facial features, and body shape (Lakoff & Scherr, 1984). Although these beauty imperatives punish all women, they especially hurt marginalized women: women of color, older women, women with disabilities, and poor women. Examining cultural reaction to these groups underscores the general lack of tolerance for any variation in beauty standards, body image, sexuality, or, ultimately, identity. Although we focus here on beauty constraints of African American women, the issue is relevant to all women of minority status.

At the turn of the century, images of the ideal beauty were accessible only to Caucasian women. Beauty was equated with white skin, straight hair, and Caucasian features. It is no surprise that the cosmetics industry equated social success and refinement with whiteness (Peiss, 1990). As a result, African American entrepreneurs developed their own section of the beauty industry by marketing products such as hair-straightening oils and skin-bleaching creams that served as a symbol of "personal success and racial progress" (Peiss, 1990, p. 156). During this time, the process of straightening hair was not only costly, but also painful and physically dangerous.

By the 1960s, awareness and appreciation of diversity had increased. African American women gained acceptance in modeling and fashion, and the saying "Black is beautiful" gained popularity. The acceptance of non-Anglo models of beauty, however, may not have been as widespread as some have portrayed. Lakoff and Scherr (1984) suggest that Black was not considered beautiful during this time, as evidenced by widespread use of skin lighteners, hair relaxers, hair extensions, and cosmetic surgery for the nose.

In contemporary times, women of color continue to be evaluated by the dominant White culture's myth of what it means to be beautiful (Lakoff & Scherr, 1984). As a result, many of these messages have been internalized. African American communities continue to consider lighter skin preferable to darker skin; "To many black men, lighter sisters are still seen as the most desirable, most worthy, and most feminine, and thus, the most in need of (male) protection" (Okazawa-Rey, Robinson, & Ward, 1987, p. 98). Marrying women of color with lighter skin is considered to be marrying "up" (Lakoff & Scherr, 1984). Indeed, Mullins and Sites (1984) found that there are significant social and economic benefits of marrying the lighter members of one's race as the inheritance of light skin color serves to increase a family's social position over time. Thus, African American women with dark skin have been considered not only less beautiful, but also less of an asset in marriage.

With regard to body shape, African American women are expected to pursue thinness. The diet and exercise industries do not discriminate. Some research has suggested that Black women of low socioeconomic status (SES) have a wider range of normal and attractive body sizes than high SES Black women or White women (Allan, Mayo, & Michel, 1993). However, in order for African-American women to reap the cultural rewards of acceptance and access to power, they must also attempt to emulate the ideal.

Ethnic images of beauty have been modestly incorporated within the past few decades (Banner, 1983). One factor influencing this change has been the marketing of the cultural conceptualization that Black women's beauty is based on a "primitive" sexuality (Carby, 1986). Constructions of African American women's sexuality as brazen and unpredictable have existed for decades. For example, during the Civil War, Caucasian southern women were believed to adhere to a strict code of chastity, while African American southern women were considered sensual and lacking in inhibitions (Good, 1989; Okazawa-Rey, Robinson, & Ward, 1987).

Josephine Baker (1906–1975) was one of the first African American women to become noted for her glamour and beauty (Haney, 1981). Her provocative bare-breasted dancing during the late 1920s and 1930s in Paris established her as a nightclub headliner. Although she eventually expanded her style to include more sultry and sensuous eroticism, she first gained status in a high-energy dance number where she appeared wearing only a skirt of bananas. Part of Baker's appeal was the presentation of her sexuality as "untamed" and "savage," and as something to be consumed by others, a presentation that did not threaten those in power.

Since that time, African American women have consistently been portrayed in magazines and on fashion runways as wild, savage beasts with overflowing sexual appetites. Black women models have been more likely than White women models to be shown in animal prints (Plous & Neptune, 1997) and are generally presented as exotic. Unfortunately, one study of over a thousand magazine advertisements concluded that racial bias not only persists in magazine advertising, but also may have increased in contemporary times (Plous & Neptune, 1997). African American women's identities are accepted into the mainstream only as they approximate the White ideal. Consequently, African American women are entitled to social and economic rewards to the extent that they accept notions of beauty and sexuality that do not threaten those in power.

This narrow range of tolerance has been costly to African American women. By looking specifically at the function of beauty ideals for women of color, the political function of these ideals for all women is made evident. In many instances, approximating the White version of beauty has increased African American women's chances for both economic and social success in an environment that valued only limited standards of beauty (Peiss, 1990; Okazawa-Rey, Robinson, & Ward, 1987). Unfortunately, meeting these beauty ideals does not provide sufficient alternatives (i.e., economic, political) for obtaining success. Approximating ideals of beauty provides access to an indirect status by virtue of being affiliated with those in positions of power and social influence.

Eventually, it becomes apparent that styles and trends do not reflect individual taste or preference but are controlled by larger forces. This dynamic suggests that the interests that are served are not primarily those of women. For example, although color-consciousness is promoted within the African American community, it is ultimately fostered and sustained by the larger society that discriminates and oppresses on the basis of color. African American women who agree to pursue the ideal as it has been defined by the majority culture are rewarded (temporarily) with status; those who are unwilling or unable to pursue the ideal are further marginalized. Ultimately, the oppression of African American women—as well as majority women—is maintained through expectations and standards of beauty, sexuality, and identity.

EFFECTS OF BEING AN OBJECT RATHER THAN AN AGENT

Whether women embody the ideal or reject it, they face detrimental consequences. The equation of beauty and sexuality creates profound effects in many areas. Here we concentrate on three: body manipulations, health effects, and implications for selfhood and identity.

Body Manipulations

To the extent that beauty ideals are internalized, women themselves are likely to see beauty work as a personal preference and to feel badly about themselves when they do not quite meet the standard. Women regularly report an ideal body image that is thinner, lighter, taller, more muscular, with larger breasts and longer hair compared with their actual physical characteristics (Jacobi & Cash, 1994). In fact girls and women are encouraged to experiment with various looks and body manipulations very much as if they themselves were objects. Although cosmetic surgery is the primary culprit—and clearly the most potentially dangerous— dysfunctional eating, tattooing, and body piercing also are forms of body manipulation.

Approximately 2 million cosmetic procedures are performed annually in the United States. Not only do these figures represent a significant increase over the past decade, but they also represent an increase in procedures being performed on younger and younger clients. For example, more than a third of face-lift patients are age 50 or younger (Hamilton & Weingarden, 1998). Cosmetic surgery fosters the notion that being unattractive is a form of pathology (Morgan, 1994). It has been suggested that cosmetic surgery exists to cure women of their ugliness, despite the fact that ugliness is not a biological disease, but rather a socially created disease (Wolf, 1991). By creating and then claiming to cure women's flawed appearance, the medical profession plays a significant role in controlling women and benefits from advising what to do to their bodies in order to combat flaws that have been socially constructed.

Because Western ideas of sexuality are projected onto women's breasts, various means of shaping and enlarging breasts have become common. Surgical breast implants were first marketed in the 1960s and have long been a means for acquiring the ideal body shape. Complications from these procedures include rupture and shrinking scar tissue around the implants that can result in a painful hardening of the breast. Implants also may limit the effectiveness of standard techniques used to screen for breast cancer. Implants filled with silicone gel have been the subject of class action suits involving 400,000 women claiming a variety of connective tissue diseases and immune disorders. Nevertheless, we continue as a society to view breast size as an important marker of sex appeal and beauty.

New technologies have expanded the range and degree of invasiveness possible in the pursuit of beauty. Liposuction (the surgical vacuuming of subcutaneous fat) is now one of the most common procedures. New techniques break up fat cells with ultrasound and suction with a smaller cannula than used in earlier methods that allow for removing pounds as well as reshaping the body. The fact that complications can include blood clots in the lung, vein collapse, shock, permanent nerve injury, skin discoloration, and increased lumpiness of skin has not kept liposuction from becoming an extremely popular procedure (Springer, 1996). Other procedures, costing thousands of dollars, involve the injection of collagen to minimize facial wrinkles. What women are getting is probably more appropriately called "psychosurgery" (Chisholm, 1996), considering the most important impact is on how women think and feel about how they look, and the real objective is a psychological comfort.

Cosmetic surgery is only the modern day approach to women's imperfections. In the Victorian era, treatment for women's pathology focused directly on their sex organs, with doctors performing clitoridectomies, hysterectomies, and ovariectomies in order to cure women of their mental illness (Ussher, 1989). Today, women have been convinced that what is wrong with them is how they look, so the knife that once removed our great grandmothers' ovaries now removes the excess cartilage from our noses, cellulite from our thighs, and wrinkles from our faces. The locus of the pathology has shifted, but the assumption is the same: Women's bodies are to blame for their inadequacies. Tragically, this message is aimed not only at women, but also at girls.

Health Effects for Adolescent Girls

The fundamental dilemma conveyed to adolescent girls is that if they develop their own autonomy and agency—and thus refuse to participate in the quest for beauty—they may risk their social acceptance and eventually jeopardize future social roles as wives and mothers. In general, these roles depend on the affirmation of a man who finds them attractive and who will choose them as a partner. Messages about the importance of attractiveness begin early, and even elementary school girls have definite ideas about how women should look (e.g., tall, thin, blonde, matching clothes) and, thus, be. Girls learn early that the most important part of who they are is their physical appearance. Magazines such as *Seventeen* continue to assume that teenage girls are, or ought to be, concerned with their physical appearance, devoting 50% of their editorial to beauty and fashion (Peirce, 1990). The result of these messages is an increasingly objectified body consciousness among young women that promotes viewing one's own body as an outside observer and that fosters the development of body shame (McKinley & Hyde, 1996).

One ethnographic study (Bell, 1989) revealed that ideals of beauty, as portrayed in the media, constitute a major theme that may block girls' success. As young women enter college, they are reminded, for example, of the importance placed, not on their education, but on their bodies. Few college women have not heard of the "freshman 15," the myth that students, especially women, gain fifteen pounds during their freshman year of college (Hodges, Jackson, & Sullivan, 1993). This myth reflects the polarity for women between attractiveness on the one hand and empowerment and independence on the other. The underlying threat is that women who choose to go to college should most fear sudden and mysterious weight gain, not academic failure. Such a myth not only warns women against losing sight of their most valued asset (i.e., their physical appearance), but also may persuade women to begin to monitor and worry about their weight, even though it had never been a problem.

Internalizing beauty ideals by merging one's sense of self-worth with physical attractiveness in order to obtain social rewards creates the potential for serious health problems for adolescent girls. Intensified focus on the body may increase the risk of eating problems and compulsive weight-management behavior. Eating disorders are alarmingly prevalent among adolescent girls (Fallon, Katzman, & Wooley, 1994), and a substantial portion of these girls will require hospitalization because they are dangerously starved.

National data indicate that 34% of girls age 12–13 perceived themselves as overweight, whereas 42% of those age 14–17 and 49% of those age 18–21 believed they were overweight (Adams, Schoenborn, Moss, Warren, & Kann, 1992). These figures compare with roughly 25% of boys in each age group who thought they were overweight. In the same survey, 50% of girls were actively trying to lose weight, and half of these were relying on restricting food to do so. By focusing on restraint and deprivation, dieting symbolically replicates messages to girls that they must deny or restrict their needs and that, ultimately, they are not entitled to nourishment or nurturance.

As are all complex behaviors, eating disorders are multiply determined, and depending on the constellation of relationships, the disorder may represent either acquiescence or resistance. In some instances an eating disorder may represent the efforts of a young girl to retain her connection to her parents, even if it means rejecting physical maturation. In other instances, the phenomenon may reflect the last means available to the girl by which she can express any form of resistance to control. Psychoanalytic assessments of eating disorders suggest that girls seek to maintain emotional and psychological attachment to their parents by perpetuating their role as a dependent child (Crisp, 1983). In this model, pubescence and associated implications of sexuality are seen as threats to the parent–child connection; girls cannot be adult, autonomous, and sexual without sacrificing the emotional bond with their parents. In this scenario, it surely is not the girls' dependency that is problematic, but rather the parents' inability to relate to daughters who are gaining authority and selfhood. Thus, eating disorders may be understood as a form of acquiescence to parental demands and needs. In this case, the adolescent negotiates with her body for continued acceptance in the role of lovable daughter.

Other models suggest that eating disorders reflect the last bastion of control for adolescent girls when parental and social pressures demand conformity in all other areas (Boskind-Lodahl, 1976). In this model, eating disorders are a form of resistance to parental and societal demands for conformity to rigid roles. Much like prisoners who become preoccupied with bodybuilding and tattooing, adolescent girls are like societal captives who restrict their self-assertion to the corporeal boundary of their own body because it is the only thing left to them. The fact that there are few other outlets for self-assertion and identity may be what makes the eating disorder so fierce. The current prevalence of tattoos among adolescent girls may be a similar kind of phenomena that provides girls a sense of assertion and autonomy.

Smoking is another health risk behavior that often coexists with dieting and efforts to control weight. Tobacco companies have associated smoking with freedom, adulthood, and sexual allure. Ad slogans such as "slim and sassy" are used to promote smoking among adolescent girls. The result is that 19% of 14–17-year-old girls are regular smokers (Adams et al., 1992). Since nicotine dependence is one of the most pernicious addictions, it is likely that girls who become regular smokers in adolescence will carry throughout their lives significant increased risks for low birth weight babies, heart disease, and lung cancer.

The ubiquitous message that external beauty is the sin qua non of sexual allure sends a parallel message to girls that the proof of their sexuality lies not in their own experience so much as the experience of others (i.e., boys and men). In some respects, girls are not considered sexual until they elicit sexual desire in others. This dynamic leads one to question who possesses girls' sexuality—girls themselves or those who are attracted to them? Contributing to this ambiguity is the fact that many girls are discouraged from masturbating. A healthy exploration of one's body for personal pleasure is often condemned in spite of the fact that initiations to erotic stimulation with boys is expected and culturally condoned. Hyde (1996) has suggested that since girls' erotic awareness often emerges within interpersonal contexts, a blurring of boundaries occurs with regard to the ownership of sexual arousal and sexuality in general.

This blurring of boundaries creates implications for health with regard to sexual behavior. Sexual experimentation and intercourse is common among teens, and national data indicate that 30% of 14–15-year-old girls and 58% of 16–17-year-old girls have had intercourse (Adams et al., 1992). Less than half of adolescent girls report condom use, and nearly one third report using no contraception at all. The normative model that seems to be operative is that sex involves little or no planning and little or no talking. The popular image is that people are swept away by the lure of romance and interpersonal intimacy. Such encounters, however, do not always represent the idyllic consummation of young love, as is indicated by the fact that approximately 20% of adolescents age 14–17 reported having between 3 and 5 partners (Adams et al., 1992).

Consequences of unprotected intercourse for adolescent girls involve high rates of sexually transmitted disease, rates that are higher in the United States than in any other industrialized country. The highest rates of gonorrhea and chlamydia are among teen females, approximately 2 million cases each year (Centers for Disease Control, 1997). Unprotected intercourse results in approximately 1 million pregnancies to unmarried teen girls annually (Ventura, Martin, Curtin, & Mathews, 1998). Some of the highest teen pregnancy rates are among southern states, where the role of demure, but seductive female is perhaps more salient (U.S. Department of Health & Human Services, 1998). Although the rate of teen pregnancy has been declining in recent years, the proportion of unmarried teens remains at 80% (Wingert, 1998). Of most concern is the fact that 39% of 15-year-old mothers say the fathers of their babies are age 20 or older (Shapiro, 1995). These disturbing statistics lead us to question the social construction of adolescent sexuality. What is negotiated in these arrangements? What are the implicit assumptions of sexuality and identity? Whose version of reality is constructed that fosters these destructive outcomes?

Fragmented Identity

Another profound effect of the social construction of sexuality and beauty is a fragmented sense of identity for both girls and women. Fragmentation occurs in part because society encourages women to be desirable according to certain beauty ideals while simultaneously encouraging them to deny their sexuality. Women are expected to be sexually attractive while at the same time being punished for being promiscuous and denied adequate access to contraception and reproductive care. In effect, women are left trying to incorporate their real experiences into a framework of fantasy. The missing images of women's realities makes women's experiences seem less valid and only vaguely visible.

An insidious effect of beauty ideals and their relation to sexuality is the transformation of women's (and men's) sexuality away from variable, emergent, and personal experiences to a sexuality that is external, impersonal, and rigidly fixed. Women learn that their sexuality is for others and that being sexual means being an object rather than an agent. Morgan

(1994) has formulated this idea in a strong statement that "women's eroticism is defined as either nonexistent, pathological, or peripheral when it is not directed to phallic goals" (p. 243). In a sense, the women themselves become invisible while the interests and desires of men become figural. To the extent that women internalize the idea that their sexuality, physical appearance, and identity are united, their sense of worth and well-being will depend in large part on their ability to meet whatever impossible standards are popular at the time.

In these circumstances of objectification, personal identity and self-worth are translated into sex appeal that is defined by and for others. Why, one may ask, do women put up with it? The paradox of why women participate in this system is answered by the omnipresent, internalized nature of the system. It is in part the attraction of power and control implicitly promised to women who meet the ideals. It is the magical power of the seductress that offers validation of the self, however temporary and fleeting.

Nevertheless, the implicit promise of affirmation and happiness is more illusory than real. The more likely consequences of buying into this system are feelings of inadequacy and failure. In fact, it is quite normative for girls and women to say they hate their bodies. Women and teen girls actually report peer pressure to express dissatisfaction and disgust for their bodies. In the process of an impossible pursuit, women are demeaned and diminished. When sexuality is objectified, a woman "is treated as if she lacked one or more of the distinctive human capacities upon which her rights to a certain level of well-being and freedom are based ... she is treated in the very way she would commonly be treated if she were an animal, body, or object" (Lemoncheck, 1994, p. 205).

We propose, along with other authors in this volume, that problems with body image, sexual dysfunction, and other psychological disorders are not the result simply of a failure to achieve the right look but are the product of striving for an impossible fantasy. Rather than feeling satisfied, affirmed, and included, women are more likely to feel vaguely anxious, inadequate, vulnerable, and needy. Rather than feeling empowered or enjoying an expanded social life, women are likely to feel insecure and defeated. Ultimately, as long as women continue to have a vested interest in their appearance for lack of another choice, they will continue to be controlled through objectification.

We should never lose sight of the fact that sexual objectification ultimately results in the dehumanization of women. For example, in a recent survey, 50% of 1,000 men said that they would not report their best friend for raping a woman they did not know ("I can't believe," 1995). Curiously enough, 71% of these same men said that women today see themselves too much as victims. These responses reveal a dangerous and dark side to objectification, issues that we will explore more fully in the final section of this volume.

REFORMULATIONS

We believe that a changed consciousness will occur when the current constructions of sexuality are recognized as relatively arbitrary and derived from oppression, an oppression that has been normalized and made invisible. An important basis for a changed consciousness is to recognize the meaning and significance of patterns that are based on status and control. Thus, the first task is to name the phenomenon as costly and based on dominance. Equally important, the task is to deny that the current definitions of women's sexuality derive inevitably from the appearance of their bodies. We hope this chapter has demystified some of the seemingly natural links of beauty and sexuality by outlining the arbitrary quality of these social arrangements and the ways in which they are maintained through everyday events. We additionally hope that a new consciousness will be liberating for women and for men.

In order to investigate sexuality and its meanings, there must be an acknowledgement of the sociopolitical structure that has shaped and sustained these meanings. The process of challenging the definition of sexuality is not simply about liberal values of more and better sex. Challenging the traditional framework of sexuality and gender is a way to challenge the system that has most benefited from that traditional framework (i.e., patriarchy). Our goal is resistance, and therefore these formulations are more political than they are dispassionate observations. However, we note along with Mary Boyle (1994) that if resistance is political, so is acquiescence. That is, accepting a system as if it were normative and benign represents adherence to politics of a certain structure, a structure that benefits some at the expense of others. In acquiescing, one contributes to the stability and pervasiveness of a harmful system. We argue that much of the current understanding of sexuality is really about the regulation of desire and the construction of a narrowed identity for women in particular. We hope to challenge definitions of women as objects and, more generally, the notion of women as Other.

The politics that control women's bodies and sexuality also control their experience, their identity, and their political role in society. The body is a medium of culture that has powerful implications for inner experience. Changing beauty ideals reflect more than intriguing (or sometimes laughable) variations of stylized beauty. They reflect messages to the self, and they shape realms of experience where political origins are disguised as personal ones. In fact, the regulation of desire is often for the purpose of social ends (Bordo, 1992; Martin, 1988).

The mechanisms that keep the sexual objectification of women in place are ubiquitous and powerful. Popular media plays a critical role in the process. Collectively, the images of women in literature, film, and commercial media help to construct common wisdom about women. These messages not only address how women should look, but also convey judgments about who women are and what they should want. These messages become internalized as part of the feelings and experiences of individual women. In this way, the political infuses the personal. It is indeed an autonomous woman who remains unaffected.

We argue along with Wolf (1991) that the pursuit of beauty is not merely based on personal aesthetics or preferences. Beauty has become a defining element in sexuality and, ultimately, a cultural feature of identity. Physical appearance mediates how women are perceived and treated by others, and it influences their own expectations for themselves. Women manipulate their bodies in an attempt to meet narrowly defined and widely shared ideals of beauty and in order to achieve social acceptance, economic security, and status. Personal choice is abrogated because alternatives are limited and because there are penalties for not pursuing mainstream dictates.

One mechanism that helps to perpetuate the high priority accorded beauty is that physical attractiveness functions in part as an alternative form of status and power; that is, physical attractiveness holds the potential to provide women access to power that is otherwise unavailable. Alternative avenues for validation and success through educational, economic, and political arenas are not only closed to most women, but also are often considered inappropriate. It is always easier to pursue goals that are approved by the larger social system and easier to use the strategies that are deemed reasonable. Success seems more attainable if one plays the game as it already has been defined. Wolf (1991) suggests that the distraction of women's attention to matters of appearance makes it less likely they will demand more power on interpersonal or political levels.

Physical attractiveness partly serves as a form of power because it is associated with goodness. It is well established that people respond more favorably to others who are attractive. Men tend to judge the attractiveness of women based on their general self-presentation and use of cosmetics. For example, women were rated significantly less attractive by male judges when they wore no makeup than when they wore a typical amount of makeup (Cash, Dawson, Davis, Bowen, & Galumbeck, 1989). People usually expect to like attractive strangers, expect them to be competent, and see them as personally successful (Dion, Berscheid, & Walster, 1972). In addition, people may be more readily swayed in their opinions by an attractive communicator (Mills & Aronson, 1965). In general, more positive qualities are attributed to attractive than to unattractive people (Moore, Graziano, & Millar, 1987). Furthermore, physical attractiveness is seen as a cue of high status (Kalick, 1988) and has been related to success in the workplace (Wolf, 1991).

Society provides certain rewards and benefits for women who most closely approximate beauty ideals. For example, attractive women who are survivors of rape and testify in court are often perceived more favorably (Deitz, Littman, & Bentley, 1984), and are perceived to be less responsible for the rape (Gerdes, Dammann, & Heilig, 1988) than are unattractive plaintiffs. Additionally, the defendants of attractive plaintiffs are more likely to be found guilty (Jacobson & Popovich, 1983) than the defendants of unattractive plaintiffs. Similarly, sexual harassment cases with attractive plaintiffs and unattractive defendants are more likely to bring in a guilty verdict (Castellow, Wuensch, & Moore, 1990). Physical attractiveness also benefits defendants; attractive defendants receive less severe punishments than do unattractive defendants (Stewart, 1985).

Although appearance is important to men, it is not considered to be their single, most important, and defining characteristic, as it often is with women. Men generally have more avenues through which they are able to obtain status, power, and social acceptance. Further, men benefit from a dynamic that emphasizes the importance of beauty for women. Unger (1979) has argued that men who are affiliated with attractive women are themselves seen as more likable and as holding higher occupational status than men who are affiliated with unattractive women. Unger termed the phenomena the "Aristotle Onassis–Jackie Kennedy effect" (i.e., a younger attractive woman paired with an older successful man). She further notes that men appear to be aware at some level that being associated with an attractive woman confers male status characteristics on them. This may be one reason why women's physical attractiveness is so salient for men. Men benefit from secondary gains in their own status among other men if they are affiliated with an attractive woman. In this way, men may derive an indirect benefit by encouraging women to continue to see themselves as objects whose value depends on being attractive to men. Men also may contribute to maintaining the equation in various common, everyday behaviors. For example, many men in the company of wives or girlfriends have little compunction about making extravagant remarks about the sex appeal of other women. Such ogling and demonstrations of arousal communicate that there is an actual ideal body-beauty-style that engenders full approval, which the woman they are with does not typify.

When women deviate from the ideal, consequences are severe. Fashion in the 1990s remains geared toward women who are young and slender; fashion for women not meeting those characteristics is largely ignored. For instance, women who wear sizes larger than 14 have a much more limited choice of clothing options, as do women who are especially short, tall, or "oddly" proportioned. Being overweight has a number of social and interpersonal consequences for women. Relative to average-weight women, overweight women tend to date less often and report that their mates are less satisfied with their body size (Stake & Lauer, 1987). Additionally, women's performance self-esteem is positively related to their perception of attractiveness (Stake & Lauer, 1987). In other words, women must be thin in order to feel competent.

Despite the consequences women face for failing to achieve beauty expectations, women who do achieve them can suffer as well. Not surprisingly, there are often double binds for women on the issue of self-display. Kleinke and Staneski (1980) found that women with large bust sizes are considered incompetent, lazy, unintelligent, immoral, and immodest, whereas women with average or small bust sizes are considered competent, ambitious, intelligent, moral, and modest. And although cosmetic use may increase the perception of physical attractiveness, it also may increase women's likelihood of being seen as less moral (Workman & Kim, 1991), less competent (Cox & Glick, 1986), and more likely to provoke sexual harassment (Workman & Johnson, 1991).

This destructive system remains stable due to promised benefits, limited alternatives, and very high costs associated with divergence. Resistance ensures negative sanctions and exclusion from the normative experiences (e.g., dating, marriage) that most women expect will provide fulfillment. How, then, will it be possible to interrupt the inertia of an entire social system?

New understanding and new theory can begin with honoring personal experience and connections (Brabeck & Brown, 1997). The process can begin by listening to the experiences of women and to the voices of those who have been oppressed in the current constructions of sexuality. As silent voices and meanings emerge, consciousness can be raised about the political nature of gender and sexual roles. From this perspective, individuals are participants in change and can be agents of change. However, we also recognize that the construction of sexuality is produced in a larger social system. Ultimately, both women and men need to understand their sexual arrangements as reflections of larger social frameworks, based on hierarchy and privilege, that meet the interests of some at the expense of others.

Therefore, we reject formulations that focus solely on the individual. Those who occupy more or less privileged positions often draft prescriptions for social change in terms of the individual: individual courage, individual morality, individual perseverance, individual choice. They admonish women for not being able to use these individual strengths in order to break free of beauty constraints. The systemic factors that nourish and engender views of self, other, and society remain invisible in such expostulations, and this approach to individual problems is thus inherently self-serving.

In contrast to traditional biological models, we propose that sexuality is socially agreed on, and as such, it is negotiated. The negotiations are based on shared, but often unspoken, understandings of reality (i.e., the meaning and significance of things). The negotiations build on the realities of each party and are used to construct the meaning of events and how they are to be appropriately experienced. In this sense, sexuality is emergent and highly contextual. Part of that context involves the status, resources, and alternatives available to each party; for example, the costs and risks of asserting one's own experience and meaning system are not equal for everyone. It is important to understand that the negotiations are seldom explicit and that they may be driven by vested interests that often remain unacknowledged by those who benefit. In the end, some realities are established as normative and natural, while others may be trivialized, silenced, or pathologized.

There are no big winners in the current arrangements of sexuality. The promises of well-being and affirmation are more illusory than real. Although it is quite clear that women are disadvantaged in the traditional system of patriarchy, it also is the case that most men are disadvantaged as well. Patriarchy promises identity, status, and control to men in the abstract, but the full benefits of masculine privilege and power fall only to a select few. Most men, as well as women, would be better served by a system more respectful of individual worth, diversity, inclusiveness, and caring—in other words, a system that conceptualizes women and men as equals. One way to find the motivation for change is to recognize that the promised benefits of the current system are not forthcoming.

Generating the emotional intensity to energize resistance will arise when women recognize the real nature of the gender contract (i.e., the trading of traditional femininity and beauty for temporary social rewards). A further step in resistance will arise when women recognize that the contract is honored in only the most shallow and fleeting way. Being beautiful will never guarantee women education, jobs, health care, child support, a home, political influence, a safe abortion, economic mobility, justice within the legal system, or personal safety. The task is to identify what will guarantee women these benefits and teach girls and women to focus their attention on opportunities and behaviors likely to bring them real security and power.

A related task is for men realize that the social contract delivers much less than is promised to them as well. It is revealing to look at the costs for men as well as for women in the current construction of sexuality. As Laura Brown points out in chapter 11, this volume, the privileges of sexual priority fall not to men in general but only to masculine men. Traditional arrangements produce an odd situation, in which men must continually seek reassurance that they are "real" men and therefore entitled to sexual expression with women. This leads to a monotonous game of one-upmanship, competition, risk taking, and aggression among boys and men. It can result in persistent feelings of isolation while simultaneously requiring that they always appear confident and in control. More specifically, we note that although they seem to privilege men, current definitions of sexuality based on the penis, erection, intercourse, and ejaculation leave most men over the age of 25 feeling as if they have passed their sexual peak.

Language is a first step toward women beginning to own their sexuality. Naming is a way to affirm and validate, and naming is a way of reclaiming value and power. Similarly, language may be used to challenge the connotations of beauty ideals. What if the word *beauty* were changed to reflect the behavior associated with such pursuits (e.g., Doll-like, made-up, fake, manipulated, painted, contorted, cut up, glued on, squeezed together, deodorized, perfumed, sprayed, darkened, lightened, bleached, pierced, chained, molded, sculpted, shaped, purged, starved).

The language of sexual relations is also revealing of a patriarchal society that has eroticized male dominance (Trigiani, 1998). Trigiani (1998) notes that the word *penetrate* to describe sexual intercourse is an example in which implicit dominance becomes more obvious and objectionable when it is applied to real people (e.g., "Bob penetrated Lisa"). Is this really the way we want to characterize intimacy, trust, and desire? In fact, there is a general fear, often unspoken, that gender equity would mean sexless relationships; that powerful women would brutalize men; that women with resources and alternatives equal to those of men would be without any libido at all; or that men in such relationships would be de-sexed and impotent. The phrase "vive la difference," expressed so playfully as a rationale for categorical distinctions between the genders, is a disguised reflection of this fear. *Cuckold* is another enlightening term (i.e., a man whose wife has committed adultery). Here is an experience that until relatively recently in many states was a justifiable defense for homicide (e.g., paramour laws). However, there is no term to recognize or name an equivalent experience, or wrong, for women; the female experience is invisible. Language that honors women's erotic life would surely look something like Lucille Clifton's (1980) poem, "Homage to My Hips":

> these hips are big hips.
> they need space to move around in.
> they don't fit into little pretty places
> these hips are free hips.
> they don't like to be held back.
> these hips have never been enslaved
> they go where they want to go.
> they do what they want to do.
> these hips are mighty hips.
> these hips are magic hips.
> i have known them to put a spell on a man
> and spin him like a top!

Another step toward transforming knowledge is to reexamine and challenge traditional assumptions about sexuality. Traditional assumptions include the idea that sexuality is encapsulated in the individual and that it reflects individual identity as opposed to socially agreed on definitions. Traditional assumptions also promote the idea that sexuality is largely, if not entirely, a matter of biology. This leads to the conclusion that sexuality is innate, invariant, and fixed. It also supports the idea that sexuality as it is currently embodied is natural, and therefore is untainted by conventions of power and privilege.

Alternative formulations of sexuality need to incorporate and value the experiences of women. Much of the empirical research on beauty and sexuality is indexed to the experiences of women who are White, middle-class, and young. Phenomenological and standpoint methodologies can be usefully applied toward building a reformulation. The objective is to allow the authority of women's experiences to construct their realities (Daniluk, 1993). Because women haven't been allowed to create a framework for sexuality based on their own experiences, they are left trying to reconcile patriarchal assumptions, myths, and lies about who they are and what is important. Dismissing the binding definitions of women in a sexist society and exploring, instead, private experience has the potential of healing individual wounds and subverting patriarchy (Brown, 1994; Brabeck & Brown, 1997). We advocate the exploration of sexuality in ways that are relevant to the lived experiences of both women and men. We additionally advocate that there be a recognition that experience is shaped by a larger framework of reality that is socially constructed. The symbols, the meanings, and the significance accorded these features reflect social arrangements of power and privilege, including the privilege to define reality. Thus, experience is the beginning point for a reflexive examination of the individual and also for the pursuit of social activism.

REFERENCES

Adams, P. F., Schoenborn, C. A., Moss, A. J., Warren, C. W., & Kann, L. (1992). Health risk behaviors among our nation's youth: United States, 1992. *Vital Health Statistics*, series 10 (12), Hyattsville, MD: National Center for Health Statistics.

Allan, J. D., Mayo, K., & Michel, Y. (1993). Body size values of White and Black women. *Research in Nursing and Health, 16(5)*, 323–333.

Baker, N. (1984). *The beauty trap: Exploring women's greatest obsession*. New York: Franklin Watts.

Banner, L. (1983). *American beauty*. New York: Knopf.

Banta, M. (1987). *Imaging American women: Idea and ideals in cultural history*. New York: Columbia University Press.

Bell, L. A. (1989). Something's wrong here and it's not me: Challenging the dilemmas that block girls' success. *Journal for the Education of the Gifted, 12(2)*, 118–130.

Bernard, J. (1972). *The future of marriage*. New York: World.

Bordo, S. R. (1992). The body and the reproduction of femininity: A feminist appropriation of Foucault. In A. M. Jaggar & S. R. Bordo (Eds.), *Gender/body/knowledge/Feminist reconstructions of being and knowing*. (pp. 13–33). New Brunswick, NJ: Rutgers University Press.

Boskind-Lodahl, M. (1976). Cinderella's stepsisters: A feminist perspective on anorexia nervosa and bulimia. *Signs: A Journal of Women in Culture and Society, 2(2)*, 342–356.

Boyle, M. (1994). Gender, science, and sexual dysfunction. In T. R. Sarbin & J. I. Kitsuse (Eds.), *Constructing the social* (pp. 101–118). Thousand Oaks, CA: Sage.

Brabeck, M., & Brown, L. (1997). Feminist theory and psychological practice. In J. Worell & N. G. Johnson (Eds.), *Shaping the future of feminist psychology: Education, research, and practice* (pp. 15–35). Washington, DC: American Psychological Association.

Broby-Johansen, R. (1968). *Body and clothes*. London: Faber and Faber.

Brown, L. (1994). *Subversive dialogues*. New York: Harper Collins.

Carby, H. (1986). It jus be's dat way sometime: The sexual politics of women's blues. *Radical America, 20(4)*, 9–22.

Cash, T. F., Dawson, K., Davis, P., Bowen, M., & Galumbeck, C. (1989). Effects of cosmetics use on the physical attractiveness and body image of American college women. *The Journal of Social Psychology, 129(3)*, 349–355.

Castellow, W. A., Wuensch, K. L., & Moore, C. H. (1990). Effects of physical attractiveness on the plaintiff and defendant in sexual harassment judgments. *Journal of Social Behavior and Personality, 5(6)*, 547–562.

Centers for Disease Control. (1997). *Sexually transmitted disease surveillance, 1996*. Washington DC: Centers for Disease Control.

Chisholm, P. (1996). The body builders. *McLean's, 109(28)*, 36.

Clark, K. (1980). *Feminine beauty*. New York: Rizzoli.

Clifton, L. (1980). *Two-headed woman*. Amherst: University of Massachusetts Press.

Cox, C. L., & Glick, W. H. (1986). Resume evaluations and cosmetic use: When more is not better. *Sex Roles, 14(1/2)*, 51–58.

Crisp, A. H. (1983). Some aspects of the psychopathology of anorexia nervosa. In P. L. Darbey, P. E. Garfinkel, D. M. Garner, & D. V. Coscina (Eds.), *Anorexia nervosa: Recent developments in research* (pp. 15–28). New York: Alan R. Liss.

Danielson, D. (1989). The changing figure ideal in fashion illustration. *Clothing and Textiles Research Journal, 8(1)*, 35–48.

Daniluk, J. C. (1993). The meaning and experience of female sexuality: A phenomenological analysis. *Psychology of Women Quarterly, 17*, 53–69.

Deitz, S. R., Littman, M. & Bentley, B. J. (1984). Attribution of responsibility for rape: The influence of observe, empathy, victim resistance, and victim attractiveness. *Sex Roles, 10(3–4),* 261–280.

Douglas, D. N. (1983). *Choice and compromise: A woman's guide to balancing family and career.* New York: AMACOM.

Dion, K. K., Berscheid, E., & Walster, E. (1972). What is beautiful is good. *Journal of Personality and Social Psychology, 24,* 285–290.

Fallon, P., Katzman, M. A., and Wooley, S. C. (Eds.). (1994). *Feminist perspectives on eating disorders.* New York: Guilford Press.

Faludi, S. (1991). *Backlash: The undeclared war against American women.* New York: Doubleday.

Firestone, S. (1970). *The dialectic of sex: The case for feminist revolution.* New York: Morrow.

Ford, C. S., & Beach, F. A. (1951). *Patterns of sexual behavior.* New York: Harper.

Frankfort, E. (1972). *Vaginal politics.* New York: Quadrangle.

Friedan, B. (1963). *The feminine mystique.* New York: Norton.

Garland, M. (1957). *The changing face of beauty; Four thousand years of beautiful women.* New York: M. Barrows and Company.

Garner, D. M., Garfinkel, P. E., Schwartz, D., & Thompson, M. (1980). Cultural expectations of thinness in women. *Psychological Reports, 47,* 483–491.

Gerdes, E. P., Dammann, E. J., & Heilig, K. E. (1988). Perceptions of rape victims and assailants: Effects of physical attractiveness, acquaintance, and subject gender. *Sex Roles, 19(3–4),* 141–153.

Gerson, K. (1985). *Hard choices: How women decide about work, career, and motherhood.* Berkeley: University of California Press.

Goldberg, P. A., Gottesdiener, M., & Abramson, P. R. (1975). Another put-down of women? Perceived attractiveness as a function of support for the feminist movement. *Journal of Personality and Social Psychology, 32,* 113–115.

Good, C. (1989). The southern lady, or the art of dissembling. *Journal of American Studies, 23(1),* 72–76.

Gray, J. (1992). *Men are from Mars, women are from Venus.* New York: Harper Collins.

Hamilton, K., & Weingarden, J. (1998, June 15). Lifts, lasers, and liposuction. *Newsweek, 131(24),* 14.

Haney, L. (1981). *Naked at the feast.* New York: Dodd, Mead.

Hewlett, S. A. (1986). *A lesser life: The myth of women's liberation in America.* New York: W. Morrow.

Hodges, C. N., Jackson, L. A., & Sullivan, L. A. (1993). The "freshman 15": Facts and fantasies about weight gain in college women. *Psychology of Women Quarterly, 17,* 119–126.

Honey, M. (1984). *Creating Rosie the Riveter: Class, gender, and propaganda during World War II.* Amherst: University of Massachusetts Press.

Hyde, J. S. (1996). *Half the human experience: The psychology of women*. Lexington, MA: DC Heath.

I can't believe you asked that! Sex answers coaxed from 1,000 men. (1995, January). *Glamour*, 136–139.

Jacobi, L., & Cash, T. F. (1994). In pursuit of the perfect appearance: Discrepancies among self ideal percepts of multiple physical attributes. *Journal of Applied Social Psychology, 24(5)*, 379–396.

Jacobson, M. B., & Popovich, P. M. (1983). Victim attractiveness and perceptions of responsibility in an ambiguous rape case. *Psychology of Women Quarterly, 8*, 100–104.

Kalick, M. S. (1988). Physical attractiveness as a status cue. *Journal of Experimental Social Psychology, 24(6)*, 469–489.

Kaltreider, N. B. (Ed.) (1997). *Dilemmas of a double life: Women balancing careers and relationships*. Northvale, NJ: Jason Aronson.

Kleinke, C. L., & Staneski, R. A. (1980). First impressions of female bust size. *The Journal of Social Psychology, 110*, 123–134.

Kilbourne, J. (1979). Beauty and the beast of advertising. *Media and Values, 4*, 121–125.

Kilbourne, J. (1994). Still killing us softly: Advertising and the obsession with thinness. In P. Fallon, M. A. Katzman, & S. C. Wooley (Ed.), *Feminist perspectives on eating disorders* (pp. 395–418). New York: Guilford.

Lakoff, R. T., & Scherr, R. L. (1984). *Face value: Politics of beauty*. Boston, MA: Routledge & Kegan Paul.

Lemoncheck, L. (1994). What's wrong with being a sex object? In A. M. Jaggar (Ed.), *Living with contradictions: Controversies in feminist social ethics*. Boulder, CO: Westview Press.

Martin, B. (1988). Feminism, criticism, and Foucault. In I. Diamond & L. Quinby (Eds.), *Feminism and Foucault* (pp. 3–19). Boston: Northeastern University Press.

Mazur, A. (1986). U.S. trends in feminine beauty and overadaptation. *The Journal of Sex Research, 22(3)*, 281–303.

McKinley, N. M., & Hyde, J. S. (1996). The objectified body consciousness scale: Development and validation. *Psychology of Women Quarterly, 20(2)*, 181–215.

Millet, K. (1970). *Sexual politics*. Garden City, NY: Doubleday.

Mills, J., & Aronson, E. (1965). Opinion change as a function of the communicator's attractiveness and desire to influence. *Journal of Personality and Social Psychology, 1*, 173–177.

Minardi, P. (1971). The politics of housework. In June Sochen (Ed.), *The new feminism in twentieth century America* (pp. 113–119). Lexington, MA: DC Heath.

Moore, J. S., Graziano, W. G., & Millar, M. G. (1987). Physical attractiveness, sex role orientation, and the evaluation of adults and children. *Personality and Social Psychology Bulletin, 13(1)*, 95–102.

Morgan, K. P. (1994). Women and the knife: Cosmetic surgery and the colonization of women's bodies. In A. M. Jaggar (Ed.), *Living with contradictions: Controversies in feminist social ethics* (pp. 305–334). Boulder, CO: Westview.

Morical, L. (1984). *Where's my happy ending?: Women and the myth of having it all.* Reading, MA: Addison-Wesley.

Morin, R. (1997, November 5). Family values a key to result: Voters concerned about morality, poll shows. *The Washington Post*, A1.

Mullins, E., & Sites, P. (1984). The origins of contemporary eminent black Americans: A three generational analysis of social origins. *American Sociological Review, 49(5),* 672–685.

Okazawa-Rey, M., Robinson, T., & Ward, J. V. (1987). Black women and the politics of skin color and hair. *Women and Therapy, 6(1–2),* 89–102.

Peirce, K. (1990). A feminist theoretical perspective on the socialization of teenage girls through *Seventeen* magazine. *Sex Roles, 23(9/10),* 491–500.

Peiss, K. (1990). Making faces: The cosmetic industry and the cultural construction of gender. *Genders, 7,* 143–169.

Plous, S., & Neptune, D. (1997). Racial and gender biases in magazine advertising. *Psychology of Women Quarterly, 21,* 627–644.

Rupp, L. (1978). *Mobilizing women for war: German and American propaganda, 1939–1945.* Princeton, NJ: Princeton University Press.

Schneider, D. (1993). *American women in the Progressive Era, 1900–1920.* New York: Facts on File.

Seaman, B. (1969). *The doctor's case against the pill.* New York: Avon Press.

Shapiro, J. P. (1995, August 14). Sins of the fathers: It is adult males who are fathering the babies born to teenagers. *U.S. News and World Report, 117,* p. 51.

Silverstein, B., Peterson, B., & Perdue, L. (1986). Some correlates of the thin standard of bodily attractiveness for women. *International Journal of Eating Disorders, 5(5),* 895–905.

Spain, D. (1996). *Balancing act: Motherhood, marriage, and employment among American women.* New York: Russell Sage Foundation.

Springer, R. C. (1996). Liposuction: An overview. *Plastic Surgical Nursing, 16(4),* 215.

Stake, J., & Lauer, M. (1987). The consequences of being overweight: A controlled study of gender differences. *Sex Roles, 17(1–2),* 31–47.

Stewart, J. E. (1985). Appearance and punishment: The attraction-leniency effect in the courtroom. *Journal of Social Psychology, 125(3),* 373–378.

Stewart, N. K. (1977). *Put down and ripped off: The American woman and the beauty cult.* New York: Crowell.

Todd, J. (1987). Bernarr Madfadden: Reformer of feminine form. *Journal of Sport History, 14(1),* 61–75.

Travis, C. (1988). *Women and health psychology: Mental health issues.* Hillsdale, NJ: Erlbaum Associates.

Trepagnier, B. (1994). The politics of white and black bodies. *Feminism & Psychology, 4(1)*, 199–205.

Trigiani, K. (1998, December 27). Power and sexuality. Listserv for Division 35, American Psychological Association.

Unger, R. K. (1979). *Female and male*. New York: Harper & Row.

U.S. Department of Health & Human Services. (1998, June 26). State-specific pregnancy rates among adolescents—United States, 1992–1995. *Morbidity & Mortality Weekly Report, 47(24)*, 497.

Ussher, J. M. (1989). *The psychology of the female body*. New York: Routledge.

Ventura, S., Martin, J., Curtin, S., & Mathews, T. J. (1998). *Report on final natality statistics, 1996*. Hyattsville, MD: National Center for Health Statistics, U.S.D.H.H.S.

Wingert, P. (1998, May 11). The battle over falling birthrates: Teenage pregnancy rate falls 11.9% from 1991–99 due to increased use of contraceptives and abstinence. *Newsweek, 131*, 40.

Wolf, N. (1991). *The beauty myth: How images of beauty are used against women*. New York: Doubleday.

Workman, J. E., & Johnson, K. K. P. (1991). The role of cosmetics in attributions about sexual harassment. *Sex Roles, 24(11/12)*, 759–769.

Workman, J. E., & Kim, K. K. P. (1991). The role of cosmetics in impression formation. *Clothing and Textiles Research Journal, 10(1)*, 63–67.

Young, C. (1998, March 11). Family values may rely on peer couples. *Detroit News*, p. A9.

11

DANGEROUSNESS, IMPOTENCE, SILENCE, AND INVISIBILITY: HETEROSEXISM IN THE CONSTRUCTION OF WOMEN'S SEXUALITY

LAURA S. BROWN

Although the phenomenology of sexuality is experienced in the body, the ways we label and define that sexual experience are heavily socially defined. What is shameful, what is acceptable, how one describes one's sexual identity to self and others, are all derived from the social discourse in general, and the discourse on sexuality in specific.

The general social discourse is one that can be described as, among other things, filled with heterosexist and antisexual minority bias. The various cultures of North America, with the exception of some Native American communities (Williams, 1987), ascribe negative value and deviant status to people whose affectional and sexual preferences are toward their own sex. Even in the face of 20 years of a political movement for the civil rights of sexual minority persons (here defined as gay men, lesbians, bisexual women and men, and transgendered people), pervasive negativity toward this population persists. In the past half decade bias-based

273

violence against sexual minority persons, a measure of such negativity, has risen sharply (Cogan, 1996) as sexual minorities have taken the place formerly held by the straw person of Communism as the cultural representation of the demonic (see Osborne, 1996; Vaid, 1995, for a discussion of the complex political issues inherent in this phenomenon). A federal law, the Defense of Marriage Act (DOMA), was passed and signed by President Clinton in 1996, proclaiming same-sex relationships to be exempt from the constitutional protections of the "Full faith and credit" clause of the Bill of Rights. Local and statewide initiatives against sexual minority civil rights continue to pass, even though their goals were defined as unconstitutional by the U.S. Supreme Court in its recent decision on Colorado's Amendment Two, one such voter-approved law.

One of the messages most powerfully conveyed by opponents of this civil rights movement is that sexual minority persons should become as we once were—silenced and invisible, ceasing to demand the so-called special rights of protections against discrimination or access to societal institutions such as legal marriage or survivor benefits from Social Security. Sexual minorities are particularly scorned when attempting to gain access to those institutions, such as marriage and parenthood, that are deemed the sole possession and right of those who identify and behave heterosexually, as demonstrated by the rhetoric that accompanied the Congressional debate over DOMA and similar bills in state legislatures. The sexuality of sexual minority persons was described as debasing and soiling the institution of marriage, thus the notion that marriage needed to be defended against same-sex unions.

The public discourse on the sexuality of sexual minority persons takes place against the backdrop of this more general heterosexist and biased milieu. The discourse on lesbian sexuality in particular takes place within the overlapping context of sexism and the larger conversation on women's sexuality. Both forms of oppression have had silencing and distorting effects on lesbians.

In English-speaking cultures, the conversation on the sexuality of gay men is more complete and rich, since sexuality has been more frequently ascribed to men, with women's sexual selves defined as subordinate or responsive to male sexuality (see Loulan, 1984, 1987, 1990, and Bright, 1990, 1992, 1995, for a more in-depth analysis of this difference). Because gay men are men, their sexuality is perceived, both by themselves and by the dominant culture, in a more overt fashion. When the radical right shows scare videos of the queer community, the images are often those of gay men in some form of sexual display (in this chapter I will not attempt to address questions of construction of gay male sexuality, since the core of my argument is that images of lesbian sexuality are commentaries on women, not on same-sex contact).

The discourse on lesbians, by contrast, is instructive for what it has historically contained and excluded. It is also of value, as I will argue here, because of its powerful but largely invisible impact on women's sexualities in general, and the interaction between images of lesbians and images of other sexually agentic women. In this chapter I explore the parameters of heterosexist discourse on lesbian sexuality, and propose that such discourse affects the sexual identities and sexual selves of nonlesbian women as well.

Heterosexism in the social construction of women's sexuality has had profound consequences for the sexual lives of lesbians. Until recently, heterosexism has served to make us invisible, or to distort our experience so that we cannot recognize ourselves in the funhouse mirrors of the dominant culture. We have been left to invent ourselves sexually using only the words and images that are available from heterosexual realities in the drawing of our lesbian images.

Not only lesbians have fallen victim to the ills of heterosexist social constructions of sexuality for women. Although most discussions of heterosexism in relationship to any variable have been confined to the effects on sexual minority women, I will argue here that all women's sexual selves are to some degree affected by the presence of heterosexism in the general discourse. Women who are sexually committed to other women are engaging in a sexuality absent men, where men are irrelevant. In consequence, commentaries on lesbian sexuality can be taken at the meta-level as forms of judgment about women's sexuality in general. Information about what is pleasurable to women, about women's sexual agency, and about the power of women to take various roles in sexual activity are all coded into the social commentary on lesbianism. These images are conveyed in various forms to all women, and become part of all women's sexual narratives (Palladino & Stephenson, 1990). When taken in uncritically, these images serve as limiting factors on the sexual selves of women who are heterosexual as well as lesbian and bisexual (Wilkinson & Kitzinger, 1993).

In this chapter I will explore the overarching impact of heterosexism on the construction of women's sexual selves. Through an examination of social narratives about lesbians and other sexual minority women, I will explore the means by which women's public and private expressions of sexual self have been constrained by heterosexist conventions. I will explore two themes that I perceive to be dominant in heterosexist narratives of lesbian sexuality—the invisibility and impotence of the lesbian, and the shaming and dangerousness of the lesbian—as a means for understanding how these constructions can train women into a colonized sexuality that is subservient to men. I will specifically explore the effects of these narratives on the sexual lives of lesbians themselves. I will then turn to questions of resistance and transformation, drawing on the personal accounts of women who have been highly sexually marginalized by the dominant culture yet able to construct vibrant and powerful sexual selves in those margins, as examples of strategies for undermining heterosexism in women's sexual self-constructions.

THE INVISIBLE AND IMPOTENT LESBIAN

The story is told that when the British legislators of Queen Victoria's era were preparing laws to criminalize sexual behaviors between adults of the same gender, they had originally planned to outlaw both male and female homosexuality. However, or so goes the story, when the Queen was apprised of these plans, she was shocked and ordered the law minister to withdraw those passages referring to lesbianism. After all, said Victoria, what would two women do together?

Perhaps this story is apocryphal; whatever its lineage, it is certainly metaphoric of the manner in which invisibility has been an aspect of the social discourse regarding lesbian sexuality. Lesbian sexuality is defined here as nonexistent; what, after all, could women do sexually without a man and his penis present? But this question could apply to any woman regardless of the object of her desire. The implications of the invisible lesbian are that all women are sexually invisible in the absence of a man. This image of lesbian sexuality as an ersatz, or incomplete sexual self, has colored the external social realities in which lesbians develop an internal sense of sexual self. Those milieux have been ones in which we have been dispossessed of the linguistic and conceptual categories with which to describe and define private sexual experiences. I am aware of no language spoken by large linguistic groups in which women are positively described as other than targets of male sexuality, rather than as actors with personal agency in the absence of men.

This invisibility of lesbian sexuality, with its subtext regarding the dependence of women's sexual selves on the presence of a man, can be found when so-called lesbian images are produced by mainstream cultures. This genre is characterized by narratives like D. H. Lawrence's *The Fox*, in which a lesbian couple befriends and then is invaded and supplanted by a man. Even literature written by lesbians prior to the introduction of a self-conscious lesbian-positive politic reflected this theme of the lesbian as incomplete and therefore sexually potentially invisible. For instance, Stephen, the hero/ine of *The Well of Loneliness* sends her beloved Mary off to a sexual relationship with a man because this will be ultimately more satisfying to her. In this collection of images, lesbian relating (and by inference, the sexual woman) is at best comforting, but neither sexual nor passionate in the way that only real (e.g., with a man present) sexuality can be.

In more recent times, there is the example of commercial (produced by men for heterosexual men and their partners) so-called soft porn (e.g., no images of violence against women) in which lesbian scenes are included. As Bright (1995) notes in her review of some of this media, even the very best and most erotic images of women pleasuring other women are inevitably, in this medium, transformed into a heterosexual scene in which the women's interactions are constructed as present for the arousal of the man who is brought into the picture, or where the women do not reach their ultimate sexual fulfillment until the man has had intercourse with them both. The inference that can be drawn from this text is that women are sexually incomplete and potentially sexually invisible when a man is not present. What is meant to be arousing about these scenes is the beauty of the women, and the anticipation of the man's appearance. The so-called lesbian of these scenes, and woman in general by implication, is sexually impotent and invalid except as an object. Even when she is using a dildo on another woman, the supposed penis substitute is defined by the story line as less sexually agentic and satisfying than the genuine article, since the levels of moaning and groaning and simulated ecstasy rise when the flesh version is used instead of the silicon one.

This sort of image is in tune with those of heterosexual relating available in almost any popular medium today. Sex for women with men is portrayed as overpowering and extraordinarily pleasurable. In feature film after feature film, the viewing audience is offered scenes of women tearing off their clothing, being pressed against walls, into muddy fields, or down on desks by a man, and coming to apparent orgasm almost immediately on penetration, which itself follows only seconds of frenzied kissing and clothing removal. Similar scenes fill the pages of novels. Here, the inference is that the mere presence of a man creates instant arousal in women, and that penetration with the penis is profoundly pleasurable and a quick source of orgasm to women, wonderful above all else. (This is not to suggest that penetration is unpleasurable—it is rather to note that this specific form of penetration, by a man's penis, is the only form so privileged by this narrative.)

The heterosexist message that can be derived from these contrasting and consistent images of male-created sexual fantasy is that women only exist sexually when a man is present. Despite all of the display of flesh and simulated sexual activity on today's screens, we appear to have come little distance from Queen Victoria in our ability to envision women as sexually potent and active when there is no man around.

The implications of this heterosexist narrative on women's sexual selves is potentially deadly and undermining. The image of lesbian impotence becomes a device for communicating several things to all women. First, it conveys that sexual relating between women, and consequently the sexuality of the individual woman, is not genuine sex. The manner in which dildos are portrayed by the heterosexist narrative is instructive and paradigmatic.

One could construct a dildo as an instrument of pleasure for a woman who chooses and enjoys penetration in her own time (e.g., not simply when a partner with a penis is capable of erection) and at her own speed, and in her own choice of company (alone or with a partner of either sex). But instead, dildos are defined as a less-than-adequate penis substitute, always joyfully put aside when the actual penis becomes available. What a woman does alone, or with another woman, is sexually inadequate in this construction. The lesser-than status of the lesbian is simply the status of the human without a penis, or a woman.

Second, there is the message that genuine pleasure is impossible for women absent a man. Women's ability to relate to themselves or other women sexually is portrayed as inferior. In a society that values speed in all things, from our computers to our sex heroes, the lengthy caresses of a woman to herself or another woman are not up to the efficient and overpoweringly pleasurable heterosexual intercourse experience offered by men. Even the terminology used in common discourse to refer to sexual relating is profoundly heterosexist; the things that women do to pleasure themselves or other women are defined as foreplay or fondling or caressing; sex always and only is shorthand for heterosexual intercourse. The language of sex is founded in the experiences of penis-bearing people.

The linguist Suzette Haden Elgin (1984) has used the device of a science fiction narrative to comment on how languages in general are shaped by the experience of men, and that the admission of women's language into a discourse potentially reshapes not only language but reality. The poverty of language in the common discourse for lesbian sexual relating is simply a version of the heavy dependence on terms that are centered in male erotic experience that include penile penetration, language informing the perceived realities of the sexual self for women. In the lives of women it is not only lesbians who lack a common language to describe sexual activity (or as one woman participant in a sexuality workshop noted, there is no female equivalent term for jerking off, leaving women to be clinical and call it masturbation, or romantic (e.g., self-pleasuring, a term that never caught on very well).

Thus, one aspect of the heterosexist narrative of female sexuality is that women are sexually nonexistent on their own. As Murphy (1991) has noted, this nonexistence extends to the social sphere, where sexuality is only implied. Two women together in a restaurant without a man's presence are women alone. The company of the other woman is rendered invisible, due to the underlying implication that a woman ceases sexually (and in consequence, socially) to exist in the absence of a man. For some feminist to have stated that "a woman needs a man like a fish needs a bicycle" was quite a revolutionary message, because it implicitly confronted multiple layers of heterosexist construction of women as only existing sexually in the heterosexual context.

THE SHAMEFUL AND DANGEROUS LESBIAN

At times, however, it has not been enough for the images of the heterosexist narrative to denigrate lesbian sexuality as impotent in order to convey to women that their sexual place was one of silence, receptivity, and response to the desires of men. When it has been necessary in the social discourse to convey the extreme undesirability of women's sexual agency, the image of the evil, dangerous, or shameful lesbian is evoked. In this version, which is most prevalent in current popular fiction and cinema and pre-1975 psychological literature (of course, we could call that fiction, too), lesbians are commonly older, often unattractive, masculine-appearing women who are stern, heavy-set, cruel, and lacking in social graces. These women can be found seducing and ruining innocent, feminine (read: heterosexual) younger women, tearing them away from the men who are their true and most appropriate sexual choices. Such lesbians are defined as rapacious, obsessed, and consumed with sex; their feelings for women are always and only sexual; there is no affection, love, or loyalty between women in this narrative. Or, they are lovely to look at (for instance, the Catherine Deneuve vampire lesbian character in *The Hunger*) but are exposed as truly ugly at the core (as does her character when it reverts to its true self).

These lesbians, like the Sharon Stone character in the film *Basic Instinct* are "killer dykes," dangerous to all who touch them. They are drunk or drugged when they have sex, and feelings of emptiness pervade their existence, like Sister George in the eponymous *The killing of . . .* These are characters who are entirely unsympathetic, lacking in common decency in their daily lives. Like the Deneuve character, they will prey on anyone, exploit any relationship and vulnerable person to meet their goals of sexual satisfaction, going so far as to commit murder repeatedly.

These images teach that lesbians can only loathe themselves and their sexuality, which in this narrative is their central defining characteristic. The inferences of these images, as of the impotent lesbian, also transcend the immediate and specific to convey information to women in general about the stigmatized and degraded nature of women's sexual agency. Women who are sexually powerful and who initiate and assert their desires become transformed in these texts into women who are "butch," masculine, dangerous, emasculating, and ugly, unless and until, like the Stone character, or Pussy Galore, the lesbian character in the James Bond films, they are "tamed," overpowered by a man. Psychoanalyst and feminist Elizabeth Young-Bruehl (1995), addressing the topic of women's homophobias (which here is equivalent to heterosexism), writes of two women, heterosexual in orientation and identity, whose rejection of their own power and criticism of their own bodies reflects these heterosexist messages:

C. (one of the clients) worries that she is unattractive to men—too tall, too heavy—and when she expresses this anxiety she says she is afraid she looks "dykey." So she has assimilated to standards for appearance that are sexist and to the culturally available idea that lesbians are substandard. (1995, p. 10)

Young-Bruehl's analysis, similar to my own, is that these images of the shameful, stigmatized lesbian can become aspects of any woman's struggle with her sexual self. I interpret the woman who worries that she is too much sexually—too demanding, too large, too powerful, too much taking the initiative—as reacting to heterosexism in the social construction of women's sexuality. And the message to the woman who is stereotypically beautiful and sexually agentic is even more devastating; these women are deadly, vampiric, not truly sexually beautiful because they have chosen agency.

These images communicate to women, lesbian and otherwise, that if we must be sexual in the absence of a man, we should do so in fear and in shame, and in hiding, because our sexuality is too disgusting and perverse to be flaunted, that the flaunting itself is perverse unless done passively for male pleasure. It is interesting to note that images of the whore as a sexually agentic woman overlap with those of the killer dyke (Delacoste & Alexander, 1987; Pheterson, 1986, 1987) in what Pheterson refers to as the "social consequences of unchastity" (1987, p. 215). The woman who wants sex, goes after it straightforwardly, is unashamed, is also constructed as a sexual predator (for instance, the Demi Moore character in *Backlash*, who becomes a dangerous sexual harasser when turned down, or the Glenn Close character in *Fatal Attraction*, who stalks her victim and his family).

THE FEMINIST LESBIAN AS "NICE GIRL"

In the initial period of White second-wave feminism, some lesbians reacted against prior negative images in a manner that has had the unintended consequences of referring back to the lesbian/woman as impotent trope. This seems to underscore my contention that the current discourse allows women to be good only when they are nonsexual, regardless of sexual object choice.

In the middle and late 1970s, the concept of the woman-loving-woman arose from a discourse among and between lesbians who were often middle class, newly self-defined as lesbian, and whose primary attachment to lesbianism could at times be described as political rather than erotic. This concept described lesbian sexuality as a gentle, nurturing, egalitarian, nonoppressive exchange between women. Desire, passion, intensity, penetration, and anything resembling butch and femme modes of sexual relating, became suspect, the bad old ways, and male-identified. (This last equation of passion with the presence of a male was another inadvertent bow to the cultural norms.) Sexual difficulties and dysfunctions were impossible because, in this version of the social discourse, merely making love to another woman was a curative; women knew what women wanted, and were presumed to be present for one another sexually in ways that no man could (Brown, 1986). With the emphasis on egalitarian modes of sexual relating, sexual practices that included penetration became stigmatized; any hint of power imbalance between sexual partners, however temporary, or indeed of any form of sexual power and agency at all was defined in this discourse on sexuality as oppressive (Bright, 1990; Nichols, 1987a, 1987b).

Nichols (1987a) describes, only slightly humorously, the image of politically correct lesbian lovemaking as, "Two women lie side by side (tops or bottoms are strictly forbidden—lesbians must be non-hierarchical); they touch each other gently and sweetly all over their bodies for several hours . . . If the women have orgasms at all—and orgasms are only marginally acceptable . . . both orgasms must occur at exactly the same time in order to foster true equality and egalitarianism" (pp. 97–98). Lesbian sexuality thus becomes desexualized, with any hint of negative or powerful images or behaviors banished. A lesbian was no longer necessarily a woman who made love to other women, but a woman who "put her entire energy" into other women, whatever that may mean. She was a good woman, and she was not a sexual being.

This construction, emerging in reaction to the heterosexist killer dyke imagery, was thus tied to it irrevocably, and served, perversely, to reinforce images of lesbian and women's sexuality as asexual, impotent, and inferior to that occurring in the presence of a man, if the women were not to be defined as dangerous and bad. This particular image of lesbian sexuality, despite its invention by women, remained mired in heterosexist conventions by finding no place for a celebratory and positive vision of women's sexual power and agency. Lesbians were here defined from within as chaste, virgins, and spinsters (Daly, 1978), images yet again of sexual impotency and invisibility, but valorized as woman-oriented ones by some lesbian thinkers and writers.

Thus, initially, the feminist discourse on lesbianism began to parallel the heterosexist and sexist discourse on women; a good woman was a sexually invisible or impotent one. A politically correct image of lesbian sexuality emerged, a reversion to the image of female impotence that was the opposite pole to the text of female sexual dangerousness previously ascribed to visible lesbians (Califia, 1983; Hollibaugh & Moraga, 1981). This idealized image of lesbian sexuality that arose from the first decade of lesbian feminism functioned partially as a curative against the overtly negative constructs of lesbian sexuality that had previously pervaded both words and images; the sexually impotent woman was, at least, a sexually good woman. This sexually impotent lesbian could be publicly visible and claim the rights and protections available to other good women. Her image contained a pleading to be treated fairly because, being desexualized, she was good and not the dangerous visible lesbian of the past.

IMPACTS OF HETEROSEXISM ON LESBIANS

Until the past 20 years, most lesbians have lived in social isolation from one another, knowing only slightly what the richness and variability of our experiences may be (Adleman, 1986; Sang, Warshaw, & Smith, 1991). The available social constructions of lesbian sexuality have often arisen from discourses of the dominant culture, in which lesbians were silenced. In the absence of a discourse between and among lesbians and other sexual minority women, the only language available to lesbians for speaking of sexuality to ourselves as we constructed sexual identities was that provided by a heterosexist narrative, and it has affected us as sexual people. As Phyllis Lyon, cofounder of early lesbian social and civil rights group Daughters of Bilitis, described it in writing of discourse on lesbian sexuality prior to the 1970s, "The subject of sex between women was almost never discussed among friends and acquaintances—and I suspect among some lovers" (1983, p. xi). Heterosexism also has pervaded the discourse in more recent times; to cite one anonymous lesbian respondent to a survey conducted by a lesbian sex researcher, "I see a butch dyke in public and I'm embarrassed. I'm staring at her and I see other people staring at her, too. I would never want people looking at me that way" (Loulan, 1990, p. 29).

Such constructions have had profound and visible effects on the actual sexual functioning of lesbians by creating external norms and images that do violence to the lived experiences of many lesbians. But there also has been resistance to the heterosexist imagery, and subversive transformations of its destructiveness into visions of lesbian and female sexual power, desire, agency, and potency. This resistance has led to struggles within and among lesbians who bring different political analyses to their understanding of these forms of resistance; some (Loulan, 1990; Nestle, 1992; Newman, 1995) have argued that such lesbian constructions of the positive, powerful, agentic sexual woman are in fact radical departures from anything contained in heterosexist imagery. Others (Kitzinger & Perkins, 1993) assert that these images are simply another manifestation of lesbian oppression.

The Phenomenology of Lesbian Sexual Identity in Heterosexist Cultures

Assume for a moment that you are an adolescent girl experiencing the dawning of sexual attraction and arousal. You find that your attractions are to other girls and women. As do your peers, you search for information that will mirror and thus shape and validate your experience; songs, movies, romance novels, advertisements, all give images of sexual, romantic, and passionate ways of being. But search as you may, you cannot find yourself in any of these places. You begin to wonder if anyone else like yourself exists. Or, you know that others like yourself exist, and you know that you and they are considered perverted, sinful, dangerous. Others like yourself appear in the pages of abnormal psychology books, or in sermons on sin; they lose their jobs, their homes, their families. People with initiative petitions come to the door of your home and encourage your parents to sign in support of laws that would declare people like yourself perverse, never to be discussed in even a neutral, much less a positive, manner. Even in the songs sung and written by artists who you know to be like yourself because you read about them in *People* magazine, you find only genderless pronouns.

Such was the social discourse that surrounded the development of a sexual self for many North American lesbians over the age of 35. For the most part, a lesbian learns that sexually she does not exist in any recognizable form within the images of the dominant culture. There are few commonly shared words and images available to the lesbian adolescent that will aid her in creating a sexual self-concept. Those emerging media examples in which lesbians are portrayed in a positive light (e.g., lesbian characters on *Friends*, *Relativity*, *Mad About You*, and *Roseanne*, [the last three all being the lesbian sisters of main characters] or in movies like *Go Fish* or *The Incredible True Adventure of Two Girls in Love*) are not universally accessible, since parents may turn off the t.v. or forbid going to the movies in question. The adolescent lesbian-to-be may even lack the words to describe her own feelings; this writer, for example, did not hear the terms *lesbian* or *homosexual* until her second year of undergraduate school. The tyranny of compulsory heterosexuality (Rich, 1980), which portrays relating to men as the only option open to women, sucks the air and life out of the sexual environment of the developing lesbian; a lesbian trying to learn on her own what two women do together is most frequently doing so outside of the context of social discourse.

Alternatively, a lesbian encounters the discourse described above, in which she is either impotent or dangerous. Lesbians learn we exist only as imitations of and adjuncts to heterosexual relating. In this text there is no authentic lesbian sexuality that arises from women's feelings and experiences. There is only a truncated heterosexuality in which the shadow of a man is omnipresent and to be deferred to.

In the literature, art, and social discourse of the dominant heterosexual culture in which all lesbians first develop our sexual selves, these images of absence, inadequacy, shame, and crime are the first reflections of ourselves that we encounter. It is thus hardly surprising that until after the lesbian and gay liberation movements of the 1970s and 1980s began to break us out of our isolation from one another, many of the images that we created of our own sexuality reflected these heterosexist ones. From *The Well of Loneliness* to Beebo Brinker in the lesbian novels of the 1950s, the images of our sexuality that we wrote about and lived within were those that contained seeds of these destructive heterosexist visions. Reading most of the books listed in Jeannette Fosters's *Sex Variant Women in Literature* (1975), which represents the most authoritative compilation of English-language books with a lesbian theme, it is nearly impossible to differentiate the lesbians written by lesbians from those invented by heterosexual authors; impotency or danger are consistently present.

Or, maintaining the heterosexist construction of lesbian sexuality as invisible, we were secret, seen by one another only if we somehow learned the codes. Grahn (1984) describes how her first lover taught her what it meant to be a woman making love with another woman: "We had a secret gay culture. We knew about the color purple . . . We knew about cunniligus, although only the boldest among us practiced it . . . We knew about tribadism" (author's note: a form of lesbian lovemaking in which women intertwine legs and surge into one another's bodies) (p. 5). As Grahn describes it, learning the words to describe lived experience was an essential part of developing an identity as a lesbian, yet for many women who behaved as lesbians during this era, both the words and the identity were unavailable. But because many of the semiotics of this secret lesbian culture were class-based, and dependent in large part on a woman's willingness to participate in bar culture, which was itself one of the most stigmatized aspects of lesbian existence in the preliberation time, middle-class and professional women who were lesbians often had no access to this information (see Sang, Warshaw, & Smith, 1991, for extensive first-person accounts) and lived in isolation with a lover, having no knowledge of the existence of any other lesbians and unable to read the signs.

In another example of the effects of lesbian invisibility, poet and author Audre Lorde (1982) writes of the first time she made love with another woman: "Until the very moment that our naked bodes touched . . . I had no idea what I was doing there, nor what I wanted to do there. I had no idea what making love to another woman meant" (p. 138). Later, after a passionate first love-making, "I finally lay quietly . . . So this was what I had been so afraid of not doing properly" (p. 139). In the absence of knowledge, desire was required to be a teacher; love-making was shadowed for many lesbians with anxiety, simply because there were no shared images of how this was done, much less done well or done right. As Lorde puts it, "There were no mothers, no sisters, no heroes. We had to do it alone" (p. 176). The heterosexist discourse had effectively banned or denied female sexual agency; for a woman to thus behave agenticly with another woman and assert her desires in the absence of a man was to enter an entirely new and different universe of meaning.

Early Forms of Resistance

What is astonishing is that within this context there also developed a rich social discourse about lesbian sexuality that did reflect the lived experiences of some lesbians. It represented attempts to recapture the narrative from heterosexist forms and redefine women as sexually present and powerful when sexual with other women. Joan Nestle (1987, 1992) has been one of our primary documentarians of that period between World War II and the lesbian and gay liberation movements. The lesbian sexuality she documents, primarily that speaking to the tropes of butch and femme, is one in which dominant images have been turned backwards on themselves, a sort of trick or joke on the invisibilities or perversions presented to us in dominant discourses. Nestle describes the images of lesbian butch and femme in which the stereotypes of heterosexual masculinity and femininity were transformed by women into uniquely lesbian ways of relating that only appeared to imitate the dominant culture. Butch, as defined by lesbians, was not a mockery of macho, or an imitation of masculinity, but rather a way of expressing female strength and the ability and willingness to sexually and emotionally nurture another woman. The ultimate butch, the "passing woman," who like Leslie Feinberg (1993) appeared to the world at large as a man, was intensely invested in the role of the nurturing gallant, and of the creator of powerful sexual experiences for her women lovers. The lesbian femme, in her turn, was not portraying passivity or defining her beauty in terms relevant to men, but instead stood for the power inherent in openness and vulnerability, and for the aesthetics of the rounded, full female body with its smells and hair and curves intact.

However, as pointed out by Grahn, these images and discourses of resistance were only at that point available to those lesbians who were able or willing to take part in the "outlaw" lesbian cultures of the 1950s and 1960s. Some of Adleman's (1986) and Sang, Warshaw, and Smith's (1991) older lesbian interviewees speak of how they never knew other lesbians beyond their own relationship until the liberation movements of the 1970s made them visible to one another. Nonurban lesbians, lesbians who felt estranged from the bar culture, lesbians who continued not to know that other lesbians existed—for all these women, the opportunity to be included in a shared social reality that included images of their ways of sexual relating continued to be absent.

THE STRUGGLE TOWARD TRANSFORMATION

The addition of feminist analysis to the social construction of women's sexuality has proven to be a mixed blessing for lesbians. On the one hand, the second wave of the U.S. White women's movement provided, after some initial prodding, a place for many White and (usually) middle-class lesbians to encounter one another in a public way, and to see more positive images of one another in both feminist and dominant media. Feminism has set the stage for the end of the pervasive invisibility of White lesbians, although lesbians of color continued to be unseen most of the time in the feminist narrative. The increased visibility of lesbians to one another has been an important development in movement toward resistance and transformation of heterosexist narratives of lesbian sexuality.

Yet feminism also developed early on a criticism of earlier lesbian ways of sexual relating, and in the process may have temporarily undermined some forms of resistance by seeking too much to leave the position of sexual outlaw and occupy that of the sexually respectable woman. Butch and femme, the archetype that dominated the discourse between and among lesbians regarding our own sexuality, was derided by many early feminists as imitative of the worst of oppressive heterosexuality (Nestle, 1987). This critique reflected both a pervasive class bias among feminists (Kennedy & Davis, 1993) and an unspoken pressure in the feminist community toward the assimilation of lesbians into the larger female population.

The attempts by some lesbian feminist authors to free lesbianism from sexuality emerged during this period; Rich's (1980) concept of the "lesbian continuum," the idea that a variety of behaviors (e.g., friendship between women) carried lesbian meanings, although popular with many lesbians by asserting that any woman could be lesbian, also carried the meta-message that lesbianism had nothing in particular to do with making love and sexual self-definition. Similar assertions can be found in the work of lesbian philosophers such as Janice Raymond (1986) or Mary Daly (1983). These authors prescribed resistance to and separation from patriarchy rather than assimilation and acceptance, but they also portrayed the lesbian as spinster, virgin, or friend of the heart rather than passionately erotic and sexual. Although this new imagery of the desexualized lesbian had the effect of conveying that lesbians were now in the social category of women to be respected in patriarchy (e.g., women who lacked sexual agency), this removal of stigma did not occur without a sexual cost.

A careful feminist analysis of the idealization of women demonstrates how such idealization is also a disguised but potent form of degradation. The ideal functions to punish those women who cannot attain it, and to constrain and stigmatize the woman who does not conform (Pheterson, 1989). Thus, as valorized and impotent images of lesbian sexuality began to emerge within the lesbian-created social discourse, so too did the image of lesbians as sexually dysfunctional, of lesbianism as "a closet for celibacy" (Frye, 1990). Lesbians began to measure our sexual functioning yet again in terms that failed to depict lesbian realities, and found ourselves wanting. The friendly but asexual lesbian described in Nichols's example above came again to be contrasted to male, heterosexual orgasmic frequency and potency, and lesbians were sexually problematic in a whole new way.

As noted by lesbian philosopher Marilyn Frye (1990), lesbians writing and reading about lesbian sexuality used criteria for evaluating the quality of lesbian sexual experiences that derived directly from heterosexist imagery. One example was that of measures of sexual frequency that were derived from models of heterosexual intercourse, and which were in turn used as indexes of good sexual functioning. From what data were available, lesbians were said to have low sexual frequency (e.g., Blumstein & Schwartz, 1983). But first, there were definitional problems; when speaking, for example, of how frequently lesbians had sex, what was being referred to? Since the heterosexist construction of lesbian and women's sexuality defined almost all sexual activity without a man as other than sex, were lesbians having any sex at all? Or, as Frye suggested, was a 2-minute episode of heterosexual intercourse as modeled by cinema, not to be made functionally or numerically equivalent to several hours spent together by two women who were sharing sexual pleasures with one another? And why was frequency of sex (whatever that was; usually agreed on to be something involving direct contact by one partner with the genitals of another partner, thus ruling out nongenital and nonpartner activities as forms of sex) an important variable for assessing quality of sexual functioning?

Furthermore, what sense did lesbians make within lived lesbian experiences of our apparent shortcoming on the sexual frequency scale? Too often, the infrequency numbers were used to convey a message of lesbians as less than, and consequently, of women as asexual in the absence of a man. As other commentators have recently noted, this application of a frequency standard for measuring sexual adequacy can be perceived as an assaultive act in which lesbian sexuality is theorized from a hostile perspective (Magee & Miller, 1995).

In the 1980s the discourse regarding lesbian sexuality was fueled by the sex wars, (Rubin, 1984), debates among public advocates of particular positions regarding sexuality. Many of these debates had their roots in feminist responses to pornography; highly polarized positions developed between lesbians who were developing radical expressions of sexuality, such as sadomasochism or a revived butch and femme erotic, and those lesbians who saw such perspectives as oppressive or violent, but who were themselves seen by the sexual radicals as anti-erotic and over-focused on women's experiences of victimization.

These debates functioned as yet another doubled-edged sword for lesbians attempting to write a sexual narrative free of heterosexism. They opened up public dialogue on sexuality between and among lesbians and made it possible for many lesbians to learn about what other lesbians think, feel, and do sexually. For example, out of this debate there arose several lesbian owned and operated erotic magazines and many lesbian-made erotic videos that directly reflect the experiences and eroticism of lesbian sex radicals from within. There also has been a recent outpouring of explicit lesbian erotica, much of it produced by women in their 20s and early 30s who grew into a lesbian identity when lesbians were visible, and who have created a medium in which an effective and joyful resistance to heterosexism prevails (Gomez & Taormino, 1997). In the remainder of this chapter I will discuss this resistance movement in the world of lesbian sex.

IMAGES OF RESISTANCE: THE SEXY PREGNANT LESBIAN MOTHER AND OTHER NEW VISIONS

The movement away from a dichotomized construction of lesbian sexuality as either impotent or dangerous has provided images of the sexually agentic lesbian that are largely divorced from the heterosexist narrative. In the pages of On Our Backs, Bad Attitude, Girljock, and other similar lesbian owned and created erotic publications are images unavailable within a heterosexist discourse, or within earlier lesbian attempts to combine social conformity with erotically charged images of sexual agency. This is a narrative of sexually potent, passionate women who take sexual risks (although always safely where sexually transmitted diseases are concerned) and experiment with sexual possibilities, that is, dangerous women. Yet at the same time these are women who are also mothers, care-givers, loving, neither impotent or nice, or dangerous or agentic, but powerful, passionate, and compassionate. The work of Susie Bright (1990, 1992, 1995) stands as one of the best examples of this development in the lesbian discourse on sexuality, as she describes the powerful sexual arousal deriving from pregnancy, childbirth, and her postpregnant bodily state as a sexually active lesbian (her "lesbian-mommy-as-sex-goddess" piece makes especially enlightening and entertaining reading, as she suggests, using her own experiences to illustrate her points, that the pregnant lesbian is the most highly sexually charged person around). Bright's work, and that of others who are redefining lesbian sexuality outside of the dominant narrative, combines images that are forbidden in the heterosexist discourse; woman, absent man, with pregnant belly or child, or both, and powerful sexual appetites, all in one.

The many women who do not identify with either polarized position emerging from the sex wars often continue to feel uncertain as to how to incorporate these new socially constructed lesbian sexualities into their own sexual selves and identities. JoAnn Loulan (1990), who has conducted the most extensive research on the sexual attitudes and practices of North American lesbians to date, describes the collective sexual self of lesbians as we entered the 1990s as a confused one, uncertain of what is right while behaving in ways that both mirror and belie the public discourse. Her work is mandatory reading for anyone attempting to understand lesbians' struggles to sexually self-define in a positive energized manner, and is a best-seller among North American lesbians. In her findings, which emerge from formal research, anecdotal data, and clinical practice of sex therapy with lesbians, the emerging tendrils of resistance to heterosexist narratives can be seen.

For example, although it continued to be somewhat suspect in some lesbian social networks to subscribe to or appear to practice butch and femme roles, most of the lesbians that Loulan surveyed could clearly identify themselves as one or the other, and had a well-defined construct for each term. Loulan herself has been quite public about being a sexually potent lesbian femme, appearing at her lectures dressed in flowery, frilly clothing, long curly hair, and makeup, then speaking directly, amusingly, and erotically of lesbian's rights to sexual joy and pleasure.

In the face of disempowering and stigmatizing social constructs, lesbians have been challenged to invent our sexuality in a vacuum. As I have commented earlier (Brown, 1989), there are both advantages and problems in having to draw your own maps of territories that are not supposed to exist, in this case the territory of the sexually potent woman who has or desires no man. As was true of the maps carried by the early European invaders of this continent, these maps can promise that which is absent, or fail to reveal essential features of the landscape. Or, as did those pre-Columbian maps, they can threaten the presence of dragons, frightening off those who must, for their own survival, engage in exploration. But such maps also can develop into accurate representations that serve as useful guides. JoAnn Loulan (1990), who has been one of the premier sexual map-makers for today's lesbians, describes what she calls a "lesbian erotic dance." Here, lesbians begin to try out combinations such as those described by Bright and discover that they can indeed fit within one woman's personal and sexual identities. New categories of lesbian sexual selves have begun to emerge and are observable in lesbian popular fiction and erotica. This trend is one in which lesbians define ourselves as both agentic and decent, sexual and maternal, powerful and orgastic, as well as altruistic and politically concerned.

A good example of this is what has happened to the social status of the dildo among lesbians. The dildo has been reclaimed in many quarters, no longer seen as a male-identified penis substitute, or something only used by outlaw sadomasochism practitioners, but as one tool available to the sexually agentic woman for her pleasure, by herself or with another woman.

The parallel emergence of woman-owned and operated dildo manufacturers, with dildos in designer colors such a lavender, pink, light blue, and gray, and in shapes such as dolphins and ears of corn as well as the traditional penis, sold in stores owned and operated by lesbians, bespeaks the power of reclamation and transformation. The phallus need no longer be a penis; the woman wielding the phallus in no manner resembles a man, but is a sexually agentic woman, down to the color coordination of phallus with bed linen.

For lesbians, this current map-making project into the realm of a nonheterosexist sexuality has been a source of interesting difficulties and challenges in constructing a sexual self. Struggles develop between that which is descriptive ("some lesbians like deep kissing") and that which is prescriptive ("a real lesbian likes deep kissing"). Activities once defined as the province only of certain groups ("only sadomasochistic lesbians do sexual role-playing") become the property of many ("I can play sexual roles if I like without doing any form of sadomasochism"). Many of these struggles toward consensual definitions of lesbian sexual identities surface within lesbian relationships, as each woman is likely to bring a different socially constructed sexual self with her to the relationship. Because there is so little shared public discourse on lesbian sexuality, each woman's experience is likely to be greatly at variance from the other's. Because of the great price that lesbians must pay to develop our sexual selves, each woman will bring powerful emotions about her sexual self with her as well. Each one will have a different version of what lesbians do; not infrequently, the differences become opportunities for polarization and dysfunction of the sort that lead to therapists' offices, in large part because there yet exist few public norms that can serve to depersonalize the argument.

The available, still somewhat skewed public discourse within lesbian communities as the struggle continues to develop nonheterosexist images of the sexually potent woman can at times add to this kind of difficulty between lesbian partners. If one woman in a couple adheres to the prescriptions of the "lesbian-sex-is-gentle-and-egalitarian" construct, and another is aroused by scenes and role-playing, their differences may not be felt to simply be personal. Rather, the public debate may be brought into the relationship; the former may be accused of wanting only vanilla sex, the latter of being oppressive and male-identified. If one woman has come out to herself in a context of shame and degradation, possessing the agentic and dangerous stereotype as the dominant voice in her inner discourse on her lesbian sexuality, and the other has developed her sexual self in tune with images of lesbian sex as impotent but uplifting and healthy, the conflicting social images may be expressed as failures of empathy or connection within the relationship. How do two lesbians communicate sexually when one is shouting danger and the other invisibility at each other in their actions? Many lesbians have still had so little nondistorted information about ourselves sexually that it becomes difficult for many women to believe Loulan's (1984) saner and highly subversive early vision that "lesbian sex is what lesbians do sexually." But encouragingly, many wish to embrace this vision, or so the standing-room only crowds at Loulan's public lectures and the rising sales of lesbian-centered erotica would suggest.

There is also the problem of what the lesbian who is not acting overtly sexually with another woman calls herself, and of how she defines her sexual self. When the public discourse on lesbians is one that defines us by our sexual behavior, it can be difficult to break through this heterosexist construction to ask if we can still find the sexually agentic woman in the picture, even if her agency is not turned to the overtly sexual and erotic in this moment. Is the celibate lesbian still a lesbian? Is the woman who has never made love to another woman aside from herself a lesbian? Is a single, unpartnered lesbian still a lesbian (a question posed to me on more than one occasion by lesbian clients in the throes of a relationship breakup who find themselves questioning their sexual identities because they are about to relinquish the only legitimate proof of its existence). If a relationship between women has no sexual component (Rothblum & Brehony, 1993), can we argue that these women are lesbian if we also wish to argue for a lesbian sexual identity that is powerful, potent, agentic? All of these women may doubt the legitimacy of their internal experience of self-as-lesbian, or have it doubted by other people, lesbians and otherwise. It is interesting to note that it would appear that the sexual identity of a celibate or temporarily unpartnered heterosexual woman is only tarnished, rather than put into question, by her unattachment to a man. It is unlikely that someone will suggest that she is not really heterosexual if she is not actively behaving heterosexually, only that she cannot get a man.

However, in the problems also lie the solutions. Lesbians are now faced with the unique opportunity of seizing control over the discourse and determining how our sexuality shall be socially, and consequently, internally, constructed. JoAnn Loulan's (1984, 1987, 1990) work is one of the better examples of this phenomenon in action. Loulan has become a tireless chronicler of the sexual experiences of lesbians; her books are snatched up hungrily and her public lectures attended by overflow crowds. Loulan gives lesbians pictures of what our sexuality is based on our own stories; she details the extraordinary diversity of lesbian experience, just as the diversity of heterosexual experience has been detailed. She serves the function of a benign external parental introject for U.S. lesbian culture, encouraging lesbians to see our sexuality as good for what it is, rather than in comparison with heterosexual norms and visions.[1] Loulan's work also

---

[1] Ironically, since this chapter was written, Loulan has publicly declared herself to be in a relationship with a man, to whom she then became married. She continues to identify herself as lesbian, but is no longer a benign figure for many lesbians, some of whom have expressed feelings of profound betrayal by her public embrace of a heterosexual relationship.

takes the public discourse on lesbian sexuality out of the polarized positions found among the sexual radicals and antipornography activists, although she is rejecting of neither. From a younger age cohort, Susie Bright's (1990, 1992, 1995) picaresque tales of life as a sexual expert, author, radical, and student are examples of what lesbians can do when their imaginations, rather than heterosexist constructions, inform their notions of sexuality. There is also an outpouring of published collections of wonderful, salacious, funny, steamy lesbian erotica beginning to be available, written by lesbians who define themselves from a lesbian center.

Some lesbian feminist commentators have found Loulan's or Bright's stances, and that of other lesbian sex writers, to be overly liberal and permissive (Kitzinger & Perkins, 1993). These authors argue against the notion that it is time to "let a thousand flowers bloom" sexually, and suggest that there are certain ways of sexual relating (for example, sadomasochism or butch and femme) that are inherently and irretrievably bound into patriarchal modes of being, thus incapable of being reclaimed or transformed satisfactorily by lesbians. Others, myself among them, argue that the positions taken by Loulan or Bright are entirely feminist and empowering to women in our resistance to patriarchal deadening, in that these authors resist the urge to be prescriptive and deny women authority over the value of their experiences. These writers provide a descriptive position, resisting the urge to become authoritative: "here are all the things that lesbians tell me that they do sexually, and thus this is what constitutes lesbian sex, and lesbian sex is fun, powerful, erotic, variable, and good" is the message of this work.

For lesbians whose sexual self-definition is painful or problematic and who bring this distress into the therapy office, the introduction of the social constructivist analysis of lesbian sexuality can an essential aspect of treatment (Brown, 1986; Nichols, 1987a, 1987b). Aside from the usual factors affecting sexual functioning in women (e.g., histories of sexual victimization), lesbians with difficulties in sexual functioning often are uncertain as to the degree of their problem, the appropriate attributions for it, and the criteria for successful outcome of their attempted change process. That is, if you have no picture of normal lesbian sexuality and are still powerfully affected by either or both of the impotent or dangerous images of lesbianism, it is difficult to know if what one is experiencing is a problem, or if the problems have to do with what one has been told about the nature of one's desires. Lesbians with sexual problems are often suffering the results of the heterosexist social discourse regarding their sexuality, seeing themselves as invisible or perverted simply for having their own desires (Brown, 1986).

Most lesbians who are neither sex radicals, philosophers, nor sex therapists have not had the opportunity to think consciously and carefully about how they experienced the social construction of lesbian sexuality, although I believe that most have intuited it and enacted it. Engaging in this level of analysis of conscious awareness and inspection can be enlightening, empowering, and often enraging, because it exposes the manner in which lesbians, both qua lesbians and qua women, have been misinformed by the heterosexist discourse. Lesbians learn how we came to nonconsciously experience our sexuality as invisible and absent, or as sick and dangerous; how we were encouraged to assume that problems in lesbian sexual functioning were indicators of a latent heterosexuality, that impotence must simply be a symptom of the absence of a man in the sexual exchange.

This increased awareness of the impact of the social construction of our sexuality on our actual sexual functioning creates a broader range of options for lesbians trying to reinvent our sexual selves. If healthy lesbian sex is that which lesbians do and receive pleasure from, and if lesbians become free to define themselves as sexually present, powerful, and valuable as women with women, eschewing the heterosexist discourse requiring the presence of a man for its completion, then a lesbian in sexual difficulties has increased degrees of freedom within which to define a nonproblematic sexual functioning.

ENDING HETEROSEXISM FOR ALL WOMEN'S SEXUALITIES

In 1989, I expressed my hunch that heterosexism created problems for heterosexual women as well as for lesbians (Brown, 1989). This hunch seems to be more accurate as the culture continues to strive to alternately rid itself of or reembrace sexist and heterosexist imperatives. Heterosexuality, as currently defined in U.S. culture, is a male-dominant experience in which women are defined as object, but not actor. The heterosexual woman who seeks sexual potency and agency runs the all-too-present risk of being labeled lesbian. In fact, a woman need only be powerful in a traditionally male sphere to achieve the honor of this title (e.g., when the radical right wing was quick to label Hillary Rodham Clinton as a lesbian —a move that many lesbians greeted with satisfaction by wearing Hillary and Tipper T-shirts with the slogan "Go girls"). And if she is not a lesbian, the agentic heterosexual woman is, as described earlier, a predator. Heterosexism is a form of sexism at its core, and neither celebrates the sexually potent, alive, passionate woman.

A clear consequence of the heterosexist hegemony of sexual definition, containing as it does the core of male superiority and construction out of male experience, has been a silencing of the genuine internal experiences of heterosexual women, experiences of agency and power that are also distorted or made absent by the dominant discourse. Thus, in the pursuit of a feminist vision of women's sexuality, it may be that when we cease to privilege the words and images of that heterosexist discourse and instead empower lesbians to speak our own sexual languages, heterosexual women may be so empowered as well (Palladino & Stephenson, 1990). It is no accident that feminist perspectives on heterosexual women's experiences of sexuality have arisen in tandem with lesbians' increased power and voice in the description of our sexual lives. Feminist questions about sexuality challenge the premises of heterosexuality by inquiring into the most fundamental aspects of the dominant images of sexual selves ascribed to women.

The accomplishment of this revolution in which we come together to undermine the heterosexist thrall in which women's sexuality has been held requires alliance between and among women. Sexual minority and heterosexual women must begin to analyze and then move away from the artificial divisions set between us by heterosexist constructions. The power of many women's voices speaking up, weaving together as theme and variation, is far more difficult to deny, or to define as peculiar, than is the voice of any one woman. In doing so, we must listen with the "loving ear" (from Frye's [1981] "loving eye") that embraces each woman's experience as genuine, that does not judge or exclude but attends carefully so as to know the details of another woman's sexual self. This collective and critical attending can wipe away the sexual fog of confusion created by the heterosexist imperative that the sexual woman exists solely in the presence of and for the pleasure of a man. In this speaking together lies the potential to create a radically different and feminist discourse about women and sex, weaving as it does the web of interactions in which women's own visions of ourselves can be constructed, and barriers between women created by the presence of heterosexism can be brought down.

REFERENCES

Adleman, M. (Ed.). (1986). *Long time passing: Lives of older lesbians*. Boston: Alyson Publications.

Blumstein, P., & Schwartz, P. (1983). *American couples*. New York: William Morrow and Company.

Bright, S. (1990). *Susie sexpert's lesbian sex world*. San Francisco: Cleis Press.

Bright, S. (1992). *Sexual reality: A virtual sex world reader*. San Francisco: Cleis Press.

Bright, S. (1995). *Sexwise*. San Francisco: Cleis Press.

Brown, L. S. (1986). Confronting internalized homophobia in sex therapy with lesbians. *Journal of Homosexuality, 12*, 99–107.

Brown, L. S. (1989). New voices, new visions: Towards a lesbian/gay paradigm for psychology. *Psychology of Women Quarterly, 13*, 445–458.

Califia, P. (1983). *Sapphistry: The book of lesbian sexuality.* Tallahassee, FL: The Naiad Press.

Cogan, J. (1996). The prevention of anti-lesbian and gay hate crimes through social change and empowerment. In E. D. Rothblum & L. A. Bond (Eds.), *Preventing heterosexism and homophobia* (pp. 219–238).Thousand Oaks, CA: Sage Publications.

Daly, M. (1978). *Gyn/Ecology: The metaethics of radical feminism.* Boston, MA: Beacon Press.

Daly, M. (1983). *Pure lust.* Boston, MA: Beacon Press.

Delacoste, F., & Alexander, P. (Eds.). (1987). *Sex work: Writings by women in the sex industry.* Pittsburgh, PA: Cleis Press.

Elgin, S. H. (1984). *Native tongue.* New York: DAW Books.

Feinberg, L. (1993). *Stone butch blues.* Ithaca, NY: Firebrand Books.

Foster, J. (1975). *Sex variant women in literature.* Baltimore: Diana Press.

Frye, M. (1981). *The politics of reality.* Trumansburg, NY: The Crossing Press.

Frye, M. (1990). Lesbian "sex". In J. Allen (Ed.), *Lesbian philosophies and cultures* (pp. 305–316). Albany: State University of New York Press.

Gomez, J., & Taormino, T. (Eds.). (1997). *Best lesbian erotica, 1977.* San Francisco: Cleis Press.

Grahn, J. (1984). *Another mother tongue: Gay words, gay worlds.* Boston: Beacon Press.

Hollibaugh, A., & Moraga, C. (1981). What we're rollin' around in bed with: Sexual silences in feminism. In A. Snitow, C. Stansell, & S. Thompson (Eds.), *Powers of desire: The politics of sexuality* (pp. 213–227). New York: New Feminist Library/Monthly Review Press.

Kennedy, E. L., & Davis, M. D. (1993). *Boots of leather, slippers of gold: The history of a lesbian community.* New York: Routledge.

Kitzinger, C., & Perkins, R. (1993). *Changing our minds: Lesbian feminism and psychology.* New York: New York University Press.

Lorde, A. (1982). *Zami: A new spelling of my name.* Watertown, MA: Persephone Press.

Loulan, J. (1984). *Lesbian sex.* San Francisco: Spinsters Ink.

Loulan, J. (1987). *Lesbian passion: Loving ourselves and each other.* San Francisco: Spinsters/Aunt Lute.

Loulan, J. (1990). *The lesbian erotic dance: Butch, femme, androgyny and other rhythms.* San Francisco: Spinsters Book Company.

Lyon, P. (1983). Foreword. In P. Califia, *Sapphistries: The book of lesbian sexuality.* Tallahassee FL: The Naiad Press.

Magee, M., & Miller, D. C. (1995, August). Assaults and harassment: The violent acts of theorizing lesbian sexuality. In M. Buttenheim (Chair), *She came in a flash: Perspectives on lesbian sexuality.* Symposium presented at the 103rd Annual Convention of the American Psychological Association, New York, NY.

Murphy, M. (1991). *Are you girls traveling alone?: Adventures in lesbianic logic*. Los Angeles: Clothespin Fever Press.

Nestle, J. (1987). *A restricted country*. Ithaca, NY: Firebrand Books.

Nestle, J. (Ed.). (1992). *The persistent desire: A butch-femme reader*. Boston: Alyson Publications.

Newman, L. (Ed.). (1995). *The femme mystique*. Boston: Alyson Publications.

Nichols, M. (1987a). Lesbian sexuality: Issues and developing theory. In Boston Lesbian Psychologies Collective (Eds.), *Lesbian psychologies: Explorations and challenges* (pp. 97–125). Urbana: University of Illinois Press.

Nichols, M. (1987b). Doing sex therapy with lesbians: Bending a heterosexual paradigm to fit a gay life-style. In Boston Lesbian Psychologies Collective (Eds.), *Lesbian psychologies: Explorations and challenges* (pp. 242–260). Urbana: University of Illinois Press.

Osborne, T. (1996). *Coming home to America*. New York: St. Martin's Press.

Palladino, D., & Stephenson, Y. (1990). Perceptions of the sexual self: Their impact on relationships between lesbian and heterosexual women. In L. S. Brown & M. P. P. Root (Eds.), *Diversity and complexity in feminist therapy* (pp. 21–254). New York: Haworth Press.

Pheterson, G. (1986). Alliances between women: Overcoming internalized oppression and internalized domination. *Signs: Journal of Women in Culture and Society, 12*, 146–160.

Pheterson, G. (1987). The social consequences of unchastity. In F. Delacoste & P. Alexander (Eds.), *Sex work: Writings by women in the sex industry* (pp. 215–230). Pittsburgh, PA: Cleis Press.

Pheterson, G. (Ed.). (1989). *A vindication of the rights of whores*. Seattle, WA: Seal Press.

Raymond, J. (1986). *A passion for friends*. Boston: Beacon Press.

Rich, A. (1980). Compulsory heterosexuality and lesbian existence. *Signs: Journal of Women in Culture and Society, 5*, 631–660.

Rothblum, E. D., & Brehony, K. (Eds.). (1993). *The Boston marriage today*. Amherst: University of Massachusetts Press.

Rubin, G. (1984). Thinking sex: Notes for a radical theory of the politics of sexuality. In C. S. Vance (Ed.), *Pleasure and danger: Exploring female sexuality* (pp. 267–319). Boston: Routledge and Kegan Paul.

Sang, B., Warshaw, J., & Smith, A. (Eds.). (1991). *Lesbians at mid-life: The creative transition*. San Francisco: Spinsters Book Company.

Vaid, U. (1995). *Virtual equality*. New York: Anchor Books.

Wilkinson, S., & Kitzinger, C. (Eds.). (1993). *Heterosexuality: A feminism and psychology reader*. London: Sage Publications.

Williams, W. G. (1987). *Spirit and the flesh: Sexual diversity in American Indian communities*. Boston: Beacon Press.

Young-Bruehl, E. (1995). Homophobias among women. In M. Buttenheim (Chair), *She came in a flash: Perspectives on lesbian sexuality*. Symposium presented at the 103rd Annual Convention of the American Psychological Association, New York.

12

A CULTURAL CONTEXT FOR SEXUAL ASSERTIVENESS IN WOMEN

PATRICIA J. MOROKOFF

The purpose of this chapter is to explore issues of sexual assertiveness and sexual decision-making for women. I will begin by presenting evidence for gender-based differences in sexual behavior followed by a discussion of how such differences are culturally assumed to derive from a biological basis. What I will refer to as the biological explanation of sexuality is consistent with the theoretical position proposed by evolutionary psychologists and recently examined by Eagly and Wood (1999). This position suggests that women and men possess sex-specific evolved mechanisms based on adaptations to "the pressures of differing physical and social environments that impinged on females and males during primeval times." (p. 410). An alternative to this assumption is a relational sexuality based on socially constructed gender roles. I will discuss the consequences of a belief in biologically derived gender differences in sexuality, including the justification of rape, impaired understanding of women's sexuality, and impaired sexual functioning for women. I will then present the difficulties in a culturally defined concept of sexual assertiveness for women, and discuss

Thank you Bernice Lett and Sheryl Gollet for your generous and helpful suggestions.

the factors that impede women's expression of sexual assertiveness, including social control of female sexuality, sexual victimization of women, and women's dependence on men. Cultural definitions of sexuality that deter sexual assertiveness of women present implications for women's satisfaction within relationships, and for women's ability to protect themselves from sexually transmitted disease.

GENDER DIFFERENCES IN SEXUAL BEHAVIOR

It is a common cultural assumption that men have a stronger sexual drive than women. In fact, numerous sources support the conclusion that men have more permissive attitudes about sex and engage in more sexual behaviors than women. In their meta-analytic review of gender differences in sexuality, Oliver and Hyde (1993) found that men had greater acceptance of casual premarital sex than women and generally more permissive attitudes toward sex than women. Men reported greater acceptance of extramarital sex than women and lower levels of anxiety, fear, and guilt than women. Men also reported greater sexual experience than women on a number of variables, including incidence of intercourse, age of first intercourse, number of sexual partners, incidence of masturbation, and frequency of intercourse.

Another data source is provided by Blumstein and Schwartz's (1983) study of American couples. The authors examined sexual behaviors in heterosexual couples, gay male couples, and lesbian couples. They found that the highest frequency of sexual behaviors were reported by gay male couples, whereas the lowest frequency was reported by lesbian couples, supporting the conclusion that women are less motivated to have sex than men.

EXPLANATIONS FOR SEXUAL BEHAVIOR

Biology is the dominant basis for understanding sexuality in our culture. By *biology* I mean evolved, physiologically based dispositions that provide explanations for sexual phenomena such as level and object of sexual desire. Thus, a reductionistic approach is assumed in which capacity for sexual desire is biologically based. Tiefer (1987; chapter 4 this book) has eloquently argued that biology has a privileged position in sexual discourse, based on the assumption that the body comes before everything else. "It is the original source of action, experience, knowledge, and meaning for the species and the individual" (p. 81). This explanation posits that both women and men are motivated by inborn biological drives. A basic tenet of Freudian psychology, for example, is that human behavior is motivated by instinctual drives, and that chief among them is the biologically based sexual instinct. Although Tiefer's argument primarily addresses sex researchers and why they have clung to a medicalized interpretation of sexuality, she also addresses motivation among the general public to understand sexuality from a medical viewpoint. She argues that a biological understanding of sexual desire, focusing on involuntary actions of hormones and blood vessels, takes responsibility away from individuals who wish to absolve themselves of traditional charges of sinful behavior.

I would like to suggest additional reasons why people support the notion that sexual motivation is biological. Sexuality, and especially gender differences in sexuality, are seen as biologically rooted in the same way that all gender characteristics are popularly believed to be biologically rooted. People focus on the inevitability, rather than the social construction, of gender characteristics. Belief in the inevitability of these differences helps support them. Thus it is popular belief not only that the gender differences discussed above exist, but also that they are biologically rooted.

Thus it is believed that men have a stronger sex drive than women and that men's strong sex drive compared with women's weaker sex drive is biologically determined. A corollary of this supposition is that it is physically harmful for men to not fulfill their sexual desires. This is especially the case once the arousal process has begun. The existence of a sex drive with these characteristics in men has various social consequences. One consequence is that men will naturally initiate sex more than women. Consequent to this is that women have some moral obligation to help men gratify their sexual desires. This view is based not only on the need to not harm men physically but also on the presumption that this strong sex drive in men is necessary for preservation of the species (the sociobiological theory) and a belief in a biological basis for male superiority, so that if men have an important physical desire, it should not be thwarted. A further social consequence is that men cannot be expected to decline irresponsible sexual behavior because their urges overwhelm them, and they will naturally have an inclination to have sex regardless of the nature of the relationship with a partner.

A second corollary is that women's bodies are intrinsically arousing to men in ways that men's bodies are not intrinsically arousing to women. In combination with men's presumed stronger sex drive based on a biological need for sex, this justifies the objectification of women's bodies for male sexual pleasure, as is found in pornography and advertising.

It is a paradox within this model that although women are supposed to have weak sex drives, their uncontrolled sexual behavior is seen as threatening. A staple of pornographic literature is the lustful woman who will stop at nothing to satisfy her powerful sexual urges. Sociobiology further explains the need to tightly control women's sexuality. According to this perspective, people are motivated to achieve reproductive success, maximizing the number of genes passed on to the next generation. If two parents are required to successfully raise children, men make a substantial investment through monogamy. It is therefore critical to make certain that the child being raised by a man is in fact his biological progeny. To assure this, his female partner must be monogamous, with any extramarital sexual activity strongly discouraged. Economic reasons further dictate that if another man can make a paternity claim to offspring, the economic value of the child may be compromised.

A relational conceptualization is an alternative to the biological explanation. This is compatible with the social role explanation for gender differences in human behavior (Eagly & Wood, 1999) in that the assumption is made that gender differences arise from the different social roles that men and women tend to occupy. However, the proposed conceptualization goes further in focusing on the relational nature of sexuality which is not explicit in the social roles explanation.

The relational approach emphasizes the importance of defining and locating sexuality primarily in personal and relational, rather than physical terms" (p. 81). If one adopts a relational conceptualization of sexual motives, then it makes sense that behaviors and even self-perception will be guided by socially, as opposed to biologically, derived gender roles. The relational model goes further in positing that individuals make sexual decisions to enact relational goals (e.g., achieve greater closeness or intimacy or assert dominance).

WHAT ARE GENDER ROLES FOR SEXUALITY?

Gender roles for sexuality are based on a heterosexual model and are consistent with a belief in the biological explanation. Gender roles prescribe an active, agentic, autonomous sexuality for men based on a sexual identity associated with characteristics of assertiveness, dominance, power, and insistence (Lott, 1987). Gender roles for women prescribe a reactive sexuality in which women's sexual response is a potential that is waiting to be released by the agentic action of her male partner. If one likens a woman's body to a harp and her male partner to a harpist, then her sexuality is the music that is produced when he plays on her. Before he does so, it is a potential with no independent existence. Thus, there is no societally appropriate autonomous sexuality for women. This lack is justified in the biological explanation by the fact that women are assumed to have a weak biological sexual drive. If one goes outside the accepted expectations for women, there is the option for women to play the masculine gender role for sexuality as the bad girl of pornography. Although exciting, this woman is perceived as damaging and ruinous to men and society at large. She is ruinous to men because she leads them away from their self-interests and social obligations. She is ruinous more generally because she fails to perform the caretaking of children and men that is the central characteristic of the female gender role. Fear of women's unchecked sexuality thus justifies the accepted gender expectations for no autonomous sexuality at all for women. It should be noted that although an agentic sexual identity is defined for men, cultural expectations for men's sexuality are nevertheless rigid. Therefore, men's sexual identity is stereotyped and not individualized.

These stereotypic gender expectations for sexuality coincide perfectly with more global gender expectations. It is a stereotypic global gender expectation for women to care for the physical and emotional needs of men (Gallant, Coons, & Morokoff, 1994). Just as women are emotional and physical caretakers for men, they also serve as sexual caretakers. It is very convenient that they have no autonomous sexuality, because autonomous sexual needs would interfere with women's ability to care for men's sexual needs. It is, therefore, women's responsibility—codified in marriage vows—to take care of men's sexual needs. Stereotypic gender expectations say that if men are hungry, sad, sexually aroused, and so forth, it is women's responsibility to attend to their needs. Thus women should not refuse sex to their legal partners. The biological explanation justifies this by the fact that men's sex drive is stronger than women's and the preservation of the species depends on it. An alternative, relational view indicates that men operate in relationships from a societally dictated position of power and use that power to have women meet their needs. If violated, men's social standing *as men* is lessened.

Another expectation is that women are gatekeepers who are held responsible for any sexual activity that occurs, even if they have no physical way to stop it. Gender roles for sexuality prescribe that women are sexually passive and, because of their passive objectivity, at the same time act as sexual gatekeepers (see McCormick, Brannigan, & LaPlante, 1984). This means that women are traditionally expected to not take the sexual initiative and are expected to prevent unwanted sexual activities from occurring. It is considered appropriate for men to initiate sex as often as they would like and to try to get partners to engage in desired sexual activities. It is the traditional obligation of women to both provide sexual satisfaction to husbands and to set limits on inappropriate sexual behaviors requested by husbands and other partners. Since men are strongly sexually motivated according to the dominant explanation, they are unable to control their sexual urges, hence the need for external controls imposed by women.

The biological explanation does not presume that men have greater power to get their way sexually than women except potentially as a result of greater physical strength. Therefore, it is not problematic to assume that women will be able to effectively exercise this gatekeeping option unless physically overpowered. As the gender with the weaker sex drive (but equal sexual power), it thus makes sense that women should simply stop men if they go too far sexually. Men should initiate sex; women should submit to sex or refuse sex. The biological explanation also asserts that it is not a gender role to be the initiator but rather that this behavior flows from the natural order in which men desire sex more than women. If women initiate sex, then men may be troubled by the need to perform sexually when they do not want to.

Women who do initiate sex play the role of the bad girl. Thus, inherent internal inconsistency of the dominant explanation is apparent because it is also clear that a social role open to women is the bad girl who does not conform to traditional gender expectations and is sexually aggressive. This role is standard fare in pornography and also represents a threat to conventional society. Men are sexually experienced and can demonstrate their sexual prowess by sexually satisfying women. Women can do the same for men when they play the role of bad girl.

CONSEQUENCES OF A BELIEF IN BIOLOGICALLY DERIVED GENDER DIFFERENCES IN SEXUALITY

Justification for Rape

Belief in these biologically derived gender differences in sexuality is consistent with rape myths indicating that it is a woman's fault if she is raped. It is her fault in the context of an expectation that women must set limits on inappropriate sexual behaviors. As discussed, it is presumed that women have the capacity to turn down unwanted sexual activity. This is consistent with the rape myth that no woman can be raped if she does not want to be. In reality, there are multiple factors restricting women's ability to set sexual limits.

One such factor is the very indoctrination into the belief system described here that trains women that it is their obligation to serve as sexual caretakers for men. Such indoctrination may even take on religious authority. Because of this indoctrination, women may go along with sex they do not desire. A second factor is men's greater potential physical strength. If a man can physically overpower a woman and is willing to do so, she may be unable to set sexual limits. Only if she puts up a sufficient fight to make clear she was physically overpowered will she be believed by some. A third is lack of support by legal structures for declining sex. Marital or acquaintance rape is difficult to prove in court and so the threat of society standing behind the word of a woman is not an effective deterrent for going against her word. Additional barriers to setting sexual limits will be discussed later in the context of barriers to sexual assertiveness.

Problems Understanding Women's Sexuality

A second consequence of these assumed gender differences is that it is difficult for a woman to determine what constitutes her own sexuality. Since man's autonomous sexuality is culturally defined and woman's is not, women (and men) may be expected to have difficulty understanding and conceptualizing women's sexuality. Women's autonomous sexuality is culturally silent and invisible. It does not exist in the culturally sanctioned biological explanation. It does not exist in cultural depictions except as it takes the masculine form of the bad girl. Further complicating women's attempts to understand their sexuality is that their sexuality (i.e., patterns of sexual arousal) may be subverted through pornography. The dominant-submissive structure to male and female sexuality frequently becomes internalized with respect to sexual arousal. Pornography graphically depicts the traditional gender roles for sexuality with men in dominant positions and women in degraded or submissive positions. Men enact their sexual will on women. This has the potential to lead to sexual arousal for women. In the biological model, arousal is a powerful force that demands its gratification, that will lead the individual to stop at nothing to satisfy. This means that the individual is sexually aroused beyond control. In the male role gratification this is accomplished through aggressiveness. In the female role, it is accomplished through self-degradation. If dominant-submissive roles are internalized, women may see their own sexuality as degraded.

What can lead women to internalize a gender role of self-degradation when sexually aroused? This may occur as a result of exposure and arousal to pornographic depictions. How would children and young women become exposed to such imagery? Such imagery is very common in the media at present, especially on MTV and advertising, especially fashion advertising. For example, in fashion advertising, women may be portrayed looking bruised or battered (e.g., "heroin chic") as a means of looking attractive. Furthermore, if women have been sexually abused or exposed to pornography as children, they will have been exposed to sexual domination and violence leading to the equation of sex and self-degradation. A consequence of this may be to internalize self-degradation in their own arousal patterns, and to find themes of dominance and submission sexually arousing. It is typical in our culture to teach adolescent boys to be aroused to these themes through masturbation to pornography. It is considered natural for young adolescent boys to get hold of pornographic pictures depicting themes of dominance and submission and masturbate to them. This is the traditional sexual initiation for boys in our culture.

This internalized fantasy structure dove tails with global cultural expectations for men but not women. Thus, although a sexuality based on arousal to dominance-submission themes may be no more natural for men than for women, it seems natural because it is consistent with the cultural belief structure of male sexuality (i.e., men are easily sexually aroused, men are the sexually dominant gender, men are aroused by seeing themselves in this role) as well as men's autonomous, agentic role as breadwinner for the family. These sexual fantasies are inconsistent with the cultural belief structure of female sexuality (nonexistence of an autonomous sexuality, passivity, lack of a strong sex drive) and with women's larger obligations of responsibility for general caretaking. These fantasies are thus confusing and discordant for women.

The woman with sexual feelings has been coopted as an image for men's sexual pleasure in pornography. There is little explicit sexual material that does not act out dominance relationships (pornography; Cowan, Lee, Levy, & Synder, 1988). As discussed, through exposure, women may internalize these images in their own fantasy. Furthermore, as demonstrated in much of women's fashion women may act out these images to please men and themselves to the extent that they have internalized these themes.

Impairment of Women's Sexual Functioning

A presumption of a weak sexuality for women also leads to the potential for lack of full sexual functioning in women. Sexual functioning, including a full experience of arousal and orgasm, seems to involve immersing oneself, self-centeredly, in a sexual experience (Mosher, 1980). As I have previously discussed (Morokoff, 1990, 1993), the gatekeeping role may prevent unwanted sexual activity, but it makes full sexual expression difficult because a woman who must constantly evaluate the appropriateness of a sexual interchange (because her partner may at any moment direct the action into an unacceptable area) cannot immerse herself in the experience. Being the gatekeeper suggests a willingness and an ability to turn off sexual feelings. "Not fully letting go involves the experience of partial arousal but the maintenance of a watchful eye on the proceedings and retention of a feeling of control over the sexual events occurring. This attitude is extremely functional for women in that one can turn off sexual arousal very quickly if needed and one can track whether the experience is in one's larger self interest, as it frequently is not. . . . This state of partial arousal, far from representing a dysfunction (as it is seen in diagnostic terms), may thus in actuality be quite functional" (Morokoff, 1993, p. 175). However, it is unlikely that a sufficient level of arousal for orgasm would occur under such circumstances. Thus the cost of the gatekeeping role for sexual self-expression in women is extremely high.

As noted by Margaret Mead (1949), societies differ greatly in their expectations of sexual responsivity for women. In contrasting the Mundugumor and the Arapesh, two South Sea societies, she reported that the Mundugumor expected both men and women to derive equivalent amounts of satisfaction from sex, whereas for the Arapesh, female orgasm was unrecognized, not reported, and had no name. She remarked, "The human female's capacity for orgasm is to be viewed, much more as a potentiality that may or may not be developed by a given culture, or in a specific life history of an individual, than as an inherent part of her full humanity."

It is clearly true that there has been a major shift in the past hundred years in expectations for sexuality of women in the United States and Western Europe. For example, it is now expected that women will experience sexual orgasm. However, this expectation clashes with a cultural reluctance to give up the assumption of a biologically based stronger sex drive in men. If sex is bound by the gender expectations discussed here it will be difficult for women to step out of the caretaking role and assume the self-centered state necessary for full sexual experience.

The inconsistency in expectations for women (to, on the one hand, have a weak sexual drive, yet on the other hand be sexually aroused and have orgasm when their partners initiate) can lead to further problems, as women may perceive they are expected to perform sexually but find they cannot. The widespread dissatisfaction of women with their sexual relationships has been documented. Morokoff (1998) reviewed literature on the prevalence of arousal disorders in women. Estimates ranged from 12% of women diagnosed with an arousal phase disorder (Levine & Yost, 1976) to 48% of a sample of normal women who indicated "difficulty getting excited" (Frank, Anderson, & Rubinstein, 1978). A study conducted by Rosen, Taylor, Leiblum, and Bachmann (1993) revealed that about a quarter of women indicated overall dissatisfaction with their sexual relationships. Lack of pleasure was the most frequently cited problem, with 61% of women indicating this was a problem at least some of the time.

SEXUAL ASSERTIVENESS

Assertiveness requires that the individual attempt to ensure her rights in a specific area or to actualize an internalized view of self through interaction with others. I will therefore posit that the extent to which women assert themselves sexually depends on the extent to which women have an accurate, nondistorted, internalized conception of their own sexuality, which they desire to actualize through interactions with others. If their internalized conception is based on socially derived stereotypes (e.g., asexual caretaker or bad girl) then women will not be able to assert an authentic sexual self.

Sexual rights for women are largely undefined, making assertion of such rights difficult. No autonomous version of women's sexuality is culturally approved, making the development of an internalized, autonomous view of the sexual self difficult. Sexual assertiveness has been defined as the ability to initiate wanted sexual activities, to refuse unwanted sexual activities, and to protect oneself against unwanted pregnancy and sexually transmitted disease (Morokoff et al., 1997). I would like to examine in detail factors that prevent women from expression of assertiveness in sexual actions and decisions.

Social Control of Female Sexuality

Women's sexual behavior is subject to social control in most if not all societies. Techniques of social control include genital mutilation, surveillance of sexual behaviors, lowered social standing for socially inappropriate sexual behavior, and increased economic value for a virginal bride. I will draw on the anthropological literature to briefly outline some common strategies for control.

In all societies where children are an economic value, the women's reproductive potential is an important resource that must be bargained for in marriage negotiations. The father is compensated for his daughter's reproductive capacity at the time of the marriage (brideprice). It is thus in his interest to negotiate the best bargain possible. In order to bargain for the strongest position, the father must be able to guarantee that there are no illicit claims to his daughter's reproductive capacity and that the future husband's paternity of their children will be undisputed. To protect his interests the father must thus be able to control his daughter's sexual behavior. According to Paige and Paige (1981), his ability to do this is strongest in societies with the greatest resources and strong fraternal interest groups. These kinsmen act as allies to the father who can help him retrieve his daughter by force, if necessary, from an abduction or elopement and can enforce payment of compensation for any damages. With greater resources the father has the ability to back up threats to kill a seducer, and ensure virginity while delaying the daughter's marriage past menarche in order to secure the best husband. He also can use ritual surveillance strategies such as genital mutilation to demonstrate how serious he is about ensuring his daughter's virginity.

In societies with low-value economic resources that do not have strong fraternal interest groups, a different strategy is used. Here there tend to be public menarcheal ceremonies lasting weeks or even months with costumes, feasting, and gifts. Paige (1983) has conceptualized these as mobilization rituals that serve to mobilize a coalition of community members who will support the father's attempt to protect the marriage value of his daughter.

In economically advanced societies where parents have attained rights to stable resources such as land, the family's economic interest lies more in ensuring that resources will be able to be inherited by grandchildren and not squandered by the husband, and that he will be of comparable wealth or social status as the family. In some societies dowries are used to help attain this goal (MacDonald, 1987). It is still the case that the daughter's sexual reputation and virginity (or relative virginity) enhance her marriageability and that the family who has the resources to control the daughter's sexual behaviors will have better chances of securing a good marriage. Paige (1983) has suggested some tactics that parents may use toward this goal, including sending daughters to sex-segregated schools or encouraging membership in sororities that participate in surveillance of sexual activities.

The advent of effective contraception has decreased the economic value of virginity and a steadily increasing percentage of adolescent women become sexually active with each new survey conducted (Morokoff, 1994). This period of social adjustment is certainly having an effect on gender expectations for sexual behavior. Evidence suggests that young women see themselves as being sexually empowered with rights to autonomy and assertiveness (Morokoff et al., 1997). More behavioral data, however, suggests that actual behavior falls far short of this ideal. Although some of society's incentive to control women's sexuality has been eroded, it has not disappeared. Thousands of years of interest in controlling women's sexuality will not disappear in a couple of decades, as this interest is rooted in gender expectations based on culture, tradition, in some cases legal statute, and religion. Subsidiary concepts such as disease prevention, self-esteem, and notions of human worth support contemporary movements designed to increase abstinence, which are primarily directed toward young women.

Sexual Victimization

Sexual victimization is one way of achieving social control of sexuality in women. Rape is often used in societies as a means of controlling women's sexuality. Sanday (1981) describes the Kikuyu, where "a band of boys belonging to a guild roamed the countryside in search of a woman to gang rape as a means of proving their manhood and as a prelude to marriage" (p. 20). Sanday concludes, based on a data set of 156 standard sample societies, that rape-prone societies generally condone violence and are characterized by male dominance; that is, in a society where women do not have power and authority. Clearly, the United States is a rape-prone society. More recently, Sanday elaborated on rape as a means of social control in fraternities (Sanday, 1990). The theory that rape is a means by which men control women was eloquently advanced by Brownmiller (1975). According to Brownmiller, "From prehistoric times to the present, I believe, rape has played a critical function. It is nothing more or less than a conscious process of intimidation by which all men keep all women in a state of fear" (p. 15). One result of that state of fear is the sexual accommodation of the individual's male partner.

Sexual victimization is more insidious when it begins in childhood.

A recent review article by Polusny and Follette (1995) documented the long-term correlates of child sexual abuse (CSA). It is now established that CSA is related to adult sexual functioning. Women with sexual abuse histories change partners more frequently, engage in sexual activities with casual acquaintances more, have more short-term sexual relationships, engage in voluntary sexual intercourse at an earlier age, and have more sexual partners than nonsexually abused women (Polusny & Follette, 1995). Finally, CSA has been shown to be related to revictimization experiences. According to Polusny and Follette (1995), "Overall, sexually abused females reported significantly more negative adult experiences, including sexual assault, physical assault, and force used in adult relationships than did nonabused women." Wyatt, Guthrie, & Notgrass (1992) found that almost half of women who had been sexually victimized before the age of 18 reported abuse in adulthood. Women who were sexually abused during childhood were 2.4 times more likely to be revictimized as adults. Other data indicate that women with CSA histories demonstrated less sexual assertiveness for refusing unwanted sexual activities (Morokoff et al., 1997). These data suggest that sexual victimization prepares the child for sexual availability and submission as an adult.

In addition to effects on sexuality, CSA can produce "intense and pervasive negative internal experiences" (Polusny & Follette, 1995, p. 157). These experiences are characterized by feelings of negative affect such as guilt, shame, fear, and rage. Strategies to avoid painful memories and emotions are reported to be used by abuse survivors. For example, emotional avoidance behaviors such as dissociation, substance abuse, and self-mutilation are thought to be reinforced by avoidance of intense affect. Emotional suppression and denial are common coping strategies used by abuse survivors (Leitenberg, Greenwald, & Cado, 1992). A wide variety of other negative sequelae to CSA have been reported including general psychological distress, depression, self-harming behaviors, anxiety, substance abuse, eating disorders, somatization, personality disorders, and impairment of interpersonal functioning (Polusny & Follette, 1995). Thus, although CSA increases women's sexual vulnerability as adults, it also leads to vulnerability in more general aspects of functioning.

Sexual victimization is unfortunately quite prevalent in American society. A national random telephone sample revealed that 27% of women and 16% of men reported having experienced sexual victimization under the age of 18 (Finkelhor, Hotaling, Lewis, & Smith, 1990). Sexual victimization of adult women is also very common, frequently reported by 1 in 4 women. If these experiences serve to intimidate women and decrease their sexual assertiveness, it can be expected that such effects occur for a substantial segment of the population.

Women's Dependence on Men

A woman may be reluctant to place sexual demands on her male partner (e.g., to use condoms, to have sex when he doesn't want to, to engage in nonpreferred sexual activities) or to refuse sex requested by her male partner (e.g., decline intercourse, refuse to perform oral sex, refuse to watch or act out scenes from pornographic videos) for fear of losing him. Commonly, male partners may threaten to seek sexual gratification elsewhere if female partners are not willing to supply sex, representing a significant threat to the relationship. Women fear losing a male partner because they fear the loss of his economic support. Many women would not be able to maintain their economic lifestyle if they were abandoned by a male partner. For some women, this may represent the difference between being able to feed their children or not. For other women, it may simply represent the difference between maintaining a lifestyle or social standing they prefer and are motivated to retain.

Women fear losing a male partner because they do not want to risk alienating their children's father, especially when society makes it clear who should accede to whose requests concerning sex. More profoundly, women are dependent on men to make them mothers in the first place. Although it is true that women can seek out an anonymous sexual encounter to become pregnant or opt for artificial insemination, thus avoiding having to please a man in order to become a mother, most women want their children to know their fathers. To achieve this goal, some accommodation of men's sexuality may be required. It may be argued that since men also are dependent on women to make them fathers, neither party has the edge in sexual bargaining. However, the argument has been made by many that women are more interested in being mothers than men are in being fathers. Chodorow (1978) offers a nonbiological explanation for this phenomenon. She argues that girls have a very close relationship with their mothers, unimpeded by a boy's need to separate in order to achieve gender identity. Thus the focus developmentally for girls is on relationships, accommodation, and caregiving, whereas for boys it is on separation, independence, and autonomy. To Chodorow, adult women seek intense relationships that replicate the psychic landscape of their childhoods. Such relationships cannot easily be achieved with men who are raised in the culture of individuation. Thus such relationships are only attained with their children, meaning that women have a greater psychological investment in having children than men do.

A third reason women fear losing a male partner is because men have traditionally served as protectors to women. According to Gates (1978), rape can be a method by which women are encouraged to remain dependent on men. Women's susceptibility to sexual or otherwise violent attack, as well as to problems in the areas that gender roles prescribe as the male domain (e.g., auto repair, appliance and household repair, finances), leave women vulnerable to feelings of dependency on men.

Conclusions

Sexual assertiveness and women's full, empowered participation in sexual decision making are clearly restricted. Each of the factors discussed here—gender expectations, social controls, childhood victimization, and the various sources of dependence on men—can be conceptualized individually, but operate in an interactive manner to limit women's sexual autonomy. Nevertheless, these factors do not determine negative outcomes for all women. A factor akin to hardiness may explain why many women, despite dismal cultural messages objectifying and demeaning women's sexuality, are able to express their own sexual interests, bargain effectively with partners for what they want sexually, and feel satisfied with their sexual expression.

LESBIAN AND BISEXUAL SEXUALITY

Does having sex with another woman avoid the problems of having sex with a man? Arguably, many of the barriers to sexual assertiveness do not exist in lesbian relationships, and no biological explanations of heightened sex drive justify predatory behavior. Thus, in theory, two women should be able to define a positive, egalitarian sexuality not based on dominance-submission or coercion. And yet, developmentally, the same cultural images available to girls who become heterosexual are available to girls who become lesbian. Examination of many sexually explicit lesbian materials reveals that they are often based on themes of dominance and submission similar to sexually explicit heterosexual materials. In lesbian relationships, women can play the role of sexual predator just as fictional women do in male-oriented pornography. In lesbian relationships, this can serve to exploit women who play the submissive role.

Recent data suggest that for women who report having had sex with both women and men in the past five years, a significantly greater percentage report histories of childhood sexual abuse than for women who had sex with only men (Quina, Burkholder, Sklar, & Morokoff, 1996). As has been discussed, a history of sexual abuse affects women's sexual behavior. It has been suggested here that women with early exposure to pornography or other forms of abuse may be more susceptible to internalizing sexual roles related to dominance and submission. Thus the fact that all women are exposed to the same negative cultural images and the evidence that bisexual women are more likely than exclusively heterosexual women to be survivors of abuse experiences suggests that at least some lesbian and bisexual women will have difficulty in defining an autonomous sexuality just as exclusively heterosexual women do.

APPLICATIONS

The effects of restrictions on women's sexual assertiveness will be examined in two situations: relationship satisfaction and sexually transmitted disease prevention.

How Sexual Assertiveness May Influence Relationship Satisfaction

Typically, a strong correlation is found between sexual satisfaction and general relationship satisfaction (Morokoff, 1994). Therefore, the question is posed, how does lack of sexual assertiveness affect sexual satisfaction and, more generally, relationship satisfaction?

It may be instructive to conceptualize some of the situations around which sexual partners may be assertive. Within the realm of initiation assertiveness, partners may be assertive in suggesting or initiating sexual activity. A woman may prefer having sex in the morning rather than evening, or on the weekend rather than a weekday. Women may prefer having sex at particular points in the menstrual cycle. If she initiates sex when she wants to have sex (rather than passively waiting for a partner to initiate at a time when she may or may not want to have sex), she is more likely to be happy with the result and satisfied with her partner. Initiation assertiveness also pertains to suggesting types of sexual activities she may prefer. She may prefer sex in a particular position or a particular type of sexual activity. If she cannot initiate these activities, she is likely to be less satisfied with the outcome.

With respect to assertiveness in refusing unwanted sex, there is potential for serious emotional distress if a woman cannot assert what she wants. If a woman feels obligated for any reason to accept sexual activities that make her feel used or evoke emotional distress, she is being sexually victimized. In many instances this will mean being sexually revictimized. This would include a sexual abuse or rape survivor experiencing subsequent unwanted sex; a woman acting out scenes from pornography without feeling she has a choice in the matter, a woman with a CSA history of forced oral sex being obligated to perform oral sex on her partner. When sexual exploitation occurs in a relationship it automatically impairs satisfaction with that relationship. Less extreme examples also can be given: A woman feels rejected by her husband because he is having an affair, but she fears that if she doesn't have sex with him it will only give him more reason to look for other women. A woman doesn't want to have sex too soon with her new boyfriend, but she fears he will think less of her if she doesn't. A woman doesn't really enjoy sex, but she feels obligated to give her husband a chance to satisfy himself. In any of these examples, damage is done to both the sexual relationship and the general relationship by (a) women not knowing what their own sexual desires are, and (b) women failing to effectively assert their desires to their partner. Of course, partners can compromise on any issue in a relationship. But when the compromise always goes in one direction or where there is an element of coercion in the compromise, damage is done to the relationship.

Research has not documented the prevalence with which women have unwanted sex with their partners or feel impeded in initiating wanted sex, but presumably it is a normative experience for most women. Such lack of satisfaction undoubtedly takes a high toll. Research is only beginning to address the impact on women of such difficult life experiences.

Sexually Transmitted Disease Prevention

There are two principal strategies currently available for women to prevent sexually transmitted disease (STD): abstinence and condom use. Both strategies require negotiation and assertiveness with a partner. This necessity is perhaps the greatest impediment to protection against disease for women. As with pregnancy prevention, negative consequences for failure to protect fall more heavily on women than men. Data suggest that women are more susceptible than men to infection as a result of unprotected sex with an infected partner by a factor of 12 to 1 (Padian, Shiboski, & Jewell, 1990).

To determine whether condoms represent an effective method of disease prevention for women, it is important to learn about how decisions related to condom use are made by couples. A study examining women's role in decision making with respect to condom use (Osmond et al., 1993) revealed that 35% of women in the sample either never discussed condom use with a partner or had no role in deciding whether to use a condom. These data made it evident that the unwritten rule among couples was that intercourse occurs without condoms and that for condoms to be used, the couple must talk. For those couples who never discussed condom use, 100% were using condoms less than half the time. If the male partner made the decision concerning condom use, only 12% used condoms more than half the time. If the decision was made jointly, 32% reported using condoms more than half the time, and if the woman reported making the decision herself, condoms were used more than half the time by 49% of the couples. The importance of this research is that it demonstrates both that a substantial portion of women do not have input into a critical sexual health decision and that many men cannot be counted on (without women's input) to make decisions that protect women.

Research supports the conclusion that when women control the use of an efficacious prevention method they will use it. The family planning literature indicates that when types of contraceptives that can be controlled by women are available, they are often used, whereas when types of contraception traditionally controlled by men are relied on, they are not used as much (Rosenberg & Gollub, 1992). These authors reviewed 10 observational studies that compared the effect of condoms, diaphragms, or spermicides on the risk of STDs (not including HIV). Nine of the 10 studies found lower risk among users of female-controlled devices than among condom users. The largest study (Rosenberg, Davidson, Chen, Judson, & Douglas, 1992) found a significantly greater risk for male-controlled (condoms) than for female-controlled (spermicide or diaphragm) methods. Such evidence leads some to recommend the female-controlled methods as more effective (taking into account compliance) than more efficacious male-controlled methods that have a lower rate of compliance (Stein, 1990, 1993). Women's reproductive freedoms over the past 20 years have relied on female-controlled contraceptives such as the IUD, oral contraceptives, and the diaphragm, as well as on abortion. The HIV/AIDS epidemic has been particularly challenging for women because it has partially set back women's reproductive health to a time when reproductive health was controlled by men.

Furthermore, research indicates that it is difficult to increase women's assertiveness for condom use. For example, Gallagher, Morokoff, Quina, and Harlow (1991) reported an increase in condom use following a five-session small group intervention with college women compared to a control group. However, a follow-up study revealed that after one year condom use for the intervention group had decreased to a level below that of the control group (Gallagher & Lang, 1993). Similarly, Deiter (1993) found no increase in sexual assertiveness as a result of a sexual assertiveness training intervention for college-age women, although the program was rated favorably by women. Part of the problem in demonstrating effectiveness of the intervention was that scores on the sexual assertiveness scale declined for women in both intervention and control groups. This interesting finding suggests that young women may initially have an unrealistic appraisal of their own level of sexual assertiveness, which they revise on subsequent test administrations.

Gavey and McPhillips (1997) found that some women reported being unable to initiate condom use despite their stated intentions not to have intercourse without a condom and despite having condoms in their possession. The author interprets this experience in the context of a socially determind sexual passivity. It is unlikely that gender roles for sexuality and social pressures on women to sexually acquiesce will dramatically change in coming years. Therefore, real questions exist as to whether the best protection for women involves teaching them to be sexually assertive concerning condom use with male partners. Alternative approaches involve speeding up the development of a female-controlled microbicide as well as focusing on heterosexual men to teach them sexual responsibility.

Toward a New Culture for Women's Sexuality

How can a culturally defined autonomous sexuality for women be created? How can the individual woman conceptualize her sexuality in more functional terms than as either nonexistent or degrading? Clearly, an important step is to work toward sexual fantasies that are not based on dominance and submission. If arousal means images of dominance and submission, the resulting sexuality is an exploitive one regardless of whether men are dominant over women, women are dominant over men, or same sex partners play the roles. It will be an interesting challenge to explore the parameters of erotica that arouses through other means than the dominance and submission themes found in pornography.

In this new vision, as a society we would let go of the biological model of sexuality. We would acknowledge a physiological component to sexual functioning, but not one that took precedence over human characteristics and capabilities. Thus it would not be assumed that men had the more powerful sexual drive. It would not be assumed that a grave disservice was done to men if they were aroused without gratification. It would be assumed that as human beings we have a measure of control over our physiological functions and can shape them to serve human goals of kindness and caring toward others.

Furthermore, it is interesting to conceptualize egalitarian sexual relationships between men and women. These would not rigidly prescribe roles based on gender for sexual interests and activities. Men would be free to be sexual caretakers, and women would be free to be sexual initiators without being cast in the role of bad girls or be seen as overly demanding. Women would be able to focus on satisfying their own needs without imposing a social threat to caring for children's needs. Such a new vision of sexuality also would encourage men to protect their own sexual interests as well as their partners. Men would be as accountable for unwanted pregnancies and disease as women, and men would serve as sexual gatekeepers similarly to women.

Overall, we are conceptualizing a society capable of defining male sexuality in relational terms, in which men have control over their sexual urges and can be held responsible for sexual transgressions. We are conceptualizing a society capable of defining female sexuality at least in part as an expression of individual interests that do not threaten the fabric of society.

We have something to look forward to.

REFERENCES

Blumstein, P., & Schwartz, P. (1983). *American couples: Money, work, sex*. New York: William Morrow.

Brownmiller, S. (1975). *Against our will: Men, women and rape*. New York: Simon and Schuster.

Chodorow, N. (1978). *The reproduction of mothering: Psychoanalysis and the sociology of gender*. Los Angeles: University of California Press.

Cowan, G., Lee, C., Levy, D., & Snyder, D. (1988). Dominance and inequality in x-rated videocassettes. *Psychology of Women Quarterly, 12*, 299–311.

Deiter, P. (1993). *Sexual assertiveness training for college women: An intervention study*. Unpublished dissertation. University of Rhode Island.

Eagly, A. H. & Wood, W. (1999). The origins of sex differences in human behavior. Evolved dispositions versus social roles. *American Psychologist, 54*, 408–423.

Finkelhor, D., Hotaling, G. T., Lewis, I. A., & Smith, C. (1990). Sexual abuse in a national survey of adult men and women: Prevalence, characteristics, and risk factors. *Child Abuse and Neglect, 14*, 19–28.

Frank, E., Anderson, C., & Rubinstein, D. (1978). Frequency of sexual dysfunction in "normal" couples. *New England Journal of Medicine, 299*, 111–115.

Gallagher, P. L., Morokoff, P. J., Quina, K., & Harlow, L. (1991, August). AIDS risk reduction training among college women. In K. Quina (Chair), *Preventing AIDS in women*. Symposium conducted at the meeting of the American Psychological Association, San Francisco, CA.

Gallagher, P. L., & Lang, M. (1993, August). AIDS risk reduction training plus 1 year follow-up. In P. J. Morokoff (Chair), *Sexual assertiveness and AIDS risk reduction in women*. Roundtable conducted at the meeting of the American Psychological Association, Toronto, Canada.

Gallant, S., Coons, H., & Morokoff, P. J. (1994). Psychological perspectives on women's health. In V. J. Adesso, D. Reddy, & R. Fleming (Eds.), Washington, DC: Hemisphere.

Gates, M. (1978). Introduction. In J. R. Chapman & M. Gates (Eds.), *The victimization of women*. Beverly Hills, CA: Sage Publications.

Gavey, N., & McPhillips, K. (1997). Women and the heterosexual transmission of HIV: Risks and prevention strategies. *Women and Health, 25*, 41–64.

Leitenberg, H., Greenwald, E., & Cado, S. (1992). A retrospective study of long-term methods of coping with having been sexually abused during childhood. *Child Abuse and Neglect, 16*, 399–407.

Levine, S. B., & Yost, M. A. (1976). Frequency of sexual dysfunction in a general gynecological clinic: An epidemiological approach. *Archives of Sexual Behavior, 5*, 229–238.

Lott, B. (1987). *Women's lives: Themes and variations in gender learning*. 2nd ed. Pacific Grove, CA: Brooks-Cole.

MacDonald, K. (1987). Biological and psychosocial interactions in early adolescence: A sociobiological perspective. In R. M. Lerner & T. T. Foch (Eds.), *Biological-psychosocial interaction in early adolescence* (pp. 95–120). Hillsdale, NJ: Erlbaum.

McCormick, N. B., Brannigan, G. G., & LaPlante, M. N. (1984). Social desirability in the bedroom: Role of approval motivation in sexual relationships. *Sex Roles, 11,* 303–314.

Mead, M. (1949). *Male and female.* New York: William Morrow.

Morokoff, P. J. (1990, August). Women's sexuality: Expression of self vs. social construction. In C. B. Travis (Chair), *The social construction of women's sexuality.* Symposium conducted at the annual meeting of the American Psychological Association, Boston, MA.

Morokoff, P. J. (1993). Female sexual arousal disorder. In W. O'Donohue and J. H. Geer (Eds.), *Handbook of sexual dysfunctions* (pp. 157–199). Boston: Allyn and Bacon.

Morokoff, P. J. (1994). Sexuality and infertility. In V. Adesso, D. Reddy, & R. Fleming (Eds.), *Psychological perspectives on women's health* (pp. 251–284). Washington, DC: Hemisphere.

Morokoff, P. J. (1998). Women's sexuality. In E. A. Blechman & K. Brownell, *Behavioral medicine for women: A comprehensive handbook.* New York: Guilford.

Morokoff, P. J., Quina, K., Harlow, L. L., Whitmire, L., Grimley, D. M., Gibson, P. R., & Burkholder, G. J. (1997). Sexual Assertiveness Scale (SAS) for women: Development and validation. *Journal of Personality and Social Psychology, 73,* 790–804.

Mosher, D. L. (1980). Three dimensions of depth of involvement in human sexual response. *Journal of Sex Research, 16,* 1–42.

Oliver, M. B., & Hyde, J. S. (1993). Gender differences in sexuality: A meta-analysis. *Psychological Bulletin, 114,* 29–51.

Osmond, M. W., Wambach, K. G., Harrison, D. F., Byers, J., Levine, P., Imershein, A., & Quadagno, D. M. (1993). The multiple jeopardy of race, class, and gender for AIDS risk among women. *Gender & Society, 7,* 99–120.

Padian, N. S., Shiboski, S. S., & Jewell, N. (1990, June). The relative efficiency of female-to-male HIV sexual transmission. *Proceedings of the VIth International Conference on AIDS* [Abstract] *Th.C.101,* 159.

Paige, K. E. (1983). Virginity rituals and chastity control during puberty: Cross-cultural patterns. In S. Golub (Ed.), *Menarche: The transition from girl to woman* (pp. 155–174). Lexington, MA: Lexington Books, DC Heath.

Paige, K. E., & Paige, J. M. (1981). *The politics of reproductive ritual.* Berkeley: University of California Press.

Polusny, M. A., & Follette, V. M. (1995). Long-term correlates of child sexual abuse: Theory and review of the empirical literature. *Applied and Preventive Psychology, 4,* 143–166.

Quina, K., Burkholder, G., Sklar, B. J., & Morokoff, P. J. (1996, March). *Bisexual women: HIV risk, psychosocial wellbeing, and abuse histories.* Paper presented at the annual meeting of the Association for Women in Psychology, Portland, OR.

Rosen, R. C., Taylor, J. F., Leiblum, S. R., & Bachmann, G. (1993). Prevalence of sexual dysfunctions in women. *Journal of Sex and Marital Therapy, 19,* 171–188.

Rosenberg, M. J., Davidson, A. F., Chen, J. H., Judson, E. N., & Douglas, J. M. (1992). Barrier contraceptives and sexually transmitted diseases in women: A comparison of female-dependent methods and condoms. *American Journal of Public Health, 82,* 669–674.

Rosenberg, M. J., & Gollub, E. L. (1992). Commentary: Methods women can use that may prevent sexually transmitted disease, including HIV. *American Journal of Public Health, 82,* 1473–1478.

Sanday, P. R. (1981). The socio-cultural context of rape: A cross-cultural study. *Journal of Social Issues, 37,* 5–27.

Sanday, P. (1990). *Fraternity gang rape: Sex brotherhood and privilege on campus.* New York: New York University Press.

Stein, Z. A. (1990). HIV prevention: The need for methods women can use. *American Journal of Public Health, 80,* 460–462.

Stein, Z. A. (1993). HIV prevention: An update on the status of methods women can use. *American Journal of Public Health, 83,* 1379–1382.

Tiefer, L. (1987). Social constructionism and the study of human sexuality. In P. Shaver & C. Hendrick (Eds.), *Sex and gender* (pp. 70–94). Beverly Hills, CA: Sage.

Wyatt, G. E., Guthrie, D., & Notgrass, C. M. (1992). Differential effects of women's child sexual abuse and subsequent sexual revictimization. *Journal of Consulting and Clinical Psychology, 60,* 167–173.

IV

SEXUALITY AND
THE SOCIAL ORDER

13

CONSENT, POWER, AND SEXUAL SCRIPTS: DECONSTRUCTING SEXUAL HARASSMENT

SUZANNE B. KURTH, BETHANY B. SPILLER,
AND CHERYL BROWN TRAVIS

We argue, along with other authors in this section, that women's sexuality is one of the arenas in which cultural beliefs about women and mandates for women's behavior permit men to exercise power over them without their consent.[1] An interesting feature of one form of this misuse of power, sexual harassment, is that it is may be both so reflective of normative gender behavior and so embedded in the activities of certain types of organizations that at least on the surface it may appear that nothing unusual is happening. Deconstructing sexual harassment is about making what is sometimes invisible visible; it involves creating labels, highlighting scripts that foster harassing behavior, and examining organizational contexts.

Identifying sexual harassment is in some ways similar to the discovery of a black hole in space. It is not so much the direct measurements that give it away as the indirect evidence of the distortion of orbits in surround-

---

[1]Although we acknowledge that men may sexually harass other men and women may harass other women and men, we focus here on the most prevalent form of men harassing women.

ing bodies. Frameworks that disguise or that make sexual harassment invisible are part of the underlying fabric of society, especially gender relations, that we hope to make more tangible in this chapter.

In American culture, those who have had the most influence in constructing the meaning and significance of such behaviors have been men whose interests are served by defining sexually harassing behavior as friendliness, humor, playful flirtation, innocent misunderstanding, or a sincere expression of sexual attraction. Men are thus able to claim, often effectively, that the sexual harassment never occurred (i.e., something else happened, perhaps a joke). They also are able to promote the idea that although something may have occurred, it was nothing of significance and no harm was done; perhaps it was a harmless flirtation. Finally, if a problem is acknowledged, it can be discounted as a problem created by the woman; that is, it is her problem because she lacks a sense of humor, misinterpreted friendly interest, or was overly sensitive and anxious about her own sexuality. The man, on the other hand, was only engaging in socially normative behavior, perhaps as an indication of his legitimate attraction.

Level of intimacy, meaning, and significance are aspects of social relations that are negotiated. But the playing field is not level for all parties. To the extent that women's own consciousness and understanding are shaped and colored by the dominant discourse of society, women are likely to have difficulty in identifying harassment as it occurs, and are likely to experience feelings of guilt, embarrassment, and helplessness in the face of it.

The shifting nature of these negotiations about meaning is underscored by the fact that the term *sexual harassment* was virtually nonexistent in print media until the mid-1970s. Even now, on the verge of a new century, what constitutes sexual harassment is being debated. Yet, as sexual harassment, rape, and pornography are subjected to increased scrutiny, "their continuity with accepted social norms has also become more obvious. Boundaries between flirtation and harassment, seduction and rape, erotica and exploitation" are fuzzy because of the links between dominant sexual scripts and the subordination of women (Rhode, 1989, pp. 230–231). As a society, Americans are relying increasingly on legal proceedings to clarify these boundaries. For example, through interpretation of Title VII, two types of sexual harassment, quid pro quo (an outright proposition for sex) and hostile work environment, are identified as employment discrimination. Through the adjudication of cases, the legal definition of sexual harassment is gradually evolving; however, we will not detail this evolution. Instead, in this chapter we focus on issues of power that underlie these social negotiations and on the interpersonal and organizational contexts that form a framework for these negotiations.

The power issues of sexual harassment may be fleshed out (as it were) in the details of gender roles and sexual scripts or as they are embedded in the structural context of larger organizations. For this reason, in this chapter we move from personal and interpersonal contexts to structural and organizational contexts. Throughout, we rely on the concepts of power, gender, and context as a means of integrating the discussion.

In the following sections we review key elements of social negotiation, including power and consent. We then discuss the ways in which interpersonal sexual scripts provide a context whereby harassment is fostered, examining both traditional male and traditional female sexual scripts. In the third section we explore organizational contexts for academia, business, and the military. We discuss organizational characteristics that foster sexual harassment in each of the three types of organizations, and how reliance on hierarchical structures is a major contextual basis for harassment in all. In particular, we argue that the preferences of men who control organizations are embedded in the organizational contexts that allow for and simultaneously ignore sexual harassment.

GENDER DIFFERENCES IN POWER

What people take for granted and what they negotiate in their interactions, as well as how they perceive their interaction outcomes, has been the subject of considerable study in social psychology. Women and men may interact with each other and perceive that interaction quite differently. For example, in interviews with married couples, Jessie Bernard (1972) found the reported experiences of the marriage to be so distinct that she referred to "his marriage" and "her marriage." Similarly, sexual harassment may occur when a man does not perceive his behavior as violating standards of conduct but a woman does, or when he knowingly elects to engage in behaviors that a woman neither seeks nor desires. This misperception on the part of the man may partly reflect unconscious defense mechanisms that hide or disguise socially unacceptable motives from those engaging in the exploitation or undermining of others.

A variety of theories and concepts can be applied to deconstruct sexual harassment. Social psychologists explaining episodes of sexual harassment as well as gender differences in cognition and behavior rely on a variety of frameworks or models (Johnson, 1993). Those who focus on differences in perception in interaction episodes may draw on symbolic interaction and social exchange theory (Jones & Remland, 1992) or consider how status characteristics affect individuals' behaviors, thoughts, and outcomes (Berger, Webster, Ridgeway, & Rosenholz, 1986). Others rely on attribution theory (Kenig & Ryan, 1986; Pryor & Day, 1988; Pryor, LaVite, & Stoller, 1993; Quinn & Less, 1984). Yet another approach is to draw on various frameworks to take a social constructionist stance (Berger & Luckmann, 1966; Gergen, 1985).

We take an eclectic approach using various components of the above approaches germane to a discussion of harassment; however, we consistently emphasize power as it is exercised in the context of interpersonal interactions (Ford & Johnson, 1998) and as it is embedded in organizational structures. Specifically, we argue that explanations of behavior need to take into account structural factors and the status characteristics of their occupants (Lach & Gwartney-Gibbs, 1993).

For example, women may behave differently and be responded to differently than men when in leadership roles, not only because of socialization but also because of their lack of organizational power compared to men in similar positions. Women traditionally occupy certain types of subordinate positions in organizations and the behaviors expected of women in those positions may be indicative both of their position in the organizational structure and expectations about gender roles (Fain & Anderton, 1987). We give credence to the proposition that the preferences of men who control organizations are embedded in the organizational structure, that organizations are gendered (Acker, 1990).

Our analysis focuses on two dimensions underlying common conceptualizations of behavior as sexual harassment, power and consent. We emphasize these because they are not merely aspects of a definition of sexual harassment, but they also suggest mechanisms by which sexual harassment is fostered and maintained.

Power

Feminists argue that to a large extent what appear to be gender differences in personal style and interpersonal relations may be explained largely on the basis of differences in status or power that are embedded in gender (Hyde, 1995; Unger & Crawford, 1996). For example, experimental studies have demonstrated that what is colloquially understood as women's intuition may be the effect of subordinate role on interpersonal sensitivity (Snodgrass, 1985). Although there are positive and legitimate ways to exercise power and authority, often referred to as empowerment or the power to, we focus here on power as control over others (Yoder & Kahn, 1992).

Power can be exercised in a variety of subtle ways (Hyde, 1995). Dominant people or groups can limit the opportunities of subordinate groups and are more likely to ignore or pay less attention to subordinates. Dominants also can deny the legitimacy of subordinates' experience.

Furthermore, power can be exercised in the course of interaction episodes and can be exercised by shaping the context in which transactions occur. For example, power can affect the availability of alternatives, and, more particularly, high-power people can prevent low-power people from developing alternatives. Social exchange theory suggests that when relationship alternatives are limited, a low cost-benefit ratio will be tolerated. That is, women may not protest sexual harassment if they perceive that they have few alternative options for employment. Recent exchange theorizing directs our attention to coercive power as well as reward power (Molm, 1997).

Power or standing may affect the interpersonal style used in negotiations. For example, high-status people often tend to negotiate directly, using forthright bargaining, direct asking, or reasoning; whereas low-status people are more likely to use indirect styles, such as, lying low, being evasive, hinting, being nice, withdrawing, and so on (Falbo & Peplau, 1980). Falbo and Peplau (1980) observed in a study of negotiating among couples that women were more likely to rely on these indirect styles. Other studies of couples (Gruber & White, 1986) have found related patterns, but observed that although men report using both male and female styles, women were more restricted in the types of strategies they adopted.

In recent decades the idea that interactants are aware that interaction is rule directed and that choices are made concerning which rules to follow has gained currency (Harre & Secord, 1973). Although commonalities in behavior exist, a female-male expressive-instrumental dichotomy appears for directness of approach, with men directly seeking to realize their ends and women wanting to develop rapport with men first (Midwinter, 1992).

One may be tempted to offer a rather simple recommendation that women could solve these problems if they would only act more like men. Besides problems with the implicit value system of such a recommendation, there are other practical difficulties. First, due to inertia as well as vested interest in maintaining the status quo, efforts to change dominance patterns are likely to be met with resistance. Furthermore, violation of expected gender roles and styles are sometimes met with negative sanctions. Experimental studies of group dynamics that varied tentative versus assertive style by gender of speaker found that women who used assertive (traditionally male styles) were liked less than women using traditional female (tentative) styles (Carli, 1989). And although tentative female speakers were judged to be less confident and less competent, they were at least more persuasive with a male audience than were women who exhibited a more expert style.

We suggest that such contrasting styles reflect differences in power (e.g., prestige, position power, access to resources, or ability to influence or orchestrate) that overlap. Thus, women as a class may generally appear more tentative, more uncertain, and more vulnerable, thereby increasing the likelihood for attempted exploitation and harassment. Serious problems arise when mechanisms for dealing with harassment impose an assertive (traditionally male) style of response on women who have been encultured with a style of low entitlement; we will discuss this in the following section on consent.

The power dimension ranges from complete equality at one end to total domination at the other (with one having complete authority over another). The specific ways in which power leads to sexual harassment have been more the subject of speculation than of research (Cleveland & Kerst, 1993). Gender arrangements in society may generate power differentials. Specifically, men may have greater power based in heterosexuality as a political institution according to feminist Adrienne Rich (1980). Differences in behavior by gender may reflect power differences (Yoder & Kahn, 1992).

The formal organizational power a person has due to occupancy of a position is central to whether unwanted sexual gestures directed at a subordinate are perceived as harassment. Researchers such as Bursik (1992) argue that this power imbalance is a crucial contextual variable shaping interpretations of situations as sexual harassment. In Bursik's research, whether behavior was perceived as harassment was linked to how blatant it was and the power of the perpetrator; more blatant behavior was consistently seen as harassment, whereas less blatant behavior was defined as harassment when committed by a more powerful person.

Consent

The inclusion of the term *unwanted* in most formal definitions of sexual harassment is reflective of the norms of social conduct in American society. By the insertion of a single word, women are made to bear the burden of monitoring their own behaviors and feelings and those of their male cohorts. Further, women may be given the additional responsibility of communicating explicitly about otherwise subtle shadings of meaning and significance to social actors (i.e., men) who would prefer to remain obtuse on the matter.

Theoretically, the consent dimension ranges from complete voluntariness at one end to total coercion at the other. The standard for harassment is whether behaviors were welcome or unwelcome, whereas for rape the standard is consent. Compliance with sexual demands does not indicate consent (Frug, 1992). For consent to be granted, the less powerful person needs to be clear about what behavior is being requested.

Consent is not always a definitive time-specific decision. Using classic foot-in-the-door technique, perpetrators may engage in small acts of social intimacy that initially seem trivial. The smutty jokes and pats are a way of eventually introducing more intimate behavior (Travis & Kurth, 1981). Because the interaction episodes typically are presented as part of normal social exchange, consent on the part of the target is assumed, and any efforts to indicate otherwise typically require a disruptive confrontation. Thus, women who have been taught to use polite styles and to rely on the goodwill of others, and who have been rewarded for being indirect and evasive, are forced into a situation in which they must use a confrontational style of interaction that is out of character, for which they may be penalized.

Furthermore, the polite, sociable manner of women is often misinterpreted by men as sexual interest. Donat and White (chapter 14, this volume) reiterate the point that men are likely to interpret demonstrations of politeness or sociability by women as an indication of sexual interest. Research demonstrates women are less likely than men to assign sexual interpretations to ambiguous friendly behaviors, which may increase the likelihood that men in various situations will perceive a woman as willing to engage in a sexual relationship (Williams & Cyr, 1992).

Other problems with consent arise from American cultural images of sexuality as part of a basic instinct that is natural and of sexual encounters as events that just happen. In the face of such images that replace intentionality with natural instinct, consent per se is not particularly relevant.

SEXUAL SCRIPTS

Examination of the sexual scripts women and men carry with them in various settings is essential for understanding the dynamics at work in social interaction episodes, and, in particular, interactions that constitute sexual harassment. The concept of scripts emphasizes the cognitive, learned, and social features of sexuality. Sexual scripts are blueprints that guide behaviors and cognitions, both our own and those of others (Rose & Frieze, 1989). Laws and Schwartz (1977) proposed that sexual scripts also include "the rules, expectations, and sanctions governing these acts" (p. 2). In other words, scripts incorporate what a culture or subculture deems as correct behavior for each sex and ensure that these gendered expectations are met by reinforcing acceptable behavior and punishing unacceptable behavior.

Acquisition

Researchers suggest that basic elements of sexual scripts are learned in childhood and that these may form the basis for more frankly outright sexual encounters (Thorne & Luria, 1986). Sexual scripts are constructed from social norms and previous social interaction. Social norms include societal expectations or rules, some of which prescribe certain behaviors for people depending on the situational characteristics, and others which prescribe behaviors based mainly on gender. Sexual scripts are acquired, reinforced, and negotiated during social interactions.

Maintenance

Sexual scripts are maintained by processes that psychologists and sociologists variously describe as social learning, socialization, and social exchange. Those who deviate from culturally dominant sexual scripts encounter sanctions or punishments, whereas those who adopt gender schema in accord with dominant sexual scripts (Bem, 1981) may receive benefits such as social approval. Gender schema theory encourages recognition that individuals' cognitive processes are reflective of their interaction with their environments (Intons-Peterson, 1988). Thus, cognitions associated with sexual scripts are actively constructed.

Before deconstructing sexual scripts, we present types of traditional male and female sexual scripts.

TRADITIONAL MALE SEXUAL SCRIPTS

The male sexual script dominant in American culture dovetails with the need to continually establish sexual competence as masculine (Tiefer, 1986). Men who engage in sexual harassment may justify their behaviors by drawing on aspects of traditional male sexual scripts. The centrality of sexuality in cultural constructions of masculinity combined with a sense of entitlement (Gilbert, 1992) may lead some men to connect dominance and sexuality and thus increase the likelihood that they will engage in sexual harassment (Pryor, LaVite, & Stoller, 1993). Changes lauded in the male sexual script in recent decades have retained the idea of sexual dominance if not exploitation, although the expectations of being a technically proficient lover have been added. Thus the potential for harassment was not reduced.

The male sexual script not only indicates what a man should do, but also carries ideas about women and their behavior. We present three male patterns linked to harassing and then complementary female patterns, that is, ones that make it difficult for women to prevent harassment.

Seducer

Some men see themselves as pursuers and appreciators of women; they define virtually all female subordinates as sexual objects. Various relationships attributed to President Clinton cast him as a man who sees women subordinates as sexual objects. Seducers may focus on one female subordinate at a time (e.g., the newest one in the setting), or they may target a number of women at the same time. These men may be charming or charismatic individuals. When their behavior is challenged they will respond that they really like women and actually have women's interests at heart, in a sense defining themselves as benevolent sexists (Glick & Fiske, 1997).

Seducers often are skilled at manipulating definitions of situations. Boundaries between friendly and sexual behavior are redefined by the seducer's strategic use of gestures that would be unquestioned if briefer (touches) or less intimate (smiles, questions). A Canadian women's track coach exemplified his charismatic ability to blur boundaries when he "convinced athletes that a particular sexual activity (the strip tease, sexual activity with the coach or with other girls on the team) [would] improve their performances because they would then be dependent only on the coach for fulfillment and not be distracted by outsiders" (Kirby, 1994, p. 234).

Initiator

Whether using a natural and biological model that assumes mens' sexual drive makes them naturally highly sexed (Tangri, Burt, & Johnson 1982) or some other model, the belief that men are the initiators of sexual relationships is widely held. The belief that men have "the exclusive role as the initiator of sexual relations and a view of women as having to discourage this initiation" may shape attitudes toward sexual harassment (Murrell & Dietz-Uhler, 1993, p. 174). The presumed burden for men is to take the risk of proposing a sexual relationship, with the possibility of being rejected; the woman's task is to fend off unwanted sexual relationships without hurting the man's self-esteem in a way that may jeopardize her job. Those who perceive men and women as having opposing positions, who hold adversarial sexual beliefs, may be more likely to harass. Men who almost automatically link power and sex possibly may be nonconscious harassers due to a lack of self-awareness (Bargh & Raymond, 1995).

Dominator

Any discussion of masculinity at some point introduces the concept of patriarchy and asks to what extent male behavior is linked to the prerogatives men receive or try to capture simply because they are men (Connell, 1987; MacKinnon, 1979).

Some men harass women who are in environments that they would like to maintain as male domains (e.g., blue-collar work environments, Gruber & Bjorn, 1982). Harassing behaviors may be seen as appropriate action against women whose presence in a particular setting is taken as a sign that they do not deserve the protective treatment accorded good women. Thus, these harassers may see women as violating the rules of appropriate feminine behavior by their presence in a traditionally male work environment and therefore proceed in a dominator mode to assert their masculinity. Men who target women workers in these settings for harassment may be attempting to maintain an implicit social norm—sex segregation of occupations. They may proceed by marking territory through acts of aggression.

Marking Territory

They may stake out (or defend) their territory by telling sexually explicit jokes or by putting up pornographic materials (hostile working environment). Tokens may be tolerated, but when real change appears to be occurring, resistance may emerge. One hypothesis in the social sciences is that as contact increases between groups, understanding may increase. Harlan and Weiss as cited in Gardner, Peluchette, and Clinebell (1994, p. 147) examined two companies and identified an initial decline in male resistance to female managers as their numbers increased, but after the number of female managers increased beyond 15%, male managers engaged in sexist behavior that the researchers attribute to frustration and fear.

Marking behavior is collective and public. "Often, the harasser needs allies, or accomplices, others to 'go along with the joke' or to 'egg him on'" (Kirby, 1994, p. 224). Tailhook involved Air Force pilots who accosted women (other officers and civilians) when they entered the hallways where they were engaging in group solidarity activities (drinking and degrading women).

Physical Aggression

Men may make women the recipients of unwanted brushes, pinches, and kisses to establish their masculinity or as their prerogative. In far too many movies, women are depicted as responding positively to men who put them in their place through physical aggression. Male politicians such as Senator Robert Packwood, who in 1995 resigned from the U.S. Senate after formal censure by the U.S. Senate Ethics Committee, may perceive they have the right to take kisses because of their position.

Targets of assault may be selected from among those perceived as more vulnerable. Self-admitted rapists were able to more accurately interpret facial nonverbal cues than control respondents (Giannini & Fellows, 1986). Those who target others for various types of sexual abuse (including sexual harassment) may choose victims based on their skills at reading nonverbal cues indicating vulnerability.

TRADITIONAL FEMALE SEXUAL SCRIPTS

Traditional female sexual scripts and accepted interaction patterns may make many women vulnerable to sexual harassment. Confronting the behavior creates a dilemma for women because viewing the phenomenon as a violation and taking steps to eradicate the unwanted behavior require going against long-standing standards of femininity and appropriate female conduct.

Sexual Objects

Women should strive to be desirable sexual objects and take responsibility for being treated as sexual objects. Women who subscribe to a traditional feminine script may find it difficult to confront more powerful men who make comments about their bodies or inappropriately touch them. They are not able to counter the argument that a woman should be flattered by sexual attention, and that if a man's attentions are inappropriate, his actions are her fault (provoked by her behavior).

Although many women think the idea of women defining themselves as sexual objects is obsolete, residual behaviors and attitudes exist that perpetuate the idea that women should strive to be desirable sexual objects and men should interact with women under the assumption that they indeed want this. Travis and colleagues (chapter 10, this volume) discuss women's concerted efforts to look attractive (to men). Receiving attention from men in the form of compliments or nonverbal behaviors, such as a touch or warm facial expressions, is considered to be flattering. The problem with this type of behavior or thinking is that women have difficulty confronting more powerful men who make unwanted comments about their body or inappropriately touch them. They find it difficult to counter the argument, either conceptually or in actuality, that they should be flattered by the male's attention.

A related issue is the common assumption that women who are harassed actually bring it on themselves through their provocative behaviors. Blaming the victim is also prevalent in incidents of rape (Rhode, 1989). In rape and harassment, the woman is said to have provoked the man by her behavior and therefore is responsible for the man's resulting actions. Such arguments release the man from any responsibility in the encounter, as well as perpetuate the myth that women want to be sexual objects and adopt styles of self-presentation for this purpose.

Some organizations may not support but rather blame physically less attractive women who are sexually harassed. Because such women are not seen as desirable sexual objects, others may argue it is nonsensical to believe that a man would pay attention to them or make sexual advances toward them. Thus, complaints from some women may be "dismissed as vindictive fantasies or wishful thinking" (Rhode, 1989). An alternative scenario used to place the blame on the victim is that an unattractive woman's efforts to gain the man's attention were rebuffed and led to the vindictive filing of a harassment complaint.

Passivity

Traditional sexual scripts may lead some women to quietly endure sexual comments and overtures because they perceive male aggression and female submissiveness as the norm or as natural (Laws & Schwartz, 1977). Women are socialized "to accept the male cultural prerogative to initiate sexual contact in virtually any situation" (Fitzgerald, 1993, p. 1072). According to the traditional script, women should endure unwanted sexual advances in recognition of men's inherent entitlement. Consequently, women often opt to ignore incidences of harassment rather than challenge tacit rules concerning men's societal prerogatives. Thus, ignoring the behavior is one of the most common coping responses to sexual harassment (Fitzgerald, Swan, & Fischer, 1995). Such nonresponse is ineffective in stopping the behavior—ignoring the harassment does little to circumvent the behavior and in some cases may result in its escalation (Silverman, 1976).

Substantial research has shown gender differences in the perceptions of sexual harassment (e.g., Gutek, 1985; Powell, 1986). Specifically, the research on gender differences supports that men hold more constricted definitions of sexual harassment and are less likely to view any interactions as examples of sexual harassment (Fitzgerald, 1993). Several studies have investigated the variables that influence these differences in perceptions. If a woman has engaged in previous friendly, informal interaction with a man, men are less likely to see the man's behavior as harassment (Williams & Cyr, 1992). Women, however, show no differences in perception, regardless of prior interaction.

Women who are harassed by men with whom they have had friendly interactions may choose to remain in the relationship and not report the harassment (Abbey, 1982; Abbey & Melby, 1986; Williams & Cyr, 1992). This response at first glance appears illogical, yet understanding the strength of traditional scripts mandates such passivity and illuminates some of the reasons behind such a response. Woman are socialized, overtly and covertly, to submit to men. If a woman on some level allows a man to interact with her (e.g., even by participating in behavior as basic as friendly exchanges), she is even less able to assert her disapproval. Not only is she normally expected to remain passive, but it also is assumed that she has given her implicit consent to the man's dominating behavior. In other words, she has lost her right to complain. It also means, in a profound way, that women do not retain the authority to negotiate how and to what extent they may express or explore their own sexuality.

Another study supporting the influence of prior interaction on perceptions is Summers and Myklebust's (1992) report that if a woman complained about harassing workplace behaviors from a man with whom she had previously been romantically involved, raters' perceptions of the seriousness of the behavior and of appropriate managerial responses shifted. Again, prior interactions mediated the perceptions of sexual harassment of men and women. Yet, in this instance men and women alike reported that prior romantic involvement weakened the severity of the harassment claim. Both sexes believe the woman "lost her right to speak up," therefore increasing the probability of the woman remaining passive and the harassment continuing.

Dependence

Women's typically more vulnerable economic position limits their freedom to complain about workplace conditions, including episodes of sexual harassment. One important reason is the fear of losing a much needed job. Burrell and Hearn (1989) state that women's lack of organizational power coupled with their need for work exacerbates the likelihood of harassment. Without these factors, they state, acts of harassment would be made more difficult.

The vulnerability of many women workers is exemplified in the story of a mother of four who was working at a steel company, earning 25,000 dollars a year. A male colleague several times over the years flirted with her. She at the time was married. Later, the woman was promoted and the man became her direct supervisor. In the meantime, she had divorced and was supporting her family on one income. She stated her supervisor knew about her vulnerable position and took advantage of it. She reported he harassed her during several months and eventually fired her because she refused to consent to his advances ("Award in Bay Sexual Harassment Case," 1985). This woman's dependence on her job, her subsequent dependence on the man, and the abuse of power provided the opportunity for sexual harassment to occur.

Even if they do not fear being fired, women may fear that a complaint will make it difficult if not impossible for them to continue to perform their jobs because of retribution from others within the organization. Instead of being rewarded for their courage, complainants may be labeled as whistle blowers and punished (Koss, 1990). When complainants suffer from retribution, double victimization has occurred. A woman who steps out of her role by reporting harassment is violating both her subordinate role as an employee, an organizational status, and her subordinate role as a woman, a gender-based status. Data from several surveys indicate women who were harassed complained of different forms of retribution, such as psychological abuse by members of the organization, public ridicule, denial of promotions, shunning by coworkers, and the loss of social support by colleagues (Koss, 1990).

DECONSTRUCTION OF SEXUAL SCRIPTS

Sexual scripts exist on multiple levels. Two levels of interest are widely known cultural scenarios—collectively held scripts such as heterosexuality, and interpersonal scripts, or expectations about behaviors to be used in a specific context (Simon & Gagnon, 1986). With their interpersonal sexual scripts, individuals may follow or violate traditionally held collective scripts. In the United States, men and women are aware that men initiate dates. Further, the man arrives at the woman's residence, takes her home, and sets up future dates (Pryor & Merluzzi, 1985); the woman's task is to respond. At the broad level, men initiate heterosexual relations and women acquiesce. On the individual level, a couple may negotiate specific aspects of a dating episode.

When people generally follow the rules or norms sanctioned for a situation, the scripted nature of behavior may be unnoticed. Problems occur when situations and the rules governing them are defined differently by the participants (e.g., a teacher-student conference is sexualized). Men may behave in ways that do not fit women's definitions of situations, and the women may experience feelings ranging from powerlessness to degradation. "What men often experience as fun or flirtation, women often experience as degrading and demanding. And, it is male experience that has shaped the law's traditional responses to sexual harassment" (Rhode, 1989, p. 233). Understanding the content of scripts and their links with gender-based role differentiation is helpful in deconstructing why some people engage in harassing behavior, as well as understanding why the targets of the behavior may choose certain responses (e.g., assertively thwarting the behaviors, ending, or enduring them).

Script Diversity

Scripts may vary on several dimensions, for example, their complexity, rigidity, and conventionality (Gagnon, Rosen, & Lieblum, 1982). Some research indicates sexual scripts that incorporate more egalitarian views of gender and sexuality are gaining validity (Weinberg, Swensson, & Hammersmith, 1983), although more conventional or traditional scripts that reflect gender differences continue to be widespread (LaPlante, McCormick, & Brannigan, 1980; O'Sullivan & Byers, 1992).

Sexual expectations may be influenced by both the perpetrator's and the target's socioeconomic standing, age, and ethnicity. We cannot separate the effects of each because they do not operate in a separable fashion (Griscom, 1992). Some circumstances may make African American women more subject to sexual harassment (e.g., stereotypical perceptions of African American women as more sexual). In addition, alternative employment may be more problematic for African American women because their educational and economic resources may be limited. This limitation in employment options may make it all the more pressing to keep their paycheck, to be perceived as not only hard working and reliable, but also agreeable, more dependent, and hence more vulnerable to harassment (Eason, 1988). Yet, African American women may be socialized to act more assertively in situations involving men's sexual advances than White women (Lewis, 1975). The intersection of race, class, and gender in African American women's sexual scripts may encourage different interpretations and responses to overt gestures than White women's. They can accept the advances and invite further interaction or reject the advances by clearly expressing intolerance. Race and social class may interact, for women with fewer economic resources are often seen as fair targets for sexual advances (Benokraitis & Feagin, 1995). More often, White middle-class women have been taught to ignore blatant sexual comments or quietly endure them.

The effects of race and ethnicity or minority status are difficult to specify in part because minority status may be associated with occupying subordinate positions in organizations. Researchers cannot assume an additive model for the effects of subordinate statuses. Also, due to the intersection of multiple statuses, researchers cannot identify whether lesbians are the target of more harassment than heterosexual women, although they may be more conscious of it.

Negotiation

The sexual scripts women and men learn shape the dynamics that operate in social interaction episodes and social relationships. A woman may view repeated unsolicited sexual overtures by a man as harassing, whereas the man initiating the advances believes his behavior to be within appropriate boundaries, with his belief actually fostering escalation of such behavior (Pryor & Day, 1988).

Individuals have to negotiate with their interaction partners what aspects of their sexual scripts are appropriate in a particular encounter. The choice of scripts is based on what the person wants to achieve in the interaction, for example, approval, acceptance, a certain identity, or to shape the other's behavior (Rose & Frieze 1989). In this sense, situation or context is important in choosing and implementing sexual scripts. Aspects of sexual scripts may either be triggered by situational cues (context) or purposefully used to create impressions (Gardner et al., 1994).

Purposeful behavior enacted to create a particular impression is the basis for impression management theory. Two interpersonal strategies are ingratiation and intimidation. Ingratiation may be used by a person for the purpose of looking attractive or being well liked by someone in power. Women may be encouraged to engage in ingratiating types of behavior because men are often in positions of power over them. Therefore, women may choose to compliment others, be agreeable, and emphasize their own physical appearance for the purpose of gaining acceptance or approval (Gardner et al., 1994).

To intimidate or coerce, people must convince target others that the initiator can make them experience negative consequences, be they physical, emotional, or professional. Men use this strategy more readily than women, perhaps because men have more power and this type of behavior is more congruent with societal expectations of men. Women are more likely to rely on other scripted behavior such as an assertive self-presentation style (Gardner et al., 1994).

Contexts or definitions of situations also play a role in the negotiation of scripts that shape interpretations of behavior and the opportunities to negotiate the interpretations. In American culture, men have a prerogative to introduce sex into an interaction regardless of context. Lack of situational variation may be evidence of the strength of certain sexual scripts. Some gender typed cultural scripts are more rigidly held and considered stronger than alternative scripts (Rose & Frieze, 1989). Another possible reason for the disregard of context in certain sexual scripts concerns the illegitimate use of power in the negotiation or lack of negotiation of sexual scripts.

More powerful people may impose their definitions on others. And people may misinterpret others' gestures to conform to what they want from the other. Nonverbal communication (e.g., smiles) may be particularly problematic, for the ambiguity of various nonverbal gestures may make it easier to assign gender stereotyped expectations to them than to verbal gestures (Johnson, 1994).

Illegitimate Use of Power

Individuals may misuse the formal organizational power they have over subordinates, but act as if what happened was an incident of negotiated interpersonal power. Recognition of sexual harassment as an illegitimate use of power reflects the questioning of rights accorded to privileged men, and even less privileged men, in a society with patriarchal structures. Those who engage in sexual harassment try to force their definition of what is appropriate on others by illegitimately using their greater power.

A perceived power differential may be based on organizational status or on status characteristics such as gender. Whatever the power basis, those who perceive they hold greater power or who may feel threatened by a woman with power may try to force an unwanted sexual definition of the situation. For example, some male patients harass female nurses (Grieco, 1987) and doctors (Phillips & Schneider, 1993). For female doctors, the risk of harassment increases when they work in emergency rooms, community health centers, and as temporary replacements, although their own offices are the typical setting in which they are harassed.

Gender Based Power

Power can be integral to a social role or position that is largely independent of the personal identities of the interacting individuals. Yet in our society power is also generally differentially accorded to the man. Occasionally, designations along these two dimensions may be contradictory, offering the possibility of contrapower harassment. *Contrapower harassment* (Benson, 1984) occurs when individuals without institutional authority select opportunities to exert illegitimate power over their superordinates (McKinney, 1990). Examples of contrapower harassment include students making anonymous harassing phone calls to faculty members, or students writing lewd or inappropriate comments on faculty members' evaluations, as well as more direct behaviors, such as explicit sexual propositions (Grauerholz, 1989). The similarity of these examples with those more traditional harassing interactions is the existence of a power differential (although only situational in some cases) in which one party attempts to force a sexual definition of a situation through enactment of aspects of a sexual script.

ORGANIZATIONAL CONTEXTS

Sexual harassment is shaped by more than personal style, gender expectations, or sexual scripts; organizational structures and overall context can make certain behaviors more likely and can provide climates that foster sexual harassment.

Organizational contexts (the structure of the organization, the social norms of the organization, and the power differentials inherent in it) play an important role in the facilitation and maintenance of sexual harassment (Acker, 1990). The prevailing organizational climate most influences a woman's overt coping response to sexual harassment (i.e., whether she uses assertiveness with the aggressor, appeases or excuses him, or seeks institutional relief) (Fitzgerald et al., 1995).

Traditionally, theoretical models of organizations assumed that organizations are and should be desexualized. With the advent of industrialization, sexuality was viewed as a distraction and a barrier to productivity (Burrell & Hearn, 1989) and thus was banned from the workplace. Policies such as those banning office romances were instituted to regulate conduct deemed inappropriate for the workplace (Taylor & Conrad, 1992). From this perspective, sexuality is unimportant and irrelevant to the organization. Workers engage in sexual behaviors on their own time and in nonwork settings.

Often the desexualizing of formal organizations is more theoretical than real. The underlying assumptions about people and relationships more common to traditional masculine models of behavior are incorporated in unrecognized ways into the structures of the organization. What actually happens is that male norms and masculine behaviors are imbedded in models of expected organizational behavior. The myth of desexualization facilitated the silent incorporation of a male model of sexuality in the underlying structures ordering participants' conceptions of how people should behave within such organizations (Taylor & Conrad, 1992). Socially constructed male attributes such as aggressiveness and competitiveness became associated with success in business. Within organizations the spillover of traditional conceptions of sex and gender led to occupations being divided into masculine and feminine, male-type and female-type jobs (Taylor & Conrad, 1992). Work organizations thus replicated the larger social context.

An alternative model of organizational theory proposes that there cannot and should not be a distinction between organizations and their social contexts. Sexuality is an integral part of the social fabric in which organizations are woven. In traditional theory, gender has been reduced to an intervening variable in the study of organizations, thus denying that sexuality is a fundamental human identity and that gender is imbedded in organizations (Burrell & Hearn, 1989). People bring with them their prescribed gender roles, with men replicating the patriarchal system and women assuming traditional roles that are congruent with the external world (Burrell & Hearn, 1989). Sexuality cannot be banned from the business arena, but rather requires recognition and response.

Taking this alternative view, feminist theorists have challenged the normalized bureaucracy with its emphasis on aggressive competition and impersonality and have looked at such suppressed feminine elements of sexuality as cooperation and dialogue as alternative ethical principles (Martin, 1988, as cited in Taylor & Conrad, 1992). Burrell and Hearn (1989) argue for the feasibility of studying sexual norms—the extent to which sexuality is an element in organizational goals, and ultimately whose sexual and other interests are being served in the organization.

Organizational Characteristics

Recognition of the overt and covert existence of sexuality in orgaizations aids understanding of how deep the seeds of harassment are planted in the soil. Certain organizational characteristics help to propagate these seeds. Drawing from Tangri, Burt, and Johnson (1982), the organizational model stipulates that authority relations that exist within a given organizational hierarchy create opportunities for sexually harassing behaviors. Characteristics such as visibility and contact in sex-integrated jobs, gender composition of the workplace, traditionalism of the job, occupational norms, job requirements, and availability of grievance procedures are several aspects of an organization that play a role in the increased likelihood of sexual harassment (Martin, 1995; Saal, Johnson, & Weber, 1989).

Visibility and contact in sex-integrated jobs affect the opportunities for sexual harassment to occur because sex-integrated jobs require both sexes to work together in either pairs or small groups. Gender composition and traditionalism are related because as the number of token women rises in a male-dominated environment, such as the automobile assembly line, so does the level of hostility toward them (Gardner et al., 1994). Occupational norms include the embedded sexual norms of the organization as discussed above. Evidence of norms can be seen by "revealing waitress costumes and by use of expressions such as 'casting couch' and 'sexcretary'" (Tangri et al., 1982). Job requirements deal with the expectations of a job whether explicitly or implicitly stated. Some occupations require overnight traveling with coworkers or late-night work sessions with colleagues. Availability of grievance procedures can affect the occurrence of sexual harassment. Explicit policies and disciplinary procedures ideally should deter potential harassers. These factors and their roles in the organizational context can best be further examined by relating these factors to three specific organizational contexts: academe, military, and consumer-oriented businesses.

Of the three organizational settings reviewed here, academia, the military, and business, all can be characterized along two dimensions that may shape the relative prevalence of sexual harassment within them. First, the extent to which organizational roles and structures emphasize hierarchy plays a critical role in shaping forms of sexual harassment. The nature of authority as it is expressed in the particular organizational context and relative power of the actors is particularly important. Second, the extent to which organizational roles and structures explicitly and implicitly reflect traditional images of men and masculinity based on ascendancy, competition, and opposition can shape not only the likelihood of sexual harassment, but also the availability of recourse once it has occurred.

Academe

Instead of academic institutions being models of ideal behavior (Strine, 1992), they may be resistant to forces that threaten the prerogatives of faculty relative to students and men compared with women. Beginning in the 1980s numerous research reports (Dziech & Weiner, 1984; McCormack, 1985; Reilly, Lott, & Gallogly, 1986) as well as many self-studies conducted by those institutions, identified sexual harassment as a not uncommon behavior on the campuses of our colleges and universities.

Academic environments have their own culture with a stratified hierarchy of power (levels of administration and academic rank, separate classes—faculty and students) and social scripts. The similarities between college and university campuses and society at large clearly outweigh the differences, yet the differences are important because their existence exacerbates the opportunities for abuses in power and exploitation (Zalk, 1990). Academia thus presents its own set of problems—specifically, the blurred boundaries between students and faculty, and the stratified hierarchy of power that is mainly male dominated. As Mezey (1992) argues, "academic harassment differs from workplace harassment because students are particularly vulnerable to faculty authority" (p. 180).

Blurred Boundaries

Performance of the professor role can incorporate elements of other roles, and boundaries can become unclear particularly if instructors engage in behaviors to reduce relational distance (Garlick, 1994). Especially for graduate students, a professor can serve as a teacher, mentor, counselor, and a friend. Each of these roles is negotiated within the context of an existing power differential. Although it may appear that the relationship (whatever the roles being played) is consensual, in fact it is not and cannot be because the faculty member has all the power (Zalk, 1990, p. 145), be it the formal power associated with assigning grades and writing recommendations or the more elusive power stemming from faculty member's control of knowledge and opportunities to shape the student's self-appraisals. Some professors do not handle the power well and take advantage of the powerless.

Faculty members may exploit their organizational power by introducing sexual content into their professorial performances acting parts, such as "the intellectual seducer," "the power broker," and "the opportunist" (see Deziech & Weiner, 1984, for a discussion of professorial roles). In the case of the opportunist, physical settings and circumstances are used to mask premeditated sexual advances (Zalk, 1990). For example, a Cornell University professor was found guilty by a faculty ethics committee of sexually harassing four former students (Goldin, 1995) who worked for him as assistants and traveled with him on various school-related trips. One student recounted a trip in which she shared a bed with the professor because he told her there were no other rooms in the hotel.

Hierarchical Arrangements

Another important characteristic of academic settings is the preponderance of men in positions of power. Although women are an increasing part of academic institutions, men still hold most of the positions of power, whether central administrative or departmental leadership positions (Zalk, 1990). At the University of Iowa and Stanford Univerity medical schools the educational hierarchy combined with the traditional occupational power of male doctors led to serious complaints from women faculty.

Inequity in the distribution of power often results in men enjoying the role of gatekeepers. Women are subject to men's wielding power through the allotment of rewards or punishments (Taylor & Conrad, 1992). Thus, the patriarchal structure of academic institutions coupled with no or weak guidelines for student-faculty relationships sets the stage for discriminatory practices and harassment against women.

Blurred boundaries work in concert with the hierarchical structure of universities in providing opportunities for sexual harassment. Particularly in their graduate training, students are very reliant on mentors or sponsors who can determine whether they will complete a degree program. The relationship boundaries may be less clear in some fields than in others. Psychology is a field in which men acknowledge sexual contacts with their students (Pope, Levenson, & Schoever, 1979). The power differential between psychology professors and graduate students is both blurred and enhanced because of the amount of time spent in clinical supervision or in research (Miller & Larabee, 1995). The focus on personal issues also may contribute, for some psychologists and psychiatrists have sexual contact with clients who have paid for their psychological services.

Methods for tracking and remediating harassment also reflect organizational contexts. Because it is difficult to acknowledge the often concealed sexual themes present in academic settings and other settings, some organizations find it easier to identify such relationships as ones involving or potentially involving conflicts of interests rather than focus on their problems as sexual relationships. Relationships in academe are assumed to be based on either a collegial or mentor model; overt exploitation is not acceptable. Therefore, formal channels are likely to exist for the processing of complaints.

Traditional female scripts that allocate consent (and therefore responsibility) to the woman are often reflected in academic organizational practices whereby no intervention can be initiated unless the female target is willing to press a formal complaint indicating her lack of consent. The responsibility for monitoring, recognizing, and actively resisting is located with the target female, as if men cannot be expected to monitor or adjust their own behavior. It is interesting, too, that interventions are almost always customized in response to a particular individual complaint. Academic administrations seldom acknowledge the structural contexts for which they may take proactive responsibility to change.

Military

Despite formal regulations prohibiting sexual harassment, its continuing high levels of occurrence may be one of the military's most open secrets based on public revelations of specific episodes and survey data collected from military personnel (Schmitt, 1993; Wilds, 1990). In 1990 the majority of military women questioned reported to investigators from the Department of Defense that they had experienced sexual harassment (Kantrowitz & Alder 1991).

Male Dominance

Military service may represent the essence of the male role for some men. Women may be perceived as the enemy invading sacred male territory who consequently deserve to be punished. When women enter into gender-integrated basic training units, their ability to successfully complete the training may be threatening to those for whom the military symbolizes the essence of masculinity.

Quasimilitary organizations may be even more vehement in their resistance to women. The various degrading and humiliating attacks Shannon Faulkner encountered when she tried to fully matriculate at South Carolina's state-supported all-male military university, the Citadel, and the jubilant cadet celebrations after she left suggested she was an enemy to be vanquished. The underlying fear may be if women can do what men can do, male dominance is undermined. Indeed, part of the identity of being male in American society is a certain superiority by virtue of the separateness and distinctiveness of the male vis-à-vis anything female.

The expectation of teamwork may elicit the male athletic model of joining together to vanquish the enemy. Kirby suggests that "in the sporting context, harassment may be intensified by the 'pack mentality', the mirror image of the term loyalty, bonding and team play coaches strive to achieve" (Kirby, 1994, p. 226). Military organizations also seek to obtain loyalty, bonding and teamwork, so some military personnel may be vulnerable to the pack mentality that may be a negative by-product of the competitive model of intergroup relations.

General reluctance to report sexual harassment may be exacerbated for military personnel because of the emphasis on the privileges associated with rank and following orders, as well as the negative perception that being female is synonymous with being weak. The limited formal sanctions levied on high-ranking male military personnel and the informal sanctions directed at their female accusers in well-publicized cases point out the challenge of trying to change gender expectations embedded in an organization.

Hierarchical Arrangements

In military organizations personnel are expected to follow orders and are dependent on those above them for positive ratings for career advancement. Problems may result from men being unwilling to take orders from women because of the belief that women should be submissive not men. Other men may illegitimately use their organizational power to sexualize interactions with female subordinates, for example, engaging in quid pro quo harassment by demanding sexual intercourse for favorable evaluations.

Business Workplaces

Traditionally, in business organizations men performed the tasks associated with the prevailing male sexual script by initiating and dominating, whereas women engaged in supportive tasks and passively awaited assignments. The expectations for women as office wives have for some incorporated acting sexy, perhaps exemplifying sex-role spillover (Gutek, 1985). Some men want young women working for them perhaps because they can continue to hold the image of themselves as sexually potent or attractive. Further, organizations may have clients who perceive that sexual by-play with female personnel constitutes another perk, a benefit like lodging and golf games, and by their actions create a hostile environment for female employees.

Yet, until more fundamental changes occur in sexual scripts, women may stand a better chance in these client serving business organizations than in others we have discussed. Businesses cannot afford negative publicity surrounding sexual harassment cases. Businesses focus on economic issues; if they are at risk of a law suit, they may lose money and customers. K-Mart spent $3.2 million in 1987 in a sexual harassment settlement, and the Marriott Corporation in 1988 spent $3 million in back pay to 3,000 female employees who claimed they had been denied promotions (Benokraitis & Feagin, 1995). Private sector employers may actually slight the due process required for the accused in the public sector to forestall legal and economic penalties (Robinson, Allen, Franklin, & Duhon, 1993). Other noticeable costs to businesses include the loss of creative personnel, increased absenteeism and turnover, low morale, and overall loss in profit (Benokraitis & Feagin, 1995). Thus in these organizations the impact of hierarchical arrangements linked to traditional conceptions of roles appropriate for men and women may persist; economic incentives provide an impetus for change.

STRATEGIES FOR PREVENTING SEXUAL HARASSMENT

To develop strategies for preventing sexual harassment, we must consider the links between sexual scripts and the dimensions underlying harassing behavior (consent, and power). Some women in corporations pursue individual solutions—trying to appear feminine enough to conform to others' expectations of how women should behave and still be professional enough to be seen as appropriate organizational members (Gardner et al., 1994). Ultimately, individual solutions may lead to role entrapment; therefore, more general changes are needed.

Consent

Requiring Consent

Rather than consent being a diffuse agreement subject to interpretation, gaining consent with an interaction partner should include the act of asking and the opportunity for the partner to freely respond. The idea of gaining consent (especially in a romantic encounter), however, has not received favorable attention. Public ridicule followed Antioch College's attempt to address consent in student-student relationships by requiring that permission be sought before a new level of intimacy was attempted. Resistance to seeking consent may occur in part because having to seek consent exposes myths of romantic love and seduction. These myths include the scenarios of the man seducing the woman who is unaware of his actions and the pair who get so carried away by passion that there is no opportunity to obtain consent.

Power

If individuals believe they can enlist the support of an organizational entity, they may be more willing to complain than when they feel like a lone lamb confronting a lion. Programs to make superordinates aware of the possible penalties also address the power dimension.

Traditionally, for women to achieve what they want, they appeal to and acquire some sort of link with individuals with more power and higher status, typically men. Lodging formal harassment complaints may require that they make the private (their sexuality, their emotions) public and challenge the hierarchical arrangements in our society. Various organizations are requiring that workers notify superiors about relationships that have the potential to involve conflicts of interest.

Sexual Focus

Although a sexual focus must be present for sexual harassment to have occurred, this dimension is not clearly developed. A wide variety of behaviors may be considered sexual, and the intent of an actor becomes an issue in concluding if a gesture is sexual. As a consequence, behaviors that may be designated as sexual harassment range from making a person uncomfortable with sexual innuendos to forced sexual intercourse. Intent is an issue because perpetrators may deny their behavior was sexual, saying

"I'm a friendly person who touches everybody," or deny it was harassing, saying "We all enjoy off-color jokes." Others may argue their behavior signified sexual attraction.

People need to engage in open negotiation of boundaries. Boundary definition often deals with ambiguous behavior (i.e., telling of jokes) that may vary in significance as a function of context, as well as very clear demarcations of categories of what is acceptable or not acceptable. In organizations, people need to talk openly about the place of sexuality rather than act as if it is something that will become an insurmountable problem if brought out into the open. At the most basic level people need to feel free to indicate in a nonconfrontational way that another person's behavior is violating their boundaries of acceptable conduct. In one U.S. army unit sexual harassment complaints were reduced by simply having people say "let's not go there" when other parties were saying or doing things that made them uncomfortable.

On university campuses faculty and students may oppose policies regulating consensual relations. Male and female opponents argue that sex is fun and that they do not want it removed from their lives. Some of the arguments brought up in defense of sex with minors or incest include the notion that the less powerful person wanted the sexual activity or the less powerful person acted so provocatively that the more powerful person either lost control or simply had no choice.

Worker norms that discourage individuals from challenging ongoing practices may serve to discourage individuals from taking action against harassing behavior from a supervisor. In many organizations, workers have the mantra, "you've got to go along, to get along." If a woman is offended by sexual remarks or behaviors, her coworkers may discourage her taking action by playing down the significance of the behavior or emphasizing the disruptive consequences for all of an accusation of harassment.

RECONSTRUCTING SEXUAL SCRIPTS

Knowledge of Sexual Harassment

Knowledge of sexual harassment has increased since the phenomenon was given a name, but such knowledge may identify only extreme behaviors as harassment (Popovich et al., 1995). There may be a gap between knowledge of formal definitions of sexual harassment and application of that knowledge to one's everyday life experiences. Bursik (1992) reported that the majority of her participants did not perceive that an instructor's numerous unsolicited requests for dates with a student constituted harassment.

Williams and Cyr (1992) note the trap of escalating commitment (based on the foot-in-the-door) technique. Once a harasser has made gestures not refused by the target, the target may find it more difficult to deal with the problem, and observers may no longer see the target as a victim of harassment.

Work organizations and universities have programs or workshops that teach employees about sexual harassment. Brochures and posters explaining formal procedures are available. Workshop leaders have people role play to make women more aware of how men may misinterpret their behaviors and to sensitize men to women's subtle efforts to rebuff them.

However, increasing knowledge or awareness is not enough. "We cannot respond adequately to harassment without responding also to the institutional conditions that sustain it—the gender stereotypes, occupational stratification, and remedial barriers that are endemic to American workplaces" (Rhode, 1989, p. 236).

Changing Sexual Scripts

We propose three changes related to sexuality. First, the link between power and domination and sexuality must be broken and people must be encouraged to associate sexuality with equality and consent. If, indeed, some men are nonconsciously harassing because they are unaware of their mentally linking power and sex (Bargh & Raymond, 1995), such a separation is imperative.

Second, we must educate people to accept a wider variety of sexual scripts (Laws & Schwartz, 1977) (i.e., alternatives to the stereotypic conceptions of women as seductive and men as dominant, Murrell & Dietz-Uhler, 1993). Rather than questioning how single mothers, the physically disabled, gays, and lesbians can fulfill the expectations associated with the dominant sexual scripts in our society, we need to recognize existing alternatives. We must provide support for those struggling to develop scripts and reaffirm that scripts are guidelines within which individuals should be able to privately negotiate with one another.

Third, being more open about sexuality may allow us to create organizations that are not shaped with patriarchal conceptions of sexuality. Discussing rather than avoiding the topic of sexuality allows opportunities for introduction of alternative scripts and negotiation of existing ones to occur. And, in turn, through such exploration and discourse new conceptualizations may be accepted.

Harassment

We also propose one mandate related to individuals, organizations, and, indeed, all of society. Harassment of all types needs to be subject to social sanction. Members of organizations and professions, whatever the level of their position, need to be held accountable for ethical conduct

(Blevins-Knabe, 1992). Some colleges and universities define sexual involvements between faculty members and students they oversee as examples of unethical behavior for members of the teaching profession or as constituting conflicts of interest (Barrett, 1993/94). Clearer and more definite boundaries such as these should be instituted in all organizational environments to ensure that sexual harassment is clearly identified and acknowledged as an abuse of power and therefore openly challenged and appropriately sanctioned.

REFERENCES

Abbey, A. (1982). Sex differences in attributions for friendly behavior: Do males misperceive females' friendliness? *Journal of Personality and Social Psychology, 42,* 830–838.

Abbey, A., & Melby, C. (1986). The effects of nonverbal cues on gender differences in perceptions of sexual intent. *Sex Roles, 15,* 283–298.

Acker, J. (1990). Hierarchies, jobs and bodies: A theory of gendered organizations. *Gender and Society, 4,* 139–158.

$265,000 award in Bay sexual harassment case. (1985, July 4). *The San Francisco Chronicle,* p. 45.

Bargh, J. A., & Raymond, P. (1995). The naive misuse of power: Nonconscious sources of sexual harassment. *Journal of Social Issues, 51,* 85–96.

Barrett, S. C. (1993/94, Winter). Compromising positions? Smith debates a ban on faculty-student sex. *Smith Alumnae Quarterly,* 12–14.

Bem, S. (1981). Gender schema theory: A cognitive account of sex-typing. *Psychological Review, 88,* 354–364.

Benokraitis, N. V., & Feagin, J. R. (1995). *Modern sexism: Blatant, subtle, and covert discrimination.* Englewood Cliffs, NJ: Prentice-Hall.

Benson, K. (1984). Comment on Crocker's "an analysis of university definitions of sexual harassment." *Signs, 9,* 515–539.

Berger, J., Webster, M., Ridgeway, C., & Rosenholz, S. J. (1986). Status cues, expectations, and behavior. In E. J. Lawler (Ed.), *Advances in group processes* (pp. 1–22). Greenwich, CT: JAI Press.

Berger, P., & Luckmann, T. (1966). *The social construction of reality.* New York: Doubleday.

Bernard, J. (1972). *The future of marriage.* New York: Bantam.

Blevins-Knabe, B. (1992). The ethics of dual relationships in higher education. *Ethics and Behavior, 2,* 151–163.

Burrell, G., & Hearn, J. (1989). The sexuality of organization. In J. Hearn, D. L. Sheppard, P. Tancred-Sheriff, & G. Burrell (Eds.), *The sexuality of organization* (pp. 1–28). London: Sage.

Bursik, K. (1992). Perceptions of sexual harassment. *Sex Roles, 27,* 401–412.

Carli, L. L. (1989). Gender differences in interaction style and influence. *Journal of Personality & Social Psychology, 56,* 565–576.

Cleveland, J. N., & Kerst, M. E. (1993). Sexual harassment and perceptions of power: An underarticulated relationship. *Journal of Vocational Behavior, 42,* 49–67.

Connell, R. W. (1987). *Gender and power.* Stanford, CA: Stanford University Press.

Dziech, B., & Weiner, L. (1984). *The lecherous professor: Sexual harassment on campus.* Boston: Beacon.

Eason, Y. (1988). When the boss wants sex. In P. S. Rothenberg (Ed.), *Racism and sexism: An integrated study* (pp. 139–146). New York: St. Martin's Press.

Fain, T. C., & Anderton, D. L. (1987). Sexual harassment: Organizational context and diffuse status. *Sex Roles, 17,* 291–311.

Falbo, T., & Peplau, L. A. (1980). Power strategies in intimate relationships. *Journal of Personality and Social Psychology, 38,* 618–628.

Fitzgerald, L. F. (1993). Sexual Harassment: Violence against women in the workplace. *American Psychologist, 48,* 1070–1076.

Fitzgerald, L. F., Swan, S., & Fischer, K. (1995). Why didn't she just report him? The psychological and legal implications of women's responses to sexual harassment. *Journal of Social Issues, 51,* 117–138.

Ford, R., & Johnson, C. (1998). The perception of power: Dependence and legitimacy in conflict. *Social Psychology Quarterly, 61,* 16–32.

Frug, M. J. (1992). *Postmodern legal feminism.* New York: Routledge.

Gagnon, J. H., Rosen, R. C., & Lieblum, S. R. (1982). Cognitive and social aspects of sexual dysfunction. *Journal of Sex and Marital Therapy, 8,* 44–56.

Gardner, W. I., Peluchette, J. V. E., & Clinebell, S. K. (1994). Valuing women in management: An impression management perspective of gender diversity. *Management Communication Quarterly, 8,* 115–164.

Garlick, R. (1994). Male and female responses to ambiguous instructor behaviors. *Sex Roles, 30,* 135–158.

Gergen, K. (1985). The social constructionist movement in modern psychology. *American Psychologist, 40,* 266–275.

Giannini, A. J., & Fellows, K. W. (1986). Enhanced interpretation of nonverbal facial cues in male rapists—a preliminary study. *Archives of Sexual Behavior, 15,* 153–156.

Gilbert, L. A. (1992). Gender and counseling psychology: Current knowledge and directions for research and social action. In S. D. Brown & R. W. Lent (Eds.), *Handbook of Counseling Psychology* (pp. 383–416). New York: Wiley.

Glick, P., & Fiske, S. T. (1997). Hostile and benevolent sexism: Measuring ambivalent sexist attitudes toward women. *Psychology of Women Quarterly, 21,* 119–135.

Goldin, D. (1995, March 23). Student claims of sexual harassment tarnish a Cornell star's luster. *The New York Times,* p. A12.

Grauerholz, E. (1989). Sexual harassment of women professors by students. *Sex Roles, 21*, 789–801.

Grieco, A. (1987). Scope and nature of sexual harassment in nursing. *Journal of Sex Research, 23*, 261–266.

Griscom, J. L. (1992). Women and power. *Psychology of Women Quarterly, 16*, 389–414.

Gruber, J., & Bjorn, L. (1982). Blue collar blues: The sexual harassment of women autoworkers. *Work and Occupations, 9*, 271–298.

Gruber, K. J., & White, J. W. (1986). Gender differences in the perceptions of self and others' use of power strategies. *Sex Roles, 15*, 109–188.

Gutek, B. (1985). *Sex and the workplace: The impact of sexual behavior and harassment on women, men and organizations*. San Francisco, CA: Jossey-Bass.

Harre, R., & Secord, P. (1973). The explanation of social behavior. Totowa, NJ: Littlefield, Adams & Co.

Hyde, J. S. (1995). *Half the human experience*. Lexington, MA: DC Heath.

Intons-Peterson, M. J. (1988). *Children's concepts of gender*. Norwood, NJ: Ablex.

Johnson, C. (1993). Gender and formal authority. *Social Psychology Quarterly, 56*, 193–210.

Johnson, C. (1994). Gender, legitimate authority, and leader-subordinate conversations. *American Sociological Review, 59*, 122–135.

Jones, T. S., & Remland, M. S. (1992). Sources of variability in perceptions of and responses to sexual harassment. *Sex Roles, 27*, 121–142.

Kantrowitz, B., & Alder, G. (1991, October 21). Striking a nerve. *Newsweek, 118*, 34–40.

Kenig, S., & Ryan, J. (1986). Sex differences in levels of tolerance and attribution of blame for sexual harassment on a university campus. *Sex Roles, 15*, 535–549.

Kirby, S. (1994). Not in my back yard: Sexual harassment and abuse in sport. In *Shades of gray: Shedding light on old struggles and new dilemmas* (pp. 226–242). 10th Annual Conference Proceedings of the Canadian Association Against Sexual Harassment in Higher Education.

Koss, M. P. (1990). Changed lives: The psychological impact of sexual harassment. In M. A. Paludi (Ed.), *Ivory power: Sexual harassment on campus* (pp. 73–92). Albany: State University of New York Press.

Lach, D. H., & Gwartney-Gibbs, P. A. (1993). Sociological perspectives on sexual harassment and workplace dispute resolution. *Journal of Vocational Behavior, 42*, 102–115.

LaPlante, M. N., McCormick, N., & Brannigan, G. G. (1980). Living the sexual script: College students' views of influence in sexual encounters. *Journal of Sex Research, 16*, 338–355.

Laws, J., & Schwartz, P. (1977). *Sexual scripts*. Hinsdale, IL: Dryden Press.

Lewis, D. K. (1975). The black family: Socialization and sex roles. *Phylon, 36*, 221–237.

MacKinnon, C. (1979). *Sexual harassment of working women: A case of sex discrimination*. New Haven, CT: Yale University Press.

McCormack, A. (1985). The sexual harassment of students by teachers: The case of students in science. *Sex Roles, 13,* 21–32.

McKinney, K. (1990). Sexual harassment of university faculty by colleagues and students. *Sex Roles, 23,* 421–438.

Martin, S. E. (1995). Sexual harassment: The link joining gender stratification, sexuality, and women's economic status. In J. Freeman (Ed.), *Women: A feminist perspective* (pp. 22–46). Palo Alto, CA: Mayfield.

Mezey, S. G. (1992). *In pursuit of equality: Women, public policy and the federal courts*. New York: St. Martin's Press.

Midwinter, D. Y. (1992). Rule prescriptions for initial male-female interaction. *Sex Roles, 26,* 161–169.

Miller, G. M., & Larabee, M. J. (1995). Sexual intimacy in counselor education and supervision: A national survey. *Counselor Education and Supervision, 34,* 332–343.

Molm, L. D. (1997). *Coercive power in social exchange*. New York: Cambridge University Press.

Murrell, A. J., & Dietz-Uhler, B. L. (1993). Gender identity and adversarial sexual beliefs as predictors of attitudes toward sexual harassment. *Psychology of Women Quarterly, 17,* 169–175.

O'Sullivan, L. F., & Byers, E. S. (1992). College students' incorporation of initiator and restrictor roles in sexual dating interactions. *Journal of Sex Research, 29*(3), 435–446.

Phillips, S. P., & Schneider, M. S. (1993). Sexual harassment of female doctors by patients. *The New England Journal of Medicine, 329,* 1936–1939.

Pope, K. S., Levenson, H., & Schoever, L. (1979). Sexual intimacy in psychology training: Results and implications of a national survey. *American Psychologist, 34,* 682–686.

Popovich, P. M., Jolton, J. A., Mastrangelo, P. M., Everton, W. J., Somers, J. M., & Gehlauf, D. N. (1995). Sexual harassment scripts: A means to understanding a phenomenon. *Sex Roles, 32,* 315–325.

Powell, G. N. (1986). Effects of sex role identity and sex on definitions of sexual harassment. *Sex Roles, 14,* 9–19.

Pryor, J., & Day, J. D. (1988). Interpretations of sexual harassment: An attributional analysis. *Sex Roles, 18,* 405–417.

Pryor, J. B., LaVite, C. M., & Stoller, L. M. (1993). A social psychological analysis of sexual harassment: The person/situation interaction. *Journal of Vocational Behavior, 42,* 68–83.

Pryor, J. B., & Merluzzi, T. V. (1985). The role of expertise in processing social interaction scripts. *Journal of Experimental Social Psychology, 21,* 362–379.

Quinn, R. E., & Less, P. L. (1984). Attraction and harassment: Dynamics of sexual politics in the workplace. *Organizational Dynamics, 6,* 35–46.

Reilly, M. E., Lott, B., & Gallogly, S. M. (1986). Sexual harassment of university students. *Sex Roles, 15,* 333–358.

Rhode, D. L. (1989). *Justice and gender.* Cambridge, MA: Harvard University Press.

Rich, A. (1980). Compulsory heterosexuality and lesbian experience. *Signs, 5,* 631–660.

Robinson, R. K., Allen, B. M., Franklin, G. M., & Duhon, D. L. (1993). Sexual harassment in the workplace: A review of the legal rights and responsibilities of all parties. *Public Personnel Management, 22,* 123–135.

Rose, S., & Frieze, I. H. (1989). Young singles' scripts for a first date. *Gender and Society, 3,* 258–268.

Saal, F. E., Johnson, C. B., & Weber, N. (1989). Friendly or sexy? It may depend on whom you ask. *Psychology of Women Quarterly, 13,* 263–276.

Schmitt, E. (1993, September 12). 2 out of 3 women in military study report sexual harassment incidents. *New York Times,* p. A12.

Silverman, D. (1976). Sexual harassment: Working women's dilemma. *Quest: A Feminist Quarterly, 10,* 346–357.

Simon, W., & Gagnon, J. H. (1986). Sexual scripts: Permanence and change. *Archives of Sexual Behavior, 15,* 97–120.

Snodgrass, S. E. (1985). Women's intuition: The effect of subordinate role on interpersonal sensitivity. *Journal of Personality and Social Psychology, 49,* 146–176.

Strine, M. S. (1992, November). Understanding "how things work": Sexual harassment and academic culture. *Journal of Applied Communication Research,* 391–400.

Summers, R. J., & Myklebust, K. (1992). The influence of a history of romance on judgments and responses to a complaint of sexual harassment. *Sex Roles, 27,* 345–357.

Tangri, S. S., Burt, M. R., & Johnson, L. B. (1982). Sexual harassment at work: Three explanatory models. *Journal of Social Issues, 38,* 33–54.

Taylor, B., & Conrad, C. (1992, November). Narratives of sexual harassment: Organizational dimensions. *Journal of Applied Communication Research,* 401–418.

Thorne, B., & Luria, Z. (1986). Sexuality and gender in children's daily worlds. *Social Problems, 33,* 176–190.

Tiefer, L. (1986). In pursuit of the perfect penis. *American Behavioral Scientist, 29,* 579–599.

Travis, C. B., & Kurth, S. (1981). Sexual harassment workshop. Southeastern Psychological Association Meetings, Atlanta, GA.

Unger, R. K., & Crawford, M. (1996). *Women and gender: A feminist psychology.* New York: McGraw-Hill.

Weinberg, M. S., Swensson, R. G., & Hammersmith, S. K. (1983). Sexual autonomy and the status of women: Models of female sexuality in U.S. sex manuals from 1950 to 1980. *Social Problems, 30,* 312–324.

Wilds, N. G. (1990). Sexual harassment in the military. *Minerva, 8,* 1–16.

Williams, K. B., & Cyr, R. R. (1992). Escalating commitment to a relationship: The sexual harassment trap. *Sex Roles, 27,* 47–72.

Yoder, J. D., & Kahn, A. S. (1992). Toward a feminist understanding of women and power. *Psychology of Women Quarterly, 16,* 381–388.

Zalk, S. R. (1990). Men in the academy: A psychological profile of harassment. In M. A. Paludi (Ed.), *Ivory power: Sexual harassment on campus* (pp. 141–176). Albany: State University of New York Press.

14

RE-EXAMINING THE ISSUE OF NONCONSENT IN ACQUAINTANCE RAPE

PATRICIA L. N. DONAT AND JACQUELYN W. WHITE

Our understanding of all forms of violence against women, including sexual assault, is embedded in our culture (Koss, Goodman, Browne, Fitzgerald, Keita, & Russo, 1994). Because cultural norms, sexual scripts, and gender roles play such a large role in defining these experiences, it is important to examine not only the dominant voice in the social construction and maintenance of contemporary definitions, but also to the factors that are marginalized by traditional definitions and by institutionalized constructions. In this chapter, we will examine the social construction of women's consent in sexual relations and challenge traditional conceptualizations of acquaintance rape based on the consent construct.[1] It is our hope that this

---

[1]Our discussion does not include cases of consensual but unwanted sex, that is, situations in which one partner overtly consents to unwanted sexual activity. For example, a partner may consent to sexual activity motivated by a desire to maintain the relationship although not desiring sexual activity at that time (perhaps because of other plans, being too tired, not being sexually aroused, or being concerned about pregnancy, etc.). For further discussion of the social construction of consent in noncoercive sexual relationships, see Muehlenhard, Powch, Phelps, & Giusti (1992) and a 1995 American Psychological Association symposium on "Consenting to unwanted sex" (O'Sullivan, 1995).

knowledge will empower us to acknowledge and reconstruct women's experiences.

DEFINING RAPE AS NONCONSENT

Most established conceptualizations of rape, particularly acquaintance rape, have been based on judgments of female sexual consent (Pineau, 1989). Acquaintance rape is usually defined as nonconsensual forced sex between persons who know each other. Traditionally, mutual consent for sexual activity, in our culture, has been determined by examining whether a woman consented to sexual intercourse. The emphasis on nonconsent is embedded in a cultural context that conceptualizes sexual consent as a woman's issue. If sexual activity occurs, it is assumed that the woman consented. Women's intent and behavior are seen as the primary indicators of mutually consensual sexual activity. Issues surrounding male consent are absent from attributions regarding mutuality. Thus, a woman is blamed if sexual activity occurs without mutual consent; she is held responsible for failing to adequately monitor the level of sexual activity. Thus, nonconsent has been crucial for determining whether an assault has occurred.

SOCIAL CONSTRUCTION OF CONSENT

The problem with conceptualizing rape around the issue of consent is that the decision whether a woman has consented to sexual intercourse rarely is determined only by the woman herself. Often, instead, a woman's consent, and ultimately her sexuality, may be determined for her by others —her partner, the community, or the court system. Women in American culture traditionally have little power to control their own bodies and their own sexuality, but, ironically, they are held responsible for the consequences. As has been noted by Weis and Borges (1973), sexual interactions are "socially structured by the culturally prescribed norms, rights, and obligations which define the expectancies for men and women and establish the rules by which [men and women] relate to one another" (p. 90). Sociocultural factors ultimately determine a woman's consent in many situations, especially in attributions made by the community regarding acquaintance rape. Women's experiences are viewed from an androcentric perspective and are lost in traditional definitions of consent and rape.

We will discuss five specific cultural factors that influence definitions of consent and attributions of acquaintance rape: cultural attitudes, cultural metaphors, societal myths, sexual scripts, and the legal system. We will argue that cultural attitudes, and their resultant metaphors and myths, lead to prescriptions for male-female relationships as reflected in sexual scripts and as codified in rape laws.

Cultural Attitudes

The belief that a woman has consented to sexual intercourse despite her objections rests on several assumptions. Martha Burt (1980, 1991) hypothesized that the status of women within American culture plays a significant role in the attitudes toward sexual violence held by persons, particularly rapists. These attitudes and beliefs may serve to facilitate sexually aggressive acts by reducing prohibitions against engaging in violent acts. Mary Koss and her colleagues (Koss, Leonard, Beezley, & Oros, 1985) proposed an early model of date rape, stating that

> culturally transmitted assumptions about men, women, violence, sexuality, and myths about rape constitute a rape-supportive belief system. Furthermore, stratified systems such as the American dating situation may legitimate the use of force by those in power and weaken resistance of the less powerful. Finally acquisition of stereotyped myths about rape may result in a failure to label as rape sexual aggression that occurs in dating situations. (Koss et al., 1985, p. 982)

Recent research has found that underlying these rape-supportive attitudes appears to be a general hostility toward women (Lonsway & Fitzgerald, 1995) that influences the likelihood that nonconsensual sexual behavior will occur. Recent models of sexual aggression have found hostile masculinity to be predictive of sexually aggressive behavior (Malamuth, Linz, Heavey, Barnes, & Acker, 1995; Malamuth, Sockloskie, Koss, & Tanaka, 1991). Hostile masculinity is defined as having two main components: (a) a hostile-distrustful orientation toward women, and (b) a motivational influence of dominance in sexual relationships.

Adversarial sexual beliefs are exemplified by some men's view of male-female relationships as exploitive and of sex as a means of achieving personal enjoyment, satisfaction, and status. Manipulation may be accepted as a common interaction strategy between men and women. Therefore, when on a date, a man's attitudes toward women and his motives for engaging in sexual behavior may influence how he perceives the woman, how he interprets her behavior, and how he chooses to behave during the date (Donat, 1995; Shotland, 1989). An underlying suspiciousness of women may prompt a sexually aggressive man to react in a hostile manner when he interprets a woman's behavior as rejecting, yet overtly sexual (Malamuth & Brown, 1994). Indeed, researchers have found that these adversarial sexual beliefs are more likely to be endorsed by men who report engaging in sexually aggressive behavior (Burt, 1980; Donat, 1991, 1995; Koss et al., 1985). Men who report interacting with women in a sexually coercive or aggressive manner are the same men who are more likely to view interactions between men and women as primarily exploitative.

Within this adversarial context, an acceptance of interpersonal violence may be tolerated in interactions with others. This acceptance of interpersonal violence may permeate all relationships, including intimate ones. This view assumes that physical force may be necessary and perhaps desirable in sexual relationships. A man may believe that force can be an effective strategy to seduce a reluctant partner (Burt, 1980). As a result, a physical struggle may not be interpreted as problematic. In fact, it may even be interpreted as arousing. Media and pornographic images often reinforce this view, portraying men and women engaged in physical confrontations that ultimately end in mutually overwhelming sexual desire. Indeed, after viewing a sexually explicit scene of a woman enjoying a rape, men report a much higher likelihood of raping a woman if they knew they would not be caught (Briere & Malamuth, 1983). The message communicated is that love conquers all, even the resistance of one's partner.

Cultural Metaphors

Similar themes are present in our language's metaphors regarding sexual activity. These cultural metaphors provide important clues about the conceptualization of sexual behavior. Language is powerful in defining the experiences of people in a society. Therefore, an examination of cultural metaphors is necessary to understand the sexual experiences of people in our culture and its implications for conceptualizations of sexual assault which rely on consent. Four metaphors will be discussed.[2]

---

[2]A number of metaphors could have been chosen. These four are particularly prominent. Analyses of portrayals of romance in magazines confirm the frequency with which men are portrayed as strong, masterful, confident, aggressive, and protective of women, whereas women are portrayed as domestic, weak, passive, and emotionally dependent (Smith & Matre, 1975). Thurston (1987) describes the classical romance novel as reflecting traditional power dynamics between women and men, and states that "the romance novel continues to reaffirm the domestic, subservient role of women in a patriarchal society" (p. 70). Even more contemporary romance novels that present "Cinderella as feisty female" or "Cinderella as virgin temptress" ultimately acquiesce to the patriarchal vision. "In fact, the heroine's militant demands are cast as threats to her own and the hero's happiness and security, and she is confronted and humbled repeatedly until she sees the error of her ways and embraces traditional male/female complementarity as a relationship style ... she is led gradually and forcefully by him to the realization that her attempts to assume power and to enjoy sexual freedom will bring her own ruin. In the end, she not only accepts his domination but rejoices in it" (Hubbard, 1985, p. 119). The complex links between sex and violence are explored in depth in a series of articles edited by Dines and Humez (1995) entitled "Modes of Sexual Representation 1: Romance Novels and Slasher Films." They state that "romance novels and slasher novels appear to have in common the presentation of women as passive victims of sadistic male victimizers. This is most obvious in the narrative formula of the slasher" (p. 162). They suggest that this remains the case because of readers' actual gendered subjectivity, defined by race, class, and other social experiences, in spite of recent critiques suggesting multiple and complex interpretations of the text.

Sexuality as a Possession

The first metaphor conceptualizes sexuality as a desired possession. It is not uncommon to hear romantic partners tell each other, "I want you" or "Tell me you're mine." Moreover, men and women use this language to describe their overwhelming need to obtain sex, using phrases such as "I gotta have it" and "I need to get me some." This language has become so common that its objectifying nature is obscured. Sexuality becomes an object to barter or sell, an object to be coveted or stolen. This analogy emphasizes dominance and control in intimate relationships. Equality between partners is subverted. Mutuality is marginalized.

Sexuality as a Competition

A second metaphor conceptualizes sexuality as a competition. Sexuality is compared with a baseball game in which the batter (i.e., the man) tries to hit a home run (i.e., obtain sexual intercourse). *Scoring*, a term often used by young men to describe a successful sexual encounter (i.e., one that resulted in sexual intercourse), also is an example of this metaphor. Mutuality is irrelevant. Scoring and winning do not require the consent of the opponent. In addition, hunting metaphors are used to describe dating relationships. Hunting and scalp collecting, historic rites of passage in some cultures, are compared with dating. The assumption is that during adolescence and young adulthood, a man will demonstrate his manhood through sexual conquests and eventually settle down into a committed relationship (Burn, 1969). This analogy supports adversarial relationships between men and women and is not a healthy analogy for mutually consensual sexual experiences. Clearly, the concept of conquest is not compatible with consent. In any competition, someone must win and someone must lose.

Sexuality as a Physical Force

A third metaphor describes sexuality as a physical force, a presence that is exerted on others. This conceptualization of sexuality is evident in such phrases as "she'll knock you off your feet," "she was giving off sexy vibes," and "she blew him away." This metaphor also can provide a basis for rape (Lakoff & Johnson, 1987). According to this metaphor, women use their sexuality (i.e., by wearing sexy clothing and engaging in flirtatious behavior) to invoke sexual responses from men, which they then must inhibit. According to Lakoff and Johnson, men who report engaging in rape may perceive women's overt expressions of their sexuality as a "physical force" to which they are unwillingly exposed and are justified in countering with a like sexual force (i.e., sexual aggression) to balance the potency of women's sexuality. Research has suggested that this metaphor is important in defining nonconsensual sexual interactions. Greater endorsement of these cultural metaphors has been found in men who report engaging in sexually aggressive behaviors (Donat, 1991). This analogy, however, denies women's sexual expression and promotes an adversarial view of sexual expression and retaliation.

Sexuality as a Contractual Agreement

Lastly, sexuality has been described as a contractual agreement. Pineau (1989) has critiqued the traditional conceptualization of consent, which "sets up sexual encounters as contractual events in which sexual aggression is presumed to be consented to unless there is some vigorous act of refusal" (p. 233). According to this view, whenever a woman's behavior is interpreted by a man as provocative, she has entered a contractual agreement to engage in sex. This analogy, however, implies that sexual activity must follow a particular progression. This sexual script is androcentric, with vaginal-penile intercourse signaling completion of the contractual activity. Why is this definition of a sexual encounter used to determine successful compliance with the contract? If we follow the contract metaphor to its logical conclusion, the only acceptable resolution to a breach of contract would be a legal one; no one has the right to enforce privately the terms of a contract. Even if a man took a woman to court because her provocative behavior did not result in sexual intercourse, the only legal resolution would be nonsexual compensation. Hence, the contract analogy perpetuates a view of sexuality that justifies sexual aggression. Societal myths and cultural attitudes contribute to this contractual view of heterosexual sexual interactions. It is to these cultural myths that we now turn.

Cultural Myths

The views of women, men, and sexuality discussed above are reflected in various cultural myths. They converge to support the conclusion that sexual assault is seduction and submission is consent (Pineau, 1989). Indeed, a review of the literature finds that acceptance of rape myths is higher among men, particularly men who report having engaged in sexually aggressive behavior (Lonsway & Fitzgerald, 1994). These myths underlie the theme that a woman must accept the consequences of her sexuality.

A commonly held myth states that men's sexual drives are greater than women's and can reach a point at which they cannot be controlled (Burt & Estep, 1981). If a woman's provocativeness arouses a man to this point, she must accept the consequences. Despite research evidence, popular culture has endorsed the idea that sex is a biological need for men, but not for women (Peplau, Rubin, & Hill, 1977). In *Better Than the Birds, Smarter Than the Bees*, a question-and-answer book about sexuality written for adolescents in 1969, Burn discusses a man's greater sexual drive and a woman's responsibility for helping him control his sexual urges. A male adolescent "has the most powerful sex drive he will ever have at a time when he has the least experience in learning to control it" (Burn, 1969, p. 51). Burn recommends that boys stay involved in vigorous physical competition with other boys, such as sports, in order to channel their overwhelming sexual energy for constructive purposes. Girls, however, are not mentioned as needing to go to such extremes to control their sexuality. Rather, girls are instructed on the importance of assisting boys in regulating their sexuality by being careful not to arouse their date's sexuality as boys who are aroused sexually are unable to think clearly (Burn, 1969).

In comparison, teenage girls may be taught that the goal of physical attractiveness is to be sexy. Media images, particularly images of women in music videos, promote the message that being a woman means being sexual. However, a woman is confronted with an irresolvable paradox—how to be attractive (i.e., appealing to the opposite sex) and at the same time avoid being provocative, lest she arouse a man to the point of no return. Once again, she must accept the consequences of her sexuality.

Myths regarding the passive nature of female sexuality are exemplified in the term *consent* itself, which carries a passive tone. A woman is not to express freely her own sexuality; her proper duty is to respond to the needs of her partner. In excluding the concept of female sexual agency, consent is relegated to a decision of whether or not to limit or control male agency, rather than acknowledge female desire (Gavey, 1992). Indeed, women may be reluctant to acknowledge their desire for sex because of the sexual double standard that prescribes unlimited sexual activity for men and limited sexual activity in women (Muehlenhard & McCoy, 1991). Any woman's behavior perceived by a man to be sexual is interpreted as consent to intercourse. Therefore, a woman dare not express herself as a sexual being lest a man determine for her the extent of her expression. This pattern of male disregard and sexual control has been supported by researchers who have found that men are less compliant to refusals of intercourse when sexually aroused (Byers, 1988). Muehlenhard and Linton (1987) found that the most common method men used to have sexual intercourse with unwilling women was to ignore their resistance.

In addition, heterosexist norms suggest that women are to be dominated by men and that male overpowerment is both desirable and pleasurable (Jackson, 1978). Researchers have suggested that power and sex may become automatically associated for some men (Bargh, Raymond, Pryor, & Strack, 1995). This association may result in sexually aggressive men exercising their need to feel powerful through sexual means (i.e., rape). Such images of male dominance and female submission are displayed repeatedly in the media. Power in intimate relationships is eroticized; dominance becomes seduction and is viewed as normative (Berger, Searles, Salem, & Pierce, 1986). Researchers have found that men who report engaging in sexually aggressive behavior are more likely to endorse dominance as a motive for engaging in sexual activity (Groth, 1979; Malamuth, 1986; Malamuth et al., 1995; Scully, 1990).

These societal myths may be magnified for women of color. Pornographic images exploit the history of racism in this country by depicting sexualized, stereotypic images of ethnic minority women (Mayall & Russell, 1993). These images communicate to viewers that ethnic minority women's claims of nonconsent are improbable and can be ignored.

Sexual Scripts

Sexual scripts are schemas that guide individuals' interpretations of, and behaviors in, sexual situations. They operate at both the institutional and individual level. Norms regarding sexuality are internalized by individuals within a culture and influence their beliefs about appropriate thoughts and actions. Before we discuss these sexual scripts, it may be helpful to first examine the ways in which gender is constructed in our culture.

Gender is created through a complex developmental process. As children develop, they internalize messages about their gender identity and appropriate gender roles through interactions with family, friends, teachers, and others around them. They also are exposed to messages about gender in schools, churches, books, movies, and other cultural products. As young girls develop, they may learn the importance of pleasing others, of yeilding to others' needs, even at the expense of their own needs and wishes. Young women also may learn to defer to men and to question their own judgment (Warshaw & Parrot, 1991). Young boys, however, may learn that they are entitled to have their needs met. In addition, they may learn that it is acceptable to use whatever means are necessary to win in a conflict, even aggression.

Sexual scripts define young men as dominant sexually (Jackson, 1978) and women as passive sexually. Men are prescribed to be seducers, whereas women are to repond with at least token resistance lest they appear loose. Men may be taught that if they honor women's hesitance and resistance, they will miss many sexual opportunities (Clark & Lewis, 1977). Men also may be taught to seek out sexual opportunities and, for young men who have internalized these masculine ideals, to engage in sexual intercourse as frequently as possible (Box, 1983). Malamuth and his colleagues (Malamuth et al., 1995; Malamuth, Sockloskie, Koss, & Tanaka, 1991) have found that an orientation toward promiscuous-impersonal sex is predictive of men who report engaging in sexually aggressive behavior. These messages also can lead to beliefs in men's sexual entitlement and women's victimization (Rapaport & Burkhart, 1984; Warshaw & Parrot, 1991). Adherence to these sexual scripts may result in a young man's persistence in engaging in sexual intercourse despite his partner's expression of nonconsent (i.e., rape). These scripts may result in a tragic combination—a woman who sincerely does not want to engage in sexual intercourse and a man who believes sincerely that a woman is only teasing even if she does protest. Indeed, some men believe women mean yes when they say no (Muehlenhard, 1988). Thus, continued sexual advances in the presence of nonconsent are justified as seduction; sexual assault becomes an extension of traditional sex role socialization patterns (Medea & Thompson, 1974).

Sexual scripts create a prototype of the consenting woman. The prototype consists of a cluster of attributes and behaviors indicative of willingness to engage in sexual intercourse. It is assumed that (a) the presence of this cluster is tantamount to consent; and (b) once this cluster is present, the woman has relinquished her right to say no. Consequently, people attend to, and find credible, certain behaviors (i.e., dress, willingness to kiss and pet, prior sexual history, etc.) while ignoring other behaviors (i.e., a woman's verbal and/or physical resistance). These sexual scripts allow men to justify their sexually aggressive behavior and define it as acceptable. They may view their coercive strategies as legitimate and feel less responsible for or deny the occurrence of a sexual assault (Jackson, 1978; Scully, 1990). The man may justify his actions by stating that "no harm was done; it was just sex," "she wanted it," or "she deserved it" (Burt, 1991). Only when the indicators of nonconsent are so extreme as to violate the prototype is the woman's resistance accepted as genuine rather than token and the man judged guilty of rape (Weis & Borges, 1973). Only then is the woman believed not to have consented to sexual intercourse and is absolved of responsibility for her victimization. Therefore, traditional views render nonconsent highly questionable. Without evidence of nonconsent, there can be no crime, and the problem of acquaintance rape becomes trivialized—it is really just sex (Jackson, 1978). The woman's experience is unacknowledged; her self-determination is denied (Griffin, 1971); her sexual expression is restricted. This script also may be internalized by women who then may fail to label an experience as rape because these traditional rape scripts do not acknowledge rape experiences between acquaintances (Kahn, Mathie, & Torgler, 1994; Kahn, chapter 15, this volume).

Historical Messages

Several factors have contributed to the present-day sexual script. These include historically rooted messages about women as property and racist and classist assumptions about sexuality.

In the colonial period, a woman's sexual purity was crucial to her ability to attract a spouse. Therefore, her value within society often was measured by her ability to marry and produce heirs (Donat & D'Emilio,

1992). Women were expected to be innocent, virtuous, and disinterested in sex. Women also were expected to use their superior morality to control men's sexuality. Therefore, a woman who engaged in sexual intercourse, even intercourse against her will, was considered a fallen woman and often was blamed for the attack (Donat & D'Emilio, 1992).

Chivalry, an often glorified tradition, particularly in the South, is itself an example of a sexual script that binds women and denies them freedom to choose their own sexuality. Women pay a high price for the chivalry extended to them. A woman is expected to remain virtuous and to defend her chastity from any "involuntary defilement." Thus, if she is raped, the assault is considered "not only a crime of aggression against the body; it is a transgression against chastity as defined by men" (Griffin, 1971, p. 32). As a result, her nonconsent may be questioned and often ignored.

> Our culture teaches men to protect women and women to look to others for safety and security. Ironically, in a chivalrous society, men are both those who commit violence and those who protect ... Chivalry promotes the man as the protector and the woman as the protected; the man as the aggressor and the woman as the victim. (White, Donat, & Bondurant, 1996, p. 551)

To an even greater extent, the sexual victimization of ethnic minority women largely has been ignored. During slavery, the African American woman was the object of sexuality for White men and the means of breeding additional slaves (Brownmiller, 1975; Simson, 1983). There were no penalties for the rape of an African American woman by a White man (Wyatt, 1992). African American women were not given the freedom to consent or refuse to consent. From this distorted context came the myth that African American women were more sexual than White women (Getman, 1984). Current stereotypes about African American women continue to perpetuate these myths of sexual promiscuity (Wyatt, 1982). Many African American women do not hold the same belief, which many White women falsely hold, that they will be believed and protected by authorities and societal institutions from sexual assault (Wyatt, 1992). Research has found that African American women are less likely to report a sexual assault to the police or rape center (Wyatt, 1992). Within this context, women of color's hesitancy to report intimate violence and their perceptions of vulnerability to sexual assault may be an accurate reflection of a society that historically has failed to protect them.

Sexual assaults against working-class women also were more common and viewed as more excusable in American history. The working-class woman openly engaged in sexual flirtation during the 1800s when middle-class values advocated sexual control. This flirtation was assumed to be the cause of the rape of working-class women because men believed that any woman walking the street at night was looking for sex (D'Emilio &

Freedman, 1988). Working women were considered closer in status to fallen women because it was believed that these women would not object to sexual intercourse with higher-status men. It was assumed that she would use her sexuality as a tool for social mobility. It was also assumed that she would consent to sexual intercourse, particularly if the relationship would increase her social status.

The Legal System

Because the law defines rape as a crime, it is important to examine historical legal definitions and past and contemporary legal processes as they relate to sexual assault.

Historically, the law conceptualized rape as the violation of a man's property. It was a man's, specifically a husband's or a partner's, personal privilege to have access to a woman's body. A husband could not be charged with raping his wife. Although the spousal exclusion rule in rape cases has been removed in all states, prosecution for rape in marriage continues to be restricted in many states. In some states, a couple must be legally separated and living in separate residences for a charge of rape to be made.

In the past, juries also may have received instruction that an accusation of rape "is one which is easily made and, once made, difficult to defend against, even if the person accused is innocent" (Berger, 1977, p. 10). The jury was cautioned to be suspicious of the victim's testimony, much more so than in other criminal cases. Even though the injunction is no longer made, this suspicion is influential particularly in a jury's decision to convict in acquaintance rape cases today. Juries are less likely to convict a man charged with raping a woman if the rapist and victim knew each other (Muehlenhard, Powch, Phelps, & Giusti, 1992). They may believe that she has raised a false accusation due to guilt, fear, or revenge.

Within the current legal system, consent remains crucial to determining whether a rape has occurred (Fuller, 1995). If a man is to be convicted of rape, the lawyer must prove not only that the woman did not consent to sexual activity, but also that the man realized that the woman was nonconsenting and continued to force her anyway. The lawyer must prove *mens rea* (criminal intent). Thus, if the defendant can present evidence of the reasonableness of his belief that the sexual activity was consensual, the prosecution lacks the required *mens rea* to convict. This process focuses on the perpetrator's rather than the victim's perception of the event. Therefore, the legal definition of consent often is determined not from the woman's perspective, but from the man's. Furthermore, nonconsent is inferred usually from evidence of resistance, which is often difficult to prove (Muehlenhard et al., 1992). For example, submission with little resistance, out of fear, may be taken as consent. Men's sexually aggressive behavior may be excused as simply a misunderstanding of the woman's desire.

Moreover, there is a tendency for juries in rape trials, which are governed by criminal law, to wrongly import the concept of contributory negligence from civil law (Bryden & Lengnick, in press). In criminal cases, the victim's behavior does not negate the perpetrator's criminal act. In a rape trial, a jury should consider the victim's behavior only insofar as it is relative to determining the likelihood that she consented. However, juries tend to use the woman's behavior to exonerate the man. Thus, they yoke blaming her with exonerating him. The concept of contributory negligence, however, is not appropriate in criminal trials. Her behavior does not excuse his behavior.

Moreover, rape, as codified in legal statutes, has been constructed from a male perspective. Sex crimes may have been defined differently if women had greater involvement in public policy and greater input into the conceptualization of what behavior constitutes a criminal act. For example, repeated psychological coercion to engage in sexual activity may be interpreted by its victims as just as hurtful or more hurtful than an isolated, minimally violent rape (Arata & Burkhart, 1996). Yet psychological coercion is not a type of crime (see Gavey, 1992, and O'Sullivan, 1995, for discussions of various forms of noncoerced, but unwanted sex).

IMPACT OF CURRENT DEFINITIONS ON RESEARCH AND PREVENTION

Defining rape primarily in terms of nonconsent has made it more difficult to come to a complete understanding of sexual assaults that occur between persons who know each other. The larger cultural context in which sexual violence occurs may be lost when research and prevention efforts become so tightly focused on issues of consent.

Research Questions

The concept of consent as definitional to determinations of rape is a recurrent theme in traditional, androcentric discourses of rape. These conceptualizations of rape suggest that either the raped woman displayed behavioral signs of consent or did not communicate clearly her nonconsent (see Crawford, 1995, for a discourse analysis of the miscommunication process in cases of rape).

The importance of miscommunication as a proximal cause of acquaintance rape and topic for prevention programs is cited often in research (e.g., Abbey, 1991; Abbey, Ross, McDuffie, & MacAuslan, 1996; Gillen & Muncer, 1995; Kowalski, 1992, 1993; Muehlenhard, 1988; Shotland,

1989). A substantial line of research has demonstrated that when considered as a whole men view the world in a more sexualized manner than women (Abbey, 1982, 1987, 1991). However, researchers suggest that only men who engage in sexually aggressive behavior, not men in general, are prone to perceiving intended friendly behaviors as sexual (Bondurant, 1994; Donat & Bondurant, 1996; White & Humphrey, 1994). This research shows that sexually aggressive men infer sexual interest on the basis of behaviors with low sexual interest cue value (such as a woman smiling). Thus, it is not the actual behaviors of women that increase their risk for victimization; it is the interpretation certain men place on these behaviors. Hanson and Gidycz (1993, p. 1051) report that "there is some evidence that women who are victimized communicate as clearly as women who are not victimized, but their perpetrators choose to ignore them and continue their aggression." Sexually aggressive men's perceptions are subjective constructions rather than objective representations of reality. Thus, miscommunication is not a plausible explanation for sexual assault. True miscommunication is based on a state of equality between a rapist and his victim (Pineau, 1989).

> Then and only then are the frequently used phrases like "negotiated order," "shared misunderstandings," or "failure to communicate" credible in that the victim presumably has the power to abort the sequence of events leading to the rapist's assault. (Schwendinger & Schwendinger, 1983, p. 68)

A rape victim, however, does not have this power. For a woman to consent, she must know that refusing is an option (Gavey, 1992). If a woman believes that her refusal will be ignored or will be met with serious consequences, her option to refuse is not a true option. Even when she explicitly refuses, verbally or nonverbally, or both, sexually assaultive men are likely to perceive it to be only token resistance and persist in inferring consent or simply ignore her refusal.

These misunderstandings may be magnified by sex role socialization in our culture (Berger et al., 1986). Men may be taught to disregard and deny the validity of women's feelings; women may be taught to question their own feelings and perceptions of sexual violation (Foa, 1977). Although men and women may not understand clearly each other's intents and behaviors, it is the social context in which sexual communication occurs, not the communication itself, that causes rape. Therefore, miscommunication may be a socially constructed correlate of sexual aggression, but not an explanation for its occurrence.

Despite evidence disconfirming the relevance of the miscommunication hypothesis, numerous research articles are published each year that discuss the gender difference in interpretations of interpersonal behavior and its possible implications for understanding sexual aggression. In addition, many rape prevention workshops also include discussion of clear communication, emphasizing its importance to female participants. Students wear buttons and t-shirts with messages stating, "no means no," as if the solution were as simple as clarifying a definition of terms. This conceptualization may serve only to distract women from challenging the larger cultural context that restricts them from controlling their own sexual expression.

Research Methods

Research methods also can influence our understanding of rape and sexual assault and how we interpret reality. Perceptions of reality can become distorted when the purposes and limitations of various methodologies are misunderstood or ignored (White & Farmer, 1992). Traditional assumptions about consent and sexual assault may influence the types of research questions asked and the methodologies used.

Scenario Research

Scenario research on acquaintance rape typically has explored various aspects of a woman's appearance and behavior while neglecting characteristics of the man (Calhoun & Townsley, 1991). One independent variable examined by researchers has been women's early versus late verbalization of refusal. This research question suggests that a woman relinquishes the right to say no to sexual intimacy if she does not express her refusal immediately. Therefore, scenario research may reinforce the assumption that victim characteristics are crucial to understanding rape and also may unknowingly contribute to victim blaming (Burt & Albin, 1981). Although theorists have emphasized the importance of not inferring that a woman is to blame for a man's assaultive behavior simply because her own behavior increased her risk of being raped (Calhoun & Townsley, 1991), scenario research continues to imply falsely that judgments of blameworthiness are more dependent on the victim than the perpetrator.

Survey Methods

Survey methods, which are used often in research on sexual assault, lose the participant's voice to define her own experience. When conducting survey research, the researcher decides how victimization will be operationally defined. Only sexual assault experiences as defined by the researcher are examined (Muehlenhard et al., 1992). Moreover, the data obtained are limited by the researcher's questions. Survey questions define the boundaries for the results that will be found and reported. Surveys decontextualize sexually assaultive behavior (White & Farmer, 1992) and give little attention to the specific circumstances under which the assault occurs. Open-ended questions, less common in the acquaintance rape literature, would permit responses unanticipated by the researcher (Burt & Albin, 1981), which would enrich our understanding of coercive sexual activity, and would allow women's voices to be heard.

Individual Predictors

In research on sexual assault, individuals rather than couples are studied typically. Therefore, individual predictors for sexual assault are identified rather than interpersonal or sociocultural factors. Research on male perpetrators focuses on the rapist's personality and behavior (White & Farmer, 1992). Penile tumescence, a measure used in some research on sexual aggression, may focus our attention on biological explanations for sexual assault. The rapist becomes pathologized. His behavior becomes the act of one man in isolation rather than embedded in its cultural context. Research on the victim focuses on characteristics that may have precipitated her assault (White & Farmer, 1992), factors that might decrease her ability to firmly resist sexual advances (e.g., self-esteem or alcohol use). As a result, the victim may be blamed. Research with the dyad as the unit of analysis is needed to better understand sexual assault (Shotland, 1989). The couple and the culture in which they are embedded must be investigated to enrich our knowledge of sexual assault and the context in which it occurs.

Prevention and Intervention

When acquaintance rape is conceptualized primarily around the issue of consent, prevention efforts also become narrowed to this specific issue. Prevention programs, especially those with college students, often focus on teaching men and women how to clearly negotiate consent and avoid miscommunication. Women are taught which behaviors and situations to avoid because of the impact such behaviors may have on others' decisions regarding her consent. For example, researchers may emphasize the importance of telling women that alcohol may impair their ability to communicate sexual intent, yet not emphasize the importance of telling men that alcohol may cloud their judgment and that extra measures may need to be taken to ensure their partner's consent.

When focusing on the issue of consent, these prevention programs become the only solution to the problem of acquaintance rape. This view suggests that couples must engage in open, verbal consent for all sexual activity. Although some may view this approach as desirable, it is unlikely to reduce the incidence of acquaintance rape because it ignores the social context in which acquaintance rape occurs. Moreover, as we discussed, consent is a socially constructed decision, a decision in which the woman's actual desire may be overshadowed by socially prescribed norms, myths, and practices. It is naive to believe that one woman can choose to position herself, as Gavey (1992) has stated, "in a feminist discourse on sexuality in an otherwise misogynist material context" (p. 330).

A FEMINIST ALTERNATIVE

Creating an alternative conceptualization of acquaintance rape is difficult because of the context in which we find ourselves embedded. However, what is needed is a new conceptualization of rape that does not focus on a woman's consent. As with other criminal acts, the focus should be on the perpetrator's behavior. A feminist perspective argues that an analysis of sexual assault's broader social context is integral to the understanding of acquaintance rape.

When we examine crimes of a nonsexual nature, it is the perpetrator's actions and their consequences for the victim that are used to determine whether a crime has been committed. In nonsexual crimes we do not ask whether the victim consented to the crime. We examine the perpetrator's behavior and its consequences. Our persistence in focusing on consent is deeply rooted in historically androcentric views of women and men.

We advocate consideration of the consequences of the assault for the victim. From research, we know that consequences can include acute medical problems (i.e., physical injuries resulting from the rape, sexually transmitted diseases), acute psychological consequences (i.e., posttraumatic stress disorder), chronic illnesses (i.e., pelvic pain, headaches), stress-related health problems (i.e., illness resulting from increased alcohol and tobacco use, and poorer sleeping and eating habits), anxiety and fear, depression, reduced sexual satisfaction and more sexual problems, poorer school and work performance, and restriction of social activity (Koss, Heise, & Russo, 1994; Koss, Goodman, et al., 1994; Koss, Koss, & Woodruff, 1991).

We also advocate consideration of the social context in which sexual assault occurs. Perhaps a more constructive conceptualization of rape should focus on control rather than consent (Muehlenhard, Danoff-Burg, & Powch, 1996, p. 133).

> A focus on control would lead us to ask questions such as, Who controls women's sexuality? Who controls men's sexuality? How free are women and men to control their own sexuality? How free are women and men to refuse to engage in unwanted sex, to engage in sex with the partner of their choice, or to engage in the type of consensual sexuality that they would like?

This conceptualization would allow analysis of power at the individual, interpersonal, and institutional levels. Constraints that inhibit an individual's ability to choose to engage in sexual activity could be examined. Rape trials would emphasize evidence of equity of power within that particular context rather than evidence of victim consent. The burden of proof would shift to the perpetrator to demonstrate that both individuals were able to exercise choice. In criminal trials, evidence regarding interpersonal power will be most relevant. Evidence of coercion, deliberate use of alcohol or drugs so that a woman is unable to resist, physical restraint (e.g., holding a woman down or blocking her escape), threats, and violence are indicators of the imbalance of interpersonal power. In research and prevention efforts, individual and institutional power also would be relevant. Individual approaches would focus on empowering women and providing them with tools of resistance. Institutional approaches would focus on public advocacy for social change as a necessary step toward creating a society in which sexual assault is not tolerated.

This conceptualization challenges researchers to identify methods for examining multiple levels of analysis (individual, interpersonal, and institutional) as they study issues of power and control in acquaintance rape. Prevention strategies also must assist young men and women to examine traditional underlying discourses regarding consent and sexual assault and to challenge these assumptions. It is hoped that this analysis will encourage us to reexamine the issue of consent and its usefulness as a definition for sexual assault.

REFERENCES

Abbey, A. (1982). Sex differences in attributions for friendly behavior: Do males misperceive females' friendliness? *Journal of Personality and Social Psychology, 42,* 830–838.

Abbey, A. (1987). Misperceptions of friendly behavior as sexual interest: A survey of naturally occurring incidents. *Psychology of Women Quarterly, 11,* 173–194.

Abbey, A. (1991). Misperception as an antecedent of acquaintance rape: A consequence of ambiguity in communication between women and men. In A. Parrot & L. Bechhofer (Eds.), *Acquaintance rape: The hidden crime* (pp. 96–111). New York: John Wiley & Sons.

Abbey, A., Ross, L. T., McDuffie, D., & MacAuslan, P. (1996). Alcohol and dating risk factors for sexual assault among college women. *Psychology of Women Quarterly, 20,* 147–169.

Arata, C. M., & Burkhart, B. R. (1996). Post-traumatic stress disorder among college student victims of acquaintance assault. *Journal of Psychology and Human Sexuality, 8,* 79–92.

Bargh, J. A., Raymond, P., Pryor, J. B., & Strack, F. (1995). Attractiveness of the underling: An automatic power → sex association and its consequences for sexual harassment and aggression. *Journal of Personality and Social Psychology,* 68, 768–781.

Berger, R. J., Searles, P., Salem, R. G., & Pierce, B. A. (1986). Sexual assault in a college community. *Sociological Focus, 19,* 1–26.

Berger, V. (1977). Man's trial, woman's tribulation: Rape cases in the courtroom. *Columbia Law Review, 77,* 1–101.

Bondurant, B. (1994, March). Men's perceptions of women's sexual interest: Sexuality or sexual aggression. In J. W. White (Chair), *The role of perceptions in relationship violence: A constructionist view.* Symposium conducted at the meeting of the Southeastern Psychological Association, New Orleans, LA.

Box, S. (1983). *Crime, power, and mystification.* London: Tavistock Publications.

Briere, J., & Malamuth, N. M. (1983). Self-reported likelihood of sexually aggressive behavior: Attitudinal versus sexual explanations. *Journal of Research in Personality, 17,* 315–323.

Brownmiller, S. (1975). *Against our will: Men, women, and rape.* New York: Simon & Schuster.

Bryden, D., & Lengnick, S. (in press). Rape in the criminal justice system. *Journal of Criminal Law and Criminology.*

Burn, H. J. (1969). *Better than the birds, smarter than the bees: No-nonsense answers to honest questions about sex and growing up.* Nashville, TN: Abingdon Press.

Burt, M. (1980). Cultural myths and supports for rape. *Journal of Personality and Social Psychology, 38,* 217–230.

Burt, M. R. (1991). Rape myths and acquaintance rape. In A. Parrot & L. Bechhofer (Eds.), *Acquaintance rape: The hidden crime* (pp. 26–40). New York: John Wiley & Sons.

Burt, M. R., & Albin, R. S. (1981). Rape myths, rape definitions, and probability of conviction. *Journal of Applied Social Psychology, 11,* 212–230.

Burt, M. R., & Estep, R. E. (1981). Who is a victim? Definitional problems in sexual victimization. *Victimology: An International Journal, 6,* 15–28.

Byers, E. S. (1988). Effects of sexual arousal on men's and women's behavior in sexual disagreement situations. *Journal of Sex Research, 25,* 235–254.

Calhoun, K. S., & Townsley, R. M. (1991). Attributions of responsibility for acquaintance rape. In A. Parrot & L. Bechhofer (Eds.), *Acquaintance rape: The hidden crime* (pp. 57–69). New York: John Wiley & Sons.

Clark, L. G., & Lewis, D. J. (1977). *Rape: The price of coercive sexuality.* Toronto: Canadian Women's Educational Press.

Crawford, M. (1995). *Talking difference: On gender and language.* London: Sage Publications.

D'Emilio, J., & Freedman, E. B. (1988). *Intimate matters: A history of sexuality in America.* New York: Harper & Row.

Dines, G., & Humez, J. M. (Eds.). (1995). *Gender, race, and class in media: A text-reader.* Thousand Oaks, CA: Sage Publications.

Donat, P. L. N. (1991, April). *Do attitudes guide behavior: Attitude accessibility in sexually aggressive males.* Poster presented at the meeting of the Southeastern Psychological Association, New Orleans, LA.

Donat, P. L. N. (1995, March). *Accessibility of rape-supportive attitudes among sexually aggressive men.* Paper presented at the meeting of the Southeastern Psychological Association, Savannah, GA.

Donat, P. L. N., & Bondurant, A. B. (1996, March). *Misperceptions of sexual intent: Effects of prior behavior and attitudes.* Poster presented at the annual meeting of the Southeastern Psychological Association, Norfolk, VA.

Donat, P. L. N., & D'Emilio, J. (1992). A feminist redefinition of rape and sexual assault: Historical foundations and change. *Journal of Social Issues, 48,* 9–22.

Foa, P. (1977). What's wrong with rape? In M. Vetterling-Braggin, F. A. Elliston, & J. English (Eds.), *Feminism and philosophy* (pp. 347–359). Totowa, NJ: Littlefield, Adams.

Fuller, P. (1995). The social construction of rape in appeal court cases. *Feminism & Psychology, 5,* 154–161.

Gavey, N. (1992). Technologies and effects of heterosexual coercion. *Feminism & Psychology, 2,* 325–351.

Getman, K. (1984). Sexual control in the slaveholding South: The implementation and maintenance of a racial caste system. *Harvard Women's Law Review, 7,* 115–153.

Gillen, K., & Muncer, S. J. (1995). Sex differences in the perceived causal structure of date rape: A preliminary report. *Aggressive Behavior, 21,* 101–112.

Griffin, S. (1971). Rape: The all-American crime. *Ramparts, 10,* 26–35.

Groth, A. N. (1979). *Men who rape: The psychology of the offender.* New York: Plenum.

Hanson, K. A., & Gidycz, C. A. (1993). Evaluation of a sexual assault prevention program. *Journal of Consulting and Clinical Psychology, 61,* 1046–1052.

Hubbard, R. C. (1985). Relationship styles in popular romance novels, 1950–1983. *Communication Quarterly, 33,* 113–125.

Jackson, S. (1978). The social context of rape: Sexual scripts and motivation. *Women's Studies International Journal, 1,* 27–38.

Kahn, A. S., Mathie, V. A., & Torgler, C. (1994). Rape scripts and rape acknowledgment. *Psychology of Women Quarterly, 18,* 53–66.

Koss, M. P., Goodman, L. A., Browne, A., Fitzgerald, L. F., Keita, G. P., & Russo, N. F. (1994). *No safe haven: Male violence against women at home, at work, and in the community.* Washington, DC: American Psychological Association.

Koss, M. P., Heise, L., & Russo, N. F. (1994). The global health burden of rape. *Psychology of Women Quarterly, 18,* 509–537.

Koss, M. P., Koss, P., & Woodruff, W. (1991). Deleterious effects of criminal victimization on women's health and medical utilization. *Archives of Internal Medicine, 151,* 342–357.

Koss, M. P., Leonard, K. E., Beezley, D. A., & Oros, C. (1985). Nonstranger sexual aggression: A discriminant analysis of the psychological characteristics of undetected offenders. *Sex Roles, 12,* 981–992.

Kowalski, R. M. (1992). Nonverbal behaviors and perceptions of sexual intentions: Effects of sexual connotativeness, verbal response, and rape outcome. *Basic and Applied Social Psychology, 13,* 427–445.

Kowalski, R. M. (1993). Inferring sexual interest from behavioral cues: Effects of gender and sexually relevant attitudes. *Sex Roles, 29,* 13–36.

Lakoff, G., & Johnson, M. (1987). The metaphorical logic of rape. *Metaphor and Symbolic Activity, 2,* 73–79.

Lonsway, K. A., & Fitzgerald, L. F. (1994). Rape myths: In review. *Psychology of Women Quarterly, 18,* 133–164.

Lonsway, K. A., & Fitzgerald, L. F. (1995). Attitudinal antecedents of rape myth acceptance: A theoretical and empirical reexamination. *Journal of Personality and Social Psychology, 68,* 704–711.

Malamuth, N. M. (1986). Predictors of naturalistic sexual aggression. *Journal of Personality and Social Psychology, 50,* 953–962.

Malamuth, N. M., & Brown, L. M. (1994). Sexually aggressive men's perceptions of women's communications: Testing three explanations. *Journal of Personality and Social Psychology, 67,* 699–712.

Malamuth, N. M., Linz, D., Heavey, C. L., Barnes, G., & Acker, M. (1995). Using the confluence model of sexual aggression to predict men's conflict with women: A 10-year follow-up study. *Journal of Personality and Social Psychology, 69,* 353–369.

Malamuth, N. M., Sockloskie, R. J., Koss, M. P., & Tanaka, J. S. (1991). Characteristics of aggressors against women: Testing a model using a national sample of college students. *Journal of Consulting and Clinical Psychology, 59,* 670–681.

Mayall, A., & Russell, D. E. H. (1993). Racism in pornography. In D. E. H. Russell (Ed.), *Making violence sexy: Feminist views on pornography* (pp. 167–177). New York: Teachers College Press.

Medea, A., & Thompson, K. (1974). *Against rape.* New York: Farrar, Straus, & Giroux.

Muehlenhard, C. L. (1988). "Nice women" don't say yes and "real men" don't say no: How miscommunication and the double standard can cause sexual problems. *Women and Therapy, 7,* 95–108.

Muehlenhard, C. L., Danoff-Burg, S., & Powch, I. G. (1996). Is rape sex or violence? Conceptual issues and implications. In D. M. Buss & N. M. Malamuth (Eds.), *Sex, power, conflict: Evolutionary and feminist perspectives* (pp. 119–137). New York: Oxford University Press.

Muehlenhard, C. L., & Linton, M.A. (1987). Date rape and sexual aggression in dating situations: Incidence and risk factors. *Journal of Counseling Psychology, 34,* 186–196.

Muehlenhard, C. L., & McCoy, M. L. (1991). Double stand/double bind: The sexual double standard and women's communication about sex. *Psychology of Women Quarterly, 15,* 447–461.

Muehlenhard, C. L., Powch, I. G., Phelps, J. L., & Giusti, L. M. (1992). Definitions of rape: Scientific and political implications. *Journal of Social Issues, 48,* 23–44.

O'Sullivan, L. F. (1995, August). *Consenting to unwanted sex.* Symposium conducted at the annual meeting of the American Psychological Association, New York, NY.

Pineau, L. (1989). Date rape: A feminist analysis. *Law and Philosophy, 8,* 217–243.

Peplau, L. A., Rubin, Z., & Hill, C. T. (1977). Sexual intimacy in dating relationships. *Journal of Social Issues, 33,* 86–109.

Rapaport, K., & Burkhart, B. R. (1984). Personality and attitudinal characteristics of sexually coercive college males. *Journal of Abnormal Psychology, 93,* 216–221.

Schwendinger, J. R., & Schwendinger, H. (1983). *Rape and inequality.* Beverly Hills, CA: Sage Publications.

Scully, D. (1990). *Understanding sexual violence: A study of convicted rapists.* Hammersmith, London: Harper Collins Academic.

Shotland, R. L. (1989). A model of the causes of date rape in developing and close relationships. In C. Hendrich (Ed.), *Close relationships* (pp. 247–270). Newbury Park, CA: Sage Publications.

Simson, R. (1983). The Afro-American female: The historical context of the construction of sexual identity. In A. Snitow, C. Stansell, & S. Thompson (Eds.), *Powers of desire: The politics of sexuality* (pp. 229–235). New York: Monthly Review Press.

Smith, M. D., & Matre, M. (1975). Social norms and sex roles in romance and adventure magazines. *Journalism Quarterly, 52,* 309–315.

Thurston, C. (1987). *The romance revolution: Erotic novels for women and the quest for a new sexual identity.* Urbana: University of Illinois Press.

Warshaw, R., & Parrot, A. (1991). The contribution of sex-role socialization to acquaintance rape. In A. Parrot & L. Bechhofer (Eds.), *Acquaintance rape: The hidden crime* (pp. 73–82). New York: John Wiley & Sons.

Weis, K., & Borges, S. S. (1973). Victimology and rape: The case of the legitimate victim. *Issues in Criminology, 8,* 71–115.

White, J. W., Donat, P. L. N., & Bondurant, B. (1996). Violence against women. In M. Crawford & R. Unger (Eds.), *Women & gender: A feminist psychology* (2nd ed., pp. 513–533). New York: McGraw Hill.

White, J. W., & Farmer, R. (1992). Research methods: How they shape views of sexual violence. *Journal of Social Issues, 48,* 45–59.

White, J. W., & Humphrey, J. (1994, March). The relationship between perceived justification for forced sexual intercourse and self-reported sexual aggression. In J. White (Chair), *The role of perceptions in relationship violence: A construc-*

tionist view. Symposium conducted at the meeting of the Southeastern Psychological Association, New Orleans, LA.

Wyatt, G. (1982). Identifying stereotypes of Afro-American sexuality and their impact upon sexual behavior. In B. Bass, G. Wyatt, & G. Powell (Eds.), *The Afro-American family: Assessment, treatment, and research issues* (pp. 333–346). New York: Grune and Stratton.

Wyatt, G. E. (1992). The sociocultural context of African American and White American women's rape. *Journal of Social Issues, 48,* 77–91.

15

UNDERSTANDING THE UNACKNOWLEDGED RAPE VICTIM

ARNOLD S. KAHN AND VIRGINIA ANDREOLI MATHIE

Until recently rape was defined in the United States as forcible sexual intercourse by a man against a woman. In almost all cases, it was assumed the victim and assailant were strangers. In the last 3 decades, feminist scholars (e.g., Brownmiller, 1975; Millet, 1970) and researchers (e.g., Burt, 1980; Koss & Oros, 1982) have determined that most rape victims know the identity of their attacker. Indeed, as a result of this research, three new phrases—*date rape, acquaintance rape,* and *marital rape*—have come into our language. Most states now define rape as vaginal, anal, or oral intercourse against a person's consent. Although rape has taken on new definitions by scholars, researchers, and legal experts, the lay public may not

We wish to thank the following individuals who were members of our research team between 1991 and 1996. Without their contributions our research could never have been completed. Sarah Baker, Shera Beadner, Paula Beeghly, Suzanne Blaisdell, Kimberly Bradley, Matthew Bruffey, Rima Bruno, Jennifer Burnfield, Susan Cather, Linh Chau, Lisa Cherry, Sarah Cheverton, Lori Dolby, Gina Feria, Debra Flickstein, Kristi Graves, Corinne Gregory, Traci Hagie, Jen Haley, Carrie Hartwell, Kathryn Hastings, Kelly Heiges, Denise Higgins, Crystal Hill, Hannah Hinely, Emily Impett, Heather Jacobs, Christine Lally, Kristi Linn, Anne McCarthy, Kathleen Palm, Dan Schaeffer, Michael Schmitt, Elaine Schoka, Wendy Schuyler, Brookie Scholten, Judith Schor, Stacey Sheetz, Martha Shute, Katie Stover, Julie Stuckey, Megan Sullivan, Marian Taliaferro, Phil Travers, Jenny Walton, Lorrin Wolf, Marchelle Yoch.

377

recognize acquaintance and date rape as acts of rape. In this chapter we survey the research regarding what has been called the hidden or unacknowledged rape victim (Koss, 1985, 1988). Unacknowledged rape victims are women who have had an experience that would legally be classified as rape, but who do not consider themselves rape victims. We review research that has been conducted from two paradigms, logical positivism and social constructionism, and try to show how the different research paradigms provide different kinds of knowledge regarding rape acknowledgment.

WHAT IS MEANT BY THE WORD RAPE?

The specific behaviors that constitute rape vary across cultures (Koss, Heise, & Russo, 1994). In the United States the meaning of rape has undergone considerable change. Donat and D'Emilio (1992) pointed out that in colonial times sex was regulated by the church and rape was considered a crime against the man who "owned" the woman, either her father or her husband. In the 19th century this view changed. "In the 19th century, women were viewed as pure and virtuous by nature, and as disinterested in sex" (Donat & D'Emilio, 1992, p. 11). A woman who engaged in sexual intercourse outside of marriage was considered an impure or fallen woman, even if the intercourse was the result of rape.

In the 20th century until the beginning of the modern feminist movement, the rapist, at least the White rapist, was viewed as someone with a mental illness (Amir, 1971; Donat & D'Emilio, 1992). In addition, the widespread belief in rape myths (e.g., you can't rape a woman who doesn't want to be raped) led to the view that women contributed to their own victimization (Burt, 1980). As Donat and D'Emilio (1992) pointed out, it was widely believed that the good woman was one who knew her place. If she strayed from her feminine role and acted as a man, one of the consequences could be rape.

In the 1970s feminist writers such as Brownmiller (1975), Griffin (1971), and Millet (1970) demonstrated how rape and the fear of rape functioned as a means by which men controlled women in a patriarchal society, a way to intimidate women and keep them fearful. Thus, over the past three centuries the meaning of rape has changed from a crime against a woman's owner (father or husband), to a defect in a woman (impurity) and a sickness in a man, to a means of social control of women by men.

As Donat and D'Emilio (1992) pointed out, it is interesting to note that almost all consideration of rape prior to the 1970s referred to stranger rape. However, once rape was reconceptualized as a means of intimidating and controlling women, it became conceivable that other men—fathers, brothers, dates, neighbors, friends—might also use rape as a means of control. Once acquaintance rape was identified as a possibility, researchers began investigating it.

The feminist reconceptualization of rape has been accompanied by changes in the rape laws of virtually every state (and across the Western world) (Donat & D'Emilio, 1992; Goldberg-Ambrose, 1992; Searles & Berger, 1987). Although rape laws vary somewhat from state to state, most states now define rape as sexual intercourse without a person's consent, and allow for various degrees of rape depending on the amount of force used.

Increasing the scope of the definition of rape has also blurred the distinction between rape and consensual sexual intercourse. What is rape? How does one know when rape has occurred? A public (Maglin & Perry, 1996; Roiphe, 1994) and scholarly (Gilbert, 1993; Koss & Cook, 1993; Sanday, 1996) debate has been ongoing regarding the distinction between acquaintance rape and bad sex (see Kamen, 1996). Muehlenhard, Powch, Phelps, and Giusti (1992) argued that this new, broader definition of rape is in the service of women. For example, if rape is narrowly defined and based on high levels of assailant force and victim resistance, it is the woman who has to prove that she was raped by showing that her experience fell within these boundaries, something that is frequently difficult to do. Muehlenhard and Linton (1987) and Rapaport and Burkhart (1984) have reported that most men do not use either high levels of force or severe threat of force to obtain intercourse against a woman's will; rather, they are most likely to ignore her protests and use their greater size and weight to continue until intercourse has been completed. Without obvious physical threat or force, it would be difficult to show that this typical situation falls within the narrow definition of rape. On the other hand, if rape is defined to include all nonconsensual sexual intercourse and is not limited by amount of assailant force or victim resistance, then the burden falls on the man to demonstrate that he did not rape.

As this brief review demonstrates, what is considered rape is influenced by society's beliefs about the roles and status of women. The definition of rape we use in this chapter is consistent with that used in most feminist research as well as most state laws. We define rape as vaginal, anal, or oral penetration of a woman by a man without her consent. Although it is possible for a woman to rape another woman, for a man to rape another man, or for a woman to rape a man, the focus of this chapter is on sexual assaults by men against women.

THE PROBLEM OF THE UNACKNOWLEDGED RAPE VICTIM

Using nonconsensual sexual intercourse as the definition of rape, researchers have discovered that rape, especially acquaintance rape, is a widespread phenomenon. The percentage of women who have experienced rape ranges between 12.7 and 25% or higher, depending upon how rape is measured (Aizenman & Kelley, 1988; Kahn, Andreoli Mathie, & Torgler, 1994; Koss, 1985, 1988, 1993; Miller & Marshall, 1987; Ward, Chapman, Cohn, White, & Williams, 1991).

Do victims of nonconsensual intercourse consistently acknowledge their experience as rape? Does the junior high student whose boyfriend doesn't stop when she says no consider herself to be a rape survivor? Does the high school student who gets drunk at a party and is unable to resist the advances of a boy believe she has been sexually assaulted? Does the college student who wakes up naked in a bed at a fraternity house consider herself to have been raped? Recent research suggests a great many of these women do not acknowledge these experiences as rape.

FREQUENCY OF RAPE ACKNOWLEDGMENT AND UNACKNOWLEDGMENT

Whether a woman has been raped or not and whether she perceives her experience as rape are usually determined by her responses to the Sexual Experiences Survey (SES) (Koss & Oros, 1982). In completing the SES a respondent anonymously checks either yes or no to a variety of sexual experiences. Some of these experiences are not rape, some are attempted rape, and some would be classified as rape under almost all state laws. At some other point the respondent is asked to respond yes or no to the direct question, "Have you ever been raped by a man?" Based on responses to these questions, participants can be classified as nonvictims, acknowledged rape victims, and unacknowledged rape victims.

The results from a number of surveys have demonstrated with remarkable consistency that many women do not acknowledge their rape experience as rape. In her initial study of the hidden rape victim, Koss (1985) found that 33% of college women indicated that they had engaged in sexual intercourse when they didn't wish to, and 12.7% of the sample responded yes to at least one of the SES questions indicating they had experienced sexual intercourse with force or threat of force. Of these women who had experienced a situation that could be classified as rape, 43% were unacknowledged or hidden victims, responding no to the question directly asking if they had ever been raped.

Using a modified version of the SES we found a consistent pattern of results regarding rape and rape acknowledgment, which are summarized in Table 1 (Andreoli Mathie et al., 1994; Andreoli Mathie & Kahn, 1995; Kahn et al., 1994). In the two studies in which participants included women at all levels of their college undergraduate careers, almost one fourth had an experience that would legally be considered rape (Andreoli Mathie & Kahn, 1995; Kahn et al., 1994). In a third study, in which the

TABLE 1
Percentages of Rape Victims, Acquaintance Rape Victims, and Unacknowledged Rape Victims Across Three Studies

Study	Total N	N and % victims	N and % unacknowledged victims	N and % acquaintance rape
Kahn et al. (1994)	198	46	22	45
		23.2%	47.8%	97.8%
Andreoli Mathie et al. (1994)	222	34	19	32
		15.3%	55.9%	97.0%[a]
Andreoli Mathie & Kahn (1995)	307	74	48	69
		24.1%	64.9%	97.2%[b]

[a]Based on 33 participants who responded to this item.
[b]Based on 71 participants who identified the relationship between the assailant and victim.

percentage was slightly lower (15.3%), most of the participants were first-semester college students. The percentage of unacknowledged victims was quite high, ranging from 47.8% to 64.9%. Table 1 also reveals that almost all the rape victims were the victim of an acquaintance rape, with the percentage of acquaintance rapes ranging from 97% to 97.8%. The few victims of stranger rape were all acknowledged victims. In other words, lack of acknowledgment that her experience was rape only occurred when the victim knew her assailant. Across the three studies, we have discovered 154 rape victims. Of these, 146 were known victims of acquaintance rape, and only 4 were known to be victims of stranger rape. Eighty-nine of the rape victims (57.8%) did not believe they had been raped.

Confirmation of this high level of victim unacknowledgment comes from Bondurant (1995) and Pitts and Schwartz (1993). Bondurant found that out of a sample of 109 college women rape victims identified by responses to the SES, 64% of them were unacknowledged victims. Likewise, Pitts and Schwartz (1993), using an instrument similar to the SES, found that in a sample of 288 college women, 19.3% had an experience since beginning college that would legally be considered rape. However, of those women who had been raped, 73% of them were unacknowledged. Finally, Phillips (1996), in interviews with 30 college students, found that 27 of the 30 women reported experiences that fit legal definitions of rape, sexual harassment, or battering. Yet none of these women considered themselves to have been raped or to have been a victim.

Why is there such a high proportion of unacknowledged rape victims? This question is not just of academic interest. If a woman does not acknowledge that a rape has occurred, she will not report the incident and the assailant will not be punished. It is quite likely the assailant will engage in additional sexual assaults on the same or other women. If we are to eliminate or reduce the frequency of rape, it is critical that both women and men recognize rape when it occurs. In this chapter we review research on rape acknowledgment from two research perspectives: quantitative methods using the perspective of logical positivism, and qualitative methods such as discourse analysis using a social constructionism perspective. After presenting a summary of the methods used and the results, we compare the two methods in terms of their usefulness for understanding the unacknowledged rape victim.

QUANTITATIVE RESEARCH AND RAPE ACKNOWLEDGMENT

Research from a logical positivist perspective searches for an explanation of events in order to predict and control them (Guba & Lincoln, 1994). Hypotheses are formulated that are supported or not through the accumulation of data or facts. In the case of rape acknowledgment, the attempt is to identify personal and situational factors that differentiate acknowledged from unacknowledged victims in order to predict the conditions under which unacknowledgment occurs. The hope is that activists could use this information to educate men and women to recognize rape when it occurs and thus prevent sexual assaults from being unacknowledged.

Possible Causes of Rape Unacknowledgment

The logical positivism approach favors the experimental manipulation and control of variables in order to identify those variables that differentiate acknowledged from unacknowledged victims. However, in the study of rape it is not possible to experimentally manipulate variables. Consequently, research in this area typically involves surveying women about their attitudes, personalities, past experiences, and the events that occurred before, during, and after their assault. The investigator then compares acknowledged and unacknowledged victims on these variables to determine whether the two groups of victims differ on any of them.

Personalities, Attitudes, and Past Experiences

Do acknowledged and unacknowledged victims have different personalities, attitudes, or background experiences that lead them to label their rape experiences differently? In an extensive investigation of this possibility, Koss (1985) found no differences between acknowledged and unacknowledged rape victims in dating behaviors, situational aspects of the rape experience, personality, or attitudes about rape. Levine-MacCombie and Koss (1986) found no differences in the resistance strategies used by acknowledged and unacknowledged victims. Finally, Bondurant (1995) found no relationship between rape acknowledgment and endorsement of romantic beliefs.

Our research also has failed to find differences in the personalities, demographics, and past experience of acknowledged and unacknowledged rape victims. Kahn et al. (1994) found no differences between types of victim in age, year in school, attendance at a rape seminar, work experience at a sexual assault agency, or acquaintance with another rape victim. Acknowledged and unacknowledged victims did not differ in their estimation of the certainty that rape had occurred in hypothetical assault scenarios. Andreoli Mathie and Kahn (1995) also found no difference between these types of victims on a measure of locus of control. The evidence to date suggests that attitude, personality, and demographic variables do not differentiate between acknowledged and unacknowledged rape victims.

Rape Scripts

Another reason for the existence of unacknowledged rape victims may be the nature of the rape scripts some women possess. A script describes the events that normally occur in a given situation (Markus & Zajonc, 1985). Fiske and Taylor (1991) summarized the evidence that people in a given culture have common scripts for a wide variety of events, including such diverse phenomena as eating at a restaurant, becoming ill, and nuclear war. It is thus highly plausible that women (and men) have fairly well-developed scripts for what happens during a rape.

When a person thinks about the events that make up the experience of rape, it is possible that one of two distinct scripts may emerge. Some people may have an acquaintance rape script in which the assault takes place indoors, involves a known assailant, and entails little force. For others, however, the thought of rape may evoke a stranger rape script, in which a woman is violently attacked out of doors by a man she has never met who wields a weapon. Given that unacknowledged rape victims are almost always assaulted by someone they know, unacknowledged victims may be women who have a rape script that is descriptive of a violent stranger rape but whose own rape experience involved an assault by an acquaintance. Under these circumstances, there would be a discrepancy between the woman's rape experience and her rape script. Given this discrepancy, the victim may come to view the incident as something other than rape (Parrot, 1991; Russell, 1975; Weis & Borges, 1973).

Under the guise of obtaining examples of how people describe a variety of events, Kahn et al. (1994) asked college women to write a description of the events occurring before, during, and after a typical rape. They found that all but one of the acknowledged victims wrote an acquaintance rape script, but 50% of the unacknowledged victims wrote a script of stranger rape. Additionally, those participants who wrote stranger rape scripts were more likely to write about a physical attack that took place out of doors and in which the assailant threatened to use or used a weapon, were more likely to mention that the victims screamed and struggled, and were more likely to inform the police. Acquaintance rape scripts generally were set indoors, involved restraint rather than an attack, and elicited verbal protests from the victim.

Bondurant (1995) provided additional support for the importance of a woman's rape script on her rape acknowledgment. Using a method in which participants were asked to think of a typical rape and then indicate the nature of their script by checking alternatives (e.g., "a typical rape is committed a. indoors, b. outdoors"), Bondurant found that unacknowledged victims were more likely than acknowledged victims to check alternatives consistent with a stranger rape.

The research by Kahn et al. (1994) and Bondurant (1995) provides strong support that at least one reason unacknowledged victims exist is because their rape experience differed from their rape script. However, the nature of one's rape script cannot account for all of the unacknowledged rape victims. Only one half of the unacknowledged victims held a stranger rape script; the other half of the unacknowledged victims did have an acquaintance rape script that likely matched, in at least some detail, their own rape experience. However, these women still did not acknowledge their experience as rape.

Force and Resistance in the Rape Itself

Perhaps the most obvious explanation for the existence of unacknowledged rape victims lies in the nature of the assault itself. It is quite possible that those victims who acknowledge the assault as rape were subjected to a higher level of physical force or threatened physical force, or displayed a higher level of resistance. There is a sizable literature showing that the perceived amount of force and resistance are the most important factors in an observer's decision as to whether or not a situation is rape (e.g., Bourque, 1989; Parrot, 1991). Perhaps the level of force and resistance are also determinants of whether a victim labels her own experience as rape.

Research on the relationship between force and rape acknowledgment has provided contradictory results. In Koss's (1985) pioneering study, acknowledged victims did not differ from unacknowledged victims on offender verbal pressure, offender physical violence, type of force, degree of force, victim resistance, or clarity of nonconsent. However, Bondurant (1995) found that level of force was significantly related to rape acknowledgment. Sixty-two percent of women who experienced physical force acknowledged their experience as rape, whereas less than 10% of women who were intoxicated or threatened with force acknowledged their experience as rape. Furthermore, when Bondurant examined various predictors of rape acknowledgment, she found that the perceived amount of assailant force accounted for more of the variance than any other factor. Bondurant's acknowledged victims also reported engaging in greater resistance and suffering more physical harm than those who were unacknowledged.

Andreoli Mathie et al. (1994) asked rape victims to check one of four alternatives—"none," "slight," "moderate," and "large"—in responding to the question, "How much force did he use?" Acknowledged victims indicated experiencing a significantly greater level of assailant force than unacknowledged victims. More than 87% of the acknowledged victims indicated that either a moderate or large amount of force was used by the assailant, whereas only 28% of unacknowledged victims reported a moderate or large degree of force. This finding was replicated by Andreoli Mathie and Kahn (1995) who asked rape victims to respond on a 7-point scale to the question, "Overall, how much force did he use in this situation?" Acknowledged victims perceived their experience as involving significantly more assailant force than did unacknowledged victims.

To explore more thoroughly differences in the amount of force experienced by acknowledged and unacknowledged rape victims, Andreoli Mathie and Kahn (1995) asked participants to indicate the extent to which the man used verbal pressure, threatened physical harm, covered her mouth, held her down, twisted her body, pushed or shoved, scratched, slapped, hit, kicked, bit, choked, threatened use of a weapon, and actually used a weapon. Participants responded to each item on a 7-point scale ranging from 0 ("not at all") to 6 ("a great deal"). A similar set of questions was asked regarding amount of victim resistance using the same response format to the stem, "What I did to resist," and included tried to leave, tried to talk him out of it, verbally protested, tried to scream, screamed or shouted, verbally attacked him, pushed or shoved him, scratched him, slapped him, hit him, kicked him, bit him, tried to use a weapon, and used a weapon.

Overall, regardless of acknowledgment status, level of assailant force and victim resistance were quite low, typically between 0 and 1 on the 0–6 scales. The only assailant force items for which the mean was greater than 3.0 were assailant's use of verbal pressure (both acknowledged and unacknowledged victims) and being held down by the assailant (acknowledged victims only). The only items for which the mean for victim resistance was greater than 3.0 were for "tried to talk him out of it" (both acknowledged and unacknowledged victims) and "verbally protested" (both acknowledged and unacknowledged victims). These findings support the conclusions of Muehlenhard and Linton (1987) and Rapaport and Burkhart (1984) that most men gain nonconsensual sexual intercourse by simply ignoring the verbal protests of the woman and refusing to stop, rather than by using high levels of force.

Although the overall level of force was low, we found significant differences between acknowledged and unacknowledged victims in levels of assailant force for some assailant behaviors. Acknowledged victims re-

TABLE 2
Percentage of Rape Victims Responding "Not at All" to Each of the Resistance Items

Item	Percentage
Tried to leave	33.8
Tried to talk her way out of it	20.5
Verbally protested	20.3
Tried to scream but was unable to do so	79.7
Screamed or shouted	75.7
Verbally attacked or swore at him	78.4
Pushed or shoved him	74.3
Scratched him	83.8
Slapped him	87.8
Hit or punched him	84.9
Kicked him	89.2
Bit him	91.8
Tried to use a weapon	100.0

ported that the assailant was more likely to have used verbal pressure, threatened physical force, held her down, and pushed or shoved her than did unacknowledged victims. When all of the individual assailant force items were combined to form an overall measure of assailant force, acknowledged victims reported significantly more force than unacknowledged victims. Unlike the victims in Bondurant's (1995) study, no significant differences were found between acknowledged and unacknowledged victims for level of victim resistance either on the individual items or on a composite score.

Although not found by Koss (1985) in her original study, the evidence seems clear from the more recent research that the amount of assailant force is an important factor in women acknowledging that they have been raped. Apparently, one way women know they have been raped is that their assailant used at least some minimal level of force. Although Bondurant (1995) found that acknowledged victims reported greater resistance to their assailant than unacknowledged victims, Andreoli Mathie and Kahn (1995) did not find a difference in victim resistance. Table 2 presents the percentage of rape victims (acknowledged and unacknowledged combined) from Andreoli Mathie and Kahn who responded "not at all" to each type of resistance. For the majority of these rape victims, resistance either did not occur or was limited to attempts to leave and verbal protests. The lack of resistance may have been due to the low levels of force used by their assailants.

Affective Reactions to the Rape Experience

Some victims may not acknowledge that rape occurred because they did not have strong emotional reactions either during the assault itself, after the assault, or both. Acknowledged victims, on the other hand, may have experienced intense emotional reactions that helped them define their experience as rape. Research has shown that women who seek assistance from agencies following a rape report severe distress, fear, anxiety, depression, lowered self-esteem, and self-blame (Branscombe, Owen, & Allison, 1995; Janoff-Bulman, 1979; Janoff-Bulman & Timko, 1987; Koss, 1993; Koss & Burkhart, 1989). These reactions are reflective of posttraumatic stress disorder (Rothbaum, Foa, Riggs, Murdock, & Walsh, 1992) and often last for several months or years (Hanson, 1990; Resick, 1987). Women who seek help from rape crisis centers, social service agencies, or hospitals also tend to label their experience as rape (Pitts & Schwartz, 1993). Thus, it appears that severe emotional reactions are associated with help-seeking behavior that in turn is associated with rape acknowledgment. We must be cautious, however, when drawing conclusions about the relationship between severity of emotional reaction and rape acknowledgment based primarily on women who have sought help because there is a confound that makes causal relationships difficult to assess. More specifically, compared with victims of acquaintance rape, victims of stranger rape are more likely to seek help or tell the police (Koss, Dinero, Seibel, & Cox, 1988; Pitts & Schwartz, 1993). Victims of stranger rape also tend to have experienced a more violent rape, feel more victimized, and are more likely to see their experience as rape (Koss et al., 1988). Thus, when using data from help seekers, it is difficult to determine whether it was their intense emotional reaction, the fact that the assailant was a stranger, or the higher level of violence that led these women to label their experience as rape.

To explore further the relationship between emotional reaction and rape acknowledgment, Andreoli Mathie and Kahn (1995) asked participants to indicate from 1 (not at all) to 7 (a great deal) the extent to which they felt a number of emotions at the time of their rape experience. These emotions and the mean endorsement for acknowledged and unacknowledged victims are listed in Table 3. The items were later grouped into three categories—self-blame, feelings of victimization, and negative affect—and the items in each group were summed to provide scores for total self-blame, total victimization, and total negative affect. Table 3 shows that acknowledged victims reported experiencing greater feelings of victimization and more negative affect than unacknowledged victims. The two groups did not differ on their feelings of self-blame. Covariance analyses also revealed that differences in feelings of victimization and negative affect remained even when level of force, whether measured by the total weighted force score, the victim's perceived level of force, or the victim's weighted resistance score, was held constant. These findings suggest that acknowledged victims differed from unacknowledged victims in their emotional reaction, with more intense reactions predictive of rape acknowledgment.

TABLE 3
Mean Affective Reactions of Acknowledged and Unacknowledged Rape Victims to Their Assault

Item	Acknowledged	Unacknowledged	Significance
Total Self-Blame	28.73	26.17	.059
Responsible	4.69	4.71	NS
Guilty	5.42	5.04	NS
Ashamed	6.39	5.09	.001
Angry at Self	5.73	5.38	NS
Regretful	6.50	6.00	NS
Total Victimized	37.19	30.44	.001
Victimized	5.69	4.11	.001
Degraded	6.35	5.36	.015
Not Strong	6.19	5.33	.036
Not in Control	6.58	6.07	NS
Violated	6.31	4.96	.002
Betrayed	6.08	4.53	.001
Total Negative Affect	46.39	34.94	.001
Sad	6.35	5.18	.005
Angry	5.73	5.04	NS
Dirty	6.08	4.53	.001
Shock	5.89	4.07	.001
Hysterical	4.15	2.33	.001
Confused	6.27	4.49	.001
Afraid	5.77	3.78	.001
Embarrassed	6.15	5.38	NS

Note. The higher the mean the more of the characteristic the women reported feeling on a scale of 1 to 7. For individual items, Multivariate $F(23,47) = 2.13$, $p < .05$. For composite scores, Multivariate $F(3,68) = 7.90$, $p < .001$.

A similar pattern of responses was found for the victims' reactions following the assault. The items and the mean responses (on 7-point scales) for acknowledged and unacknowledged victims are shown in Table 4. Table 4 shows that acknowledged victims reported stronger and more negative reactions to their assault experience than did unacknowledged victims. Acknowledged victims not only reported feeling worse after the assault, but also reported more life disruptions (nightmares, lost time from work and school, and suicidal thoughts). It is not clear whether labeling their experience as rape led to these negative reactions following the assault, or whether the negative emotional experience and life disruptions led these women to acknowledge their experience as rape.

Sexual Experiences

Although we had no prior hypotheses regarding sexual experiences and rape acknowledgment, in each of our studies (Andreoli Mathie et al., 1994; Andreoli Mathie & Kahn, 1995; Kahn et al., 1994) we examined whether acknowledged and unacknowledged victims differed in their responses to each item of the SES, such as those who indicated consensual

TABLE 4
Mean Reactions of Acknowledged and Unacknowledged Victims Following Their Assault

Item	Acknowledged	Unacknowledged	Significance
Felt guilt	5.65	4.96	NS
Felt devastated	5.92	3.43	.001
Kept thinking about incident	6.04	4.94	.018
Was depressed	5.96	3.92	.001
Felt angry	6.31	4.79	.001
Had lowered self-esteem	5.73	4.32	.008
Afraid of what others thought of me	5.46	3.64	.001
More fearful of men	4.69	4.04	NS
Saw world as scarier place	3.92	2.98	NS
Difficulty relating with others	4.58	2.32	.001
Had nightmares	4.65	1.98	.001
Lost time from school or work	2.81	1.40	.001
Had suicidal thoughts	2.35	1.26	.003

Note. Multivariate $F(13,59) = 4.79$, $p < .001$. The higher the mean, the greater the reaction the woman experienced on a scale from 1 to 7.

sex, force during petting, and attempted rape. As can be seen in Table 5, acknowledged victims reported greater frequencies of sexual experiences involving force than unacknowledged victims in their nonrape experiences, including forced kissing and petting, and the threat or actual use of force when intercourse did not occur. Thus, compared with acknowledged victims, unacknowledged victims appear to have had a less violent nonrape sexual history.

Counterfactual Thinking

Counterfactual thinking is another cognitive process that may lead women to not acknowledge their experience as rape. As applied to rape, counterfactual thinking would involve mentally changing or reconstructing the events that culminated in rape in such a way that something other than rape occurred (Kahneman & Miller, 1986; Kahneman & Tversky, 1982). Unusual or negative events, such as nonconsensual sexual intercourse, elicit more counterfactual thinking than mundane or positive events (Davis, Lehman, Wortman, Silver, & Thompson, 1995; Kahneman & Miller, 1986; Kahneman & Tversky, 1982; Miller & McFarland, 1986; Wells, Taylor, & Turtle, 1987) because alternatives, including more typical or desired outcomes, such as nonconsensual intercourse not occurring, can be readily brought to mind.

Andreoli Mathie and Kahn (1995) suggested that some rape victims may engage in upward counterfactual thinking (Markman, Gavanski, Sherman, & McMullen, 1993), and think about how they could have avoided

TABLE 5
SES Items on Which Acknowledged Rape Victims had Signficantly Higher Levels of Endorsement Than Unacknowledged Victims

SES Item	Kahn et al. (1994)	Andreoli Mathie et al. (1994)	Andreoli Mathie & Kahn (1995)
Man misinterpreted sexual intimacy you desired	.06	NS	.02
Man used force in kissing or petting	.01	.001	NS
Man threatened force, but intercourse did not occur	.02	.001	NS
Man used force, but intercourse did not occur	.03	.001	NS
Man obtained sexual intercourse after you asserted no	NA	NA	.001
Had sexual intercourse because man threatened force	NS	.001	.01
Had sexual intercourse because man used force	.001	.001	.001
Had anal or oral intercourse because of threat or actual force	NS	NS	.003

Note. NA = not asked; NS = not significant.

the rape or made it less traumatic (e.g., "If only I had not had so much to drink, this never would have happened"). Other victims may engage in downward counterfactual thinking, and think about how the situation could have been worse case (e.g., "At least he didn't beat me up or it would have been worse"). Upward comparisons produce more intense negative affect (Gleicher, Kost, Baker, Strathman, Richman, & Sherman, 1990; Johnson, 1986; Kahneman & Miller, 1986; Kahneman & Tversky, 1982; Landman, 1987; Miller & McFarland, 1986; Wells et al., 1987), more feelings of deprivation and resentment (Folger, 1987; Folger, Rosenfield, & Robinson, 1983; Hemphill & Lehman, 1991; Markman et al., 1993; Roese, 1994; Taylor, Buunk, & Aspinwall, 1990), more regret and self-blame (Boninger, Gleicher, & Strathman, 1994), and poorer adjustment (Bulman & Wortman, 1977; Burgess & Holmstrom, 1979; Taylor, Wood, & Lichtman, 1983) than downward comparisons. However, upward comparisons also can provide information about how to change the situation in the future and this may make the person better prepared for and more hopeful about the future (Boninger et al., 1994; Roese, 1994; Taylor et al., 1990; Taylor & Schneider, 1989; Taylor et al., 1983).

Rape acknowledgment may also be influenced by whose behavior is changed in the counterfactuals, the victim's own behavior or that of her assailant (Branscombe, Owen, Garstka, & Coleman, 1996; Miller &

McFarland, 1986; Wells & Gavanski, 1989). When participants imagined what a rape victim could have done (but did not do) to avoid rape (Branscombe et al., 1996) or to impose justice on the assailant (and hence make it better for her) (Nario-Redmond & Branscombe, 1996), they assigned a greater percentage of blame to the victim, saw her as more responsible, and perceived the situation as less serious than when a change in her behavior did not alter the outcome. Similarly, the more counterfactual thoughts rape victims had in which they changed their own behavior to avoid the rape, the more self-blame they reported (Branscombe et al., 1995). It appears that the more people think they *could* have changed their behavior to alter the outcome, the more they think they *should* have done so. This may be what leads to the guilt and self-blame (Miller, Turnbull, & McFarland, 1990).

Based on these findings, Andreoli Mathie and Kahn (1995) hypothesized that the more women engaged in upward counterfactual thinking, especially upward counterfactual thinking that altered the assailant's behavior, the more intense the negative feelings they would have about the incident, the less self-blame they would experience, and the more likely they would be to acknowledge their experience as rape. On the other hand, the more women engaged in downward counterfactual thinking, the less traumatized they would feel about the incident and the less likely they would be to acknowledge the situation as rape.

To examine what counterfactual thoughts victims had about the incident, they were asked in an open-ended question if they had replayed the event in their mind such that the outcome was better or worse, and if so, to list the thoughts they had. All counterfactual thoughts were coded by their direction (upward or downward) and whose behavior changed (victim, assailant, or other).

Our data provided little support for the importance of counterfactual thinking in rape acknowledgment. Acknowledged and unacknowledged victims did not differ on the total number of counterfactual thoughts or on the various types of counterfactual thoughts. The 56 women who listed their thoughts reported an average of 2.66 counterfactual thoughts, with a range of 0 to 8. However, almost all of these thoughts were upward and victim-focused counterfactuals (e.g., "if only I had done something different, things would have been better"). Forty-eight women reported one or more upward victim-focused counterfactuals (M = 2.13), eight women reported one, and one woman reported two upward assailant-focused counterfactuals. Only two women reported one downward victim-focused counterfactual, three women reported one, and two women reported four downward assailant-focused counterfactuals. There were no significant correlations between any of the types of counterfactual thoughts and the total affect, total self-blame, or total victimization scores.

Reaction of Peers

As Festinger (1950) noted many years ago, other people help us define reality. This can also be true in defining an experience as acquaintance rape. If a woman tells her friends about an assault experience and they label the experience as rape, the victim will more likely acknowledge the experience as rape then if her friends say something like, "well, you shouldn't have been in that place at that time." Pitts and Schwartz (1993) presented evidence that peer reactions were a determinant of rape acknowledgement. In a sample of 288 women they found 19.3% of the respondents reported to have had an experience since entering college that would legally be classified as rape in Ohio. However, only 27% of these women acknowledged that they had been raped; 73% were unacknowledged. These participants were asked if they told anyone about the experience, and if so, whether their friend helped them establish blame. Thirteen participants mentioned that their friend helped them establish blame. All four of the victims who stated that their friend told them it was not their fault were acknowledged victims. All nine of the victims who stated that their friend held them at least partially responsible did not acknowledge victimization.

Use of Alcohol or Drugs

A situational variable that may influence rape acknowledgment is the use of alcohol or drugs. Richardson and Campbell (1982) found that when the victim was intoxicated, college student observers viewed her as more responsible for the rape than when she had not been drinking. Similarly, Abbey (1991) found that observers rated a woman more sexually available and responsive to sexual overtures when she had been drinking alcohol than when she had been drinking soda. These findings suggest that if the victim had been drinking at the time of the rape, she may be more inclined to see herself as responsible for what happened and be less likely to acknowledge the incident as rape. Results from the Andreoli Mathie and Kahn (1995) study lend some support to this logic. Significantly more unacknowledged victims reported they were impaired by alcohol or drugs during the incident (54.2%) than acknowledged victims (28%).

Summary of Quantitative Research

The quantitative research reported thus far suggests there are at least seven variables on which acknowledged and unacknowledged rape victims differ—the nature of her rape script, the amount of force experienced in nonrape sexual experiences, the amount of force used by the assailant in the rape, the amount of negative affect and feelings of victimization experienced during the rape, whether she used alcohol or drugs prior to the rape, the amount of negative affect experienced after the rape, and the influence of peers following the rape. Researchers examining these variables suggest the cognitions and experiences that a woman brings to the assault situation (rape script, previous sexual experiences, use of alcohol), the cognitions and experiences that occur during the assault (level of assailant force, amount of negative affect), and the cognitions and experiences that occur after the assault (amount of negative affect and behavioral disruptions, reaction of peers) are all likely to affect rape acknowledgment. Putting all of these variables together suggests the following composite of a rape victim who is likely to be an acknowledged victim. Thinking of rape as a violent assault committed by a stranger out of doors predisposes a woman to define her subsequent nonconsensual sexual intercourse with someone she knows as something other than rape. Her rape script and her sexual experience do not match. This discrepancy is heightened if she experienced little force in her nonassaultive sexual experiences as well as in the actual rape. Drinking alcohol and being intoxicated at the time of the incident are additional factors reducing the likelihood of labeling the incident as rape. Unacknowledgment is even more likely if she did not experience intense negative emotions at the time or subsequently, and if her peers suggested she was at least partially to blame for what happened.

On the other hand, acknowledged victims are more likely to think of rape in terms of an acquaintance, and to have experienced force in nonrape sexual situations. Their assailants were more likely to have used at least some level of force, and the victim was less likely to have been intoxicated. She was likely to have had intense negative emotional reactions both during and after the assault; and if she told her peers, they were likely to tell her she was not to blame.

QUALITATIVE METHODS AND RAPE ACKNOWLEDGMENT

Although quantitative methods search for explanations, qualitative methods seek understanding (Comstock, 1994; Guba & Lincoln, 1994). Knowledge consists of consensus among informants regarding the meanings of their experiences. One method of gaining such knowledge is discourse analysis. Discourse refers to a "system of statements, practices and institutional structures that share common values" (Hare-Mustin, 1994, p. 19). People know what they know because they share common discourses about the nature of the world. A dominant discourse within a society defines what is true and why it is true. From this perspective, often referred to as social construction (Gergen, 1985; Schwandt, 1994), people construct the world around them by learning the meanings given by language, history, and culture. Discourse analysis, then, is a qualitative method of analyzing the themes that occur when people talk about how they define what has happened to them and why it happened. It is a means for understanding subjectivity, the construal process (Ross & Nisbett, 1991), or the way a person understands and interprets her world. Qualitative methods adhere to the position that in order to address problems of everyday life we must first understand the social situation (Comstock, 1994).

Although quantitative research on rape acknowledgment asked women about their own experiences, the participants were not free to tell their own stories in their own words. For example, although Kahn et al. (1994) asked participants to write their rape scripts, they did not allow for multiple scripts. The assumption was implicitly made that women have a single, dominant rape script. Likewise, Andreoli Mathie and Kahn (1995) asked participants what happened during and after their assault, but provided them with categories and dimensions on which to make check marks; participants were not given the opportunity to use their own words, categories, and dimensions. Furthermore, the data gathered about women's experiences using a quantitative approach do not allow the researcher to see the context in which the assault occurred. The complexity of a woman's actual rape experience is ignored when a single aspect of that experience, such as assailant force, is measured alone without taking into account the woman's relationship with the man, her past relationships and experiences, her goals and fears, her beliefs and attitudes about men, women, love, and sex, and so much more that put her experience in context.

A growing body of research suggests women's sexual experiences cannot be understood by looking at isolated categories and classifications of experience (e.g., Thompson, 1995; Tolman, 1994), and that methods such as discourse analysis may be superior to traditional empirical methods in psychology for understanding the complexities of women's experiences, including sexual assault. Lynn Phillips (1995) recently conducted 2- to 5-hour in-depth interviews of 30 women college students to learn about their experiences with romance, sex, and violence. The participants were all self-defined feminists. All but a few participants had one or more experiences that would legally be considered rape, but none of them called themselves a rape victim. In other words, most of these women were unacknowledged victims. Through her interviews, Phillips extracted a number of dominant discourses these women possessed about sex, love, victimization, and gender. She found three interrelated themes: how to be a "good woman," the nature of sexual danger, and the nature of victimization. For each theme she found two conflicting dominant discourses. These are listed in Table 6.

Phillips' (1995) use of discourse analysis leads to a very different way of viewing the unacknowledged rape victim than is found with quantitative research. We quote her at length:

TABLE 6
Themes and Dominant Discourses Relating to Sex, Love, Victimization, and Gender Found by Phillips (1995, 1996) in Her Interviews With Women

Theme	Dominant Discourse	Example
Good woman	Pleasing woman discourse	"A woman is feminine, virtuous, pleasing to men," which is in conflict with
	Liberated woman discourse	"A woman is entitled to be sexual and to full equality in a relationship."
Sexual danger	Normal vs. dangerous sex discourse	"Normal sex and coercive, dangerous sex are completely different and clearly distinct," which is in conflict with
	Male sexual drive discourse	"Men possess an instinctive sexual drive that once aroused must be satisfied."
Victimization	Sex as victimization discourse	"Sex is inherently victimizing to girls and young women," which is in conflict with
	True victim discourse	"Real victims are virtuous, good girls who avoid danger and fight back assailants."

Explaining their reluctance to consider themselves victims, the women pointed to the complicated circumstances surrounding their own experiences. Echoing the *normal/danger dichotomy discourse* and the *true victim discourse*, they suggested that "real" victimization was clear-cut, leaving their sometimes murky, and always contextualized, experiences somehow outside that category. While they were quite willing to describe the pain, fear, and humiliation they endured, they stopped short of labeling their experiences, except to say that things "went badly." Here we see an unexpected twist on the well-intentioned, popularized feminist notion that rape is about violence, not about sex. Since these women's encounters were seldom *simply* about violence, they did not count them as real cases of victimization.

At the same time, confronted with the victim/agent dichotomy posed by the *sex as victimization discourse*, these women express a compelling dilemma: they can be either a victim or an active subject, but not both. Within the terms of this discourse, then, an acknowledgment of their victimization would require them to forfeit their "status" as an agent. Coming of age in an era where the *liberated woman discourse* tells them to be strong and autonomous, these young women place a premium on their ability to appear "together," in control, and "grown up." If victimization and agency are dichotomous, then naming themselves as victims would represent a threat to their sense of self.

Thus, we see women's reluctance to name personal victimization fueled by at least two inter-locking phenomena: 1) the need to preserve agency, encouraged by the *liberated woman discourse*; and 2) the lack of fit between their complex interactions on the one hand, and the simplicity presumed by both the *normal/danger dichotomy discourse* and the *true victim discourse* on the other. These two concerns come together dialectically to inform the woman's thought process: their situations are complicated, so they must not be real victims. And as agents they cannot allow themselves to be framed as victims, so the complexities of their own experiences must preclude them from falling into that category. Viewed in light of their development into young womanhood in an individualistic society, the tendency to minimize one's victimization begins to make sense. Rather than representing an acceptance of male aggression, this tendency may be seen as a strategy for preserving a sense of self within a culture which seeks to oversimplify such complex phenomena as selfhood, gendered power, and sexual violence. (Phillips, 1996, pp. 10–13)

Walker, Gilbert, and Goss (1996) offered further evidence of the existence of the male sexual drive discourse. They found that men and women shared the common beliefs that men have uncontrollable sexual drives when they are aroused and women should acquiesce to the men's needs. When role playing negotiating a date or sexual intimacy, these beliefs were common discourse themes. By making women feel obligated to fulfill men's needs, the male sexual drive discourse may lead women to see themselves as fulfilling their role rather than seeing themselves as a victim of rape. Having the man continue his sexual advances through to intercourse may be viewed as the natural progression of events, rather than as a violation of the woman's desires.

Comparison of the Quantitative and Qualitative Approaches to Rape Acknowledgment

Taken together, the qualitative and quantitative approaches give a more complete picture of why many women do not acknowledge their assault experiences as rape than data using only a single research paradigm. "For a positive social science, knowledge is constituted by the theoretical ordering of empirical observations of an objective reality. The data are descriptions of social behaviors and the subjective beliefs, attitudes, and values of individuals" (Comstock, 1994, p. 627). The goal of such a science is a causal analysis, explanations of what produces something else (e.g., scripts are associated with rape acknowledgment). Using the quantitative methods of logical positivism described in this quotation, we have identified some factors on which acknowledged and unacknowledged victims differ. The end goal is to use this knowledge to help us predict when a woman will or will not acknowledge a sexual assault experience as rape.

From the quantitative data we discovered some of the conditions that make a woman less likely to label her experience as rape, such as possessing a stranger rape script, using alcohol prior to the assault, or the assailant using some level of force. From qualitative research we learned why a rape victim does not label her experience as rape. Discourse analysis, for example, reveals the interpretations people give to their experiences and events; it reveals the norms, values, motives, and meanings shared by the community within which the individuals live. From Phillips' (1996) research we gain insights into why large numbers of women are unacknowledged rape victims—we learn the reasons, meanings, and implications associated with acknowledging or not acknowledging their experience as rape. Phillips' qualitative data inform us that for a college woman to acknowledge an experience as rape, she must change her conception of herself. The research shows why it is important for college women to avoid thinking of themselves as victims.

The qualitative approach underscores the importance of the woman's constructed social reality and her constructed place in that reality. There may be pressures operating to lead a rape victim to construe her rape experience in such a way that it does not threaten the reality she has constructed. Although it is possible for women to change their constructions of reality and the discourses to which they adhere, this process is not easy. For example, Walker et al. (1996) reported that even when they provided an alternative context and an opportunity to change the male sexual drive discourse, their efforts were not effective. Guba and Lincoln (1994) suggested that although constructions may change, such change is most likely to occur when individuals are exposed to different constructions and given the opportunity to compare and contrast them through social interaction. Because women are not likely to discuss their rape experiences with others, the opportunities to change their discourses or perceptions of social reality are limited. Furthermore, even when they do discuss such experiences with friends, these friends are likely to reinforce the dominant discourses identified by Phillips (1996). Hence, the constructed reality that there is a natural progression leading to the man's fulfillment of his sexual arousal despite the woman's desire to avoid this is not likely to change, and women may feel pressure to interpret their rape experience to be consistent with this reality.

CONCLUSION

Both quantitative and qualitative research methods lead to the conclusion that what constitutes rape for college women is complex, multiply determined, and complicated. Phillips (1996) and Walker et al. (1996) found this complexity in their participants' conflicting discourses on what it means to be a good woman, the nature of sexual danger, and victimization. Quantitative research comparing acknowledged and unacknowledged rape victims has identified several variables on which these groups differ. However, the extent to which these variables lead to rape acknowledgment or are by-products of how the woman labeled her experience is not clear. Because we cannot manipulate these variables systematically, causal relationships are difficult to establish.

Clearly, further research is needed to enhance the understanding of why some women do not label rape experiences as rape. From the quantitative research perspective, there may be additional variables not yet identified that are important predictors of rape acknowledgment. New statistical procedures also may be helpful. For example, larger samples of unacknowledged and acknowledged rape victims would permit the use of sophisticated statistical methods such as discriminant analysis or structural equation modeling. These statistical procedures could help researchers identify which variables are most important in predicting whether or not women would acknowledge their experiences as rape.

From a qualitative perspective, we need to expand our knowledge of the dominant discourses in our society, particularly of those dealing with relationships between women and men. Analyses of men's dominant discourses and how their shared beliefs and values compare with those of women would be useful. This research could shed light on the reasons men engage in sexual intercourse after a woman has indicated she does not want to participate. Perhaps through research of this sort, women and men can come to share common dominant discourses about love, sex, and relationships such that all nonconsensual sex is acknowledged as rape.

REFERENCES

Abbey, A. (1991). Misperception as an antecedent of acquaintance rape: A consequence of ambiguity in communication between women and men. In A. Parrot & L. Bechhofer (Eds.), *Acquaintance rape: The hidden crime* (pp. 96–111). New York: Wiley.

Aizenman, M., & Kelley, G. (1988). The incidence of violence and acquaintance rape in dating situations among college men and women. *Journal of College Student Development, 29*, 305–311.

Amir, M. (1971). *Patterns in forcible rape*. Chicago: University of Chicago Press.

Andreoli Mathie, V., Kahn, A. S., Baker, S., Cherry, L., Feria, G., Gregory, C., Heiges, K., Hinely, H., Linn, K., & Scholten, B. (1994, April). *Counterfactual thinking in women's perceptions of their rape experiences*. Poster presented at Southeastern Psychological Association, New Orleans, LA.

Andreoli Mathie, V., & Kahn, A. S. (1995). *The role of counterfactual thinking in rape acknowledgment.* Unpublished manuscript, James Madison University, Harrisonburg, VA.

Bondurant, A. B. (1995). *University women's acknowledgment of rape: Individual, interpersonal, and social factors.* Unpublished doctoral dissertation, Greensboro, North Carolina State University at Greensboro.

Boninger, D. S., Gleicher, F., & Strathman, A. (1994). Counterfactual thinking: From what might have been to what may be. *Journal of Personality and Social Psychology, 67,* 297–307.

Bourque, L. B. (1989). *Defining rape.* Durham, NC: Duke University Press.

Branscombe, N. R., Owen, S., & Allison, J. A. (1995). *Effects of counterfactual thinking on adjustment in rape victims.* Unpublished manuscript, University of Kansas.

Branscombe, N. R., Owen, S., Garstka, T. A., & Coleman, J. (1996). Rape and accident counterfactuals: Who might have done otherwise and would it have changed the outcome? *Journal of Applied Social Psychology, 26,* 1042–1067.

Brownmiller, S. (1975). *Against our will: Men, women and rape.* New York: Simon and Schuster.

Bulman, J. R., & Wortman, C. B. (1977). Attributions of blame and coping in the "real world": Severe accident victims react to their lot. *Journal of Personality and Social Psychology, 35,* 351–363.

Burgess, A. W., & Holmstrom, L. (1979). *Rape: Crisis and recovery.* Bowie, MD: Robert Brady.

Burt, M. R. (1980). Cultural myths and supports for rape. *Journal of Personality and Social Psychology, 38,* 217–230.

Comstock, D. E. (1994). A method for critical research. In M. Martin & L. C. McIntyre (Eds.), *Readings in the philosophy of social science* (pp. 625–639). Cambridge, MA: MIT Press.

Davis, C. G., Lehman, D. R., Wortman, C. B., Silver, R. C., & Thompson, S. C. (1995). The undoing of traumatic life events. *Personality and Social Psychology Bulletin, 21,* 109–124.

Donat, P. L., & D'Emilio, J. (1992). A feminist redefinition of rape and sexual assault: Historical foundations and change. *Journal of Social Issues, 48,* 9–22.

Festinger, L. (1950). Informal social communication. *Psychological Review, 57,* 271–282.

Fiske, S. T., & Taylor, S. (1991). *Social cognition* (2nd ed.). New York: McGraw-Hill.

Folger, R. (1987). Reformulating the preconditions of resentment: A referent cognitions model. In J. C. Masters & W. P. Smith (Eds.), *Social comparison, social justice, and relative deprivation* (pp. 183–215). Hillsdale, NJ: Erlbaum.

Folger, R., Rosenfield, D., & Robinson, T. (1983). Relative deprivation and procedural justifications. *Journal of Personality and Social Psychology, 45,* 268–273.

Gergen, K. J. (1985). The social constructionist movement in modern psychology. *American Psychologist, 40,* 266–275.

Gilbert, N. (1993). Examining the facts: Advocacy research overstates the incidence of date and acquaintance rape. In R. J. Gelles & D. R. Loseke (Eds.), *Current controversies on family violence* (pp. 120–132). Newbury Park, CA: Sage.

Gleicher, F., Kost, K. A., Baker, S. M., Strathman, A. J., Richman, S. A., & Sherman, S. J. (1990). The role of counterfactual thinking in judgements of affect. *Personality and Social Psychology Bulletin, 16*, 284–295.

Goldberg-Ambrose, C. (1992). Unfinished business in rape law reform. *Journal of Social Issues, 48*, 173–185.

Griffin, S. (1971). Rape: The all-American crime. *Ramparts, 10*, 26–35.

Guba, E. G., & Lincoln, Y. S. (1994). Competing paradigms in qualitative research. In N. K. Denzin & Y. S. Lincoln (Eds.), *Handbook of qualitative research* (pp. 105–117). Thousand Oaks, CA: Sage.

Hanson, R. K. (1990). The psychological impact of sexual assault on women and children: A review. *Annals of Sex Research, 3*, 187–232.

Hare-Mustin, R. T. (1994). Discourses in the mirrored room: A postmodern analysis of therapy. *Family Process, 33*, 19–35.

Hemphill, K. J., & Lehman, D. R. (1991). Social comparisons and their affective consequences: The importance of comparison dimension and individual difference variables. *Journal of Social and Clinical Psychology, 10*, 372–394.

Janoff-Bulman, R. (1979). Characterological versus behavioral self-blame: Inquiries into depression and rape. *Journal of Personality and Social Psychology, 37*, 1798–1809.

Janoff-Bulman, R., & Timko, C. (1987). Coping with traumatic life events. In C. R. Snyder & C. E. Ford (Eds.), *Coping with negative life events* (pp. 135–159). New York: Plenum Press.

Johnson, J. T. (1986). The knowledge of what might have been: Affective and attributional consequences of near outcomes. *Personality and Social Psychology Bulletin, 12*, 51–62.

Kahn, A. S., Andreoli Mathie, V., & Torgler, C. (1994). Rape scripts and rape acknowledgment. *Psychology of Women Quarterly, 18*, 53–66.

Kahneman, D., & Miller, D. T. (1986). Norm theory: Comparing reality to its alternatives. *Psychological Review, 93*, 136–153.

Kahneman, D., & Tversky, A. (1982). The simulation heuristic. In D. Kahneman, P. Slovic, & A. Tversky (Eds.), *Judgement under certainty: Heuristics and biases* (pp. 201–208). New York: Cambridge University Press.

Kamen, P. (1996). Acquaintance rape: Revolution and reaction. In N. B. Maglin & D. Perry (Eds.), *"Bad girls/good girls": Women, sex and power in the nineties* (pp. 137–149). New Brunswick, NJ: Rutgers University Press.

Koss, M. P. (1985). The hidden rape victim: Personality, attitudinal, and situational characteristics. *Psychology of Women Quarterly, 9*, 193–212.

Koss, M. P. (1988). Hidden rape: Sexual aggression and victimization in a national sample in higher education. In A. W. Burgess (Ed.), *Rape and sexual assault II* (pp. 3–25). New York: Garland Press.

Koss, M. P. (1993). Detecting the scope of rape: A review of prevalence research methods. *Journal of Interpersonal Violence, 8*, 198–222.

Koss, M. P., & Burkhart, B. R. (1989). A conceptual analysis of rape victimization: Long-term effects and implications for treatment. *Psychology of Women Quarterly, 13*, 27–40.

Koss, M. P., & Cook, S. L. (1993). Facing the facts: Date and acquaintance rape are significant problems for women. In R. J. Gelles & D. R. Loseke (Eds.), *Current controversies on family violence* (pp. 104–119). Newbury Park, CA: Sage.

Koss, M. P., Dinero, T. E., Seibel, C. A., & Cox, S. L. (1988). Stranger and acquaintance rape: Are there differences in the victim's experience? *Psychology of Women Quarterly, 12*, 1–24.

Koss, M. P., Heise, L., & Russo, N. F. (1994). The global health burden of rape. *Psychology of Women Quarterly, 18*, 509–537.

Koss, M. P., & Oros, C. J. (1982). Sexual experiences survey: A research instrument investigating sexual aggression and victimization. *Journal of Consulting and Clinical Psychology, 50*, 455–457.

Landman, J. (1987). Regret and elation following action and inaction: Affective responses to positive versus negative outcomes. *Personality and Social Psychology Bulletin, 13*, 524–536.

Levine-MacCombie, J., & Koss, M. P. (1986). Acquaintance rape: Effective avoidance strategies. *Psychology of Women Quarterly, 10*, 311–319.

Maglin, N. B., & Perry, D. (1996). *"Good girls/bad girls": Women, sex, & power in the nineties*. New Brunswick, NJ: Rutgers University Press.

Markman, K. D., Gavanski, I., Sherman, S. J., & McMullen, M. N. (1993). The mental simulation of better and worse possible worlds. *Journal of Experimental Social Psychology, 29*, 87–109.

Markus, H., & Zajonc, R. B. (1985). The cognitive perspective in social psychology. In G. Lindzey & E. Aronson (Eds.), *Handbook of social psychology* (Vol. 1, pp. 137–230). New York: Random House.

Miller, B., & Marshall, J. C. (1987). Coercive sex on the university campus. *Journal of College Student Personnel, 28*, 38–47.

Miller, D. T., & McFarland, C. (1986). Counterfactual thinking and victim compensation: A test of norm theory. *Personality and Social Psychology Bulletin, 12*, 513–519.

Miller, D. T., Turnbull, W., & McFarland, C. (1990). Counterfactual thinking and social perception: Thinking about what might have been. In M. P. Zanna (Ed.), *Advances in experimental social psychology* (Vol. 23, pp. 305–331). Orlando, FL: Academic Press.

Millet, K. (1970). *Sexual politics*. New York: Avon.

Muehlenhard, C. L., & Linton, M. A. (1987). Date rape and sexual aggression in dating situations: Incidence and risk factors. *Journal of Counseling Psychology, 34*, 186–196.

Muehlenhard, C. L., Powch, I. G., Phelps, J. L., & Giusti, L. M. (1992). Definitions of rape: Scientific and political implications. *Journal of Social Issues, 48,* 23–44.

Nario-Redmond, M. R., & Branscombe, N. R. (1996). It could have been better or it might have been worse: Implications for blame assignment in rape cases. *Basic and Applied Social Psychology, 18,* 347–366.

Parrot, A. (1991). Institutionalized response: How can acquaintance be prevented? Recommendations for college policies and procedures to deal with acquaintance rape. In A. Parrot & L. Bechhofer (Eds.), *Acquaintance rape: The hidden crime* (pp. 355–367). New York: Wiley.

Phillips, L. (1995). *Flirting with danger: A study of the multiple meanings of male aggression in women's hetero-relations.* Doctoral dissertation, Graduate School of Education, University of Pennsylvania.

Phillips, L. (1996, August). *Constructing meanings in hetero-relations: Young women's experiences of power and desire.* Paper presented at the XXVI International Congress of Psychology, Montreal, Canada.

Pitts, V. L., & Schwartz, M. D. (1993). Promoting self-blame in hidden rape cases. *Humanity & Society, 17,* 383–398.

Rapaport, K., & Burkhart, B. R. (1984). Personality and attitudinal characteristics of sexually coercive college males. *Journal of Abnormal Psychology, 93,* 216–221.

Resick, P. A. (1987). Psychological effects of victimization: Implications for the criminal justice system. *Crime & Delinquency, 33,* 468–478.

Richardson, D., & Campbell, J. L. (1982). Alcohol and rape: The effect of alcohol on attributions of blame for rape. *Personality and Social Psychology Bulletin, 8,* 468–476.

Roese, N. J. (1994). The functional basis of counterfactual thinking. *Journal of Personality and Social Psychology, 66,* 805–818.

Roiphe, K. (1994). *The morning after: Sex, fear and feminism on campus.* New York: Little, Brown.

Rothbaum, B. O., Foa, E. B., Riggs, D. S., Murdock, T., & Walsh, W. (1992). A prospective examination of post-traumatic stress disorder in rape victims. *Journal of Traumatic Stress, 5,* 455–474.

Ross, L., & Nisbett, R. E. (1991). *The person and the situation: Perspectives of social psychology.* New York: McGraw-Hill.

Russell, D. (1975). *The politics of rape: The victim's perspective.* New York: Stein & Day.

Sanday, P. R. (1996). *A woman scorned: Acquaintance rape on trial.* New York: Doubleday.

Searles, P., & Berger, R. (1987). The current status of rape reform legislation: An examination of state statutes. *Women's Rights Law Reporter, 10,* 25–43.

Schwandt, T. A. (1994). Constructivist, interpretivist approaches to human inquiry. In N. K. Denzin & Y. S. Lincoln (Eds.), *Handbook of qualitative research* (pp. 118–137). Thousand Oaks, CA: Sage.

Taylor, S. E., Buunk, B. P., & Aspinwall, L. G. (1990). Social comparison, stress, and coping. *Personality and Social Psychology Bulletin, 16,* 74–89.

Taylor, S. E., & Schneider, S. K. (1989). Coping and the simulation of events. *Social Cognition, 7,* 174–194.

Taylor, S. E., Wood, J. V., & Lichtman, R. R. (1983). It could be worse: Selective evaluation as a response to victimization. *Journal of Social Issues, 39,* 19–40.

Thompson, S. (1995). *Going all the way: Teenage girls' tales of sex, romance, and pregnancy.* New York: Hill and Wang.

Tolman, D. L. (1994). Doing desire: Adolescent girls' struggles for/with sexuality. *Gender & Society, 8,* 324–342.

Walker, S., Gilbert, L., & Goss, S. (1996, August). *Negotiating sex in heterosexual dating: Challenging the dominant discourses.* Paper presented at the annual meeting of the American Psychological Association, Toronto, Canada.

Ward, S. K., Chapman, K., Cohn, E., White, S., & Williams, K. (1991). Acquaintance rape and the college social scene. *Family Relations, 40,* 65–71.

Weis, K., & Borges, S. S. (1973). Victimology and rape: The case of the legitimate victim. *Issues in Criminology, 8,* 71–115.

Wells, G. L., & Gavanski, I. (1989). Mental simulation of causality. *Journal of Personality and Social Psychology, 56,* 161–169.

Wells, G. L., Taylor, B. R., & Turtle, J. W. (1987). The undoing of scenarios. *Journal of Personality and Social Psychology, 53,* 421–430.

AUTHOR INDEX

Numbers in italics refer to listings in the reference section.

Byne, W., 38, 40, 41, *53*
Byrd, J. M., *180*

Cado, S., 310, *317*
Caggiula, A., *207*
Calhoun, K. S., 156, *164*, 368, *372*
Califia, P., 281, *295*
Call, V., 169, *180*
Callan, V. J., 123, *134*
Campbell, J. L., 392, *402*
Cantor, A., 187, *206*
Cantor, M. G., 100, *104*
Carby, H., 253, *268*
Carli, L. L., 327, *350*
Carroll, J. L., 118, *134*
Carter, D. B., 146, *161*
Casas, J. M., 158, *163*
Cash, T. F., *161*, 255, 262, *268*, 270
Castaneda, X., 141, *161*
Castellow, W. A., 263, *268*
Cate, R. M., 118, 131, *134*
Caulfield, M. D., 143, *161*
Centers for Disease Control, 259, *268*
Cervantes, R., 158, *164*
Chambless, D. L., 187, *206*
Chan, C., 159, 160, *161*
Chapman, K., 380, *403*
Chen, J. H., 315, *319*
Cherfas, J., 38, *53*
Cherry, L., *398*
Chilman, C., 117, *134*
Chin, J. L., *162*
Chisholm, P., 256, *268*
Chodorow, N., 58, *74*, 117, *134*, 311, *317*
Chrisler, J. C., 185, *203*
Christensen, H., 117, *134*
Christensen, R. B., 123, *137*
Christopher, F. S., 118, 131, *134*
Christopherson, C. R., 129, *134*
Clark, K., 243, *268*
Clark, L. G., 362, *372*
Clark, R., 171, *180*
Clark, R. D., 68, *74*
Clark, S. B., 148, *163*
Cleveland, J. N., 328, *350*
Clifton, L., 266, *268*
Clinebell, S. K., 332, *350*
Clinton, K., 230, *233*
Coates, J., 225, *233*

Cogan, J., 274, *295*
Cohen, J., 67, *74*
Cohn, E., 380, *403*
Colburn, D. W., 189, *203*
Colditz, G. A., 188, *203*
Cole, E., 192, *203*
Coleman, J., 390, *399*
Coleman, L. M., 192, 202, *203*
Coles, R., 118, *134*
Collins, P. H., 16, 29, 156, *162*
Comas-Diaz, L., 158, *164*
Comfort, A. C., 187, *203*
Comstock, D. E., 393, 394, 396, *399*
Connell, R. W., 79, 93, *104*, 331, *350*
Conrad, C., 339, 340, 343, *353*
Cook, S. L., 379, *401*
Cooke, D. J., 196, *205*
Coons, H., 303, *317*
Corner, G. W., 88, *104*
Costa, F., 115, *136*
Costello, E., *207*
Cowan, G., 192, *204*, 306, *317*
Coward, R., 100, *104*
Cox, C. L., 264, *268*
Cox, S. L., *401*
Crabb, C., 39, *53*
Crawford, M., 5, 8, 17, 29, 116, *134*,
    214–217, 219, 224, 233, 234,
    326, 354, 366, *372*
Crews, D., 42, *53*
Crisp, A. H., 257, *268*
Crohan, S. E., 192, 202, *203*
Crowley, M., 62, *75*
Crowley, S. L., 148, *162*
Cubbins, L. A., 156, *165*
Cullen, M., 121, *134*
Cunningham, F. G., 170, 171, *180*
Cupach, W. R., 100, *104*
Curtin, S., 259, *272*
Cutler, W. B., 193, *204*
Cyr, R. R., 329, 334, 347, *354*

Daly, M., 46, *53*, 281, 286, *295*
Dammann, E. J., 263, *269*
Dan, A. J., 192, *204*
Danielson, D., 245, *268*
Daniluk, J. C., 267, *268*
Danoff-Burg, S., 370, *374*
Datan, N., 196, 199, *204*
Davidson, A. F., 315, *319*

Russo, N. F., 156, *164, 355, 370, 373,*
  378, 401
Ryan, J., 325, *351*
Ryff, C. D., 192, 197, *208*

Saal, F. E., 341, *353*
Sadock, B. J., 173, *180*
Sadock, V. A., 173, *180*
Sakamoto, I., 160, *164*
Salem, R. G., 361, *372*
Salgado de Snyder, V. N., 158, *164*
Samuelsson, S., 187, *205*
Sanchez, S. D., 197, *206*
Sanchez-Ayendez, M., 192, *208*
Sand, G., 185, *208*
Sanday, P. R., 309, *319, 379, 402*
Sandberg, D. E., 148, *165*
Sandin, K., 188, *207*
Sang, B., 282, 284, 285, *296*
Sarrel, P. M., 187, 188, *208*
Saudargas, R. A., 126, 127, *137*
Savvas, M., 194, *204*
Scherr, R. L., 247, 250, 252, 253, *270*
Schlossberg, N., 197, *208*
Schmitt, D. P., 59, 60, 72, *74*
Schmitt, E., 344, *353*
Schneider, D., 243, *271*
Schneider, M. S., 338, *352*
Schneider, S. K., 390, *403*
Schoenborn, C. A., 257, *267*
Schoever, L., 343, *352*
Schofield, M., 117, *139*
Scholtem, B., *398*
Schwandt, T. A., 393, *402*
Schwartz, D., 250, *269*
Schwartz, M. D., 381, 387, 392, *402*
Schwartz, P., 70, *75, 128, 133, 169, 180,*
  287, 294, 300, 317, 329, 334,
  348, 352
Schwendinger, H., 367, *375*
Schwendinger, J. R., 367, *375*
Scully, D., 362, 363, *375*
Seaman, B., 248, *271*
Searles, P., 361, *372, 379, 402*
Secord, P., 327, *351*
Seibel, C. A., 387, *401*
Selman, R. L., 112, *139*
Semmelroth, J., 72, *74*
Serbin, L. A., 146, *165*
Seymore, C., 158, *162*

Shah, F. K., 131, *140*
Shapiro, J. P., 259, *271*
Shedler, J., 116, *139*
Sheehey, G., 185, *208*
Shelden, R., 189, *203*
Sherif, C. W., 88, *106*
Sherman, S. J., 389, *400, 401*
Sherwin, B. B., 189, 191, *208*
Sherwin, S., 198, *209*
Shiboski, S. S., 314, *318*
Shotland, R. L., 357, 366, 368, *375*
Shotter, J., 219, *235*
Shuttleworth, S., 8, 15, *31*
Siebrecht, K., *354*
Silver, R. C., 389, *399*
Silverman, D., *353*
Silverstein, B., 248, *271*
Simms, M. C., 129, 130, *138*
Simon, W., 63, 75, 336, *353*
Simpson, G. G., 44, *55*
Simson, R., 364, *375*
Singer, F., 194, *206*
Sites, P., *271*
Sklar, B. J., 312, *318*
Slipp, S., 27, *32*
Smith, A., 282, 284, 285, *296*
Smith, C., 310, *317*
Smith, E. A., 125, 130, *139, 140*
Smith, J., 148, *165*
Smith, M. D. Q., 358, *375*
Snodgrass, S. E., 326, *353*
Snyder, D., 306, *317*
Snyder, M., 217, *235*
Sockloskie, R. J., 357, 362, *374*
Somers, J. M., *352*
Sommers-Flanagan, J., 150, *165*
Sommers-Flanagan, R., 150, *165*
Sorensen, R., 117, *139*
Sourander, L. B., 188, *209*
Spain, D., 250, *271*
Speizer, F. E., *203*
Spelman, E. V., 59, *76*
Sporakowski, M., 127, *138*
Sprecher, S., 61–63, 69–71, *76, 169, 180*
Springer, R. C., 256, *271*
Stack, C. B., 156, *165*
Stake, J., 263, 264, *271*
Stampfer, M. J., *203*
Stanback, M. H., 226, *235*
Staneski, R. A., 264, *270*
Staples, R., 158, *165*

SUBJECT INDEX

Basic Instinct, 279
Beal, Carol, 148
Beauty-sex equation, 237–267
  in 1910s/1920s, 244–246
  in 1940s/1950s, 246–247
  in 1960s/1970s, 247–249
  in 1980s/1990s, 249–252
  African American women and, 252–254
  and cosmetic surgery, 255–256
  development of, 242–243
  health effects of, 256–259
  and identity fragmentation, 259–260
  and social construction of sexuality, 238–242
  at turn of the century, 143–144
Bernard, Jesse, 247
Bias, 13, 16, 196
Biological models of sexuality, 23–52, 95–97, 300–302.
  See also Menopause
  deconstructionist view vs., 51–52
  and gender roles, 36
  and hormonal influences, 41–44
  and LeVay neuroanatomy study, 36–41
  social/political implications of, 49–51
  sociobiology, 44–49
Biological view of sexuality, 19–21
Birth control, 248, 314–316
Birth control movement, 114–115
Bisexuality, 312–313
Blackwell, Elizabeth, 90
Black women. See African American women
Blaming the victim, 142, 231–232, 364
Bohan, Janis, 215
Boundaries, 347
Brain, 19, 20, 96
  and gender differences, 38
  and homosexuality, 37–41
Breast-feeding, 175
Breasts, 247
Brecher, E. M., 90
The Bridges of Madison County, 183–184
Bright, Susie, 288, 292
Bronfenbrenner, Urie, 125
Bullough, V. L., 91
Burt, Martha, 357
Business workplaces, sexual harassment in, 345
Buss, D. M., 60–61
Byne, William, 40

Calvin Klein, 152
Catholic church, 158
Chamorro, 168
Cheyenne, 65
Childhood sexuality, 27–28
Child sexual abuse (CSA), 310, 313
Chodorow, N., 58–59, 311
Christianity, 155
Chronicle of Higher Education, 39
Chung, Connie, 185
Citadel, 344
Civil rights movement, 247
Class, 25–26
Clifton, Lucille, 266
Clinton, Hillary Rodham, 293
Clinton, Kate, 230
Cognitive ability, 111–112
Colombia, 47
Colorado, 274
Comfort, Alex, 187
Commitment, 131
Competition, sexuality as, 359
Comstock Laws, 245
Condoms, 26, 314, 315
Confucianism, 159–160
Consent, 328–329, 346, 356–366
Constructionism. See Social construction/constructionism
Contractual agreement, sexuality as, 360
Cosmetic surgery, 255–256
Counterfactual thinking, 389–391
Cross-dressing, 23–24
CSA. See Child sexual abuse
Cuckold, 72, 266
Cultural metaphors, 358–360
Cultural myths, 360–362
Culture, 22–23, 130

Dating, 131
Daughters of Bilitis, 282
Davis, Angela, 247
Declaration of Sentiments, 57
Deconstruction, 15
  as alternative to biological models of sexuality, 51–52
  of childhood sexuality, 27–28
  of Freud on incest, 27
  of sexual scripts, 336–339
Defense of Marriage Act (DOMA), 274
Dependence/dependency
  in feminist theory, 64

in neoanalytic theory, 58
as traditional female sexual script, 335
of women on men, 311–312
Development
in adolescent girls. *See* Adolescent
girls, sexuality of
ego, 126–127
normative, 120–122
personality, 219
Developmental theories
feminist theories of, 219
of menopause, 197
of sexual roles, 145–146
Dharma, 158–159
*Diagnostic and Statistical Manual of Mental
Disorders*, 96
Dildos, 277–278, 289–290
Dirty jokes, 220–221
Discover, 40
Dolls, 147
DOMA. *See* Defense of Marriage Act
Dominator (traditional male sexual
script), 331–332
Double standard, 60, 62–63, 117
Drosophila, 45
Drug use
among adolescents, 116
and unacknowledged rape, 392

Eastern Pomo, 168
Economic dependence, 59
Egg, 42
Ego development, 126–127
Elders, Jocelyn, 3
Elgin, Suzette Haden, 278
Ellis, Havelock, 25
Empiricism, feminist, 15–16
Environment, and hormonal levels, 42–
44
Epistemologies, 12, 16
Essentialism, 214, 215
Estrogen, 188–189
Ethnicity, 25–26
and adolescent sexuality, 130
and gender differences, 67–68
and sexual roles, 153–160
Evolutionary psychology, 59–61, 72
Eysenck, H. J., 48–49

Family, and adolescent sexuality, 128–129

Family values, 251–252
Fantasy, gender differences in sexual, 70–
71
Faulkner, Shannon, 344
Feelings, sexual, 122–125
Feinberg, Leslie, 285
Feldman, S. Shirley, 123–124
Fellatio, 173
The Feminine Mystique (Betty Friedan),
248
Feminism
challenges to sexological model by,
101–103
and humor, 228–232
and social construction, 15–18
Feminist lesbian, 280–282
Feminist standpoint epistemologies, 16
Feminist theories
acquaintance rape in, 370–371
and gender differences, 64–65
of menopause, 198–201
of personality development, 219
Foster, Jodie, 152
The Fox (D. H. Lawrence), 276
Frankfort, Ellen, 248
Frequency of sexual behavior, and age,
187–188
Freud, Sigmund, 25, 27, 90, 98
Friedan, Betty, 248
Frum, David, 249

Gay men, 24, 37–41
Gender differences, 57–74, 215–220
feminist approach to, 64–65
as justification for rape, 304
mate selection, 69–70
neoanalytic theory approach to, 58–59
popular misconceptions about, 49–50
in power, 325–329
script theory approach to, 63–64
in sexual behavior, 300
in sexual fantasies, 70–71
in sexual jealousy, 72
social construction approach to, 65
social learning approach to, 61–62
Gender differences (*continued*)
social role approach to, 62–64
sociobiological approach, 59–61
studies of, 66–69
Gender expectations, 302–304
Gender identity, 143

Religion/religious beliefs, 18, 50–51
Roberts, Cokie, 185
Robinson, P., 90
Romanticism, 59
Romantic relationships, 130–131
Rosie the Riveter, 246
Russell, Jane, 247

Sambia, 23
Sand, Gayle, 185
Sanday, P., 309
Sanger, Margaret, 57, 245
Schmitt, D. P., 60–61
School, gender socialization at, 148
Science, 36, 38, 40
Science, biologically based, 35–36
Science News, 39
Scientific American, 40
Scientific method, 15–16, 18–21
Scientific progress, 13
Script theory, 63–64. *See also* Sexual
    scripts
Seducer (traditional male sexual script),
    330–331
SES. *See* Sexual Experiences Survey
Seventeen, 256
Sexological model, 79–103
    feminist challenges to, 101–103
    fragmentation of bodily components
        in, 97
    individualism in, 97–00
    influence of, on sexual consciousness,
        99–101
    origins of, 89–92
    pre-eminence of biological variables in,
        95–97
    and sex research, 83–89
    and social context of researcher/re-
        search participant, 94–95
    social impact of, 99
    tenets of, 82–83
    universal mechanisms of sexuality in,
        92–93
Sex research, 83–89
    with animals, 88–89, 93
    definition of, 83
    favored methods in, 84–85
    and gender, 102–103
    individualistic bias in, 97–99, 118–119
    pre-Kinsey, 87–88
    on rape, 366–369

social context of, 94–95
    thematic elements in, 84
    validity of, 85–87
Sexual assertiveness. *See* Assertiveness,
    sexual
Sexual behavior
    biological explanation for, 300–302
    gender differences in, 300
Sexual drive, 360–361
Sexual Experiences Survey (SES), 380,
    381, 388
Sexual fantasy, gender differences in, 70–
    71
Sexual functioning, and belief in biologi-
    cally derived gender differences,
    306–307
Sexual harassment, 323–349
    in academic environments, 341–343
    in business workplaces, 345
    and gender differences in power, 325–
        329
    identification of, 323–324
    knowledge of, 347–348
    linguistic reference to, 17
    in military, 343–345
    organizational contexts of, 339–345
    and sexual scripts, 329–339
    strategies for prevention of, 345–347
    as term, 324
Sexual humor. *See* Humor
Sexual identity, 259–260
Sexual intercourse
    equation of sexuality with, 117–118
    in postpartum period, 170–171, 173
    during pregnancy, 169–170
    premarital, 123
    quantification of, 95
Sexuality (term), 11
Sexually transmitted diseases (STDs), 26,
    120, 149, 314–316. *See also* Ac-
    quired immunodeficiency syn-
    drome
Sexual object (traditional female sexual
    script), 333
Sexual orientation, and adolescent sexu-
    ality, 127–128
Sexual roles, female, 141–160
    in adolescence, 149–153
    among Asian women, 159–160
    among Black, 155–158

ABOUT THE EDITORS

Cheryl Brown Travis, PhD, is a professor of psychology at the University of Tennessee, Knoxville. Her scholarship has been guided by feminist ideals to re-examine and to question the status quo. She has pursued this focus in the areas of the psychology of women and health psychology, particularly where these two areas intersect with respect to social justice in health care planning and medical decision making. She is also interested in environmental issues and environmental decision making. She has authored two books on women and health psychology and has numerous other papers and presentations on equity and medical decision making. She is a past president of the Society for the Psychology of Women, Division 35 of the American Psychological Association (APA). She is a Fellow of several APA divisions, has chaired the Board of Scientific Affairs for the APA, has served as an associate editor of *American Psychologist*, and is the first editor of the APA's Division 35 book series. She is an enthusiast of back-country mountain biking and orienteering that frequently involves segments better understood as hike-a-bike.

Jacquelyn W. White, PhD, is a professor of psychology and director of women's studies at the University of North Carolina at Greensboro. Her research focuses on gender issues and aggression using research techniques ranging from laboratory experiments to surveys and interviews. She has published numerous articles and chapters in the area of gender and aggression and is a frequent speaker at national and international conferences.

In addition to her research activities, Dr. White serves as the editor of the *Psychology of Women Quarterly* and is an associate editor for *Aggressive Behavior*. She recently completed a term as president of the Southeastern Psychological Association. She also is a consultant on a project with the US Navy examining the impact of pre-military experiences with physical and sexual abuse on military experiences. She has been the recipient of a number of awards, including the Women's History Committee Service Award given by the Commission on the Status of Women and the Greensboro Young Women's Christian Association and the Senior Research Excellence Award from the University of North Carolina at Greensboro. She is a Fellow of the American Psychological Association.